PRACTICAL
BOAT
MECHANICS

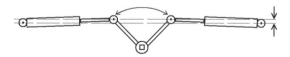

PRACTICAL
BOAT

Commonsense Ways to Prevent, Diagnose

MECHANICS

and Repair Engine and Mechanical Problems

BEN L. EVRIDGE

International Marine / McGraw-Hill

Camden, Maine • New York • Chicago • San Francisco • Lisbon • London • Madrid • Mexico City •
Milan • New Delhi • San Juan • Seoul • Singapore • Sydney • Toronto

The **McGraw·Hill** Companies

1 2 3 4 5 6 7 8 9 DOC DOC 2 1 0 9

Library of Congress Cataloging-in-Publication Data
Evridge, Ben L.
  Practical boat mechanics : commonsense ways to prevent, diagnose, and repair engine and mechanical problems / Ben L. Evridge.
    p. cm.
  Includes index.
  ISBN-13: 978-0-07-144505-4 (pbk. : alk. paper)
  1. Boats and boating—Maintenance and repair. 2. Motorboats—Motors—Maintenance and repair. 3. Sailboats—Auxiliary engines—Maintenance and repair. I. Title.
  VM322.E87 2007
  623.82'020288—dc22
                        2007024456

ISBN 978-0-07-144505-4
MHID 0-07-144505-6

Questions regarding the content of this book should be addressed to
www.internationalmarine.com

Questions regarding the ordering of this book should be addressed to
The McGraw-Hill Companies
Customer Service Department
P.O. Box 547
Blacklick, OH 43004
Retail customers: 1-800-262-4729
Bookstores: 1-800-722-4726

Photographs and illustrations by the author unless otherwise credited.

This book is dedicated to my former students at Kodiak College, who had a way of asking the right questions.

CONTENTS

ACKNOWLEDGMENTS

First and most important, my thanks go to Irene, who keeps a happy home.

Next, to Jon Eaton and the staff at International Marine/McGraw-Hill who kept the book on course.

For giving their time, for contributing photos and technical resources, and for sharing their experience, my deepest thanks go to Bob Allen and the crew of MER Equipment, Seattle, Washington (see www.merequipment.com, and see also MERPOWER Technical Support Blog: http://merpower.wordpress.com).

My thanks go also to Dwight Allen, for great technical insight; to Pearl, Hank, and Chuck Burkhardt; to Jack Chafee of Jack's Truck and Equipment, Gillette, Wyoming; to Don Clark of Clark Marine, Dutch Harbor, Alaska; to Andy Denham, Master Mechanic; to Ralph Endresen of Endresen Diesel Service, Seattle, Washington; to Bob Evridge; to Jim Evridge of Jim's Equipment Repair LLC, Anchorage, Alaska; to Gerald Gardner; to Betty and Richard Geddes; to Bob Gil, Master Mechanic; to Jerry Grant, Master Mechanic; to Paul Hansen, Kodiak logger; to KJ and Jim Herman; to Al Herrington at www.fuelspillprevention.com; to Tim Hess of Cascade Engine LLC, Seattle; to Cecile and Todd Hiner; to Pat, Jake, and Theresa Jacobson; to Dave Jensen; to Mark Jochems, of Shoreline Marine Diesel Inc.; to David Pflaum; to Meryl Snavely; to Lowell Stambaugh, owner of Deflector Marine Rudder (www.rudderpower.com); to Jim Tully; to Randy Weber, Master Mechanic; to Glenn White; to Bob Wilkison of Wilkies Equipment, Anchorage, Alaska; to Kathy and Thom Wischer; and to Stanley Wolrich.

INTRODUCTION

There is a large gap between the information marine manufacturers provide in their manuals and the information mariners need to keep their boats motoring along. This book was written to fill the gap.

I've been troubleshooting and repairing Kodiak fishing boats since I worked for a diesel equipment company in Anchorage, Alaska, in 1980. Later I settled in Kodiak and opened a marine engine repair shop, where I also began receiving calls to repair motoryachts, pleasure boats, and sailboats. Soon after, I was asked to instruct night classes in marine engine repair at Kodiak College. The next twenty years found me in the company of these students, often mariners, who were wrestling with maintenance problems.

I found the best approach to answering my students' troubleshooting questions was through an ever-expanding collection of one-page handouts. Each handout summarized a particular problem with marine equipment, then offered solutions. The summaries focused on the sights, sounds, sensations, smells, and tastes associated with mechanical problems.

The handouts often spurred conversations in the class. My students would recount their own "war stories"—real-life, hair-raising near misses. Most of their stories had happy endings, and the enthused students explained how they averted catastrophe and returned safely to port.

These classroom discussions resulted in more topics that could be distilled into one-page summaries, but it didn't stop there. Topics would arise outside the classroom as well. For instance, a former student might see me at the grocery store and say: "Hey, Ben, I've got a good one for you." Then we might get a napkin from the deli and draw a diagram of the solution to a particular marine equipment problem.

The number of summaries grew to 50, 200, 400, and then I lost count. *Practical Boat Mechanics* grew out of this collaborative process.

HOW TO USE THIS BOOK

Most of us are familiar with traditional methods of troubleshooting. When something goes wrong, it becomes painfully obvious. There is a horrifying noise, a burning smell, a mysterious appearance of water in the bilge. At that moment, your primary concern is to know what happened and how to fix it; however, good troubleshooting is much more than a gut-level reactive response.

The first step toward becoming a seasoned troubleshooter is to know your boat's systems. Part 1 of this book will enhance your understanding of how your boat works, and thus provide valuable context when you notice something out of the ordinary. It will also provide maintenance advice to help you avoid problems altogether.

Eventually, however, something will break down. Part 2 presents a unique approach to troubleshooting and maintenance by putting your five senses to work. We start with Chapter 10, which, for those who like the familiar, tackles troubleshooting in the traditional fashion of symptom analysis. The remaining chapters in Part 2 have been crafted to ease your access to the information. For example, Chapter 11 is divided by subsystems related to your diesel engine. Under each subsystem you will find a series of symptoms organized by the five senses. If, for instance, you see black smoke billowing from the exhaust pipe, you'd flip to the section "What You See."

Following each symptom is the subhead "Urgency." This will indicate if the situation is dire, or if you have the luxury of fixing the problem when you return to port, or if you can ignore it altogether.

Next, you'll see the heading "Suggested Actions." This will list steps you can take to solve the problem, and it will offer background information on its nature.

Throughout the book you'll also find helpful sidebars. Some sidebars are called "Work-Around Solutions." These sidebars offer stop-gap measures if distance from shore services makes a proper repair impractical or impossible. Other sidebars are called "For the Workboat." These sidebars deal with topics that are specific to big-rig commercial vessels, master mechanics, or anything beyond the scope of the average recreational boater.

PART 1: SYSTEMS OVERVIEW

CHAPTER 1

THE NATURE OF THE BEAST

Before you begin caring for your boat's mechanical health and diagnosing and treating its mechanical symptoms, you should meet the patient. Chapters 1 through 9 offer a tour of your boat's mechanical mysteries and make a number of suggestions for routine maintenance. Caring for your boat's mechanical systems is not only the best way to keep them functioning reliably, it's also the best way to learn how they function and to prepare yourself for problem solving if and when something does go wrong.

This chapter covers a few of the basics. Your boat may be brand-new, it may simply be new to you, or it may be a mechanical mystery even though you've owned it for several years. Whatever the reason, it's time to meet your boat and to familiarize yourself with a few of the techniques and circumstances you'll encounter again and again as you work with mechanical systems aboard.

THE BOATOWNER'S CHECKLIST
Before you use your boat, gather the information and make the inspections noted in this section. You need to be familiar with all the important systems on board to properly maintain them and to know what to do if something goes wrong. You'll be able to respond more quickly if you do your homework ahead of time.

1. Record the information from all engines and transmissions. *Note: The transmission,* which conveys engine power to the propeller shaft, is often called the marine gear, the gearbox, or simply the gear.

Every engine and transmission leaves the factory with a serial number plate (Fig. 1-1) to enable the ordering of parts and service work. Most often these plates are attached with four small rivets. This same plate often provides the engine's power rating as well.

If no serial number plate is visible, begin looking for its original place on the cylinder block. You'll know you've found it when you see a flat rectangular area roughly two inches by three inches in size, framed either by four chiseled-off rivets or by the epoxy glue that once held the plate. When this is the case, you will have to get serial number information from the boat's previous owner. If this is not possible, an experienced marine mechanic can inspect the equipment and determine what was stamped on the plate.

If the plate is missing and there is no other way, it is worth hiring a mechanic to get you the information that was stamped on it. Don't be tempted to just let it go. You'll need the model and serial number whenever you call a mechanic for help. Your mechanic must have accurate information to know how your equipment is configured, especially if he or she hasn't worked on that type of engine or transmission before. It's also vital information when ordering parts.

Fig. 1-1. The serial number plate.

2. Determine if the boat's transmission has a come-home feature. If it does, know how to engage it. This information will be found in the transmission service manual. (See also Figure 14-3 and Chapter 6.)

3. Locate and clean the transmission oil suction screen and filter, if so equipped. Most hydraulic transmission clutch failures start with a plugged suction screen. A failure is easy to spot early by monitoring any accumulation of metallic debris in the suction screen.

4. Find and check the oil dipsticks for both the engine and the transmission.

5. Learn how to check the coolant level (Fig. 1-2), and in cold climates keep track of the level of protection provided by the antifreeze. The coolant should be protected from freezing at temperatures as much as 20°F colder than the expected local minimum temperature.

In addition, you should monitor the coolant conditioner, an additive that minimizes the possibility of galvanic corrosion in the engine. You should do this in warm and cold climates. Fuel supply docks and most auto parts stores sell coolant test kits.

A large part of cooling system maintenance involves keeping the pH of the coolant slightly alkaline instead of acidic. Acidic coolant acts as an electrolyte, conducting corrosive

THE COME-HOME FEATURE

Imagine that the transmission in your car has failed, leaving you stranded on the side of the road. Now imagine that you could get going again by making a simple adjustment. Unfortunately, that isn't possible with a car, but it is for some boats!

Normally, a transmission in good condition connects the *power-absorbing* propeller to the *power-producing* engine. The connection is made in the transmission clutch pack. Some transmissions rated for under 100 hp use a mechanically activated clutch pack. However, transmissions mated with more powerful engines use a hydraulically activated clutch pack.

Until the hydraulic clutch is applied, the engine's crankshaft and the propeller shaft turn independently; there is no connection. When the control lever in the wheelhouse is pulled into gear, pressurized oil flows into the clutch pack and moves the clutch piston, which applies (locks) the clutch. After the clutch is applied, the two shafts turn together.

The come-home feature allows the forward clutch pack on transmissions to be mechanically clamped together to cause the clutch to lock up, regardless of whether the clutch is normally applied mechanically or hydraulically. This manual lock-up is done by turning two screws to force the clutch discs together, in effect connecting the engine crankshaft to the propeller even though the forward clutch pack may have failed.

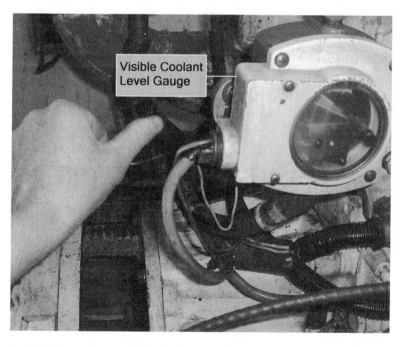

Fig. 1-2. Checking the coolant level indicator on a workboat. Many diesel power and sailing yachts also have this feature. If yours doesn't, you'll need to check the coolant level in an expansion tank as in Figure 1-6. (Courtesy MER Equipment, Seattle, Washington)

currents between the dissimilar metals that exist in any engine's cooling system. Such currents, if unchecked, can cause galvanic corrosion that destroys metal and any non-silicone rubber coolant hoses.

6. Check the engine's direct current (DC) electrical system, including the starter motor, alternator, batteries, starter switch, the DC breaker or fuse panel, the engine and transmission gauges, all interconnecting wires, and often electronic engine and transmission controls. *Note: If your boat has an AC system as well as DC, the two electrical panels are probably next to each other. Do not under any circumstances poke around behind an AC panel unless you know with absolute certainty that no power is flowing to the panel from a shore connection or from an onboard generator set.* If you have any doubts about your ability or the system, call a marine electrician.

Write down the part numbers and operating voltages for the engine's starter motor and alternator. Also record the starter motor's direction of rotation (abbreviated on the starter motor plate as DOR or sometimes DIR), which will obviously be either clockwise (CW) or counterclockwise (CCW). *Note: Alternators don't care which way they turn.*

WORKBOAT ONLY: Some workboats require the engine to power two alternators of two different voltages.

Next, find the boat's battery selector switch or switches. There are two different styles—the kind that *can* be switched with the engines running, and the kind that *cannot*. If your switch has two small wires running

to it in addition to the battery cables, then it is the type of switch that can be operated (or turned) with the engine running. If there are no small wires running to the switch, then it must not be turned with the engine running. Failure to observe this limitation will result in destroying the alternator. The boat may even have both kinds of switches.

7. After turning off any battery chargers (called constavolts in some parts of the U.S.) and all electrical loads, check the electrolyte levels in all liquid-electrolyte batteries with a good light. (This step does not apply to gel and absorbed glass mat, AGM batteries, which are also generically called sealed or no-maintenance batteries.) If a battery's electrolyte is below the top of the battery plates, add distilled water.

If the batteries are alike, with the same warranty date on each sticker, you have found a sign of good maintenance. Dissimilar batteries should be replaced by a matched set when it is convenient.

8. After turning off all battery chargers and loads, disconnect, clean, and reconnect all battery terminals. Inspect all battery cables for cracked insulation, which can result in short circuits or leak power to the electrical ground and discharge the batteries over time.

Also, check the ends of the cables by lifting an edge of the insulation and looking for green (copper) corrosion at the terminals. If corrosion is present, it may be a clue that the cable has been chronically wet or even submerged. If so, the cable must be replaced.

9. If your boat has a fire suppression system, find its sensors and controls and verify that

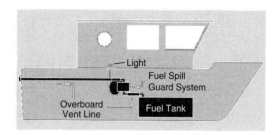

Fig. 1-3. The Spill Guard stops fuel spills.

the bottles are full. If you have any doubt about the system, have it inspected by a fire and safety professional. If your boat has fire extinguishers rather than a suppression system, verify that the extinguishers are fully charged, properly inspected, and properly secured in their brackets.

10. Assuming the boat has a diesel engine or engines, locate all valves for both sides of the fuel system (suction and the return). Note whether the fuel lines to and from the boat's fuel tanks are plumbed and valved to allow the engine or engines to pull fuel from the tanks on one side of the boat and send the return fuel to the other side of the boat. This type of system is only found on larger boats. It is used to adjust trim as fuel in a port or starboard tank is depleted. *Note: If the fuel system is plumbed this way, then it is also possible to return fuel to a full tank and thereby overfill the tank, sending fuel out the tank's vent and causing a fuel spill.* The Spill Guard by Herrington Marine Technologies stops fuel spills by alerting the crew with a flashing light when the tank is full.

11. Verify that all external fuel tank fill openings are properly sealed. If there is an O-ring seal on the fill cap, check it for visible damage and replace it if needed. This will help keep water out of the fuel. Likewise, find the fuel tank vents and be sure they are clear of obstructions.

12. Find the stuffing box (Fig. 1-4) and learn the best way to adjust it. The stuffing box is where the boat's propeller shaft exits the hull. The stuffing box contains the propeller shaft seal, and the job of the assembly is to keep the ocean out of the boat while allowing the shaft to turn. Most stuffing boxes are designed to admit a slow drip of water, which lubricates the shaft, and the purpose of adjustment is to obtain the proper drip rate. If the drip is too fast, the bilge fills with water; if it is not fast enough, the shaft overheats. *Note: Newer boats are often equipped with so-called dripless propeller shaft seals.*

13. Locate and check the condition of the boat's freshwater tank or tanks, and also look for leaky or damaged hoses or fittings. The boat's freshwater system should include a replaceable activated charcoal filter with an exterior label indicating the date it was last changed.

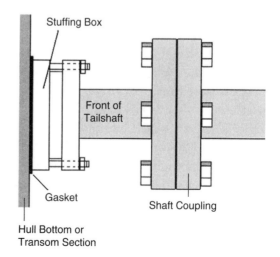

Fig. 1-4. Representative stuffing box.

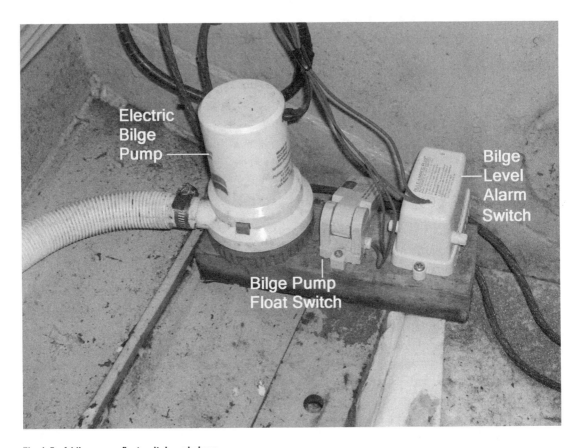

Fig. 1-5. A bilge pump, float switch, and alarm.

14. Find the best method for an emergency engine shutoff on your boat. See Chapter 2 for more on this.

15. Locate the bilge pumps and bilge pump switches (Fig. 1-5), together with their fuses or breakers. Bilge pumps have two possible settings—manual or automatic. Verify that each pump works properly on either setting.

16. Locate the engine cooling system's raw-water strainer and its valves, if so equipped. Check the freshwater (antifreeze) side of the system (Fig. 1-6) for evidence of leaks, damage to the plumbing, or chafing of these critical hoses. Replacing depleted sacrificial zincs is also important to prevent damaging

WORKBOAT ONLY: If your boat is very large, it may be worthwhile to obtain a gasoline-powered pump capable of rapidly pumping out the bilge. Practice starting and priming the pump, and identify the best location for it when it is in use and the best way to tie it in place during rough weather. If your boat has a watertight lazarette housing the steering mechanism, you may also need to figure out where to place your pump should it be necessary to pump water out of this compartment.

galvanic corrosion. Check the zincs and replace them as needed.

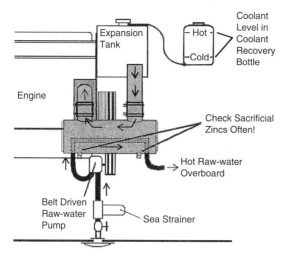

Fig. 1-6. A freshwater cooling system, showing a simplified heat exchanger. There is antifreeze in the freshwater side.

17. Locate all openings that pierce the hull and check for visible leaks, signs of corrosion (Fig. 1-7), and adequate tightness of the related fittings and hose clamps.

WORKBOAT ONLY: On a workboat engine that is raw-water cooled (a boat with a keel cooler instead of a heat exchanger), check the system for leaks, damaged hardware, or damage to the hoses.

---

18. Outboard engines: Check the engine mounting bolts for adequate tightness, fuel lines for kinks or chafing, and steering linkage for excess wear. Also, check all controls and electrical connections for any

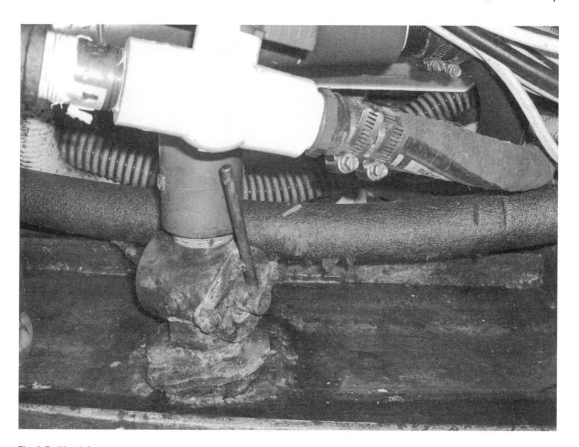

Fig. 1-7. Watch for corrosion where dissimilar metals meet.

apparent damage before starting the engine. If the engine is a newer four-stroke outboard, remember that the intake and exhaust valves do need to be adjusted periodically. If the engine is a two-stroke outboard, confirm whether it has automatic oil injection or not. If not, you will have to mix the oil into the fuel with each refueling. Read the engine manual to find the mixing ratio and the type of oil to add to the gasoline. Stock plenty of two-stroke oil on the boat.

ENGINE START-UP PROCEDURES

The previous section showed you what to check on a boat you are just getting to know. At the risk of some redundancy, here are procedures to follow each time you start your gasoline or diesel engine(s) to ensure long, trouble-free service:

- Check the engine and transmission oil levels.
- Check the coolant level.
- Remove the cover from a vertical

ROUTINE MAINTENANCE OF OUTBOARDS AND OUTDRIVES

The lower unit oil must be checked and changed regularly to keep water out of the gear lube in the lower unit. Because the outdrive is vented to eliminate pressure buildup, there is just no other way to keep atmospheric humidity out.

Fig. 1-8. Notice the oil drain plug.

Each outboard has its own system of zinc anodes to control corrosion. Waterborne electrical activity in a harbor can eat them up quickly. Be sure to monitor the life of the zincs throughout the unit while you are getting to know it. In time, you will know when to change them according to local conditions.

dry exhaust stack, if your boat is so equipped.

+ Check the battery charge.
+ Now crank and start the engine(s), keeping your eyes on the oil pressure gauge to verify that the oil pressure is correct.
+ Inspect the engine and transmission for leaks and excess noise.
+ Idle the engine up to 1,000 rpm in neutral.
+ Make note of the exhaust sound, and note the exhaust gas color; it must not be white.
+ Unless your boat has a dry exhaust, make sure a healthy flow of cooling water is coming out with the exhaust.
+ When the water (coolant)

temperature reaches 100°F, you can put the engine into gear and idle away from the dock.
+ When the water (coolant) temperature reaches 180°F, you can throttle up the engine to cruising speed.

TOOLS AND EQUIPMENT TO HAVE ON BOARD

This section is not meant to list a complete inventory of the tools you might need aboard. The focus is on a few items that have repeatedly proven their value. Here they are:

1. Jumper cables
2. A multimeter (electrical tester), along with the knowledge to use it (Fig. 1-9)

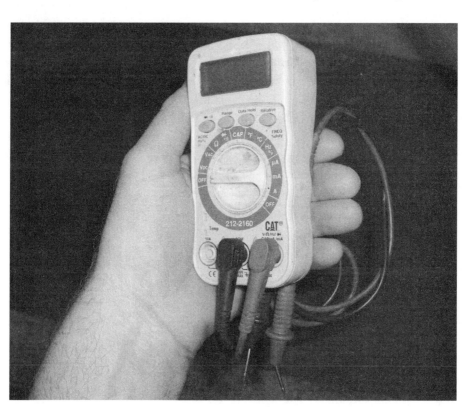

Fig. 1-9. Become familiar with the multimeter electrical tester.

Note: NAPA auto parts stores sell an excellent booklet that explains how to test electrical items with a multimeter. Strangely enough, it is titled Burn Baby Burn, *and it explains why so many electrical components are needlessly replaced due to ignorance of good electrical testing procedures.*

3. LED flashlights

4. A shut-down paddle for stopping a runaway engine (see page 15)

5. Left-handed drill bits and Easy-Outs for removing broken bolts (see below)

6. A battery-powered Dremel tool (die grinder) and battery-powered carbide burrs (rotary files)

OTHER ITEMS TO HAVE ON BOARD

In addition to the foregoing, the following materials, spares, and fasteners may come in handy. They are so easy to carry that it would be a shame not to have any of them should the need arise.

1. You should have conversion charts to switch measurement units for bolt-tightening torque and for any other application.

2. Ultra-Gray Silicone Sealer is heat resistant and is especially useful because it sets up very firm. Good silicone sealants will replace many paper and fiber gaskets.

3. Rolls of gasket paper in various grades and thicknesses are essential for maintenance and repairs. Both $1/_{32}$ and $1/_{16}$ inch are good thicknesses to have on the boat. In a pinch, however, a temporary gasket can be made from cereal box paper. Just cut open a Cheerios box and cut the gasket's shape from the paper, then put a light coat of silicone sealer on both sides and install. In addition, any paper suitable for a gasket will also make a good shim.

4. Speaking of shims and shim stock, remember that some shims must be made of metal, such as steel, stainless steel, aluminum, brass, or copper. In a pinch, aluminum pop cans make a good shim. Galvanized and stainless steel stove pipe are also commonly available and make good shims.

5. Marvel Mystery Oil is an "upper cylinder lube," which means it is a good lubricant for valve guides and piston rings. It is available at most fuel docks and auto parts stores and can be added to both the engine lubricating oil and the fuel tank for use with either a gasoline or diesel engine.

6. It's important to carry both stainless steel and high-strength bolts and hardware on oceangoing boats. Engine bolts and fasteners, such as those that mount the alternator, are high-strength. In the United States, a high-strength bolt such as one of the ones attaching an alternator to an engine is called a Grade 8 bolt in the hardware and auto parts stores that sell them.

Spare fasteners come in ready-made kits from marine suppliers, or you can buy a case with many compartments and make your own selection. Other boaters will have good suggestions based on their own experience.

7. Carry spare oil pressure and water temperature gauges and senders (Fig. 1-10). Engines have been rebuilt when all that was wrong was a failed oil pressure sender that showed no oil pressure. At the first sign of high water temperature or low oil pressure, be sure to consider a failed sender. On the other hand, you should definitely consider that the gauge is accurate until you know otherwise. Trust but verify; verify the alarming readings with mechanical gauges

Fig. 1-10. Carry spare gauge senders.

that provide a reading with no electrical input.

If you don't have mechanical gauges installed on the engine, consider carrying pressure and temperature test kits. These kits are available from Snap-on Tools.

8. Carry high-quality black and red electrical tape for insulation purposes and for marking positive and negative electrical conductors.

9. You'll want to carry assorted sizes of crimp-on electrical terminals and heat-shrink tubing. The latter is plastic tubing that shrinks around electrical wires when heated. Small electrical supply kits are available at auto parts stores and offer a good assortment of terminals and heat-shrink tubing.

10. Aquarium-grade silicone sealant is handy to have for emergency repair of the boat's drinking water plumbing. If it won't harm fish, it won't harm you either!

11. Thread-locking compound (Loctite) keeps bolts and nuts from vibrating loose and is highly useful stuff to have around.

12. Spare engine-cooling system thermostats are important to have when an engine is running too hot or cold.

ROUTINE MAINTENANCE PROCEDURES

Know how to do the following routine procedures:

+ crimp electrical terminals
+ adjust your engine's valves
+ adjust the fuel injection timing
+ replace the water pump
+ change the engine and transmission oil and filters
+ change the engine air filter
+ drain water from the fuel tanks
+ switch from one fuel tank to the other while under way

EMERGENCY RESPONSE SCENARIOS

There are a few emergency topics you should consider at length well ahead of time. If you do your homework regarding these potential problems, odds are you'll never have to apply the knowledge. If you don't prepare for them, you know how Murphy's Law works.

1. First, unless your diesel engine is self-bleeding, learn the procedure for bleeding air from its fuel system.

Note: All gasoline engines and some diesel engines have self-bleeding fuel systems.

2. Learn the procedure for bleeding air from your engine's cooling system after the coolant has been drained and refilled.

3. Know all the possible sources of water that can sink or damage your boat, and know how to halt each one.

Rainwater can flood a boat that has a vertical exhaust stack, a problem limited to workboats for the most part. Sailboats and recreational powerboats with horizontal exhaust systems can also suffer damage from water ingress through the exhaust system,

though in this case the water has gotten in due to wave action against the stern. A rubber flap on the outside of the hull will prevent water from entering the exhaust system when a following sea washes against the exhaust outlet.

With water-lift mufflers, proper installation of the exhaust system will keep water out of the boat. The engine's raw cooling water flows through a hose from the heat exchanger to the exhaust elbow, where it is injected into the exhaust. This hose should be looped at least 6 inches (preferably 12 inches) above the waterline, with a siphon break in the top of the loop. This will prevent water from siphoning from the muffler back into the exhaust manifold and then to the cylinders.

WORK-AROUND SOLUTION

Turn Your Engine into a Bilge Pump

By replumbing your engine's raw-water pump, it is possible to take water from the bilge and pump it overboard. Simply detach the raw-water intake hose from its seacock (after closing the seacock) and plunge it into the bilge as shown in the illustration. Of course, this will only work on relatively slow leaks.

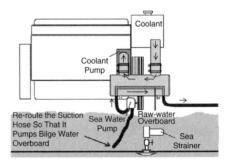

Fig. 1-11. Replumb the freshwater cooling system to pump the bilge.

WORK-AROUND SOLUTION

Stop a Runaway Diesel Engine

A runaway engine is usually a diesel engine that is out of control and revving beyond the top speed limit of the engine's governor. High speed is far more destructive to a diesel engine than a gasoline engine for one very good reason: the rods and pistons are far heavier for a given bore size in a diesel. As speed increases, forces of inertia multiply quickly. The crankshaft throws the piston toward top dead center for the last time. The rod or rod bolts break and the engine fails!

One way to quickly stop a runaway diesel engine is to cut off its air supply with a fabricated metal paddle. **Caution: Do not under any circumstances use a hand or any other part of your body for this.** Alternatively, if you lack the time or means to shut off the air, the next best thing to do is to break off a vital fuel fitting in the incoming fuel supply plumbing.

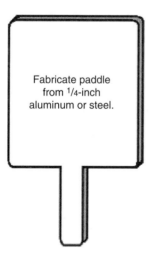

Fabricate paddle from 1/4-inch aluminum or steel.

Fig. 1-12. Use a metal paddle to stop airflow to the engine.

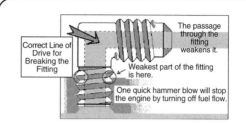

Correct Line of Drive for Breaking the Fitting

The passage through the fitting weakens it.

Weakest part of the fitting is here.

One quick hammer blow will stop the engine by turning off fuel flow.

Fig. 1-13. Break the fuel fitting with a blow from the side.

Further, on sailboats, the engine's exhaust outlet from the exhaust manifold is sometimes well below the vessel's waterline. There should be a high, above-the-waterline loop in the exhaust line between the water-lift muffler and the exhaust outlet to stop water from siphoning in.

The propeller shaft stuffing box is another source of water coming into the vessel. Since the stuffing box seal is low in the boat and usually tucked out of sight, it can be dripping without being noticed right away. This makes adjustment of the stuffing box seal important. The gasket behind the stuffing box can also leak. See Figure 1-4 earlier in this chapter.

Another possible source of water in the bilge is a leaking freshwater tank. Rain can enter the boat in other places besides a vertical exhaust stack, such as through poorly caulked areas on deck. Suspect one of these sources if the water in your bilge tastes fresh.

Leaks along the keel and planking of a wooden hull or at the outside of poorly sealed through-hull fittings are another place where water can enter the boat.

Of course, hitting a rock and punching a hole in the hull will quickly sink a boat. If there is time for coast guard personnel to respond, they will often drop gasoline-powered pumps on board so you can attempt to pump out the boat. Even these may not be big enough, however, unless the leak is slowed or stopped.

REPAIRING AND REPLACING DAMAGED FASTENERS AND FITTINGS

1. Broken steel engine exhaust bolts or studs that are broken off in a blind hole

If possible, start the engine and get it up to operating temperature, then turn it off and disassemble as necessary to the point where candle wax can be dripped on the exposed threads of the exhaust bolt or on the bolt stub. The wax will melt and find its way along the bolt threads. If there is a stub sticking out, an effort must be made to grab it with Vise-Grip locking pliers. If it can't be gripped, then it is a good idea to first weld a washer onto the stub, and then weld a nut to the washer. Next, attempt to turn the stub out by the nut that was just welded (Fig. 1-14).

A bolt remnant that has broken off flush or recessed below the surface of the work piece (Fig. 1-15) will usually be loose in the threads. In such a case, it often works to carefully use a punch or chisel and drive on the outer perimeter of the bolt to turn it counterclockwise. If this won't move it, use a left-handed drill bit to

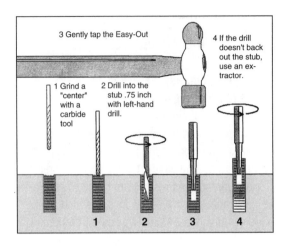

Fig. 1-15. Removing below-flush broken bolts.

drill a hole in the bolt so that an Easy-Out may be driven into the freshly drilled hole to remove the bolt.

Just starting to drill a broken stud with a left-handed bit will typically be enough to turn the bolt out of the threads.

2. A rounded-off bolt head or a head that has rusted away

First, try an undersized 6-point box-end wrench as shown in Fig. 1-16. If this does not

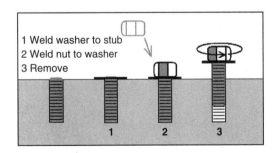

Fig. 1-14. One way to break out a fastener stub that is standing proud of the work surface.

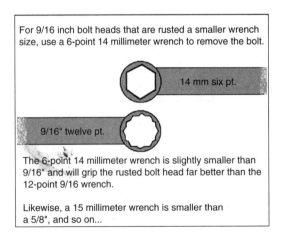

Fig. 1-16. Use a slightly undersized 6-point wrench to remove rounded fasteners.

work, dress off the rounded head and press or drive a larger nut over the head of the bolt, then weld the larger nut to the bolt head.

3. A bolt used for through-bolting is broken off

If the back of the bolt can be accessed, it can sometimes be turned by gripping with pliers after treating it with candle wax or penetrating oil.

4. A threaded bolt used for through-bolting is broken off, but not in a blind hole

A broken threaded bolt in this state (Fig. 1-17) can, with practice and skill, be blown out with a cutting torch, leaving the threads undamaged. After the bolt is blown out, use a thread tap to clean the holes.

5. A threaded brass (yellow metal) fitting is broken off in a blind hole

An internal pipe wrench (Fig. 1-18) or large extractor (Fig. 1-19) will usually remove this kind of fitting. The internal pipe wrench fits inside the piece to be removed. As the wrench is turned, it expands. This action saves collapsing and damaging the fitting during removal.

6. A pipe nipple is to be removed

The nipple will sometimes collapse under the jaw pressure of a conventional external pipe wrench, especially if it is thin-walled. To prevent this, insert a solid, snug-fitting object into the nipple before using the pipe wrench (Fig. 1-20). Even a piece of wood can be driven inside the pipe.

7. A threaded steel (gray or bright metal) or aluminum fitting is broken off in a blind hole.

Use an internal pipe wrench to remove a larger broken fitting, and an Easy-Out style extractor to remove a smaller one. In Figure 1-21, an aluminum coolant pipe fitting was broken off in an aluminum coolant passage boss on an intake manifold. A large-diameter extractor was first driven into the broken-off stub of the threaded fitting. Then the outside of the threaded boss in the manifold was heated to expand the metal around the broken fitting, and finally the broken remnant

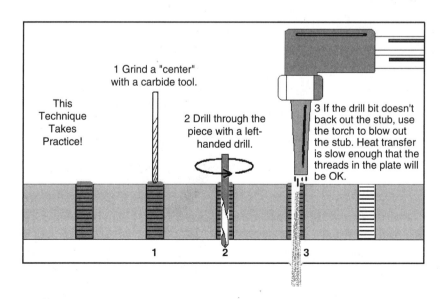

Fig. 1-17. Removing a broken through-bolted stub.

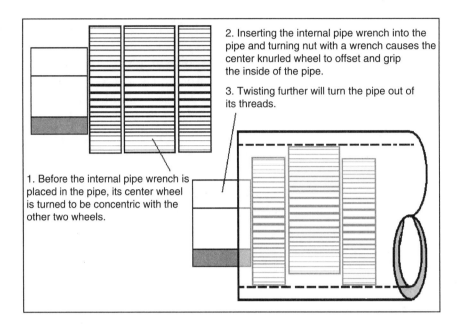

2. Inserting the internal pipe wrench into the pipe and turning nut with a wrench causes the center knurled wheel to offset and grip the inside of the pipe.

3. Twisting further will turn the pipe out of its threads.

1. Before the internal pipe wrench is placed in the pipe, its center wheel is turned to be concentric with the other two wheels.

Fig. 1-18. Using an internal pipe wrench.

Fig. 1-19. An extractor for broken bolts and fittings, showing the helical grooves in its business end. Figure 1-21 shows it in use.

was turned counterclockwise (with a box-end wrench on the extractor) and removed.

MATERIAL SAFETY DATA SHEETS

There is a material safety data sheet (MSDS) available free of charge for any chemical product sold in the United States, and product manufacturers are required by law to provide one upon request.

Because the marine environment is harsh, chemical products (lubricants, cleaners, paints, etc.) used to maintain boats must be of industrial strength, as opposed to consumer strength, to provide the required strong cleansing and protective action. What this means to the boatowner is that certain chemical compounds or dust particles found on boats can easily and irreversibly harm you or your children before you know you have been hurt! Strong detergents, the contents of fire extinguishers, solvents, polyurethane compounds, and even the fumes from charging batteries are just a few items to consider. Protect yourself and especially any children who may be on the boat by obtaining and reading the MSDS for the products you are using on board.

KEEP YOURSELF SAFE

Take the necessary and commonsense safety precautions when working on boats. For

Fig. 1-20. Preventing pipe nipple collapse. (Courtesy MER Equipment, Seattle, Washington)

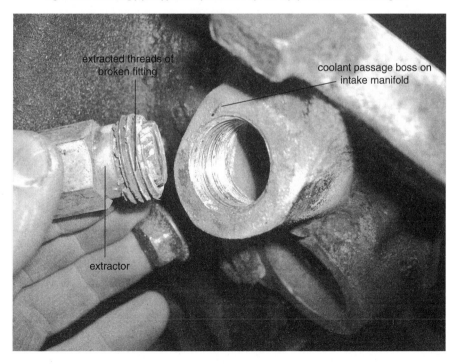

Fig. 1-21. An extractor in action.

example, you should obtain solvent-resistant or vinyl gloves to protect your hands and skin from chemical compounds. When your work will create loud noises, wear earplugs or other types of ear protection.

When you're grinding or using hazardous chemicals, wear safety glasses and use a full-face shield over the glasses. When you're grinding or welding, wear leather gloves to protect your hands.

Finally, for breathing protection from dust particles and mist, use a respirator with the correct cartridge inserts for the job you are doing. Get a chemical cartridge when appropriate, and a dust and particulate cartridge for grinding wood, fiberglass, or metal.

CHAPTER 2

UNDERSTANDING MARINE ENGINES

There is no more critical piece of machinery on your boat than its engine, so this where we'll start our tour of mechanical systems. This chapter introduces both gasoline and diesel engines, showing how they're similar and where they differ.

Like marine gasoline engines, marine diesel engines come with either a single cylinder (often called a one-lunger), in-line cylinders (2, 3, 4, 5, or 6), or V configurations. The cylinders in an in-line engine are arrayed in a single row, whereas a V engine has two banks, or rows, of cylinders.

Both gas and diesel engines come in V-6, V-8, and V-10 configurations, and diesels can also have a V-12 or even a V-16 configuration. Those are big engines indeed. However, most diesel engines found on recreational sailboats are typically less than 50 hp and have up to four cylinders. The more powerful marine gasoline engines, including inboard/outboard and common outboard engines, are often V configurations, whereas very small inboard/outboard and outboard engines have in-line configurations.

Inboard/outboard engine installations (stern drives), keep the engine inside the hull like a true inboard, but a rotating shaft pierces the transom and connects the engine to an outdrive (leg) through the transom of the boat. The outdrive usually contains the unit's forward and reverse gears as well as the propeller. On the other hand, an outboard engine is obviously mounted entirely outside the hull. Please see Chapter 12 for more on outboard engines and stern drives. This chapter will focus on diesel and gasoline inboard engines.

IN-LINE ENGINES

Most in-line engines are easy to maintain and keep clean, largely because all the cylinders are lined up in a single row, making them easier to access than on V engines. In-line engine designs vary, as shown in Figure 2-1, but regardless of design differences the working principles remain the same for either diesel or gasoline models. A key difference between them, however, is that marine diesel engines can have multiple heads, whereas in-line gasoline engines have only one cylinder head per engine. The cylinders on an in-line engine are numbered starting from the front end, where the water pump is located. The first cylinder is the one closest to the water pump.

The locations of the timing gears and fuel system components in in-line engines vary widely. Figure 2-2 shows the timing gears on a John Deere diesel. (In marine engines, the front of the engine is always the end opposite the flywheel, and the transmission is always at the rear end, outside the flywheel. In a standard propulsion system the front of the engine is forward, but in a V drive it's aft.) This is the ideal location for the timing gears because it allows for quick "in-frame overhauls" when an

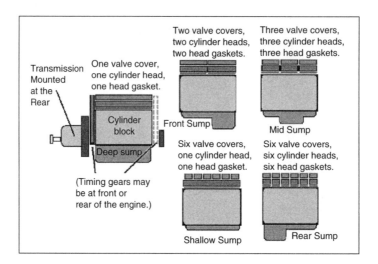

Transmission Mounted at the Rear

One valve cover, one cylinder head, one head gasket.

Cylinder block

Deep sump

(Timing gears may be at front or rear of the engine.)

Two valve covers, two cylinder heads, two head gaskets.

Three valve covers, three cylinder heads, three head gaskets.

Front Sump

Mid Sump

Six valve covers, one cylinder head, one head gasket.

Six valve covers, six cylinder heads, six head gaskets.

Shallow Sump

Rear Sump

Fig. 2-1. In-line engine configurations.

Fig. 2-2. Front-mounted diesel engine timing gears.

THE IN-FRAME OVERHAUL

The term "in-frame overhaul" originated with trucks and heavy equipment, and it usually applies to diesel engines. When an in-frame overhaul is performed, the engine remains bolted to the boat. Leaving the engine in place is quick and inexpensive compared to removing it for a complete rebuild. In-frame overhauls will restore full power to the engine, and most diesels can be in-framed twice before a full reconditioning is necessary.

Although an in-frame overhaul is quicker than a complete rebuild, it still takes work. The first step involves removing the coolant pump, cylinder head, oil pan, and lube oil pump. The piston and connecting rod assemblies, along with the cylinder liners, have to come out, and the block and all gasket surfaces must be cleaned. To finish the job, you'll need a cylinder kit. A cylinder kit includes the piston, rings, wrist pins, and cylinder liners. Install these new parts and replace the coolant pump. Replacing the lube oil pump is optional, depending on its condition.

Diesel engines are rugged, and many parts can be reused, as specified by the engine manufacturer. If the crankshaft bearing journals are in good condition and the manufacturer's specifications say it is OK, the crankshaft and even the existing bearings can be reused. You can often order specialized manuals from engine dealers that provide details on which parts are acceptable for reuse. For example, if you own a Caterpillar diesel, you could order the *Engine Bearings and Crankshaft* manual (publication number SEBD0531).

Front-mounted timing gears also allow better access for camshaft repairs or replacement when the engine loses efficiency due to wear. Easy access means it is less time-consuming and less expensive to do the work, always a big plus. In addition, the timing gears often drive the fuel injection system, and when they are front-mounted it is much easier to uncouple the engine from the transmission to replace the camshaft or repair the timing gear train.

The timing gears on all new four-stroke marine gasoline engines in North America, the market I'm familiar with, and many marine diesel engines are front-mounted. On four-stroke outboards, the timing gears are positioned at the top of the engine.

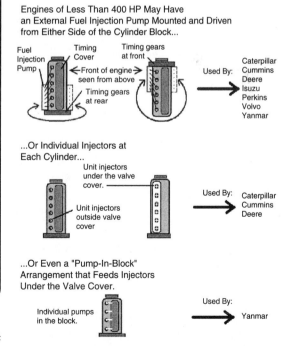

Fig. 2-3. **Various fuel system configurations for in-line diesel engines.**

engine rebuild is required; it eliminates the time-consuming and expensive job of uncoupling the engine from the transmission.

V ENGINES

A V engine has two rows of cylinders, called the left and right banks. The term "bank" refers to one side of a V engine, hence the right- and left-handed designation, and it can only be used to describe the cylinders on this type of engine. In-line engines don't have banks, since there is only one row of cylinders, not two.

Identifying the first cylinder of an in-line engine is pretty simple. It is a little trickier on a V engine because the location varies. On one, the first (No. 1) cylinder may be on the left bank and on another it may be on the right bank. However, as a general rule,

cylinder numbering usually starts at the front end (i.e., the water-pump end) of the engine. The cylinder closest to the water pump is the first (No. 1) cylinder.

It does get interesting here, though, because the two forwardmost cylinders on a V engine both share one "crank pin" on the crankshaft. However, because of the cylinder offset required for two connecting rods to fit on one crank pin, one of the two cylinders will be ahead of the other. The forwardmost one is cylinder No. 1.

It definitely matters which cylinder is first in the firing order. Engine manufacturers usually start with that one for timing and firing-order purposes, and shop manuals will require you to identify it before going to work.

Again, every V engine has one bank of cylinders offset forward or aft of the other (when viewed from overhead) by the thickness of the big end of the connecting rod, as shown in Fig. 2-4.

Cylinder heads, valve covers, and head gasket systems (Fig. 2-5) also vary by manufacturer. Some companies will install one

---

TERMINOLOGY FOR IN-LINE AND V ENGINES

When ordering parts for a V or in-line engine, pretend you are facing the flywheel mounted on the rear of the engine. Then refer to either the right or left *side* of an in-line engine, or the right or left *bank* of a V engine. Don't mix up the terms *side* and *bank*; it will cause confusion at the order desk. Simply say you need a part for the left side of an in-line engine or for the left bank of a V engine, and take it from there.

The reason for visualizing yourself standing at the flywheel end of either type of engine when ordering parts is simple: engines can be mounted with the flywheel facing the bow or stern, depending on the driveshaft configuration (V drive or straight). A generator can be mounted athwartships, further complicating matters. If you always use the flywheel as a reference point, you won't confuse left with right, and you will receive the correct parts when your order arrives.

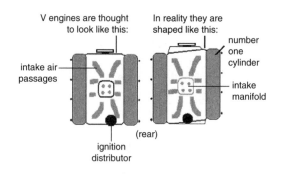

Fig. 2-4. On V engines, one bank of cylinders is offset forward or aft of the other when viewed from overhead. In this gasoline V-8 schematic, the distributor shows as a black dot at the rear of the engine.

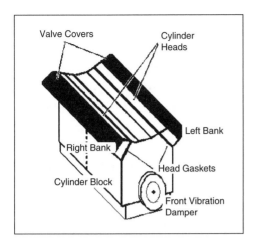

Fig. 2-5. Diesel V-engine construction. In this schematic we're looking at the engine's front end, where the water pump would be located.

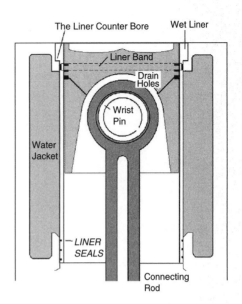

Fig. 2-6. Wet cylinder liner.

cylinder head for each bank, whereas others will install multiple heads. There are other variations too, such as multiple head gaskets, heads, and valve covers, and each diesel engine manufacturer has its own type of cylinder configuration. Cylinder design and construction materials determine the cost of the engine, its length, weight, longevity, efficiency, and ease of maintenance and repair. The many variables won't pose a problem as long as you know your particular engine.

WET CYLINDER LINERS

Just what is a wet cylinder liner? The term describes a diesel engine where engine coolant is in direct contact with the outer diameter of the replaceable cylinder liner (a wet liner). See Figure 2-6 for an example. Some diesel engines have wet liners, but you won't find them in marine gasoline engines in North America.

Diesel engines with wet liners can be rebuilt a number of times before the cylinder block becomes worn and the liner counter bore requires a trip to the machine shop.

The liner counter bore is the step machined into the cylinder block; the cylinder liner flange rests on the step. When the cylinder head bolts clamp the head gasket between the cylinder head and the top cylinder liner flange, the force exerted on the cylinder liner counter bore is considerable. Once tightened (torqued) according to specification, the head bolts stretch a little and in effect become powerful springs.

While the wet liner design does provide for cylinder replacement that brings the engine back to the level of power and efficiency it had when new, the design does have one major drawback. Wet liners can allow coolant to leak into the oil pan if the liner counter bore doesn't fit properly, if the liner develops a pinhole, or if the liner seals fail.

THE DRY CYLINDER LINER

Engines that have a replaceable sleeve (wear surface) to house the piston and rings are described as dry liners. In contrast to wet

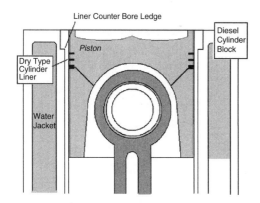

Fig. 2-7. Dry cylinder liner.

liners, dry liners are not in direct contact with coolant, so there will never be a coolant leak into the oil pan (Fig. 2-7).

PARENT BORE CYLINDER BLOCKS

Engines that have the cylinder bore cast and then finished in the cylinder block (Fig. 2-8) are said to be parent bore engines, that is, they have no replaceable cylinder liner. The advantage of this common automotive gasoline engine design is that it makes for a lighter and less expensive cylinder block. The parent

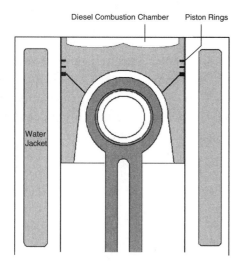

Fig. 2-8. Parent bore cylinder block construction.

bore block design is also used in relatively light, high-speed diesel engines.

DIRECTION OF ROTATION (DOR)

To understand engine crankshaft rotation direction, consider a chicken slowly turning on a rotisserie at the deli. To a person viewing the head end of the now headless chicken, the bird will appear to be turning clockwise. However, if we change our vantage point to view the bird from the other end of the skewer—i.e. from the tail end of the featherless fricassee—it will appear to be turning counterclockwise.

As with a rotisserie chicken, standard engine crankshaft rotation is counterclockwise as viewed from the rear, for the sake of consistency when ordering engine-driven accessories such as hydraulic pumps and air compressors. And, similarly, looking at the crank's movement from the other end will show it is turning clockwise as seen from the front.

Now let's turn our attention to the direction the cam turns (Fig. 2-9). The reason to do this is in case we must order and install an accessory that drives off the cam instead of the crankshaft.

The cam and crank turn the same direction when a chain or belt drives the camshaft, as seen in engine No. 1 in Fig. 2-9. The cam in engine No. 2, however, rotates in the opposite direction from the crank. Yet a third application, engine No. 3, uses an idler gear to drive the cam, and as shown, the cam turns the same direction as the crankshaft.

ENGINE MECHANISMS AND SYSTEMS

Every marine engine, regardless of its configuration, has mechanisms and systems that support its operation. Some of the systems are

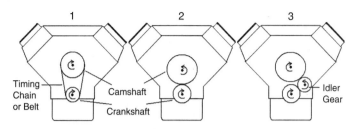

Fig. 2-9. Direction of crankshaft and cam rotation.

parasitic and draw power from the engine but still permit it to run well. In fact, the engine won't run without some of the parasitic systems. The oil pump, for example, draws power, and it's a necessity.

While designs vary, every reciprocating engine (those with pistons traveling up and down) must have the following twenty mechanisms and systems, many of which absorb power:

1. fuel system
2. cooling system
3. air intake system
4. exhaust system
5. lubrication system
6. starting and electrical system
7. engine cover system (the valve cover, for example)
8. emission control system
9. fastening system (head bolts and other fasteners)
10. sealing system (consisting of gaskets, O-rings, and lip-type seals)
11. plumbing system
12. filtration system
13. control system
14. engine mounting system
15. camshaft and timing gear mechanism
16. piston, connecting rod, and cylinder mechanism
17. valve operating mechanism
18. cylinder head mechanism (including valves, seats, springs, and retainers)
19. cylinder block and crankshaft mechanism
20. flywheel mechanism

To learn the troubleshooting skills that apply to your boat's engine, you must take the time to get familiar with it. The first step is to become acquainted with the engine manual. Go through it, focusing on each system common to all reciprocating engines. Learn the particulars of yours. This is important because spare parts and maintenance procedures are specific to each brand and model of engine. Use the list of twenty mechanisms and systems as a guide. Let's take a look at an interesting example that will illustrate how different one engine can be from another.

In the 1970s, banjo fittings, fuel fittings shaped like banjos, were only found in engines manufactured in Japan or Europe (Fig. 2-10). In North America at that time, most engine manufacturers used either pipe threads or flanges. Sometimes the flange required a gasket or O-ring seal. Thus, the parts and procedures to deal with an emergency leak differed, depending on where the engine was made. Does your boat need spare pipe fittings (North American), or does it need spare

hose carrying air, oil, fuel, or coolant

Fig. 2-10. A banjo fitting like this can carry fuel, air, oil, or coolant. In practice the bolt threads into a port (note the threads at top left), and the banjo bolt is tightened until the port in its shank, which is visible in the photo, is recessed into the fitting. The fluid then flows from the engine block or accessory into the banjo bolt, then makes a right-angle turn through the banjo bolt's port and is distributed to its destination.

copper washers (European or Japanese) for banjo fittings? It's a good idea to find out.

Consider the engine fasteners. Are they metric bolts or standard ones based on the criteria set by the Society of Automotive Engineers (SAE)? Do the heads of the bolts use metric or SAE sockets? Should your spare O-ring seal kit be metric or SAE? How is the front crankshaft pulley retained on the crankshaft? Is it fixed to a tapered shaft or a keyed tapered shaft? Is the shaft straight and keyed, or is it straight but not keyed? Paying attention to details like these will enable you to effectively deal with any trouble that might come up while you are on the water.

COMBUSTION CHAMBERS

The combustion chamber configuration constitutes an important difference between gasoline and diesel engines. Gasoline engines have the chamber above the top of the piston as shown in Figure 2-11, while most diesel engines have the chamber below the top of the piston. This is especially important after an engine is submerged or develops a hydraulic lock, meaning there is fluid in the cylinder above the piston.

If a gasoline engine develops a hydraulic lock, most of the fluid above the rings will, in time, leak into the crankcase through the gaps at the ends of the piston rings. You would remove the excess fluid by simply draining the crankcase oil.

However, when the combustion chamber is in the piston, as is the case with many diesel engines, the fluid must be removed from the piston crown before attempting to start the engine. For complete directions on clearing a hydraulically locked diesel engine, see Chapter 11.

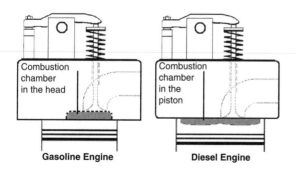

Fig. 2-11. **Gasoline and diesel engine combustion chambers.**

When a hydraulically locked diesel engine is to be drained and restored after submersion, it can be done without removing the heads. However, as mentioned above, the engine will require special measures to clear the fluid in the piston crown. If this is not done, severe overpressurizing of the cylinder will occur when the starter motor is energized. For more on this, please see Chapter 11.

DIESEL ENGINE OPERATION WHEN STARTING

When you start a diesel, the engine turns and each cylinder fires in succession. During this process the engine must overcome the increasing power demand from parasitic loads, especially when the engine is cold. When a 12-volt starter motor begins cranking a large cold diesel engine, voltage at the starter can drop from 13.8 volts to only 10. Amperage does the opposite, going from zero to well over 1,500 amps in an instant. The sudden, strong electromagnetic field around the starter cables may make them twitch or seem to crawl. Add parasitic loads into the equation and you can see why a cold start can sometimes be troublesome. The following are examples of parasitic loads during engine start-up.

Power is needed for

1. overcoming inertia (resistance to motion) and turning the heavy flywheel and related components;
2. turning the fuel transfer pump;
3. the fuel injection equipment (or ignition system);
4. the engine oil pump;
5. the engine coolant pump;
6. the alternator;

7. moving the column of cold air in the exhaust pipes and muffler;
8. moving the pistons in cylinders that are not yet firing, along with their valve mechanisms.

Another big energy draw includes starting an engine with a power-take-off engaged. This will greatly increase the load on the starter motor. (A power-take-off, or PTO, usually powers a hydraulic pump that drives a pot hauler, rigging hoist, etc., on a workboat.)

DIESEL FUEL INJECTION

While the piston is approaching top-dead-center on the compression stroke, the fuel injection system quickly builds high pressure to inject fuel into the cylinders. The fuel bursts into each cylinder and ignites in the hot, freshly compressed air in the cylinder. The heated air results from compression. This process happens one cylinder at a time, based on the engine's firing order. Plenty of fuel is injected into the cylinders to get the engine turning at start-up, but the amount the governor delivers quickly diminishes as the engine accelerates to its preset low idle speed.

LUBRICATION

Prior to start-up, when the engine was turned off the night before, the lubricating oil slowly receded from between many of the components that depend so much on it. As the engine begins to turn, the oil pump quickly lifts a column of oil from the oil pan and forces all the air from the lubrication system. With the air gone, the vital lubricating oil flows in and around and through the engine, within seconds of starting. In addition to providing lubrication, the oil film centers the big end of each connecting rod around its crankpin on the crankshaft.

As the oil pressure increases, the crankshaft seems to levitate and soon rises to the center of its bore in the cylinder block. It is lifted to and supported in this position by the oil wedge that acts between the crankshaft journals and the engine bearings. It would not be far-fetched to say the crankshaft surfs on a film of oil.

If the crankshaft main bearings have four thousandths (0.004) of an inch oil clearance, then the combination of oil pressure and the rotation of the crankshaft will lift the crankshaft half this distance, or 0.002 of an inch, to the center of its bore. This weight can be several hundred pounds, depending on the weight of the crankshaft, flywheel, and the vibration damper. If the engine has a front-mounted power-take-off clutch, the oil film must lift this additional weight as well. On larger engines this weight can exceed one thousand pounds.

THE EXHAUST SYSTEM

When the engine was at rest, the exhaust system and muffler were full of cool, dense air. This heavy column of air in the exhaust system initially resists movement. But after the engine starts, it does move, though slowly at first, like molasses. Soon the exhaust gases, which can be as hot as 250 to 600°F soon after starting, push the cold air out of the system. Later, as the engine warms, these gases will become even hotter and expand, losing density and becoming much easier to pump through the exhaust system. The two main types of marine exhaust systems are covered in Chapter 8.

HORSEPOWER AND TORQUE

A basic understanding of horsepower and torque is essential to broadening your working knowledge of marine engines. Let's start by briefly defining them both. As shown in

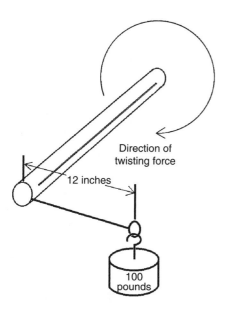

Direction of
twisting force

12 inches

100
pounds

Fig. 2-12. One hundred foot-pounds of torque.

minute (rpm) is the term in common use. To clarify torque, consider what happens when you attempt to remove a stuck screw: twisting force with no movement of the screw is purely torque.

James Watt, an Englishman, defined horsepower in quantifiable terms by learning what a good horse could lift with a block and tackle, and also how long it took the horse to do a certain amount of work. He found a horse could raise 200 pounds of ore 165 feet in one minute. This is equal to lifting 33,000 pounds to a height of one foot in one minute, which he defined as 1 hp.

In a boat with a displacement hull, the engine always "thinks" it is going up a steep hill. Therefore, the power ratings for a marine propulsion engine in this application will usually be a continuous rating rather than an intermittent rating. In other words, the engine will be rated at a level of power that it can sustain the majority of the time it is running.

To illustrate this concept, let's examine some important differences (Table 2-1) between two 350 hp engines. One is a gasoline engine

Figure 2-12, torque is a twisting force, and the common unit of torque in North America is the foot-pound.

Horsepower describes how fast a shaft with a known load and measure of torque will turn in a specific time period. Revolutions per

Table 2-1. Comparison of 350 HP Gasoline and Diesel Engines		
	1970 Vintage Hot Rod	**Common Truck**
	350 hp V-8 gasoline engine	350 hp diesel engine
Cylinders	8	6
RPM	6,300	2,100
Cruising rpm	2,000–3,000	1,300–1,650
Highest torque	300 ft.-lb. at 2,800 rpm	1,400 ft.-lb. at 1,300 rpm
Bore size	4 inches	5½ inches
Stroke	3½ inches	6 inches
Engine displacement	350 cubic inches	855 cubic inches
Engine weight	600 lb.	2,000 lb.
Fuel consumption	½ lb. of fuel per hp per hour	⅓ lb. of fuel per hp per hour
Fuel economy	8 mpg with 4,000 lb. rolling load	7 mpg with 75,000 lb. rolling load
Miles between tune-ups	20,000	50,000
Engine life	100,000 miles	1,000,000 miles +

in a small car, and the other is a heavy-duty diesel engine in a truck.

POWER RATINGS

Both engines in Table 2-1 have excess power available. Neither of them will produce maximum power all the time. The hot-rod enthusiast wants excess power to accelerate quickly. However, the truck driver needs excess power to accelerate with a heavy load, often bucking a headwind or climbing a hill. The table compares these two different types of engines to show how horsepower relates to engine speed and torque. It is easy to see that a low-torque engine can do a lot of work quickly when rpm is increased. While increasing engine speed does raise horsepower, it also reduces engine life. The table can be summarized another way: engine efficiency equals power produced (work done) based on fuel type.

ENGINE RATINGS

The truck engine in Table 2-1 has an intermittent rating—that is, it can't produce 350 hp every hour it is running, but only when the truck is briskly accelerating or climbing a hill. The driver watches the exhaust temperature gauge and must downshift and ease off the throttle when the exhaust temperature climbs too high. Once the top of the hill is reached, the driver downshifts and also throttles back for the downgrade, and the engine cools off as indicated by the exhaust temperature gauge, otherwise known as the pyrometer.

HORSEPOWER RATINGS IN BOATS

Small powerboats, such as those used for waterskiing or brief sprints across a lake, have pleasure craft ratings for those short bursts of speed. Oceangoing sailboats use far less power per foot of length than, say, a commercial

FOR THE WORKBOAT

Strategy for Avoiding Wet Stacking

While gasoline engines tolerate a wide range of loads within their power rating, diesel engines are much more finicky about how they are used. One of the most challenging aspects of operating diesel engines on the water is dealing with the problem of running them without sufficient load, resulting in wet stacking and fuel dilution.

Wet stacking simply means that unburned fuel is leaving the cylinder and going into the exhaust manifold and out the stack. When this happens, black leaks develop in the joints of the exhaust system and make a terrible mess. Wet stacking also forces unburned fuel past the piston rings and into the engine oil, causing fuel dilution of the lube oil. When an engine is in good condition, the cure is to work it harder. If the engine is in poor condition, it must be rebuilt and then worked harder.

fishing boat, and have engines with either intermittent or continuous ratings.

A continuous marine rating is a level of power that the engine can sustain the majority of the time it is running.

Diesel engine ratings determine not only what an engine is capable of, but also the way it must be used. For example, to get the longest life out of an engine rated for generator use, it must carry a load that is no less than 80 percent of its maximum rating 80 percent of the time. Also, the speed range for most diesel generator sets is only 1,800 rpm, quite a difference from the rating for the same engine in a truck that might be set to run at a maximum of 2,300 rpm. Following this

80 percent rule, a 100-kilowatt marine generator set would not be allowed to produce less than 80 kilowatts.

Conditions occur when there just isn't enough load to put on an engine. One example of this would be a main propulsion engine rated at 400 hp that is periodically used to power hydraulics at the low idle speed of 700 rpm. A few minutes of this isn't so bad, but hours of producing only 20 hp, or 5 percent of its rating, will harm the engine, because the unburned fuel (soot) will flow past the piston rings and dilute the engine oil.

Here's another example: A generator set engine is rated at 60 kilowatts to cover a vessel's heavier electrical loads, but it only produces 12 kilowatts at night when the crew is using the electric range and doing laundry. In both these cases, problems will eventually crop up because unburned fuel will create soot, which is bad for engines.

Extended light loading will do two things to your engine: First, incompletely burned fuel, due to the lower cylinder pressure, will exit the cylinder through the exhaust valves. This fuel will paint the inside of your exhaust manifold with a thick black ooze. It will soon find any leaks in your exhaust system. On the outside of the engine this fuel looks a lot more like lubricating oil than diesel fuel, and its appearance has been the trigger for unneeded repair jobs.

Second, as mentioned above, the unburned fuel will dilute the oil with fuel, reducing the viscosity of the oil. This will prematurely clog the engine's oil filter with soot, which in turn will cause the filter bypass valve to open (if so equipped). This necessary but unfortunate event will result in the engine being lubricated with unfiltered oil!

Some engines can tolerate operating under a light load better than others. There is a qualifier for this statement, though, and it is that most boat engines are ten to fifteen years behind the state-of-the-art in fuel efficiency. The following list focuses on older engines in the 20 to 500 hp range, and it contains general rules for the most efficient features for diesel engines that must handle extended periods of light loading:

1. Newer engines are better at operating under light loads than older ones because of improved designs and materials. Another reason is that increasingly stringent emission standards are helping to ensure that all engines do a better job of burning fuel in the cylinder, and not in the exhaust manifold, even during light loading conditions.

2. Four-stroke engines handle light loads better than two-stroke engines because there is more time for the fuel to burn before the exhaust stroke.

3. Four-stroke engines with cast-iron pistons do better under light loads than those with aluminum pistons. At lower cylinder temperatures, the cast-iron piston-to-cylinder-wall clearance is less than it would be with aluminum pistons.

4. Direct fuel-injected engines do better under light loads than precombustion-chamber engines because the injection pressure is much greater and the fuel is more finely atomized.

5. Air-cooled engines do better than water-cooled engines under light loads because the cylinder temperature of an air-cooled engine tends to be 10 to 15 percent greater.

6. Electronically controlled engines perform better under light loads than mechanically governed engines because they inject fuel

at higher pressures. The electronic engine's control system quickly cuts back the amount of fuel injected as the load tapers off.

7. **Square-cut piston compression rings often work better for lightly loaded engines than the tapered keystone-style rings.** The reason for this is that square-cut rings are not as dependent on cylinder pressure to force the rings against the cylinder wall during light loads.

8. **Three-ring pistons seal better than two-ring pistons when an engine is under light load simply because they seal compression more efficiently.** Two-ring engines are now quite rare.

9. **Naturally aspirated engines generally work better for light loads than turbocharged engines because their compression ratios are one or two points higher than a turbocharged engine.**

10. **Small-bore engines will work better than large-bore engines because it is easier to control piston ring leakage in a small cylinder.**

If we add all of the above together, we can come up with the ideal marine diesel engine for handling significant periods of operation under light loads. The engine would be technologically advanced, air-cooled, electronically controlled, four-stroke, direct-injected, naturally aspirated, and it would have cast-iron three-ring pistons and square-cut compression rings!

It's too bad there is no such engine in production, although the air-cooled Deutz diesel engine is closer than most to this ideal specimen for extended use under light loads. However, few boats have space for an air-cooled engine.

As engines are reconditioned or replaced, though, it's important to keep the above attributes in mind as part of a strategy to address problems associated with running an engine under light loads.

FUEL QUALITY AND BACK-PRESSURE

If you regularly buy your fuel from a single supplier, it makes sense to verify its quality. Consider sending a sample of the fuel to a lab and ask for a test to determine the cetane number. Some fuel suppliers have this information available for each shipment they receive. All engine manufacturers publish fuel specifications for their engines, and the fuel must conform to these specifications to ensure long engine life.

Fuel additives are available from the Stanadyne Corporation and many other companies. Stanadyne also tests fuel for their customers. Marvel Mystery Oil improves the lubricating qualities of any fuel in either gasoline or diesel engines and also works well in the engine crankcase oil. Cleaning and water removal from diesel fuel can be done with a centrifuge or with fuel-water separators. While a centrifuge is expensive and requires

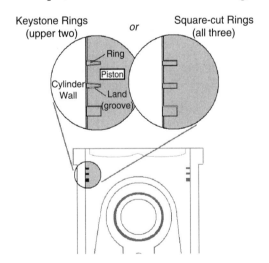

Fig. 2-13. Comparison of keystone and square-cut rings.

constant maintenance, it is the method of choice for cleaning fuel.

Restricting the flow of exhaust gases in the exhaust system creates back-pressure, making it difficult for the gases to escape from the cylinders. Excess back-pressure mimics a plugged air filter, which causes intake airflow restriction. Fresh air must get into the cylinders for combustion, and the spent gases, depleted of oxygen, must get out. Anything that hinders air and gas flow will cause problems, such as low power, and on older engines it will cause black smoke.

Testing exhaust back-pressure is done with a mercury-filled manometer. Engine manufacturers publish their specification for exhaust back-pressure in inches of mercury (hg). This is covered in detail in Chapters 8 and 16.

MARINE ENGINE ENERGY EFFICIENCY

For the foreseeable future, diesel engines will remain significantly more efficient (Fig. 2-14) than gasoline engines. This would probably be less true if there were more gasoline engines with direct injection of fuel into the cylinders. In other words, if these engines worked more like diesels, they'd be better at burning fuel. Another reason why a diesel is more efficient

stems from the greater energy content of each gallon of diesel fuel. However, the best marine diesel engines still harness the smaller part of the energy in each gallon of fuel. The energy that is *not* wasted as heat to the exhaust and cooling systems does the work of moving the boat through the water or powering a generator set.

To save fuel after starting a cold diesel engine, idle it long enough to get good oil pressure and then get the boat moving with low rpm, light throttle, and light load until the engine is up to temperature. Never use full power until the engine is all the way up to operating temperature. Marine and heavy equipment engines take more time to warm up than a truck engine because their cooling system capacities are much larger.

These additional items will also increase fuel efficiency:

1. Remove barnacles and keep the bottom of the boat painted.
2. When possible, reduce wind resistance.
3. Use the maximum allowable pitch and prop diameter that will allow the engine to get up to its rated full-load speed.
4. Bevel skegs and underwater supports, if so equipped.
5. Good shaft alignment reduces friction losses.
6. Be sure the exhaust system is unrestricted.
7. Engines are more efficient with plenty of cold air coming into the engine room.
8. Precisely tune your engine.
9. Use the lightest allowable weight of lube oil, or, better yet, use synthetic oil.
10. Use the smallest allowable generator set for house power; try to size it to operate at over 85 percent of its rated capacity.

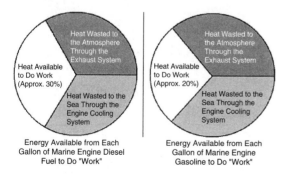

Fig. 2-14. Diesel engine (left) and gasoline engine (right) fuel efficiency compared.

11. Wherever possible, use 3-phase motors for the best electrical efficiency instead of single-phase motors.

12. For larger boats, if light loading is not a problem, use waste heat from the engine water jackets to warm the vessel, rather than electric heaters.

13. A little-known cause of excess fuel consumption is poor tracking while the vessel is under way, which results from poorly designed rudders and/or faulty autopilot adjustment.

ENGINE MOUNTING

Engine mounting is not a short-term efficiency improver, but it is a necessity to ensure maximum engine and transmission longevity.

Bolting a square (symmetrical) engine into a boat's crooked or uneven engine bed rails will actually bend the engine. We are using the term *square* as a carpenter uses the word. Houses can be out of square, and so can the area of a boat into which the engine or any other piece of equipment is bolted. Rigidly mounted marine engines, especially longer ones, can be installed in such a way that extreme force is exerted on the cylinder block. This twisting force can be so great that the cylinder block and the crankshaft bore inside actually bend enough to warp the crankshaft.

When the crankshaft warps like this it is called crankshaft deflection. Crankshaft deflection is the cause for the more spectacular and expensive engine failures that occur, especially for those failures that are harder to explain.

For smaller, lighter engines, avoiding the soft foot, which we will now define, easily eliminates crankshaft deflection. Marine engines have four mounting feet that sit on the engine bed mounting rails. Sometimes

BARRING AN ENGINE OVER

Barring is the word used to describe rotating the engine crankshaft slowly by hand without energizing the starter motor. There are times that engines, both gasoline and diesel, need to be barred. This is true during engine installation, tune-ups, when doing valve adjustments, or when an engine is hydraulically locked due to fluid above a piston.

Because there are so many engine configurations, there are several ways to turn an engine manually. The guidelines for barring an engine are as follows: Turn the crankshaft by any means that won't harm the engine or yourself.

Many engine manufacturers make provisions for the use of an engine turning tool that engages either the flywheel ring gear teeth or the timing gear train teeth on the front of the engine.

When these options aren't available, there is sometimes a timing window on the flywheel housing that allows the use of a pry bar on the flywheel teeth. When there is a mechanical power-take-off (PTO) on the front of the engine, a pipe wrench can be used to turn the PTO shaft after the PTO clutch has been engaged. Also, the starter can be removed to allow the use of a pry bar on the flywheel teeth.

Fig. 2-15. Barring over an engine. The photo shows a bar attached to a socket wrench on the end of the crankshaft. Some engines are fitted by the manufacturer with an opening through which a specially designed turning tool can be inserted.

On small engines, turning can often be accomplished by putting a wrench on the crankshaft hub retaining bolt or even on the alternator's pulley retaining nut.

the transmission will also have two mounting feet. If any of these feet shows a gap between it and the engine bed before the foot is tightened, then it is a soft foot. A soft foot will need to be shimmed as described in Chapter 17. Otherwise, it's easy to picture what would happen if this soft foot were violently pulled down by being bolted to the engine bed: the mounting bolt tension would put the engine in a bind as the bolt is tightened.

For large, long, heavy engines, the span is much greater and the effect of being bolted down in a bind is much more serious. The procedure for dealing with crankshaft deflection on large engines is more complex. A marine mechanic can follow the simple test procedure published by Caterpillar for checking and correcting crankshaft deflection.

A USEFUL ENGINE PROCEDURE

There will come a time when you will want to turn the engine over without engaging the starter motor. On smaller engines you can do this with a turning tool supplied by the manufacturer. On larger engines the procedure is somewhat more complex. In either case, though, turning an engine without engaging the starter is, in the lingo of the trade, called *barring* the engine over.

CHAPTER 3

MARINE ENGINE COOLING SYSTEMS

The cooling system on your boat's engine is critical. If it malfunctions, the engine will overheat, potentially causing severe damage. The cooling system is also particularly vulnerable. Plenty can go wrong and often does. In this chapter, you will learn about various types of cooling systems: freshwater cooling, the common method used on pleasure craft; keel cooling, which is mostly found on workboats; and intake-air aftercooling, a feature used on all high-performance diesel engines. Topics such as engine cooling components, expansion tanks, and engine overheating will also be discussed.

It is important to clarify cooling system terms. As often happens in industries or trades, certain nomenclature will "stick" to a part or a system even though, strictly speaking, it isn't very accurate.

The term "heat exchanger" is a good example; it's a catchall for many things. You probably wouldn't think of your car's radiator as a heat exchanger, but it is. On a boat, an engine's oil cooler, aftercooler, intercooler, keel cooler, and freshwater (heat exchanger) cooler are all heat exchangers of one sort or another because they remove excess heat from the engine and direct it elsewhere. Therefore, throughout this chapter, key terms will be defined to clarify matters, and where necessary an illustration will be included. Figure 3-1 shows how a basic marine heat exchanger works.

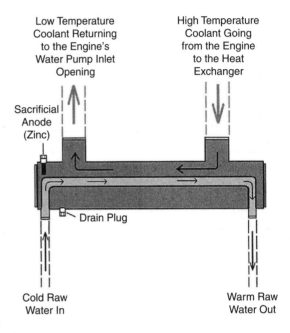

Fig. 3-1. Heat exchanger construction and action.

FRESHWATER COOLING

Freshwater cooling is a somewhat misleading description of how the system really works. It's not fresh water that cools the engine, but raw water. Raw water is water from the ocean or a lake pumped into the boat with a raw-water pump, also called a seawater pump. The raw water passes through a strainer and an intake hose and circulates through a heat exchanger before it is pumped overboard, often through a water-cooled exhaust system (see Chapter 8), where it mixes with exhaust gas. The raw-water side of the system removes heat from the fresh water, or closed-cooling, side.

The term "closed-cooling" describes what is happening inside the engine block. The coolant, usually an equal mixture of antifreeze and distilled water, circulates through passages in the engine in a never-ending closed cycle. Closed-cooling and freshwater cooling can be used interchangeably. The so-called freshwater coolant is in fact a mixture of fresh water and antifreeze. In a pinch you could fill the block with fresh water and the cooling system would still work, though you wouldn't want to leave it in the block for long. Apart from preventing the block from freezing in cold climates, antifreeze inhibits rust and corrosion and enhances cooling, which is why it's used in freshwater cooling systems.

The heat exchanger is a vital component in a freshwater cooling system. It facilitates the ability of raw water to remove heat from the coolant circulating inside the engine. Heat exchangers are usually made of corrosion-resistant copper-nickel alloy rather than straight copper tubing, and replaceable sacrificial zincs are incorporated into the design to further prevent galvanic corrosion. These units can be mounted remotely or directly on the engine. While a coolant recovery bottle is often used with a heat exchanger, no supplemental expansion tank, other than the one that came with the engine, is needed in a freshwater cooling system. See Fig. 1-6 for a simplified schematic illustration of a freshwater cooling system.

The raw-water pump is also an important part of a freshwater cooling system. Without it, the system would fail because the raw water could not circulate through the heat exchanger. The raw-water pump draws water into the system with a a rubber impeller; water flowing inside lubricates it. Most raw-water pumps

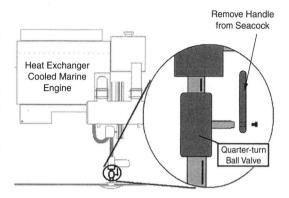

Fig. 3-2. Remove the ball valve handle from the raw-water intake seacock to avoid accidental opening.

are self-priming, meaning they will lift water a short distance and pull it into the pump.

Note: When doing service work on freshwater cooling systems or on any other system that uses quarter-turn ball valves, be sure to remove the handle from the raw-water intake seacock so the valve cannot be accidentally opened (Fig. 3-2).

KEEL COOLERS

Although most pleasure boaters have never heard of a keel cooling system, it is common on workboats. A keel cooling system routes the engine coolant through a loop of pipe outside the hull below the waterline. The water the vessel travels through cools the coolant circulating in the submerged pipe. Every keel cooler must be connected to the engine through the hull, with either a single or double opening. The double-stem (double opening) keel cooler is constructed of steel, aluminum, brass, or copper-nickel tubing. Careful design is needed to ensure adequate heat transfer, to minimize pumping losses inside the cooler, to allow expansion and contraction as temperatures change, and to minimize corrosion of the unit inside and out. For a schematic of a single-stem keel cooling system, see Figure 3-3.

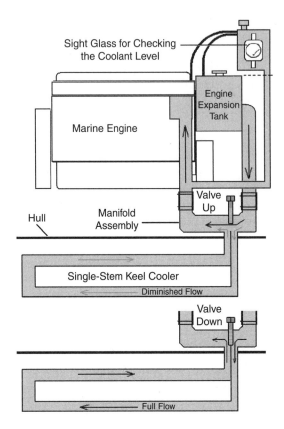

Sight Glass for Checking
the Coolant Level

Engine
Expansion
Tank

Marine Engine

Valve
Up

Hull

Manifold
Assembly

Single-Stem Keel Cooler

Diminished Flow

Valve
Down

Full Flow

Fig. 3-3. Single-stem keel cooler with flow adjusting screw.

**Fig. 3-4. A Murphy coolant level alarm switch is just visible
on the bottom rim of this coolant level gauge. When
the coolant level gets dangerously low, the switch
activates an alarm (propulsion engine) or shuts
down the engine (if a generator). See also Chapter 7.**

An option for keel coolers, as shown in Fig. 3-3, is a flow-bypass adjusting screw incorporated into the manifold on top of the through-hull fitting. This adjusting screw provides the option of recirculating coolant back to the inlet pipe on the water pump without sending it all out to the keel cooler. For large cooling systems operating in cold waters, adjusting the screw on the manifold will help the system get up to adequate temperature. The opposite is true as well; the adjustment valve can be closed to provide more cooling if it's needed.

KEEL COOLER SIZING

Well-designed cooling systems will have enough capacity to cool the boat's engines worldwide, even in equatorial waters. Therefore, boats operating in colder waters are frequently going to have more cooling capacity than is needed. Over the years and during the course of repairs, as keel coolers are damaged and replaced, skippers and boatowners operating in cold waters realize that their keel coolers are often providing more cooling capacity than is necessary, so they just order a slightly smaller unit and save a few dollars. The best way to repair the cooling system is to check with the manufacturer of the equipment and follow their guidelines.

KEEL COOLING SYSTEM VOLUME AND THE RESULTING EXPANSION

Marine keel cooling systems have at least twice the volume of a comparable truck engine's cooling system. This is important, because unless the keel cooler is very efficient, the coolant can expand five percent in volume as it warms up. Since engine manufacturers have no way of knowing the capacity of your keel cooler, they expect the person installing

CHRONIC ENGINE OVERHEATING

Ely's 425 hp diesel engine had been periodically overheating since the boat and engine were brand-new. The engine had been rebuilt twice, and a huge amount of fishing time had been wasted. In spite of the rebuilds, repeatedly overheating the engine finally caused it to seize up. Ely had taken it to several marine mechanics. Mechanics from the engine dealer had even flown in to the fishing grounds to help. He had spent thousands of dollars on travel expenses for the several mechanics that had flown to his remote location in Alaska, not to mention their repair charges. It wasn't until the engine failed and he decided to try a different brand that the problem was found.

His original engine was a 425 hp high-performance diesel. That is, to maximize the power from the engine, it was not only heavily turbocharged, but it was also aftercooled.

High levels of turbocharging are used on high-performance diesel engines to supply more available oxygen in the cylinder, so that more fuel can be injected. This allows the engine to produce more power. However, in the process of highly pressurizing the air entering the cylinders, the air is excessively heated, which makes it expand, thus reducing volumetric efficiency. The solution to this dilemma is provided by an aftercooler, which cools the air back down and makes it denser, thus restoring its volumetric efficiency.

Ely's boat had been built with two keel coolers—a large one to cool the engine, and a smaller one for the aftercooler circuit. After the boat was hauled and cribbed up in the boatyard, it was easy to see what had caused the years of overheating problems. When the boat was built, the aftercooler had been mistakenly

plumbed to the larger keel cooler, and the engine had been connected to the smaller keel cooler! The main engine had been operating for eight years with less than half of its needed cooling capacity.

the engine to add a supplementary coolant recovery tank when it is needed. Coolant recovery tanks add to the volume of the engine-mounted expansion tank and provide for this change in volume. As the engine cools after it is shut off, the cooling system will draw coolant back from the coolant recovery tank; it does this by way of the pressure cap on the expansion tank.

AFTERCOOLERS

High-performance turbocharged diesel engines require additional cooling of the intake air. This is done with aftercoolers, which are also known as intercoolers. Figures 3-5 and 3-6 show the

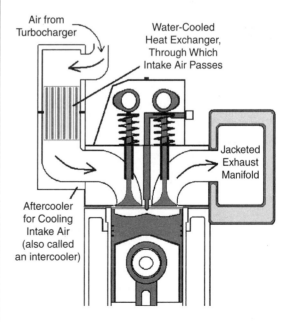

Fig. 3-5. Marine engine aftercooler action.

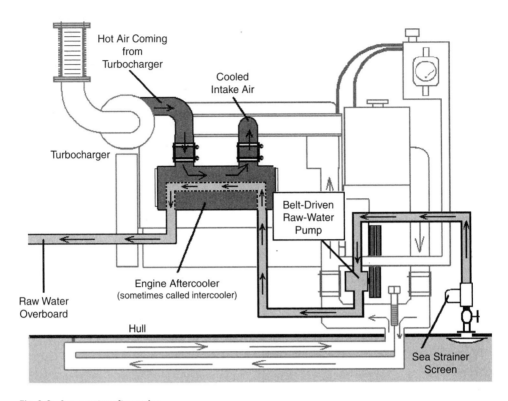

Fig. 3-6. A raw-water aftercooler.

air and raw-water flow through a heat-exchanger aftercooler. Some workboats use fresh water in the aftercooler and cool that water through a keel cooler. *Note: An aftercooler that is too large will overcool the engine intake air to the point that it will hinder combustion of the fuel.* An example of higher volumetric efficiency is simply packing more of the oxygen-bearing atmosphere into the cylinder when the intake valve opens. An example of something that hinders volumetric efficiency is a plugged air filter. Aftercooling improves volumetric efficiency by cooling the air that is going into the cylinders—thus making it denser—and it is a good and necessary practice. On keel-cooled high-performance diesels, the aftercooler will often have its own separate keel cooler and pump for taking heat from the intake air and putting it into the water beneath the boat.

HEAT EXCHANGER AFTERCOOLER

Another option for cooling engine intake air is to use a raw-water-cooled aftercooler. This type of unit (Fig. 3-6) can be engine-mounted or mounted remotely.

ENGINE COOLING COMPONENTS

Every engine cooling system has key components such as pumps, thermostats, and hoses, to name just a few. Let's take a look at some of the more important ones to broaden your working knowledge of what makes a cooling system function properly.

Cooling System Hoses

Coolant hoses, though pretty basic in function, are nevertheless vital parts of the cooling system. They must be protected from oil,

AFTERCOOLING ON LAND AND SEA

Marine engines are expensive, and to save money boatowners, particularly owners of workboats, sometimes install heavy-duty truck engines in their boats. Air emissions regulations in some nations prohibit such installations, but some boatowners do it anyway.

The incentive is easy to understand. A truck engine, regardless of the manufacturer, costs 10 to 15 percent less than a marine engine with the same horsepower. However, even putting aside the issue of exhaust emissions, there is a problem with using a truck engine in a boat, one that fortunately can be easily overcome. Most, if not all, heavy-duty truck engines are built with air-to-air aftercooling, which differs drastically from the type used on boats. These engines will not produce full power in a boat unless the intake air is adequately cooled.

Herein lies the difference: While marine engines come with an engine-mounted aftercooler, truck engines use a chassis-mounted air-to-air aftercooler placed ahead of the truck's radiator. The truck type of aftercooler depends on a prodigious flow of air to cool the intake air as the truck moves along the road. The manufacturer of the truck supplies the air-to-air aftercooler, not the engine manufacturer. Thus, if a boatowner ordered a 300 hp truck engine for use in a boat, the engine would come without the vitally important aftercooler. The simple solution to the problem is to buy and install a raw-water-cooled aftercooler. A truck engine equipped with one will work just fine in a boat.

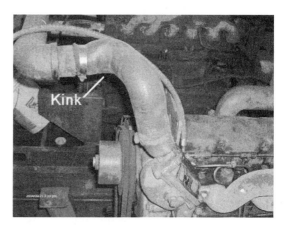

Fig. 3-7. Kinked coolant hose.

Coolant Pumps

The coolant pump (Fig. 3-8) serves an important purpose. It moves hot coolant from the engine to the heat exchanger, where the coolant can shed its heat, and unlike a raw-water pump, it is not self-priming. In fact, a coolant pump is a submersible pump and must be submerged to work. When all is well with the system, the coolant pump moves hot coolant from inside the engine and the engine

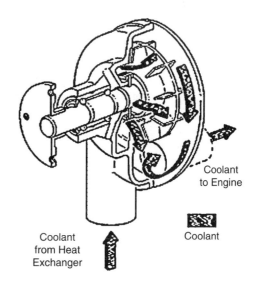

Coolant to Engine

Coolant

Coolant from Heat Exchanger

Fig. 3-8. The inner workings of a coolant pump.

fuel, heat, and abrasion. They must also be installed so they are not stretched or kinked such as the hose in Figure 3-7.

oil cooler, and circulates the coolant through the heat exchanger and back to the engine. The coolant returns to the engine at a much lower temperature than it had before passing through the heat exchanger.

Oil Coolers

The engine oil cooler (Fig. 3-9) is another form of heat exchanger within the cooling system. It is designed to take excess heat from the engine oil and dispose of it by transferring the heat to the engine coolant. Oil coolers are often used regardless of how the boat engine is cooled.

The oil cooler is mounted on the side of most diesel engines, and under the oil filter on gasoline engines. While generally trouble-free, sometimes the coolant passages within the oil cooler become plugged and the cooler must be removed from the engine for cleaning. Normal servicing is usually done during an engine rebuild, and consists of cleaning the water passages and replacing all O-rings and gaskets.

In extremely cold climates, in a truck or a piece of heavy equipment, the engine oil cooler is, at times, an oil warmer. If the engine is at operating temperature and the oil pan happens to be cooled too much by the windchill, the cooling system transfers heat, by way of the oil cooler, into the engine oil. However, in boating applications the oil cooler's purpose is always to transfer heat away from the lube oil.

Here's how an oil cooler works. Thin-walled copper or stainless steel tubes (round or flattened in cross section) wind through the oil cooler body, or core. In some engines the body contains the coolant and the tubes contain the oil, and in other engines the opposite is true. Either way, the object is to facilitate heat transfer from the oil to the coolant through the thin walls of the tubing. Whenever there is a leak in an oil cooler, the fluid flows from the high-pressure side of the oil cooler tubing to the low-pressure side.

Thermostats

When the engine is cold, the thermostat (Fig. 3-10) closes to recirculate coolant inside the engine. When the coolant reaches the thermostat's rated temperature, the thermostat opens to send coolant out to the cooling loop. Thermostats are temperature-controlled

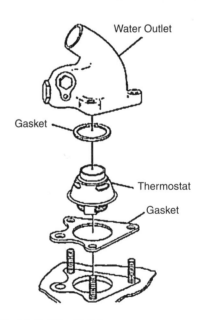

Fig. 3-10. A typical thermostat.

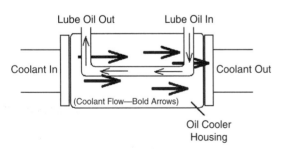

Fig. 3-9. Overview of oil cooling.

OIL COOLER LEAKS

The relative pressure of the two fluids becomes important if the cooler fails and an internal leak develops between the oil side and the coolant side. The pressure on both sides of the cooler tubes is usually different, which means that oil or coolant will travel from one side of the core to the other due to the pressure difference. There is a case where the pressures will nearly equal out, though, such as with a worn engine with low oil pressure running at low idle speed with the coolant up to full temperature and pressure.

When the engine is operating at full speed, the pressure on the oil side of the tubes is much greater than the pressure on the coolant side. The pressure balance can go the other way, too, such as when an engine (at operating temperature and coolant pressure) is turned off at the end of the day. The oil pressure suddenly drops to zero, while the cooling system still maintains the radiator cap's rated pressure until the engine cools.

This discussion isn't important unless the oil cooler tubes begin to leak. If the pressure on the oil side is higher when a leak develops in the core, then oil will travel across the leak and into the cooling system. Under these conditions, opening the radiator cap will reveal oil in the coolant. If a leak develops after the engine is turned off, while the cooling system pressure is higher, coolant will travel into the engine's lubrication system and the oil pan. At this point, checking the engine lube oil level will show the oil level to be higher than normal. Pressure testing the oil cooler is your next step.

To test an oil cooler, first plug one of the two coolant openings to the cooler and then pressurize the other coolant opening to no more than 20 psi. This test is illustrated in Figure 11-15, and pressure tests are discussed further in Chapter 16. If the oil cooler holds pressure, there must be some other way that one fluid is invading the other. But if the oil cooler fails to hold pressure, it must be replaced.

coolant flow valves, and their job is to keep the coolant in the ideal temperature range as determined by the engine manufacturer.

As the coolant nears its ideal temperature, the thermostat begins to open gradually, thereby helping avoid abrupt changes of temperature in the engine coolant. Abrupt changes in coolant temperature stress the engine castings. Of course, a thermostat that opens late or not at all will cause engine overheating.

Thermostats are easy to test. Heat some water in a saucepan and place a meat thermometer in it. Simply watch to see when the thermostat opens and note the temperature when it does. Each thermostat has a temperature rating stamped on it, in degrees Fahrenheit or Celsius. If the thermostat doesn't begin opening at its rated temperature, then it's time to replace it.

THE EXPANSION TANK

As coolant warms, it expands. For example, a cooling system holding 100 gallons of a water and antifreeze mixture will expand roughly 5 percent, or 5 gallons, between cold and hot extremes.

Keel coolers sometimes need more expansion tank capacity than the engine-mounted expansion tank provides. The reason for this is that the cooling system volume for many keel coolers is at least two or three times the volume of the cooling system of a truck that happens to use the same engine.

Marine engine manufacturers usually have very little information about the types of vessels in which their engines will be installed. They send the engine-mounted tank that will accept the expansion of coolant up to a certain volume. The manufacturer might include a tank, for example, that will accept the expansion (and contraction) of all keel coolers up to 40 gallons of total system volume. Systems with more volume will require a supplemental expansion tank.

In older boats, the cooling systems, if not properly serviced, will acquire a buildup of rust and precipitated dissolved solids (minerals). Some of this contamination will find its way into the cylinder block and settle around the cylinders as shown in Figure 3-11. This buildup will eventually reduce keel cooler heat transfer and result in far more expansion of the coolant than will occur in an efficient cooling system. For this reason, inefficient cooling

systems run higher coolant temperatures and will need larger expansion tanks.

It is important to change coolant periodically as suggested by the engine manufacturer and to add distilled water rather than tap water for the 50–50 mix if possible. Using distilled water will keep the mineral content low in the coolant and reduce the likelihood of problems developing over time.

It is vital to have a pressure cap (see below) on the cooling system. The pressurized system not only raises the boiling point of the coolant, but it also prevents the coolant from evaporating through the opening on the expansion tank and precipitating minerals.

COOLANT RECOVERY BOTTLES

Coolant recovery bottles are sometimes used instead of supplemental expansion tanks. There are several differences between supplemental expansion tanks and coolant recovery bottles. Unlike a supplemental expansion tank, a recovery bottle has no make-up line coming out the bottom and has only one small line from the engine's expansion tank pressure cap that runs to the bottom of the recovery bottle.

The recovery bottle cannot deaerate the coolant in the upper parts of an engine as an expansion tank can. Pressure caps are made so they allow coolant to run into the recovery bottle as the coolant expands. The pressure cap also allows the vacuum, created as the system cools down, to pull coolant from the bottom of the recovery bottle and back into the system. After the engine cools, you will notice the level in the recovery bottle is down—this is normal.

Unlike a supplemental expansion tank, the coolant recovery bottle can be mounted below

Fig. 3-11. **Contamination in the cylinder block.**

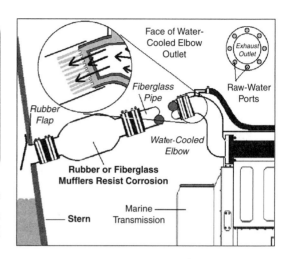

Fig. 3-13. A horizontal wet-exhaust system.

WORK-AROUND SOLUTION

Failure of the Raw-Water Pump
During a dire emergency, when the raw-water pump fails at sea, you might try using the bilge pump to circulate bilge water for limited engine cooling.

---

the top of the engine's expansion tank. The coolant recovery bottle is an elegant solution for many applications that just need a small amount of additional room for expansion.

WATER-COOLED EXHAUST

A water-cooled exhaust system is more often used with freshwater cooling systems than with keel coolers. The water-cooled exhaust system uses raw water flowing from the freshwater system's heat exchanger to cool the engine's exhaust gases (Fig. 3-12). This water is sprayed into the stream of hot exhaust gases exiting each cylinder, rapidly cooling these gases so that they may safely leave the boat through a horizontal exhaust system. Horizontal exhaust systems usually exit through the stern as shown in Figure 3-13.

COOLING SYSTEM CONDITIONER

Diesel engines with wet cylinder liners must have adequate cooling system conditioner in the coolant to protect the outer surface of the

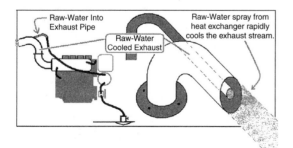

Fig. 3-12. A water-cooled exhaust system.

liner from corrosion. For engines with dry liners, or no liners at all, conditioner is still important to limit corrosion between dissimilar metals in the system. It's a good idea to learn what your engine manufacturer suggests you use as a cooling system conditioner.

To neutralize acids in coolant that cause corrosion, chemicals are added to the conditioner formula. These additives keep the coolant pH slightly alkaline. Conditioner can be purchased in any quantity, and for the best results it is wise to use the manufacturer's test kit. Always test coolant before making any changes to the strength of the mixture.

Conditioner also comes in a spin-on cartridge that is plumbed to keep some coolant flowing through when the engine is running. You can tell when a conditioner cartridge is used up by spinning it off and comparing its weight to a new cartridge. A depleted cartridge will be much lighter than a new one.

ANTIFREEZE COOLANT

Because modern engines often have aluminum components in the cooling system, it

Winterizing the Raw-Water Side of a Freshwater-Cooled Engine

The following method assumes that the coolant side of the system has adequate antifreeze protection according to a hydrometer tester. Testers are available in any auto parts store.

Raw-water cooling systems can be tough to thoroughly winterize because pockets of water sometimes remain in the system. If it gets really cold, the water will freeze, damaging the system. Follow the engine manufacturer's instructions whenever possible. If such instructions are unclear or unavailable, the following drawing will help.

If the boat is in the water, begin by shutting off the valve (seacock) below the sea strainer. *Caution: Again, always remove the valve handle so that it cannot be bumped open accidentally later on and sink the boat!*

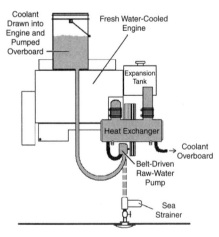

Fig. 3-14. Winterizing a freshwater-cooled system.

After closing the valve and removing the handle, remove the suction hose to the belt-driven

raw-water pump and connect it to a 5-gallon bucket as shown. Fill the bucket with pure, undiluted antifreeze. (Use propylene glycol, which is nontoxic, rather than the highly toxic ethylene glycol.) Start the engine and pump the bucket dry before shutting off the engine. Refill the bucket and pump it dry one more time. Finish by thoroughly inspecting the engine and cooling system and removing all drain plugs from the raw-water side of the system. If possible, put a small, fan-driven electric heater under the engine cover. This will help minimize condensation inside and outside the engine.

is important to use coolant that is compatible with aluminum. Coolant is also available pre-mixed. The advantage of the pre-mixed variety is that the water quality is better for your engine than most local freshwater sources. Use distilled water if at all possible to reduce the buildup of minerals in the cooling system.

PRESSURE CAPS

The pressure cap's main job is to cause the coolant to boil at a temperature well above 212°F. This happens because the cap raises the pressure in the cooling system and prevents the formation of air bubbles that would otherwise cause small, localized hot spots, which in time destroy parts of the cooling system.

Secondly, pressure caps stop the evaporation of water and coolant. When water evaporates, make-up water must be continually added. In time, hundreds of gallons of water evaporate in systems aboard large boats, leaving behind the water's dissolved solid (mineral) content. High levels of dissolved solids cause sludge to form in the cooling system, blocking the small internal passages.

So, take care of the cap by visually inspecting it periodically to be sure the neoprene washer on the bottom is in good shape.

MIXING COOLANT

As previously mentioned, the best water to mix with antifreeze is demineralized or distilled water. Cooling system conditioner must also be added to this mixture. It is important to test the effectiveness of the conditioner and the freezing protection of the coolant after the engine has been warmed up and the coolant has thoroughly circulated through the boat's cooling system. For small pleasure boats, one hour of running at full temperature will be enough to mix the antifreeze and the conditioner with any existing coolant in the system. For vessels with greater cooling system capacity, eight hours of running time may not be enough to mix the coolant and conditioner sufficiently to get an accurate test result. In situations like this, the levels must be retested until the same reading is obtained twice in a row.

Avoid using more than fifty percent because antifreeze is harder to pump than water.

TROUBLESHOOTING COOLANT CONSUMPTION

When the coolant level in an engine keeps going down it is time to find out where it is going. First, check for water leaking to the outside of the engine by pressurizing the cooling system to 15 to 20 psi. Find a pipe plug high in the cooling system and connect a pressure source, such as a test pump or air compressor hose, to it. Auto parts stores sell cooling system test pumps. Care must be taken to verify

that you are indeed tapped into the cooling system and not the lube oil or fuel system. Check the engine manual for clues on where to make the connection. (There is more detail on pressure tests in Chapter 16.)

Once the system is pressurized, begin following all external coolant lines to check each joint. Sometimes it helps to turn off the engine room lights and examine each joint with a bright flashlight. At this point, if no leaks are obvious, it is time to see if coolant is going into the engine oil pan by way of the engine oil cooler.

Loosen the oil pan drain plug a little and watch carefully. If coolant is leaking into the oil, you will see coolant drip out of the plug threads before oil. If you just see oil, check the transmission oil cooler next using the same approach. Another possibility is that coolant is going out the exhaust stack with the exhaust gases. To check this, isolate the engine from the keel cooler or heat exchanger and pressurize the engine. If the engine will not hold pressure, there is an internal leak. The possibilities for internal leaks include:

1. The aftercooler (intercooler), if so equipped
2. Cylinder liner coolant seals, if so equipped
3. Faulty head gasket
4. A cracked cylinder head
5. An internally cracked jacketed exhaust manifold
6. An internally cracked jacketed turbocharger, if so equipped

Another quick test for an engine sending coolant out the stack is to remove the exhaust

FOR THE WORKBOAT

Coolant Consumption

In 1980 I was called to fly to Kotzebue, Alaska, where a 280-foot seismic survey vessel was anchored twelve miles offshore; it had lost electrical power to its hydraulic steering system.

Arriving at the boat, I found that one of the two Cat generators (Unit A) had a bad engine, and the other (Unit B) had a bad generator (electrical) end. Because flashlights were the only source of light in the engine room, it was important to start the generator set with the bad engine and keep it going long enough to let us remove the old generator from the good engine.

The problem with Unit A was that it had been severely overheated, and cooling water was flowing from the cooling system into the engine's oil pan nearly as fast as water could be added.

To keep it going temporarily, we made sure it had plenty of oil in the oil pan and filled the cooling system with water. We instructed Eddy, the one-armed engineer, to continually add water to the cooling system once the engine was running, and to open the drain valve on the bottom of the oil pan and let the water flow out as fast as it was going in, as shown in the accompanying drawing.

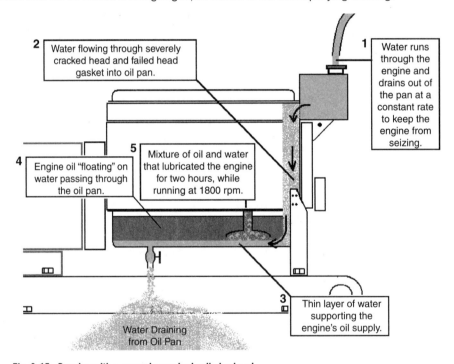

2 Water flowing through severely cracked head and failed head gasket into oil pan.

1 Water runs through the engine and drains out of the pan at a constant rate to keep the engine from seizing.

5 Mixture of oil and water that lubricated the engine for two hours, while running at 1800 rpm.

4 Engine oil "floating" on water passing through the oil pan.

3 Thin layer of water supporting the engine's oil supply.

Water Draining from Oil Pan

Fig. 3-15. **Running with a severely cracked cylinder head.**

Eddy succeeded in doing this for three hours while we removed the faulty generator end from the good engine. We then shut off the bad engine and, by flashlight, starting at 2:00 a.m., removed its good generator end. As we were moving the 400-pound armature with a chain hoist, the boat pitched and one of the two chains that held the armature slipped. The armature came hurtling across the engine room at me and I dove to the left just in time. The man behind me didn't see it coming and had his leg badly crushed. He was taken to Kotzebue by an Air National Guard helicopter and then flown to Anchorage for treatment.

By 6:00 a.m., we had the good generator installed on the good engine, and all was well while we waited for parts to be flown in to repair the other engine and generator.

manifold and check the exhaust ports visually for any sign of rust. Rust in an exhaust port is a sign of a coolant leak in the corresponding cylinder. Beyond this, if no leak is found, it is time to isolate the engine's keel cooler or heat exchanger from the engine for a pressure test.

SEVERE ENGINE OVERHEATING

When severe overheating occurs, it is often due to lack of coolant, which impacts the cylinder head first. As heat increases, the pistons soon expand and actually get bigger than the bores through which they travel. Tremendous friction and heat are then generated between the pistons and the cylinder walls. This can cause the piston material to transfer (weld) to the cylinder wall, and the piston becomes a brake that tries to stop the motion of the crankshaft. If it gets hot enough, the engine will suddenly stop because the braking action between the piston and the cylinder wall has locked the crankshaft.

If the piston seizes on the downstroke, the motion of the crankshaft will break both connecting rod bearings. If the piston seizes on the upstroke, it will stop the engine. As soon as the engine stops, any cooling benefit from the water pump ceases, and there is usually a serious temperature spike in the engine, especially in the cylinder head and exhaust manifold.

If you see such a temperature spike (it can reach well above 210°F) on the temperature gauge, or if your engine suddenly stops, begin assessing how much damage has been done. If the engine has locked up while it was running, you know that the pistons have expanded due to heat and lodged in the bores. Excessive heat in the engine room and darkened paint on the outside of the engine are other indications of severe overheating. Check coolant and oil levels, and if you find both are normal, your engine may not have been damaged. However, you must track down what caused the overheating, be it a faulty raw-water or coolant pump, an obstruction in the raw-water intake line, or some other cause.

Often, after an engine has cooled down after overheating, it will start and run, sometimes surprisingly well. In a case like this, cut open the oil filter and check the oil filter media to learn if aluminum piston material (shards of metal called glitter, see Figure 11-11) is present in the lubricating oil. If the oil filter has aluminum in it, the piston damage is serious. If the oil filter has no aluminum in it, the engine may be fine. The engine may be equipped with cast-iron pistons, which will produce darker (magnetic) iron particles. To further check the engine, pull a clean magnet through the filter media to check for the presence of iron from the cylinder walls or pistons, if the engine is equipped with iron pistons.

When nothing is apparently wrong, perform an oil analysis to watch for wear metals or antifreeze coolant in the oil. The second problem that can occur after severe overheating is that the cylinder liner seals, if the engine is so equipped, can begin to leak coolant into the crankcase. If this has happened, the coolant and water mixture will go to the bottom of the oil pan. If the leak is small, the engine may have to be left shut off for an hour or so before coolant will accumulate in the pan. When water is present, simply loosening the oil pan drain plug will allow water to leak out first, making it easy to spot.

With very long use, liner seals can harden and shrink slightly, allowing coolant to leak. This can happen without the engine ever overheating. When the engine is severely overheated, water-cooled exhaust manifolds, cylinder heads, and even the cylinder block can crack, causing coolant leaks into the oil pan.

CHAPTER 4

BELTS AND HOSES

If you consider the many systems on your boat, you'll see that rotation plays an important part in making things work. Belts affixed to raw-water pumps, alternators, and coolant pumps all spin and transfer power to these components. From the viewpoint of manufacturers and boatbuilders, drive belts are attractive for their simplicity, low cost, and convenience. Engine designers know that it will cost more to build an engine with a gear-driven coolant pump than one that is belt-driven. A disadvantage of the belt-driven pump, though, is that it will need the belts changed periodically.

Hoses are another important part of a vast array of boat systems. Hoses, or lines, carry fuel, oil, coolant, raw water, potable water, propane gas, engine exhaust, and sewage. There are many types, each with its specific application. Maintaining belts and hoses is one of the most basic ways to avoid trouble on the water. It pays to know something about them.

WATER PUMP AND ALTERNATOR BELTS

Raw-water, coolant, and alternator belts live in the engine room, where heat is a concern. High heat greatly reduces belt life. Too much or too little belt tension is another area to watch. Either extreme will harm the belts, and overtightened belts will ruin water pump and alternator bearings. Be sure to tighten V-belts as specified in the engine manual. The belt shown in Figure 4-1 has been loose

and "throwing rubber," as you can see by the black material on the engine.

If information on proper belt tension isn't available, push firmly on the belt with a force of ten to fifteen pounds and adjust the belt tension, usually by moving the alternator, to allow $1/2$ inch of belt deflection for every foot of length between pulleys. When it comes to belts, it is obviously important to inspect them regularly, and if you see any signs of cracks, loss of pliability, or wear, replace them immediately. Don't wait for a belt to fail.

EXTRA BELTS

Because marine engines on larger workboats often have front-mounted power-take-offs (PTOs) driven by crankshafts, it is necessary to remove the entire front PTO system to replace alternator and water pump belts. For this reason, it's a good idea to tie in an extra set of belts any time the belts are changed or the PTO is serviced. Nylon cable ties work well for tying in extra belts. To tie in an extra belt when the pump is removed, simply route the extra, unused belt where it will not interfere with any moving equipment and attach it there with the cable ties.

SIDE LOADS

Engine manufacturers specify the amount of side load their engine's crankshaft will safely carry, and these guidelines must be followed, as must those for the mechanical component the belts are powering. By placing belt- or

Fig. 4-1. Inspect your belts regularly for signs of wear and to monitor tension. The black deposits on this engine indicate that this belt is loose, throwing rubber onto the engine. (Courtesy MER Equipment, Seattle, Washington)

chain-driven loads on both sides of the crankshaft pulley, you can get the driven elements to oppose and partially cancel out one another's side load effect on the crankshaft.

It is also important when engines are mounted on flexible engine mounts to mount belt- and chain-driven loads on the engine block, not the engine beds (Fig. 4-2). Otherwise, as the engine moves on the mounts, belt and chain tension can get too slack or overly tight from the movement of the boat and engine. Eventually, the belt will fail.

If you lose a belt on a water pump or alternator and you don't have a spare, follow the instructions in Figure 4-3 to make a temporary repair with a Push-Loc hose or some other material. This type of hose, when used

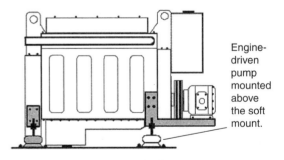

Engine-driven pump mounted above the soft mount.

Fig. 4-2. Mounting engine-driven accessories on the block of an engine with flexible mounts.

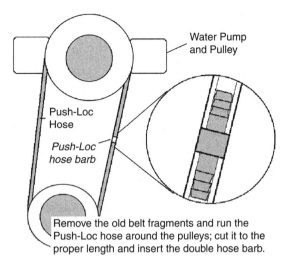

Water Pump
and Pulley

Push-Loc
Hose

Push-Loc
hose barb

Remove the old belt fragments and run the
Push-Loc hose around the pulleys; cut it to the
proper length and insert the double hose barb.

**Fig. 4-3. A Push-Loc hose, duct tape, or even a nylon
stocking will temporarily replace a V-belt.**

with a Push-Loc barbed fitting, requires no
hose clamps. *Note: Due to resistance to turning, it is difficult to drive an alternator with a
Push-Loc hose. If the hose slips on the pulley, in
spite of being well tensioned, try driving only the
water pump. (You can get home without electronics but not with an overheated engine.)*

REPLACING POLY V-BELTS

A poly V-belt is a wide, flat belt that has several small V ribs on the drive side of the belt.
These are often found on boats and will eventually require replacement. To do so, make a
diagram before removing a poly serpentine
V-belt so that you can put it back on with
the same routing. Never cut the old belt off
to remove it; save it in case the new one is the
wrong size.

FUEL HOSES AND AIR IN THE FUEL

The presence of air in the fuel reduces engine
power and can cause hard starting. To check
for air entering the fuel due to a suction leak,
put a sight glass in-line between the engine's

STRIPPED CAM TIMING (COG) BELTS

Engine cam timing (cog) belts fail when the
belt gets old and three or four cogs in one
area of the belt "strip" or peel off. When this
happens the cam ceases to turn, and on some
engines will also bend valves, resulting in the
need for a valve job. To learn if your broken timing belt has resulted in bent valves, remove the
valve cover and notice if there are large gaps
between some of the valve tips and their corresponding rocker arms, but not on others. Large
gaps indicate those valves that are bent.

If, however, your engine has no bent valves,
replace the timing belt according to the
engine maker's directions.

The cam drive cog belts that power most
overhead cams in diesel and gasoline engines
should be replaced after 1,500 hours of use. If
your belt snaps before you can replace it and you
can't get a new one, you can use the technique
in the illustration to get the engine started.

To get the engine going again without a new
cam belt, begin by removing the failed belt.

Next, cut right down the center of the belt, all
the way around the belt until you have made
two belts from the one.

*stripped area
of belt*

Now install the first belt.

Then put on the second belt with the
stripped cogs several cogs away
from each failed section, and both
failed sections on the slack side of
the crankshaft cogs.

When the engine starts, don't turn it
off until you arrive at your destination.

fuel transfer pump and the injection pump.
Caterpillar sells a special sight-glass kit that
will stand considerable pressure, but verify
that it will stand the level of pressure your
transfer pump produces before using it.

Start the engine and watch for air bubbles. The slightest amount of visible air coming in with the fuel indicates at least a 5 percent power loss! More bubbles mean more power loss. To eliminate the air, start working backward from the engine and tighten all fittings. If needed, reseal them with a sparing application of pipe sealant. Tighten the stem packing on all valves in the system. These valve stem packings can be a source of air entering the fuel system too. As you go along, watch for collapsed, chafed, or damaged fuel hoses as well.

When replacing hoses, be sure to purchase only those that are U.S. Coast Guard–approved.

TRANSMISSION HOSES

Beware of a suction leak that allows the transmission oil pump to draw air with the oil (Fig. 4-5). Aerated oil won't provide proper lubrication. Suction leaks occur when the suction hose to the pump gets hard (difficult to bend). When this happens, replace it.

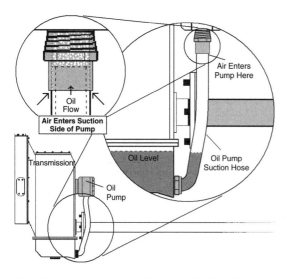

Fig. 4-5. Suction hose leaks will draw air into the oil flow and kill your transmission.

OIL COOLER FLOW DIRECTION WHEN CHANGING HOSES

When changing oil cooler hoses, keep the oil flowing through the cooler in the same direction (Fig. 4-6) as it was before the hose change. The oil flow direction is important because contamination and debris will sometimes get caught on the upstream side of a cooler. If the flow direction is suddenly changed, contaminants will be released directly into the transmission, quite likely resulting in damage. *Note: This also goes for the hoses on engines with remote, bulkhead-mounted oil filters. Accidentally reversing oil flow direction through a remote oil filter will eventually reduce engine lubrication.*

Hydraulic hoses can have pipe fittings crimped to both ends, or they can have any combination of pipe threads crimped to one end and a straight threaded coupling on the other end.

WET EXHAUST SYSTEM HOSES

The exhaust pipe for horizontally positioned wet exhaust systems is usually made of fiberglass. The small amount of expansion in a wet exhaust system is absorbed by the hoses that connect the parts of the system together.

Periodically check the inside of the wet exhaust elbow where the exhaust hose is

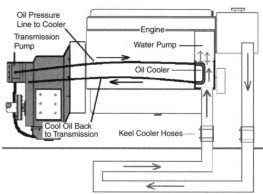

Fig. 4-6. Flow of transmission oil cooler.

Fig. 4-7. Check the wet exhaust elbow for coking buildup. (Courtesy MER Equipment, Seattle, Washington)

attached for signs of coking (carbon). Coking occurs on some engines because the exhaust gases get cold so quickly that the hydrocarbon residue in the gases can solidify and build up inside the elbow.

Installed in-line with the wet exhaust system is a silencer (muffler) that is either fiberglass or a rubber-like compound. The entire exhaust system must angled downward, toward the stern, where the exhaust exits. This allows water inside the exhaust pipe to flow, with the exhaust gases, out of the boat. Be sure to check your engine's installation guide to verify that the installation is correct. The through-the-stern fitting should have a

rubber flap on the outside that will close if a large wave hits the transom. The flap prevents water from entering the exhaust system from the wrong direction, possibly resulting in the introduction of water into the engine. When exhaust cooling water gets into the engine, it will rust the cylinders and cause a hydraulic lock.

All wet exhaust systems must be monitored for hot spots during operation. Hot spots will occur if water flow stops. The entire system must be well supported on both small and large boats. Sagging hoses can restrict exhaust flow and cause back-pressure. On larger boats, crew may actually step on hoses and other parts of the system as they maintain the boat.

COOLANT HOSES

If your conventional coolant hoses (the black ones) seem to age, dry out, and fail prematurely, consider upgrading them to silicone hoses. In the long run you'll save money, and don't forget the safety implications if a coolant hose bursts when the boat is in a close-quarters maneuver or near rocks or other hazards.

Heat and the effects of galvanic corrosion, the result of electrochemical action, cause many hose failures. The damage usually happens right at the connecting point between the hose and the metal pipes in the system, such as the water pump inlet pipe.

Consider this interesting scenario: The pump inlet pipe becomes an anode, the hose becomes a cathode, and the coolant circulating inside the hose becomes an electrolyte because of higher-than-normal acidity. What you have is a form of battery, or, more properly termed, a galvanic cell generating low voltage that will shorten the life of the hose.

To combat such problems it is important to keep enough conditioner in the coolant to prevent the coolant from becoming acidic. Hose manufacturers have also developed chemical additives for their rubber compounds that resist electrochemical degradation (ECD). These additives enable hoses to carry the ECR rating, which stands for electrochemical resistant.

Another way around such hose problems as mentioned above is to use silicone rubber hoses. While expensive and not as resistant to abrasion as conventional hoses, silicone hoses don't harden over time and are not affected by ECD. When clamping silicone

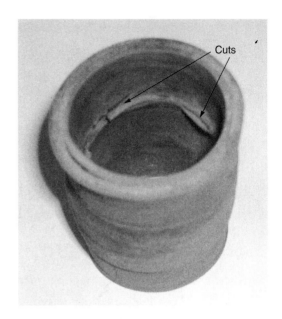

Fig. 4-8. Too much clamping force cut the inside of this silicone rubber hose. (Courtesy MER Equipment, Seattle, Washington)

hoses, use constant-tension clamps to avoid overclamping.

Non-reinforced suction hoses can collapse and totally stop circulation of the coolant when they are used on the suction side of the coolant pump. *Note: Avoid overclamping all hoses, especially silicone hoses (Fig. 4-8), to eliminate cutting the inside of the hose.*

PREFORMED HOSES

There are times when nothing but a preformed hose can bend tightly enough to connect components at extreme angles. Preformed hoses aren't always available in remote communities. If you're stuck, visit an auto parts store—you may find what you're looking for hanging on a wall (Figure 4-9).

If you get lucky and the auto parts store carries preformed hose, carefully examine the inventory for any hoses that match the bend you need; you can always cut it to make it fit.

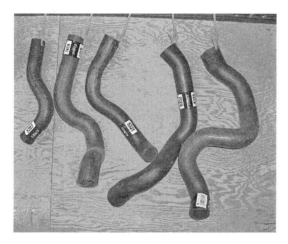

Fig. 4-9. Cut sections from preformed hoses to get the right bend.

However, care must be taken to avoid kinking a hose when installing it; otherwise, flow restrictions will occur. As previously mentioned, hoses must be protected from high heat.

Many boats have hoses that are nearly impossible to access. Removing an old hose is the easy part, because it can be cut off.

When new hoses are tough to install, use oil or dish soap as a lubricant to help the hose slide into place. If the hose just can't be reached, fashion a hook from an old screwdriver and pull it into place (Fig. 4-10).

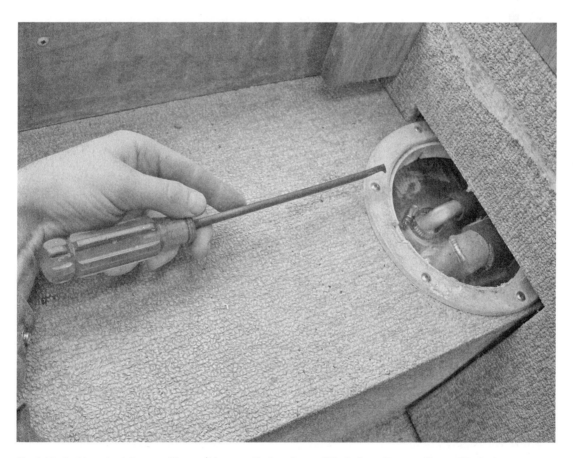

Fig. 4-10. Fashion a hook from an old screwdriver to pull a hose into a difficult place. (Courtesy Thomas Wischer)

CHAPTER 5
FUEL, LUBE OIL, AND FILTRATION SYSTEMS

The importance of avoiding contamination of fuel and lube oil with water, dirt, and other substances cannot be emphasized enough. Water in diesel fuel will create havoc, and it doesn't do a gasoline engine any good either. Water or coolant in oil degrades its lubrication ability, counteracting its benefits. These are just two examples of what can happen when the vital liquids of your boat's engine and transmission are compromised. Let's take a close look at some of the problems you may encounter, and how good filtration and constant vigilance will help you avoid unpleasant and potentially costly surprises.

WATER IN THE FUEL

Whether you have a gasoline or a diesel engine, the most common type of fuel contamination is fresh water. It can get into fuel through condensation in the fuel tank or rain entering tank vents and the fuel fill.

GASOLINE ENGINES

Dealing with water in the fuel of a gasoline engine is much easier than it is with a diesel. With a gasoline engine, all you have to do is drain the tank and replace the fuel. Water can go through the gasoline fuel system with little harm, though it's important to get most of the water out. Pour a water-dispersing additive into the tank to remove the final residue of water.

DIESEL ENGINES

Closely fit mechanical parts in a diesel fuel system depend on the lubricity of the fuel and will be harmed by the passage of water through the system if dispersant additives are used. *Note: Water dispersants must not be used in diesel fuel!* If there is a low drain point in the tank, water must be drained from there. If there isn't a good drain system, the choices come down to either processing the fuel with a filter buggy or removing the tank for cleaning.

A filter buggy (Fig. 5-1) is a two-wheeled cart with an electric pump and two large Racor fuel-water separator-type filters plumbed after a small pre-filter. The suction hose from the pump is connected directly to the fuel tank's outlet fitting, and the hose that carries the filtered and dewatered fuel is routed to the boat's fuel fill. To prevent fuel spills, this hose is tied in place, and the buggy's pump is turned on.

WATER OR COOLANT IN THE ENGINE OIL

When water or coolant leaks into the engine crankcase, it migrates to the bottom of the oil pan because it is heavier than the engine's lube oil. It will stay on the bottom until the engine is started. When the engine is running, water is pulled from the bottom of the pan into the engine oil pump. From there it is sent throughout the engine lubricating oil system.

Fig. 5-1. A filter buggy removes water from fuel.

Note: Engines equipped with a good partial-flow oil filter, like the COMO filter, manufactured in Janesville, Wisconsin, can temporarily tolerate a small amount of antifreeze in the oil. The COMO filter element is made of cellulose, which absorbs and holds water (coolant) while trapping wear-causing particles. Partial-flow oil filters are discussed later in this chapter.

Unless coolant is removed from the oil, the oil and coolant emulsify into an oily black substance. That is worse than water alone mixing with the oil, because the resulting sludge (Fig. 5-4) is so thick it plugs the lube oil passages in the engine on both the suction and pressure side of the oil pump (Fig. 5-5).

Plugged oil passages result in a loss of lubricating oil to the entire engine. This condition is first revealed at the crankshaft (Fig. 5-6).

Some engine manufacturers suggest flushing the engine with a special compound to remove the coolant residue, or completely dismantling the engine for piece-by-piece cleaning. Others recommend changing the oil twice in a short period of time and then sampling the oil. Let's look at the options.

WORK-AROUND SOLUTION

Dealing with Water in Fuel

In the accompanying photo, boatowner Thomas Wischer of Kodiak, Alaska, monitors progress after the two fuel lines were connected to his 26-foot Volvo-Penta diesel-powered Olympic.

Fig. 5-2. The filter buggy in action.

In this case, we were drawing the fuel from the rear of the tank, and we ran the filter buggy until the fuel appeared to be clean. As a precaution, we jacked up the tongue of the boat trailer to make any remaining water run to the back of the tank, where the filter buggy could treat it. Jacking up the trailer helped the filter buggy pick up more water.

However, on two subsequent sea trials the water just kept coming. We realized that the fuel tank baffles were trapping water, and we were forced to cut the deck to allow removal of the tank.

Angle cuts were made so that the piece removed would be self-aligning when it was replaced. The 83-gallon tank had to be pumped out to allow its removal.

The tank's bay was then thoroughly cleaned to remove any debris that might puncture the tank when it was reinstalled. After the

Fig. 5-3. Cutting a deck open to remove a fuel tank.

tank was pressure-washed and air-dried, we "flanged" the piece of deck that had been cut out. Aluminum flat bar and angle were used here, thereby turning it into a removable hatch.

Next, both the fill and vent hoses were replaced with U.S. Coast Guard–approved hose.

The clean tank was put back in place, and aluminum angles were fitted, full length to the tank bay, to help support the hatch.

Finally, the hatch was installed using 3M 4200 quick-drying sealant. In addition to this, we drilled and screwed the hatch flanges to the deck.

The last step was to replace all filters and drain all fuel lines between the fuel tank and the engine before the sea trial, which was successful. Just to be sure there would be no unexpected water coming into the fuel through the filler neck, we installed a new O-ring seal on the plug.

Picture for a moment the instant when the first drop of antifreeze leaks into the engine oil. This first drop activates the engine failure clock. There is no way that the engine operator can immediately discern from the engine's performance, sound, or appearance that coolant

Fig. 5-4. An example of sludge created by antifreeze leaking into crankcase oil.

is leaking into the oil. While there is now an engine failure in progress, the engine still performs well.

Unless someone intervenes, the failure will proceed as if it were a large stone rolling

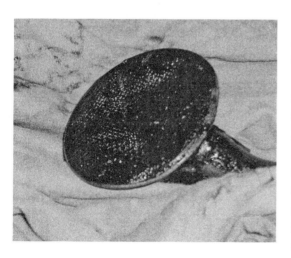

Fig. 5-5. A partially plugged oil pump suction pipe.

down a steep mountainside. Two things will happen: (1) the failure will gather momentum, and (2) it will become increasingly noticeable as it proceeds. The best approach for stopping the large (and soon to be very destructive) stone from rolling down the mountain is to stop its movement while it *can* be stopped—that is, before it gathers momentum.

This brings us to several ways of dealing with antifreeze leaks into the engine oil, starting with the ideal and working down the list to the least desirable outcome:

1. If the operator is diligent about regularly checking oil and coolant levels and notices that the system is losing coolant, engine damage can be avoided. Then, by following up with pressure testing, the source of coolant leaking into the oil can be found and repaired.

Fig. 5-6. Congealed oil and coolant can block an oil supply. This engine is upside down with its crankshaft removed, and the screwdriver has just been withdrawn from the crankshaft oil supply port that is just beneath the screwdriver tip. Coolant got into the oil in this engine, turning the oil to sludge.

In this ideal situation, after the leak is stopped, all that is needed is to bring the engine up to full operating temperature and change the engine oil. This must be done twice, two hours apart. Following up by sending an oil sample to a lab should then verify that the engine is OK.

2. The coolant leaking into the oil pan begins to congeal the oil (Fig. 5-7). If it is caught before the engine's internal oil passages are plugged, you can use butyl cellosolve as suggested by the engine manufacturer. Butyl cellosolve is a harsh, toxic chemical compound

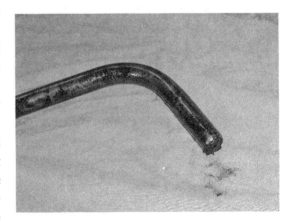

Fig. 5-7. A plugged outlet tube from an oil pump.

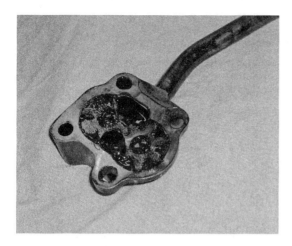

Fig. 5-8. Congealed oil in an oil pump is clearly visible in this photo of the pump's endcap.

FLUSHING A CRANKCASE WITH BUTYL CELLOSOLVE

While it is a judgment call, a marine mechanic may sometimes opt to try flushing the engine crankcase with the strong (and toxic) solvent butyl cellosolve. This is done by mixing 20 percent of the solvent (by normal lube oil volume) with 80 percent engine oil. Next the engine must be idled at 1,000 rpm until it reaches operating temperature. Finally, the engine oil and filters must be changed. The filters that are taken out with the oil change must be cut open for inspection to determine if engine damage has occurred, as revealed by shards of aluminum or iron. Sample the oil again after twenty hours of running time.

that is sometimes used to clean coolant from the engine lubricating system after the source of a leak is located and repaired. Use of butyl cellosolve is not advised for weekend boaters, but this treatment is used by professional diesel mechanics (see sidebar).

3. When the oil congeals, however, no amount of clean oil or butyl cellosolve can *reach* the extremities of the system to dissolve the sludge. Therefore, the engine must be taken apart (Fig. 5-8) and meticulously cleaned. Every plug must be removed from the lube oil system, and all lube oil passages must be brushed and cleaned. If the engine continues to run while lacking lubrication, it will self-destruct.

In the final seconds of an engine failure, the engine damage, cost of repairs, length of downtime, and potential danger to those nearby all rapidly increase.

AIR-INTAKE CONTAMINATION

When all parts of the intake air plumbing system are in good condition, regular air filter maintenance will keep dust out of the engine. Many air filters may be gently washed from the inside out with warm soapy water and then rinsed in the same direction. Check with the filter manufacturer first, though, to be sure your air filters are washable. Both disposable and cleanable air filters are available.

Most engine air filters made of paper may be gently washed twice in mild, warm detergent from the inside out. Never blow a filter clean with compressed air, because the risk of tearing the paper is too great. After cleaning, shine a light through the filter media (paper) and inspect for tears or cracks. There can be a lot of dust over lakes, and streams, as well as the ocean. Monitor the condition of your air filters.

Besides being extremely hard on the boat's occupants, nothing is worse for an air filter than an exhaust leak in the boat's engine room. After a filter is plugged, the restriction can get high enough to pull the filter media into the turbocharger!

AIR-INTAKE PLUMBING

There is an easy way to test for leaks in the intake air system plumbing between the air filter and the turbocharger. Begin by starting the engine and letting it idle, then lightly spray all the joints in the air plumbing with starting fluid and see if the engine speed suddenly changes. Engine speed will fluctuate if the starting fluid enters the engine through a leak. This indicates a leak that will allow dust to get into the cylinders and damage them.

AIR FILTERS

Always check for an air filter restriction in response to a low engine power complaint. Most air-intake systems have a filter restriction indicator plumbed into the system. Air filter vacuum gauges can be installed in the instrument panel and will provide an early warning of air filter plugging. Black smoke is a dead giveaway for a restricted air filter. It can also indicate an internally collapsed muffler.

FUEL AND CONTAMINANTS IN THE OIL

Engine oil is thinned when fuel leaks into the crankcase, thereby diminishing its lubrication qualities. Checking the oil level and quickly noticing a rising oil level will help you spot this problem before damage is done. Consult the engine manual for fuel dilution sources for each engine. The following general list will be helpful:

1. plugged air filters
2. fuel transfer pump leaks
3. leaks on the injection pump drive shaft seal
4. leaking fuel lines inside the crankcase

Periodic oil sampling will verify that the problem has been found and cured.

AIR FILTERS ARE CHEAP

It took a day to get to Prudhoe Bay from Anchorage with 450 pounds of tools and engine parts, and upon arriving I asked to look at a Caterpillar 3306 engine that the owner wanted rebuilt.

The oil level was slightly above the full mark, and it did drip too freely from the end of the dipstick, even in the cold. I took this to indicate possible dilution of the crankcase oil with fuel. The coolant level was just right. When I started the engine, it billowed black smoke even at idle. Sure enough, the engine's power output was very low.

An inspection of the engine showed no big oil leaks and no burned or darkened paint, a sign of severe overheating. The hour meter showed a low number of hours for a rebuild, but I didn't put too much stock in it, thinking that a previous hour meter may have failed and been replaced. Then I noticed that the air filter restriction indicator device was in the red, an indication of a restriction. Pulling the lid off the air cleaner, I found an air filter that was caked and plugged with dust! Replacing the air filter cured all problems on this engine, including the fuel dilution.

CONTAMINATION OF NEW OIL

There is plenty of opportunity for contamination of new engine oil on most vessels. This is especially true when a vessel is large enough to have a bulk (built into the boat) oil storage tank. These tanks are subject to the same problems that affect marine fuel tanks, such as condensation of water and the collection of dust, rust scale, and algae in the bottom. In addition to this, there is nothing worse than a dirty oil bucket being used to transfer oil from an oil spigot on the tank to the engine!

After an oil tank is opened and cleaned thoroughly, all it takes to keep these problems under control is to drain condensed water from the low part of the tank. If there is no drain at the bottom, it's important to install one.

A second preventive measure involves installing an oil filter on the outlet of the lube oil tank to filter all new oil that is going into the engine. It can save time in the long run to install a filter base that will accept the same spin-on oil filter that the engine uses. Finish this upgrade by installing a brass gate valve on the end of the oil filler hose. This will enhance safety and prevent an accidental spill if the hose falls on the engine room floor. Unlike a ball valve, a brass gate valve takes more than an accidental bump to open. Often, the boat's engineer will put a pipe cap on the end of the tube coming from the gate valve to stop airborne contamination from entering the filler tube.

What can you do to protect your engine if your boat is too small to have a lube oil reservoir? The answer is as simple as keeping any funnels or pouring buckets spotlessly clean, and storing them in clean plastic bags.

FILTER INVENTORY

Every boatowner has several filters to keep track of. Care must be taken to ensure proper storage, ratings, filter type, filter quality, and change intervals. Since a filter is a device that removes unwanted particles from a fluid, proper maintenance is critical. Abrasive particles in the air, oil, and fuel cause damage and actually generate more particles.

All filter ratings are measured in microns, one micron being a millionth of a meter. A filter rated at 10 microns is finer and will remove smaller particles than a coarser 20-micron filter. Along with micron ratings, filters are rated as either nominal or absolute. A filter rated at 20 microns nominal will remove many of the 21-micron particles that reach the filter, but not all of them. Nominal ratings on filters mean they are rated at the best performance that could ever be hoped for. An absolute rating means that a 20-micron filter will pass no particles larger than 20 microns.

Those manufacturers that make high-quality filters always advertise what kind of filter media they are using as a selling point. Each manufacturer has brochures explaining its filters' construction. Oxygen takes a toll on paper filters, and inexpensive ones degrade quickly. Better-quality filters last longer.

ENGINE OIL FILTERS

Besides being made of good materials, a good engine oil filter will hold more soot than an inferior one. Soot is incompletely burned fuel that gets past the piston rings and ends up in the crankcase. Diesel engines produce more soot when they are in poor condition, are idled for too long, or are run with insufficient load.

The two major types of filters (Fig. 5-9) are (1) full-flow and (2) partial-flow (bypass). The former filters all the oil that comes to it until it reaches its maximum capacity to hold soot, at which point a bypass valve opens and the engine runs with unfiltered oil. Proper oil change intervals prevent this from happening. Filling a new full-flow filter with oil prior to installation is a good move.

Partial-flow filters are much less common but will extend engine life when used to assist full-flow filters. A partial-flow filter is

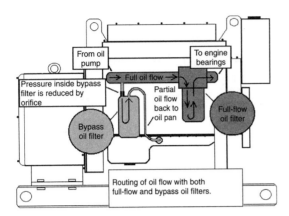

Fig. 5-9. Full-flow and partial-flow oil filters.

finer—i.e., it has a lower micron rating than a full-flow filter—and is teed-in to the main oil gallery. Generally, a partial-flow filter only filters one quart in ten, but the oil it does filter is rendered very clean. The oil from a bypass filter goes back to the oil pan and not directly to the engine's bearings.

Use of a partial-flow oil filter can also save fuel, enhance horsepower, or both—even

if only slightly. There is a qualifier for this statement, though: The partial-flow filter must pass enough oil to reduce the oil pressure gauge reading by 2 or 3 psi, yet maintain sufficient oil pressure when the engine is at operating temperature. If you install a partial-fill filter of proper size, the engine will waste less fuel and power pressurizing lube oil.

Partial-flow filters work well on transmissions and hydraulic systems as well as engines. The filter media inside the housing is tightly wound cellulose paper. Cellulose has a strong affinity for water, and the unit will hold a considerable amount of it while the cellulose fibers allow oil to slowly pass through and return to the sump.

Note: When upgrading a system by installing a partial-flow filter, like the COMO filter, use a wet- or dry-vacuum cleaner to change the drain plug without completely draining the hydraulic reservoir (Fig. 5-11). With the new,

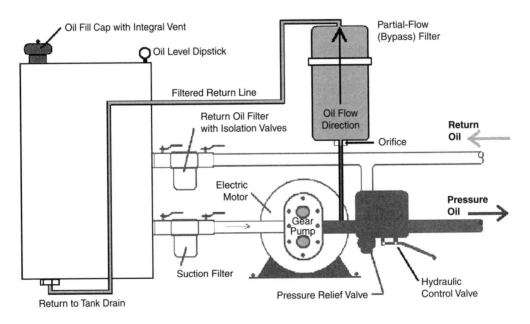

Fig. 5-10. A partial-flow filter installed on a workboat hydraulic system.

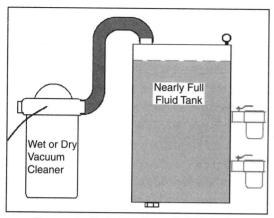

Remove the Drain Plug from a Full Hydraulic Oil or Fuel Tank Without Losing the Fluid

Fig. 5-11. Use of a wet- or dry-vacuum cleaner to keep fluid in a reservoir while a drain plug is removed. This trick can be used on engines, transmissions, and hydraulic tanks.

predrilled fitting standing by, pull a vacuum on the tank, switch plugs, and then connect the line to the bottom of the tank.

FUEL FILTERS

Coalescing fuel-water separators are available in several micron sizes and will remove water from fuel. Many vessels use a 10-micron fuel-water separator, which can be overwhelmed if a big slug of water hits it. Dark-colored material in the transparent filter bowl indicates an algae problem. Algae cannot live without water, so the presence of algae is a danger signal suggesting that there is more water coming into the tank than condensation alone could account for.

Several companies are now making fuel and hydraulic filters that absorb water and stop the flow when the filter's water-absorbing capacity is reached. They have a cellulose core that will absorb water but not fuel. As the core absorbs water, it swells until it finally stops the flow through the filter.

Filling a new diesel fuel filter before installation is a *bad move*, because unfiltered fuel flows to the filtered side. This gives the unfiltered fuel a straight shot into the fuel injection system.

MARINE TRANSMISSION FILTERS

Older transmissions have a cartridge-style filter, while newer gears use spin-on filters. Regular service of either type is important. Most transmissions also have a screen on the suction side of the pump. Metal particles in the suction screen filter indicate a failure of the clutch discs or bearings in the transmission.

Small transmissions often have no filter and are fitted only with a suction screen to monitor and clean. Very small transmissions, such as those on diesels under 40 hp, may not even have a screen.

FILTER INSPECTION

Most used oil filters can be inspected after they are drained. Filters can be inspected periodically for safety's sake or especially if a new noise develops in a piece of equipment.

It's easy to cut open a filter to see how your equipment is functioning and whether or not metal fragments are appearing due to a failure. Clamp the threaded end of the filter into a vise and cut the threaded end from the filter with a hacksaw. Remove the inner pleated filter media and cut out a 2-inch section (see also Fig. 10-20). Cutting several pleats out, opposite the end you opened, is also a good idea. There may be iron particles present from when the filter was cut open. Snap-on Tools makes a filter cutter that will open a filter without creating any metal particles.

Squeeze the test section in a vise to remove all the oil, then open the pleats for inspection. Aluminum particles are easy to spot.

In an engine, aluminum particles mean piston damage. These show up in the filter after severe overheating. Iron particles are not as easy to spot, but they can be picked up with a clean magnet. Black soot particles don't always indicate damage but may mean that oil and filters need to be changed more often.

DON'T WASTE OIL AND FILTER CHANGES

Because equipment manufacturers have no control over the conditions under which their units are used, they often specify very conservative oil and filter change intervals. Your application may not be as severe as the ones envisioned when the intervals were specified. You may be wasting oil and filter changes. There are three ways to find the best change interval for your equipment. While these checks are often used for engines, they have application to equipment such as marine transmissions as well.

1. Pressure differential gauges: The efficiency of many filters improves dramatically just before the media clogs because larger particles plug the bigger holes in the media that smaller particles could have gone through. As a filter begins to clog, it will restrict the flow of oil or it will bypass, depending on how it is constructed. Many filter manufacturers provide pressure gauges on the inlet and outlet ports of the filter housing that allow the user to see when the filter is beginning to clog. For example, if the inlet gauge indicates 50 psi and the outlet gauge says 46 psi, it is apparent that the filter is at the end of its useful life.

2. Oil analysis: Testing used oil lets boatowners see engine, transmission, and hydraulic system failures coming. For most diesel engines, the most important wear metals to watch for are iron from cylinder liners and aluminum from pistons. Also, by doing engine oil analysis and watching soot levels in the report, it is possible to see if filters are being changed too seldom or too often.

3. The Exxon Mobil Viscosity tester: This is a clever plastic device with two grooves on the upper surface, allowing users to compare the change in viscosity between new oil and oil that is about to be changed. When soot levels in engine oil get too high, it increases the oil's viscosity, and it is time for an oil change, regardless of how few or how many hours have passed since the last one. (See Figure 5-12.)

To use the portable tester shown, begin by laying it flat and filling each of the two reservoirs. One is to be filled with oil from your engine and the other with new oil that is the same brand, weight, and temperature as the old oil.

Next tip the tester up on its beveled end and watch the two oils race to the bottom. If the old oil is a lot slower than the new,

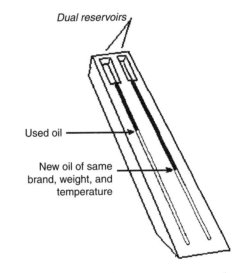

Dual reservoirs

Used oil

New oil of same brand, weight, and temperature

Fig. 5-12. A portable viscosity tester. Exxon Mobil makes one, or you can make one with a router and a piece of wood.

there is probably soot in the oil. To correct this, shorten the oil and filter change interval by fifty hours and eliminate all idling below 1,000 rpm.

If the old and new oil travel at the same speed, lengthen the oil and filter change interval by fifty hours and retest.

If the old oil gets to the bottom first, there is probably fuel in the oil, the source of which must be found.

Note: Spin-on oil filters can be tough to remove. Kodiak pilot and mechanic Randy Weber suggests using silicone lubricant on the oil filter seal (Fig. 5-13) and then tightening the filter exactly as the engine manufacturer suggests.

Some engine manufacturers suggest a specific torque for tightening the filter, while others suggest tightening the filter three fourths to one complete turn after the filter seal makes contact with the base.

With longer oil change intervals, ease of pumping, and resistance to degradation, synthetic oil is a high-quality product that can help reduce engine wear. Use synthetic oils and extended drain intervals only after engine oil analysis proves it is safe for the engine.

There are, finally, many good additives for oil. One that works especially well is an old product with a most unlikely name: Marvel Mystery Oil. It comes in a red can and is

Fig. 5-13. Lube the oil filter seal with silicone grease.

CALIBRATING THE OIL DIPSTICK ON A NEWLY INSTALLED ENGINE

When repowering with a marine engine different from the one you are replacing, it is important to calibrate the dipstick. Engineers at the factory knew how much oil the new engine required, but they couldn't know at what angle the engine would be installed. This is an important consideration in recreational sailboats, which often have engines installed at an angle.

To begin, drain all oil from the engine. The manufacturer will specify how many gallons represent the low oil mark. Usually the low oil mark will be 90 percent of full. Therefore, if the engine holds 10 gallons, adding nine gallons and marking the stick at nine gallons will represent the low oil mark.

To find the full mark, add the final gallon and mark the stick at the full mark. Marking can be done by lightly marking the dipstick with a file or with a center punch. After all the specified oil is added, this level of oil represents the full mark. Wipe off the dipstick and insert it in the engine, draw it out, and mark this level as the high mark.

Modern oil has very good wetting ability. Therefore, an engine at rest overnight can give the oil time to wick above the full mark. Just wipe the stick and reinsert it for an accurate reading. The same procedure works with engines that must have their oil checked while the engine is running. Note: Don't exceed the engine manufacturer's maximum engine installation angle.

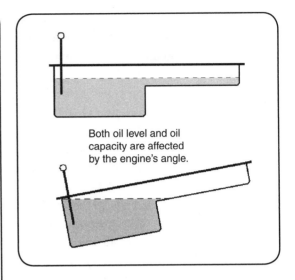

Both oil level and oil capacity are affected by the engine's angle.

also helps prevent sticking of the piston rings in their ring grooves. Marvel Mystery Oil is very good in gasoline and diesel fuel systems as well as in the crankcase oil. It is a super lubricant that can extend engine life.

WATER FILTERS

Domestic water filters are important for the crew's health. In remote areas, you don't know about the quality of the water you're putting in the tank. Many workboats have questionable potable water tanks, as do pleasure craft. For inboard water filtration, an activated charcoal filter is the minimum, and a reverse osmosis (RO) filter system is far better.

Reverse osmosis units have pores in the filter membranes that are so small only water molecules can pass through. These units then flush contaminants overboard, so they do require a little more plumbing, and, like any other filter, they do require filter cartridge changes. All water filters need to be connected between the boat's freshwater (domestic) pump and the galley tap where the crew gets their drinking water.

available in most auto parts stores. It is an upper cylinder lubricant, which means it works well in lubricating the valve guides and

Marine engines spin far faster than a propeller should turn, and engines turn in just one direction. The function of the marine transmission is to reduce the engine speed to a usable shaft rpm while enabling the propeller to spin in reverse as well as forward. It sounds obvious, but sometimes the most basic functions related to a boat's machinery are taken for granted until a vital component fails.

The following discussion will focus primarily on marine transmissions for inboard gasoline and diesel engines, but it will also provide information about engine power-take-offs (PTOs). A PTO is essentially a means by which power from the engine is harnessed to run other equipment on board. While most smaller recreational vessels don't have PTOs, it is still good to know about them, because the knowledge will broaden your overall understanding of what an engine can do in addition to moving a boat through the water.

MARINE TRANSMISSIONS

As mentioned above, transmissions do more than allow you to shift into forward, neutral, and reverse. The transmission, also known as a reduction gear, slows the propeller to a useful speed. In other words, it helps control the power transfer from the engine to the propeller, acting as a middleman. The transmission is often referred to as a marine gear to distinguish it from automotive transmissions (Fig. 6-1).

The transmission performs four vital duties:

1. It provides reverse for backing the boat and also for sudden braking
2. It reduces propeller shaft speed for maximum efficiency
3. It transmits the fore-and aft-thrust from the propeller to the boat. Just as the mast on a sailboat transmits the wind's force on the sails to the vessel, the transmission transmits the propeller's force to the vessel through the engine bed, while isolating the engine from the destructive power of the propeller's thrust. If this thrust acted directly on the engine's flywheel, it would immediately destroy the crankshaft's main thrust bearing and cause engine failure.
4. It dissipates heat, both by radiation and through the oil supply to a heat exchanger (oil cooler). This heat is caused by friction inside the gearbox.

Propeller thrust, even in a small boat, can be considerable. For example, a 16-foot seine skiff, such as an Alaskan salmon fisherman uses, might have a 130 hp, four-cylinder diesel engine and easily achieve a bollard pull of 3,000 pounds. (Bollard pull is measured with a heavy-duty scale tied between the skiff and the dock. It is defined as the pulling ability of a boat measured in pounds or tons exerted when the boat is tied to and pulling against an immovable object.)

Fig. 6-1. This small marine transmission has no oil filter and no suction screen on the oil intake. The lever arm in the foreground controls the shifting between forward, neutral, and reverse. This transmission would be matched with a two- or three-cylinder diesel of less than 40 hp. (Courtesy MER Equipment, Seattle, Washington)

GEAR RATIOS

When a diesel engine turns at 2,000 rpm and the propeller shaft turns at only 1,000 rpm, there is a drive ratio through the transmission of 2:1 (Fig. 6-2). Put another way, 2,000 rpm is going into the front of the transmission, but only 1,000 rpm comes out the back. This is accomplished by using two gears inside the transmission, running together. From the ratio we can see that the driving gear, the one from the engine, must have half the number of teeth as the gear that drives the propeller shaft. Gear reduction is what allows the engine, transmission, and propeller shaft to work together to move the boat efficiently through the water.

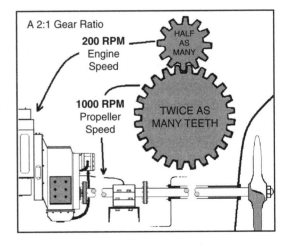

Fig. 6-2. A 2:1 transmission reduction ratio.

MAINTENANCE

As always, the first essential step in mechanical maintenance is to read the manual carefully. Examine your transmission manual and check for the proper type of oil to use. If synthetic oil is compatible with your equipment, use it because it has better film strength and is easier to pump than conventional oils. While you have the manual in hand, also note the manufacturer's recommendations for oil change intervals.

Watch for oil leaks, especially from the front end of the transmission. There are two possibilities for oil leaks in this area. Be sure to make the correct call between an engine rear crankshaft seal leak and a seal leak in the front of the transmission. To distinguish between them, just remember that the transmission oil is always honey-colored, unless you're using automatic transmission fluid (ATF), in which case the fluid will be red. Engine oil, on the other hand, is normally black. It is honey-colored immediately following an oil change, but blackens as soon as the engine is started. One problem with an oil leak in this area is that the oil can deteriorate the rubber coupling that connects the input shaft of some transmissions to the engine flywheel.

Always monitor oil temperature and pressure as you operate the boat. Some transmissions have lower pressure in neutral than when they are in gear. If so, always wait to increase the throttle setting until sufficient drive pressure comes up on your gauge to show that the transmission is fully engaged.

GLITTER

Many transmissions have a suction screen on the gear pump's incoming oil supply line. This screen needs to be checked when you change the oil and filter or if your transmission develops problems. It is not uncommon to find metallic fuzz consisting of very fine, short strands of metal in this screen in a new gear or following a rebuild. Use caution when checking your screen because these strands are very sharp!

If you begin to see metal fuzz in the screen on a transmission with a high number of hours, you need to check further. Remove the oil filter and cut it open to inspect for metallic glitter.

Glitter is composed of small chunks of recently destroyed machinery, and more than half a thimble of this stuff in a small transmission indicates that your gear is about to die or is already dead. With glitter you will often see the lubricating oil take on an appearance as of metallic paint. Glitter is also self-perpetuating—that is, when the metallic particles start flowing through a transmission, they run through the gears and bearings and cause even more damage.

COME-HOME SCREWS

Several manufacturers of marine transmissions, including Twin Disc and ZF, provide come-home screws as a means to keep going if a clutch pack fails. Check your manual or ask your transmission or engine dealer to demonstrate the come-home feature before you need it.

While coming back to port on the come-home screws, it is advisable to be on the radio lining up a possible tow, because the failed clutch will contaminate the gear case with clutch material and may result in a complete transmission failure. See Fig. 14-3 on page 245 for more information on the come-home feature.

LOCKING THE SHAFT

If your workboat must be towed, be sure to stop the propeller shaft rotation. This can be done by hanging a pipe wrench on the propeller shaft to prevent it from turning. When the shaft freewheels from the rear with the engine turned off, a hydraulic transmission will not receive lubrication, which is why a spinning output shaft can be harmful. Some hydraulic workboat transmissions have shaft brakes that lock automatically when the transmission is in neutral or the engine is shut down. Be sure to check the manual for your unit to understand what is required. Small mechanical transmissions with toothed gears, such as those on sailboats, do receive some lubrication whenever the output shaft spins, so shaft freewheeling does not harm the transmission.

FRONT AND REAR COUPLINGS

Each transmission has one coupling at the front and one at the rear. They are alike in name only.

The coupling between the engine and the transmission is designed to be flexible enough to absorb rotating impulses of torque coming from the engine. However, these front couplings are not designed to absorb fore-and-aft thrust. They are sometimes made of a combination of steel discs and springs to absorb torque, though they can also be made of a rubber-like compound that absorbs vibrations from firing impulses common to all engines. These rotary vibrations are called torsional vibrations. As previously mentioned, an oil leak between the engine and the transmission will seriously weaken a rubber coupling and cause it to fail.

Output shaft couplings usually come installed from the factory, with rigid couplings

FOR THE WORKBOAT
Trolling Valves on Workboats

Sometimes the need arises to go slower than the vessel travels in gear at its lowest engine rpm, which is why many transmissions on workboats have provisions for a trolling valve. The trolling valves that Twin Disc sells, for example, can be added to many of their transmissions after the sale.

A trolling valve reduces the application oil pressure to the forward clutch pack, allowing the clutch to slip a little while maintaining lubrication to the discs to carry away excess heat caused by slippage in the forward clutch.

The downside to a trolling valve is that you can't use full engine power unless the valve is closed. Using the trolling valve at high engine rpm will quickly burn out the forward clutch.

designed to take a small amount of torsional vibration and a huge amount of propeller thrust. Flexible couplings for the output end of the transmission are available and do have their place. Lighter, high-speed boats with high propeller shaft speeds benefit from a flexible output shaft coupling. They are used on motoryachts and lobster boats, which are light vessels with much higher power levels than is typical of commercial fishing boats of the same length.

THE POWER-TAKE-OFF (PTO)

As mentioned in the introduction of this chapter, a power-take-off (PTO) harnesses the engine to power other equipment.

Conservatively speaking, there are more than one hundred ways to do it.

Figure 6-3 shows several ways to use an engine to drive pumps:

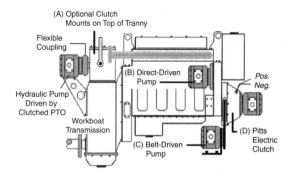

Fig. 6-3. Various power-take-off (PTO) systems. Option A, for workboats, requires a clutched PTO mounted on the transmission.

+ With the engine's flywheel, through a mechanical clutch (A)
+ With a clutchless side-mounted pump direct-driven from the engine's timing gears (B)
+ With a belt driving a pump from the engine's front crankshaft pulley (C)
+ With a D-shaft driving a pump remotely through a Pitts electric clutch (D)

The PTO is used to power hydraulic pumps, steering pumps, refrigeration compressors, or an extra alternator. Usually mounted at opposite ends of the engine, PTOs and boat transmissions share common mounting requirements: they all must be centered with the engine's crankshaft. Caterpillar engine service manuals provide a very clear explanation of how to check to see that the flywheel and PTO housings are round and centered with the crankshaft.

CRANKSHAFT END FLOAT

Most engine manuals spell out how to check crankshaft end float, another important aspect of mounting transmissions and PTOs on an engine. Crankshaft end float, otherwise

known as end play, allows the crankshaft to move forward and aft in the cylinder block. It must have enough end float to allow the crankshaft thrust bearing to receive proper lubrication. Too little prevents oil from getting to the thrust-bearing surface, which will destroy the crankshaft and cylinder block.

MEASURING YOUR FLYWHEEL HOUSING

When ordering an engine-driven unit such as a marine transmission or a new PTO, you have to know the size of the flywheel housing on the engine. This seemingly simple information isn't always easy to obtain. Follow the measurements on Figure 6-4 to determine the size and bolt pattern of the flywheel housing on your engine.

EXTRA BELTS

When replacing alternator or fan belts on an engine with a front-mounted PTO, always tie in an extra set of belts around the crankshaft snout so the whole PTO won't need to be removed for future belt changes. See Chapter 4 for more details.

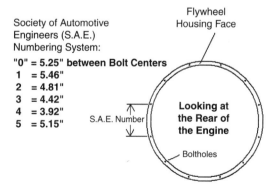

Fig. 6-4. The SAE flywheel housing size is simply the straight-line center-to-center distance between two adjacent bolts.

REMOVING PROPELLERS

Using an acetylene torch is a good way to remove a larger propeller. A Mapp gas torch gets warm enough to do small propellers.

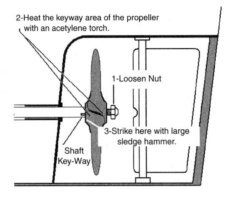

CHAPTER 7

THE MECHANICAL/ELECTRICAL INTERFACE

Many boats have two electrical systems, one operating on direct current (DC) and one operating on alternating current (AC). The two systems are quite different, but they both deliver electrical power and do work on board, and this saves the crew's time and muscle power. I am not an electrician, and this book does not attempt to guide you through the ins and outs of onboard DC and AC electrical system maintenance and troubleshooting. For that you can study one of the several good marine electrical manuals available. For example, basic 12-volt DC coverage is provided by *The 12-Volt Bible for Boats*, Second Edition (Miner Brotherton and Ed Sherman, 2003) and by *Sailboat Electrics Simplified* (Don Casey, 1999). For intermediate coverage of DC and AC systems, your choices include *Powerboater's Guide to Electrical Systems*, Second Edition (Ed Sherman, 2007); *Boatowner's Illustrated Electrical Manual*, Second Edition (Charlie Wing, 2006); and *Boatowner's Mechanical and Electrical Manual*, Third Edition (Nigel Calder, 2005). And advanced onboard troubleshooting and electronics installation guidance is available from *Advanced Marine Electrics and Electronics Troubleshooting* (Ed Sherman, 2007).

This chapter will focus on the electromechanical connections in noncomputerized mechanical components—in other words, our concern here is mechanical malfunctions that have an electrical origin. We'll also emphasize devices that enhance safety and protect propulsion and generator engines, as well as tips for maintaining these devices.

Before we begin, please note that working around electricity on boats can be dangerous, and this is particularly true of AC power. Where DC power might shock or arc (neither being a pleasant thing by any means), AC power can kill. You must be absolutely certain that no power is supplying any AC components you handle or work on. If in any doubt about what you are doing, hire a marine electrician.

SWITCHES, ALARMS, AND SHUTDOWN SYSTEMS

The alarm and shutdown systems that protect propulsion and generator engines typically operate with DC power and use electrical switches, such as an oil pressure switch that detects faults (Fig. 7-2). The system then activates an alarm or shutdown mechanism.

Alarm and shutdown switches are designed to respond to "inputs" from temperature, pressure, or liquid level fluctuations, and they do one of two things in response to abnormal inputs: In the case of a propulsion engine, since sudden engine shutdown is undesirable, the switch will send power to an alarm, which is either a horn or warning light, and the engine will keep running. In the case of a generator engine, the switch will power a normally non-energized actuator (or depower

USING A MULTIMETER TO CHECK SWITCHES

Even inexpensive multimeters come with helpful documentation. Start by reading the booklet that came with yours.

To check for the presence of voltage at a DC switch, turn the system on without starting the engine. Turn the multimeter dial (Fig.7-1) to "Volts DC" (in other words, put the multimeter in its voltmeter mode) and ground the tip of the black lead to ground. Next touch the tip of the red lead to each terminal on the switch. One of the terminals should provide a voltage reading on the multimeter display.

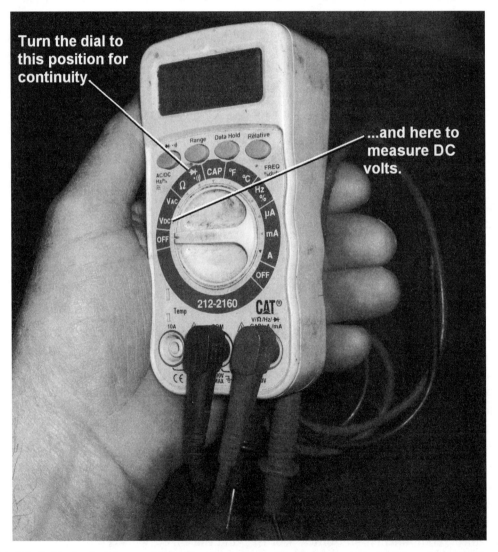

Turn the dial to this position for continuity.

...and here to measure DC volts.

Fig. 7-1. **Multimeters include several dial settings for use in checking electrical systems. Read the meter instructions carefully to learn how yours works.**

To check for continuity through a switch or wire, first be sure that power to the switch is off. Confirm this by testing for voltage as described above. Next, turn the multimeter to ohmmeter mode by switching the dial to "Ohms" or "continuity" (depending on how the dial is labeled). Connect the black probe to one terminal on the switch and the red probe to the other terminal, and watch the meter display for a change in reading. If the meter shows continuity (resistance near zero ohms), then the contacts are closed. If the meter shows infinite ohms or OL (overload), the contacts are open.

Note: Some multimeters have an audible "beep" for continuity that helps to quickly check switches.

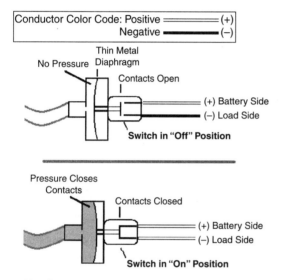

Note: Both conductors attached to a switch are in the "supply" circuit to the load. However, the conductor to the load is electrically dead until the contacts close.

Fig. 7-2. This normally open switch allows no current flow until its contacts are closed by oil pressure.

a normally energized actuator) to shut down the engine. (It may or may not activate an alarm at the same time.) The actuator may be an electrical solenoid valve that closes to turn off the fuel, or it may be an electromechanical solenoid actuator that pushes or pulls a linkage to turn off the fuel. One brand of the latter is the Trombetta actuator, which we'll cover shortly.

For example, you can wire a switch to sound an alarm in response to low oil pressure

in a main propulsion engine. Meanwhile the engine keeps running, leaving the decision of when to shut it down to the skipper. If the boat is close to rocks or other hazards, the skipper may decide to operate the engine just a little longer to get away from the hazard. In the case of low oil pressure in a generator set, however, a shutdown system can be configured to first sound an alarm and then stop the engine shortly thereafter.

At a minimum, generators require protection from low oil pressure and high coolant temperature. There are more elaborate options as well, including high or low oil level, low coolant level, and even overspeeding protection.

A FEW DEFINITIONS

Defining a few terms will simplify the work of understanding the concepts that follow.

The term *shelf-state* refers to the position of a switch's internal contacts—open or closed—when unaffected by external pressure or temperature—i.e., when the switch is still in its box on the store shelf. Both the designers of a system and the technicians who repair it later need to know the shelf-state of each relevant switch.

A *normally open switch* is one in which the contacts are open in shelf-state. That is, the electrical circuit through the switch is normally open, and no current will pass through the contacts. A *normally closed switch*, on the other hand, does maintain continuity in normal operation, because the contacts are closed in shelf-state, thereby allowing current flow.

An automatic shutdown system can be either an *energize-to-run* or an *energize-to-stop* variety. An energize-to-run system is one in which a solenoid-style actuator must oppose a spring in order to keep the engine running. When electrical current is interrupted at the switch due to a fault (for example, low oil pressure), the spring either closes a valve or moves a mechanical linkage to stop the engine. An energize-to-stop system works in the opposite way; that is to say, a spring will keep the engine running unless the shutdown solenoid is activated in response to a fault detection and overcomes the spring.

Normally open and normally closed switches are used in various combinations depending on the complexity of an engine-protection system, which includes an alarm and/or, for a generator, an automatic shutdown. For example, a normally open oil pressure switch is often wired in series with a normally closed coolant temperature switch in an energize-to-run shutdown system. If the contacts in either switch open due to a fault, the engine will shut down.

A simple *two-terminal switch* must be either normally open or normally closed. (See, for example, the normally open switch in Figure 7-2 and the normally closed switch shown in Figure 7-3.) Since there is only one circuit through the switch, it must be dedicated to just one task.

Though nearly identical to a two-terminal switch, a *three-terminal switch* provides two

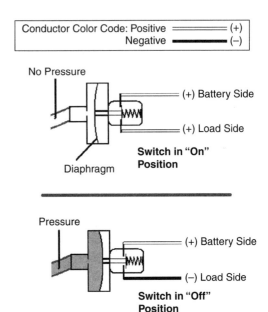

Fig. 7-3. A simple normally closed pressure switch has closed contacts in the shelf-state, before engine oil pressure acts on it. In use, a fall in oil pressure allows the contacts to close. This then sounds an alarm and/or, in the case of a generator, supplies power to an energize-to-stop mechanical solenoid-type actuator, which shuts down the engine.

circuits through the switch and can do two jobs simultaneously if needed. One circuit is normally open and the other is normally closed. The connections are as follows: (1) the common wire brings power in; (2) the normally closed terminal connects to components operated by the normally closed side; and (3) the normally open terminal connects to components operated by the normally open side.

A three-terminal switch can be operated on one side only if that is all that is needed. The common terminal is always used, but either the normally closed terminal or the normally open terminal can remain unused. The advantage of this is that the vessel owner can carry three-terminal spares for a variety of applications rather than having to carry normally open switches for some applications and normally closed switches for others. If the three-terminal switch is adjustable, that's all the better.

ALARM SYSTEMS

To build a very simple oil pressure alarm for a propulsion engine with a normally closed oil pressure switch, first plumb the switch into the engine's oil passages and then connect one of the switch's terminals to a battery through the boat's ignition switch in the wheelhouse. Connect the other terminal to a grounded horn (Fig. 7-4).

When connected this way, the horn will sound anytime the engine's ignition switch is on and there is insufficient oil pressure acting on the oil pressure switch's internal contacts. Normal oil pressure is required to open the contacts and break the alarm circuit. As the engine operates, this spring-loaded oil pressure switch is poised to sound the alarm at the instant oil pressure drops.

SHUTDOWN SYSTEMS

Let's return to the subject of automatic shutdowns in generator engines. As we've noted, a generator shutdown system requires a device, known as an actuator, that positively stops the engine when a switch trips. The type of shutdown system employed (energize-to-run or energize-to-stop) dictates the combination of normally open and normally closed switches to be used.

Simple Shutdown Systems

The simple shutdown system shown in Figure 7-5 has an energize-to-run solenoid valve on the injection pump. This means the engine will not get fuel and therefore will not run unless there is electrical power to the solenoid valve. (Solenoid valves open or close against a spring, depending on electrical input.)

In contrast with a solenoid valve, an electromechanical solenoid actuator (Fig. 7-6) moves a mechanical linkage in response to electrical input (energize-to-run) or interruption of electrical input (energize-to-stop). Trombetta is a common brand name of

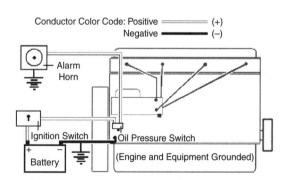

Fig. 7-4. A simplified oil pressure alarm system for a propulsion engine. Using a normally closed oil pressure switch, this system sounds a horn alarm in response to falling oil pressure, but does not turn off the engine.

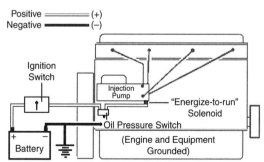

Fig. 7-5. In this simplified energize-to-run shutdown system schematic, a normally open oil pressure switch will open in response to low oil pressure and interrupt the electrical supply to an energize-to-run solenoid valve on the injection pump, closing the valve and shutting down the generator engine.

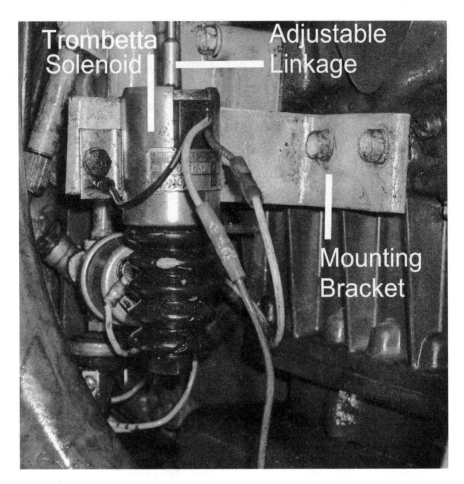

Fig. 7-6. This Trombetta actuator uses electrical power to oppose a spring, thus allowing fuel into the injection pump and permitting the generator engine to run. In the event of a fault, the power to the actuator is interrupted, and the generator shuts down.

electromechanical actuator. A simple electromagnet moves an iron pin when the solenoid is energized (magnetized). In the energize-to-run system shown in Figure 7-6, the actuator opposes a spring when energized, allowing fuel into the injection pump and thus permitting the engine to run. When a fault occurs, power to the actuator is interrupted and the opposing spring cuts off the fuel and turns the engine off. An electromechanical actuator in an energize-to-stop application works in the opposite fashion—i.e., when energized,

the actuator moves a lever, cutting off fuel to stop the generator.

The solenoid actuators discussed in this chapter, such as the Trombetta, are continuously rated (as opposed to momentary rated). That is, they can run day in, day out, without overheating or malfunctioning. These actuators have both pull-in and hold-in electrical windings. In either an energize-to-run or an energize-to-stop application, the pull-in windings use high amperage to pull in a mechanical linkage in opposition to spring pressure. In an energize-to-run application only, once the linkage is pulled in, lighter-duty hold-in windings that use far less current take over to hold the linkage in the run position, and the pull-in windings are switched off at this point. In fact, solenoids operating on 12 volts can take from 50 to 80 amps to pull in the mechanical linkage, depending on their size; hold-in windings take just a fraction of that amperage to hold the linkage in place. Always follow the manufacturer's recommendations regarding wire or conductor sizing.

The length of the linkage from a Trombetta solenoid to the injection pump shutdown lever must be precisely adjusted. When there is trouble with this type of shutdown system, check this linkage length first. Having the linkage adjusted perfectly allows the sliding iron pin inside the solenoid body to advance to the point within the magnetic field created by the hold-in windings at which it will be held securely. If the linkage is too short and the solenoid pin cannot reach the hold-in position, the solenoid will not keep the engine running when the starter quits cranking.

A Trombetta solenoid has three wires: (1) the black ground wire; (2) the white, high-current pull-in wire; and (3) the red, low-current hold-in wire. When wiring the solenoid, it's vital to carefully follow the printed directions that come with the solenoid, because none of the wires is interchangeable with the others. If the hold-in and pull-in wires are mistakenly reversed, the solenoid will quickly overheat and be destroyed.

The solenoid actuators discussed above— including the Trombetta—mount on the outside of the fuel system, but this arrangement, while common, is by no means universal. For example, Stanadyne diesel fuel injection systems, like those on some John Deere engines, mount the solenoid actuator inside the injection pump lid.

Finally, some generator engines are manufactured without shutdown systems but can be protected by an aftermarket system that includes a Trombetta or some other actuator. Other engines, however, are manufactured with shutdown systems in place and will not run without them. For example, CAV distributor-type fuel systems, such as those used on Cummins engines, mount an energize-to-run or energize-to-stop solenoid valve under the pump body (Fig. 7-7).

When solenoid valves like the one shown in Figure 7-5 are energized, they emit an audible "click," and this can be helpful when troubleshooting. If you don't hear a click, the solenoid may not be getting power.

However, in a noisy engine room, when you don't even have access to a multimeter, it is still possible to learn if a solenoid valve is energized. When a solenoid valve is energized, its exterior is magnetized. Just lay a steel screwdriver against the outside of the solenoid to learn if it is magnetized and therefore receiving power.

More Elaborate Shutdown Systems

To build a more elaborate shutdown system, one that responds to abnormally high coolant temperature as well as abnormally low oil pressure, we would add the second switch (coolant temperature) in series so that a fault at either the oil pressure *or* coolant temperature switch will stop the engine, as shown in Figure 7-8.

Direct Current (DC) Relays

If the design of a shutdown system calls for the use of a more powerful mechanical

Fig. 7-7. Location of the fuel solenoid on a CAV distributor-type diesel fuel system. Small Cummins engines sometimes use this type of fuel system.

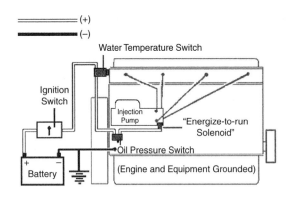

Fig. 7-8. This simplified view shows a generator shutdown system with pressure and temperature switches wired in series and designed to power an energize-to-run fuel system solenoid valve.

actuator, the system will require higher amperage. When the amperage gets above 5 amps at 12 volts, it is time to incorporate a relay (Fig. 7-9). A *relay* is a device that uses a *small* amount of electrical current to control a *larger* amount of current (Fig. 7-10).

This type of DC relay is rated as either momentary or continuous. Energize-to-run systems must have a continuously rated relay, whereas an energize-to-stop system or alarm needs only a relay with a momentary rating. Relays are often used to power (control) solenoids like the Trombetta actuator. The control power to the relay (Fig. 7-11) is in

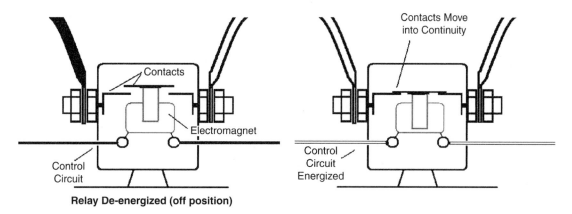

Relay De-energized (off position)

Fig. 7-9.   This simplified view of a DC relay shows how its contacts move inside the relay's metal jacket. The small-gauge wires at the bottom of the relay carry the energizing current that closes the relay's contacts. The large-gauge wires at the top of the relay carry the heavy electrical load that the relay controls. In the left view, the relay is not energized and the contacts are therefore open, interrupting the electrical load. In the right view, the relay is energized, closing the contacts and permitting the heavy electrical current to flow.

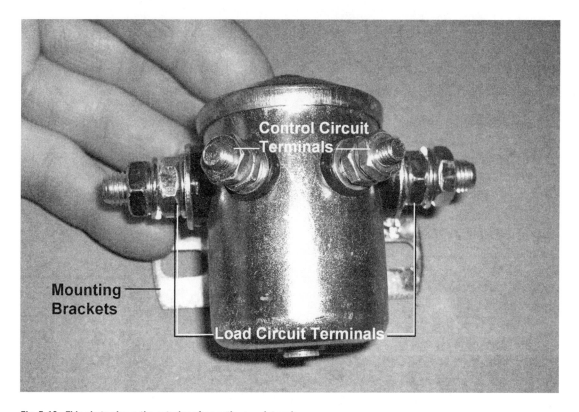

Fig. 7-10.   This photo shows the exterior of a continuous-duty relay.

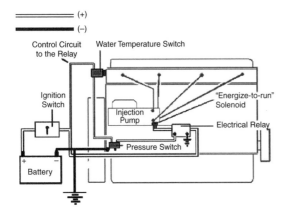

Fig. 7-11. **This shutdown system is equipped with a relay and is able to power heavy-duty actuators.**

turn routed through the shutdown system's switches.

OTHER POSSIBLE ENGINE-PROTECTION SWITCHES

Switches are available with a wide range of settings, and some are adjustable so that they can be reset in the field. The switch shown in Figure 7-12 is adjustable with an Allen wrench after the rubber plug is removed.

Some engine-protection systems use, in addition, a coolant-level switch on the cooling system expansion tank. This is usually wired to sound an alarm and/or (in the case of a

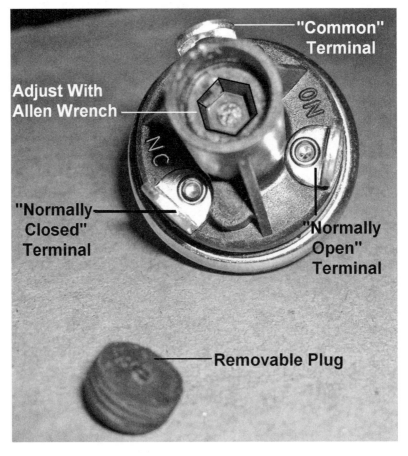

Fig. 7-12. **This three-terminal adjustable oil pressure switch can be reset in the field when a higher or lower tripping pressure is needed.**

generator engine) to stop the engine when the coolant level drops below a specified threshold. Yet another option is an oil level switch in the oil pan, which is usually set to sound an alarm and/or stop a generator engine when oil rises above or falls below a specified operating range, the idea being that running out of oil and "making oil" must both be guarded against. ("Making oil" means simply that the oil level is rising, which can only be caused by either fuel or coolant leaking into the oil pan.)

Electric tachometer senders, also known as magnetic impulse pickups, constitute yet another engine-protection option for generators. A tachometer sender mounts just 0.050 inch from a generator flywheel and measures the rpm of flywheel teeth through its magnetic field. In the event of an engine overspeed, it sends an electric signal through an overspeed switch to the generator's energize-to-run or energize-to-stop shutdown solenoid.

Tachometer senders come in a number of diameters (Fig. 7-13). In North America, $3/_8$-inch national fine (NF), $5/_8$-inch NF, and even $3/_4$-inch NF are common sizes. Follow the engine maker's directions for installing and adjusting these components.

Whatever additional switches are in an engine-protection system, they all act as monitors to safeguard the engine while it is running.

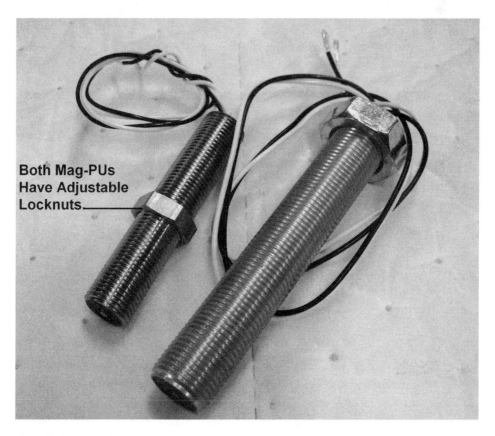

Both Mag-PUs Have Adjustable Locknuts

Fig. 7-13. Electric tachometer senders, also known as magnetic impulse pickups, are used in generator engine speed-control systems.

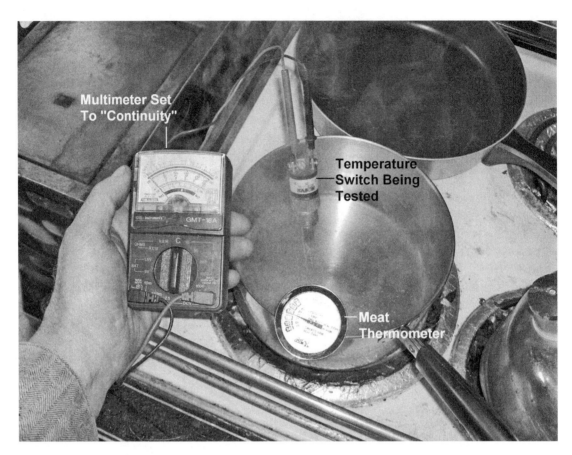

Fig. 7-14. A stovetop testing of a temperature switch quickly shows when and if the switch contacts are tripping.

TESTING SWITCHES

You can test a coolant-temperature switch on a stovetop in the same way you test an engine thermostat. Heat water in a one-quart saucepan and use a thermometer to check the temperature at which the switch contacts move. A meat thermometer works just fine, as shown in Figure 7-14.

Attach an ohmmeter to both contacts of the switch and wait for the contacts to move. If the contacts don't trip near the rated temperature, the switch must be replaced or adjusted (if adjustment is possible).

Murphy coolant-level alarms have a small knob on the face of the unit that can be turned by hand for testing purposes.

Testing oil pressure switches is a little more difficult, because it requires a pressure source. If you have access to a compressed air system, connect air pressure to the switch. The regulator on the air compressor should be turned down to 30 psi to avoid overpressurizing the switch. When the pressure switch is connected to air pressure, use an ohmmeter to tell if the switch is tripping, proceeding as in the test of a temperature switch described above.

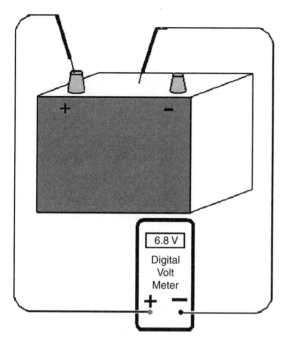

Fig. 7-15. Test the battery for self-discharge due to surface deposits. If you register a voltage difference between the positive post and the battery surface, clean the battery surfaces and posts.

BATTERY MAINTENANCE

Keep the tops of batteries clean and dry to avoid unwanted discharging through electrically conductive deposits between the positive and negative posts of a dirty battery. Test for a dirty battery with a voltmeter as shown in Figure 7-15. If you get a voltage reading between the positive post and any surface of the battery, you are losing charge. To clean the tops of your battery, dust the surface with a fine coat of baking soda to neutralize any acidic residue. Wash the baking soda off with water.

THE MECHANICAL SIDE OF AC POWER GENERATION

Generators have an electrical (generator) side and a mechanical (engine) side. The engine turns the generator, and this movement causes a magnetic field to revolve. The revolving magnetic field moves past a current-carrying conductor at great speed. This action results in useful electrical power flowing to the boat's breaker panel.

Every generator set has two identification plates, one for the engine and one for the generator. For some strange reason, these plates are often made of aluminum rather than stainless steel. In the marine environment, the corners of the identification plates soon corrode where the rivets pass through the tag to attach them to the engine and generator. If they don't corrode and fall off, somebody will surely paint over them! Be sure to record all information from each identification plate while you can.

LEAKY CRANKSHAFT SEALS

One of the more important maintenance items to watch with generators is the engine's rear crankshaft seal (Fig. 7-18). When the seal fails, engine oil leaks into the flywheel housing between the generator windings and the engine. A quick inspection of the air discharge end of the generator will indicate if there is a buildup of oil and dust. This should serve as a red flag, signaling the need for maintenance. If there is a buildup of dirt, it is time to look deeper for the source of contamination.

In pleasure boats and sailboats, generator engines turn at either 1,800 or 1,200 rpm. Any oil that leaks past the rear seal is flung outward by the spinning of the flywheel. The oil is then picked up by the air coming from the generator fan and becomes an airborne mist. This oily mist is carried throughout the engine room because of the tremendous amount of cooling air that the generator fan moves through the generator.

TEMPORARY REPAIR OF A BAD BATTERY POST

When battery cable terminals are loose on battery posts, and cranking the engine demands high amperage, the arc and heat will cause the posts to disintegrate. It is possible to temporarily rebuild a post and get home by making a post mold and pouring a new post.

But first some precautions! The battery must be disconnected and carried out on deck, where there is good ventilation. Without ventilation, hydrogen gases inside the battery can explode. Wear gloves and eye protection, and further, put a transparent face shield over your safety glasses. *Also, avoid using open flames near batteries!*

You can make a mold by drilling a piece of hardwood or aluminum and tapering the hole to the size of the damaged post. It is not too hard to make a post mold in a piece of 1-inch-thick hardwood—begin by drilling a hole through the hardwood, then enlarge the hole by whittling. Remember that the positive post is always larger in diameter than the negative post. Before pouring, clean the damaged post with a wire brush. If most of the post is gone, thread a short sheet-metal screw into the old post before you fit the mold over the post (Figure 7-16), and pour molten lead around the screw. A source of lead is found in lead sinkers used for fishing. While this remedy isn't something an average recreational boater would wish to do, it just might get you out of a bind, especially if you're caught in a pinch in a remote locale. *Use extreme caution when handling molten lead; the lead will be hot, and it is poisonous.*

Needless to say, this is a short-term solution. You will need to replace the battery as soon as possible.

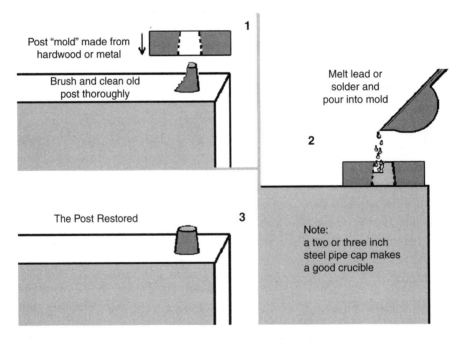

Fig. 7-16. Making a mold and pouring a new post to temporarily repair a battery.

WORK-AROUND SOLUTION

Bypassing a Failed Indicator in a Manually Controlled Glow-Plug Starting System

Some diesel engines use glow plugs to aid starting. The amount of time the glow plugs are supposed to be energized is measured in seconds, and if glow plugs are energized too long, they overheat. When this happens, the tips are prone to melt and break off, causing them to fall into the cylinders, where they can do terrible damage to an engine. One diesel owner told me that he never worried about this because his mechanic had assured him that glow plugs are made of soft materials so that an engine can pulverize them and spit them out the exhaust! Engine manufacturers don't buy this concept.

To prevent overheating of glow plugs, most manually controlled glow-plug systems provide an indicator in the control panel that glows red when it's time to turn off the glow plugs and start the engine. If your indicator has failed, it is possible to "jump" your glow plugs for starting by temporarily connecting a wire from the battery to the glow-plug harness. To jump glow plugs without an indicator, however, is to risk expensive damage to the engine. You need some other means of determining when it's time to turn off the glow plugs.

Roy Maddocks, owner of Alaska Diesel Service in Anchorage, Alaska, suggests the following temporary fix. Since it is often a lot easier to find a spare glow plug than to find a new glow-plug indicator, his system (Fig. 7-17) uses an extra glow plug installed in a holder behind the instrument panel. Careful installation is required to

avoid fire hazard. The system also uses a spring-loaded push button (momentary switch). When the glow plugs are energized, the extra plug glows red. When you see that slight red glow behind the instrument panel, turn off the glow plugs and start the engine.

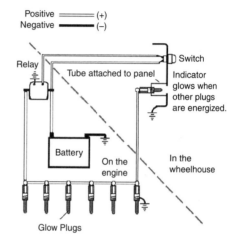

Fig. 7-17. Roy Maddocks's work-around glow-plug control system.

Many generators move between 500 and 1,200 cubic feet of cooling air per minute (CFM). In a small engine room, twice the volume of air in the entire enclosure can pass through the generator every minute.

The mist recirculates to the air-intake portion of the generator and is repeatedly pulled inside. This puts a uniform coat of oil on every part of the generator. The airborne oil is also pulled into the generator engine's air filter. In fact, any engines running nearby will draw oil into their air filters, causing premature airflow restriction.

Oil on the generator windings acts as an insulator and prevents them from cooling.

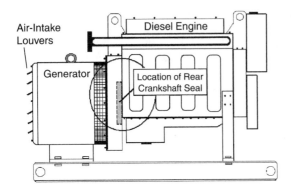

Air-Intake
Louvers

Diesel Engine

Generator

Location of Rear
Crankshaft Seal

Fig. 7-18. Rear crankshaft seal.

Once the windings are coated with oil, any dust that comes through will stick to them, further reducing their ability to cool.

Any amount of water or salt spray coming into the generator airstream will soon find its way inside. Even splash from bilge water in rough seas will find its way into the generator's airstream. Because water contains minerals that will carry electrical current, a short circuit will occur if a crack develops in the winding insulation. Bilge water also carries microorganisms that eat the winding insulation. Generator winding insulation is degraded when anything other than cool, dry air passes through the generator.

If you see oil leaking from the rear crankshaft seal, it is time to find out why the seal failed and then replace it. First check the engine oil level to learn if the level is too high. A high oil level can cause even a good seal to leak. Someone may have overfilled the engine with oil, or perhaps the engine is mounted at an extreme angle (more than 15 degrees of fore-and-aft inclination). It is also possible that you need to check the dipstick calibration. Each engine manufacturer has a suggested method for calibrating the oil dipstick in its marine engines (see Fig. 5-14). Refer to

your engine manual. Fuel or coolant leaking into the oil pan can also explain a high oil level in the engine.

Engines that have wet boltholes in the flywheel mounting crankshaft flange can leak through one or more boltholes when not sealed according to the engine maker's instructions. Some engines also have wet boltholes in the flywheel housing (going through the block into the crankcase) that can mimic a rear seal failure, though this type of arrangement is rare. (A wet bolthole is one in which the bolt is turned into threads from outside the engine and penetrates any of the engine's fluid systems, such as the crankcase or the cooling system.)

One additional reason for rear seal failure is excessive wear of the rear main bearing in an engine with many hours of service. In this case, the crankshaft can wobble as it turns while the engine is being started, and this wobble will cause the rear seal to leak. In a generator engine, the rear main crankshaft bearing will often wear more than other engine bearings because the engine must start dry with the weight of the generator's revolving member hanging on the heavy flywheel.

Never clean or wash a generator when it is running or when the electrical junction box is open. Before servicing any generator, have a qualified electrician confirm that there is no power running to it. Disconnect all electrical leads to the generator. Both propulsion and generator engines must have the battery cables removed from the starter to avoid accidental turning of the crankshaft during repairs.

Clearly tag the instrument panel or control panel so that all personnel will see that the unit is out of service. Disconnect the battery from the starter and turn off fuel to the engine. If it looks like the engine position will be disturbed, disconnect the exhaust system plumbing as well. Detaching the exhaust system will avoid damaging the exhaust pipe or flex when the engine is moved to facilitate the repair.

To become familiar with the area between the engine and the powered unit, make note of three things inside the flywheel housing:

1. the drive device that couples the transmission or generator to the flywheel;
2. the engine's flywheel;
3. the engine's rear crankshaft seal.

Looking forward from the rear of the engine (i.e., the generator end), you will see three concentric rings of bolts that you must remove to gain access to the rear seal:

1. The largest-diameter ring of bolts fastens the transmission or generator housing to the engine's flywheel housing.

2. The next smaller ring of bolts fastens the transmission or generator drive to the engine's flywheel. After removing the first two rings of bolts you can pull the transmission or generator away from the engine.

3. Next the flywheel-lifting brackets bolted to the flywheel and the third, inner ring of bolts can be removed. This allows the flywheel to be lifted away from the engine and provides access to the rear seal. Before removing the flywheel, however, mark the position of the flywheel on the crankshaft to aid its reinstallation.

Once you gain access to the seal, drill a small hole in the outer metal surface of the seal body and use a slide hammer to remove

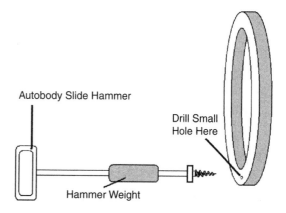

Autobody Slide Hammer

Drill Small Hole Here

Hammer Weight

Fig. 7-19. Removing a lip-type seal with a slide hammer. First drill a small hole in the seal's metal body, sizing the hole so that the threads on the tip of the slide hammer will grip in it. Twist the slide hammer into this hole, then tap away from the seal with the slide hammer weight. The seal will quickly be pulled from its bore.

the old seal as shown in Figure 7-19. Clean the area thoroughly, and then install the new seal as directed in your engine service manual.

SINGLE BEARING DAMAGE

Older generators used bearings that had to be oiled daily. Modern marine generators use a single or rear bearing, sealed and lubricated at the factory. It is important to visually inspect the bearing now and then to watch for a leaky seal. If and when you see evidence of grease leaking from the bearing, it needs to be changed. The bearing is located opposite the engine (Fig. 7-22). After this type of bearing runs without lubrication for a short time, it will lock and cause the entire bearing to spin with the rotating member of the generator. This will seriously damage the bearing's support plate, and serious vibration or even electrical arcing will result. Change the bearing by removing the rear generator cover, which is also the rear bearing carrier.

WORK-AROUND SOLUTION

Tightening Oil-Seal Tension Springs

Lip-type seal tension springs can be tightened (Fig. 7-20) if a replacement seal isn't available and the engine must be used. They can also be tightened if a shaft running through the seal has become undersized from wear or is wobbling as it rotates due to bearing wear. Front and rear crankshaft seals, as well as other lip-type seals, often wear a groove in the adjacent shaft the seal runs against. Tightening the tension springs may work even when the shaft or bearings are badly worn.

To shorten (and thereby tighten) a seal tension spring, begin by removing the spring from its groove in the back side of the seal's neoprene lip. Next find the joint in the spring, and gently turn both ends in opposite directions to pull the spring apart.

For seals under 1 inch in diameter, cut ¼ inch from the blunt (non-pointed) end of the spring. For larger seals, cut ½ inch from the blunt end. Screw the ends back together and install the spring back in its place in the lip seal.

It is important to note that the recommended shaft size for a given seal is not always set in stone. This means that you may be able to get a seal that fits the inner diameter (ID) of your application, but the suggested shaft size for the lip may have leeway, both ways. For example, you can often run a 1.345-inch shaft in a seal recommended for a 1.338-inch shaft, and so on.

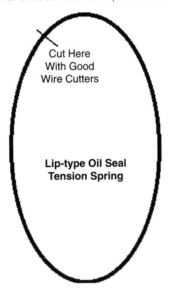

Cut Here
With Good
Wire Cutters

**Lip-type Oil Seal
Tension Spring**

Fig. 7-20. Shortening a seal tension spring increases the lip seal pressure against the shaft, thereby stopping leaks.

When shafts and their lip-type seals are leaking, position the new lip-type seal on an unworn portion of the shaft (Fig. 7-21). Done properly, this technique restores sealing integrity if the shaft or bearings are not excessively worn.

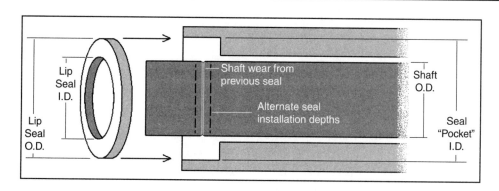

Fig. 7-21. Install the new seal to a different depth than the old seal.

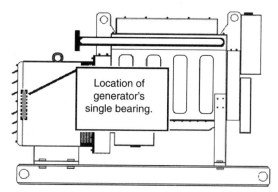

Fig. 7-22. Single bearing generators have just one bearing
opposite the engine. They are sealed and lubricated
for life.

EXCEPTIONAL TROUBLESHOOTING

One of my customers noticed that one of his fishing vessels was burning out more lightbulbs than usual. He called and said he felt funny asking me to check his generator because he was spending more on light bulbs, but it seemed like there might be an electrical problem and he wanted to know what might be causing it. When I checked the generator I found a problem with the fuel transfer pump that allowed air to mix with the fuel. The pump problem was actually triggering brownouts, a low voltage condition that causes the lights to dim. Brownouts will damage electric motors and are an indicator of governor, regulator, or fuel problems (see Chapter 1).

CHAPTER 8

MARINE EXHAUST SYSTEMS

Every engine requires an exhaust system to remove gases and heat to achieve optimal performance. On vehicles, this system is fairly straightforward. On boats, however, the system must function in the harsh marine environment and fit into a confined space below. There are different types of systems for a given vessel and engine configuration. This chapter will guide you through the basics of marine exhaust systems, with a special emphasis on diesel engines.

ENGINE FUEL EFFICIENCY

Not all the fuel a diesel engine burns is used to spin the propeller shaft. In fact, approximately one-third of every gallon is used to turn the crankshaft, and even more of that same gallon, about two-thirds, is converted into wasted heat that must be disposed of as quickly as possible through the cooling and exhaust systems.

Consider this for a moment: A gallon of No. 2 diesel fuel, when burned, produces over 130,000 British thermal units (Btu) of heat. Now, let's take a look at a 42-foot motoryacht with a 400 hp diesel engine running at full power for one hour. The yacht will burn 20 gallons of fuel, and two-thirds of it will be wasted in the production of heat equaling roughly two million Btu. Roughly half of this heat will be transferred into the ocean via the engine's cooling system, and the other half will be released into the atmosphere by the exhaust system.

At times, the exhaust temperatures in diesel engines can exceed 1,000°F. Jacketed exhaust manifolds reduce exhaust temperatures, knocking them down to 450°F as the exhaust exits the manifold (Fig. 8-1). Downstream of the exhaust manifold, it takes a well-designed system to safely carry the remaining heat away.

The hottest parts of the system are the exhaust manifold and turbocharger. They are constructed of heat-resistant materials and will usually last the life of the engine. New marine diesel engines come with either water-jacketed or dry-wrapped (Fig. 8-2) exhaust manifolds, and each has its own distinct advantages.

Dry-wrapped manifolds control surface temperature with insulation that coats the exterior to keep heat from escaping into the engine room. It takes power to pump exhaust gases through the boat's exhaust system, and hotter exhaust is easier to pump. Thus, an engine with a dry-wrapped exhaust manifold can be slightly more efficient because the exhaust gas temperatures are higher and easier to pump than those from an engine equipped with a water-jacketed exhaust manifold.

Water-jacketed exhaust manifolds are heavier and more expensive than the dry-wrapped type. They absorb heat from the exhaust and transfer it to the engine cooling system. The gases aren't as hot as those

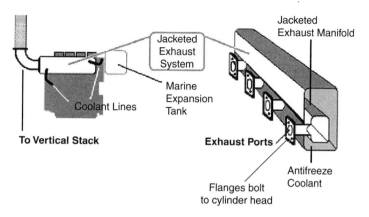

Fig. 8-1. A jacketed exhaust system. The upward-turning elbow at the aft end leads to a dry stack. In a wet exhaust this would be replaced with a downward-turning mixing elbow where the raw water is injected into the exhaust.

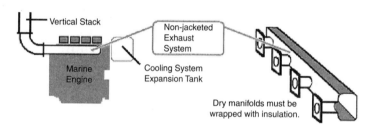

Fig. 8-2. Manifolds without a water jacket are often wrapped with a heat-insulating material to guard against fire and injury.

passing through a dry-wrapped exhaust manifold, making the gases slightly harder for the engine to pump. The outer surface of water-jacketed manifolds is made of cast iron or various steel alloys. This makes the manifold more durable and more resistant to bumps and abrasion than the dry-wrapped type.

WET AND DRY EXHAUST SYSTEMS

There are many variations on exhaust system designs, but in spite of the numerous configurations you'll find on boats, the systems will either operate wet or dry. A wet exhaust system mixes cooling water with exhaust gases, and a dry exhaust system doesn't. Horizontal systems, such as the ones that exit at the transom, can be either wet or dry. Vertical systems, where exhaust exits from a stack, are always dry.

WET EXHAUST SYSTEMS

Most recreational boats are equipped with horizontal exhaust systems plumbed out the transom or the side of the hull. The exhaust gas exits the jacketed exhaust manifold at nearly 450°F, then travels to the water-cooled elbow where cold raw water is sprayed into the hot gas. The raw water rapidly cools the exhaust to a temperature that makes it safe to run the mixture of exhaust and raw water through the stern of the boat. This cooling will reduce the volume of exhaust gases by at least half.

However, the amount of water coming through with the exhaust requires that wet exhaust systems usually must go up one pipe size, rather than down a size, when compared to a dry exhaust system. See Fig. 3-10 of a water-cooled exhaust elbow. Figure 8-3 shows an application of a wet exhaust system in a boat with its exhaust outlet above the water-line. The muffler is a simple in-line type that the water and exhaust gases flow through.

The top two drawings in Figure 8-4 show water-lift mufflers in boats with engines below the waterline. Both of these systems require a siphon break line designed to stop water from entering the engine through the exhaust manifold when the engine is turned off. The bottom of the three drawings shows a water-lift muffler in an application where the engine is well above the waterline. Be sure to consult a specialist with your exact requirements.

DRY EXHAUST SYSTEMS

Vertical exhaust systems are always dry and constructed from steel pipe or tubing. They are ideal for performing the following five functions:

1. Remove exhaust gases from the engine *and* **take them away from the boat**

2. Keep sound levels low

3. Allow heat from the engine room to escape by rising alongside the exhaust pipe and muffler (silencer). The accompanying drawing (Fig. 8-5) shows several features of a complete exhaust system going up the stack.

4. Keep the surface temperature of the entire exhaust system low, by way of insulation, to avoid fire hazards and injury to crew. The system must be insulated high enough, sometimes including the muffler (silencer), so that heat is prevented from being radiated into the galley wall or other living spaces.

5. Allow the entire assembly to lengthen and shorten as the system warms and cools through the use of flexible tubing joints. Any flexes used in a horizontal run of pipe incorporate an inner shield made of tubing. This tube is only welded all the way around the upstream portion to allow for expansion and contraction of the system. The purpose of the inner liner is to keep the bellows of the flex from filling with soot and breaking.

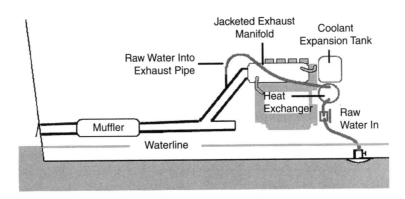

Fig. 8-3. A wet exhaust system with in-line muffer.

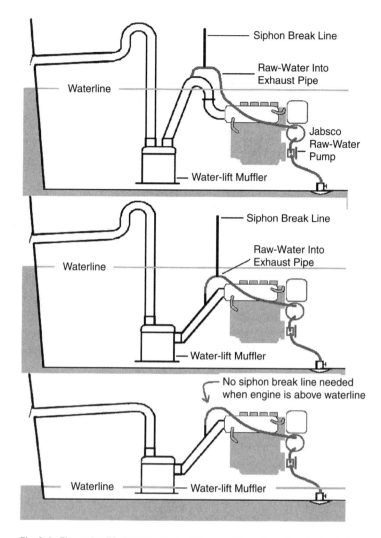

Fig. 8-4. Three simplified applications with water-lift mufflers. Top: Engine below waterline; exhaust loops above waterline; raw water injected above waterline with siphon break. Middle: Engine below waterline; raw water injected below waterline with siphon break. Bottom: Engine and exhaust above waterline. Note: These are generalized—be sure to consult a specialist.

Exhaust systems in boats are far heavier than those used in trucks. For example, let's compare a fishing boat or large motoryacht with a truck. Each is powered by a Caterpillar 3406 diesel engine. The exhaust system in the boats can be *ten* times heavier and *five* times longer than the one in the truck, requiring

careful design for the mounting and support system.

Expansion

Dry exhaust systems typically vent gases up a vertical stack. The main consideration with this part of the system is expansion

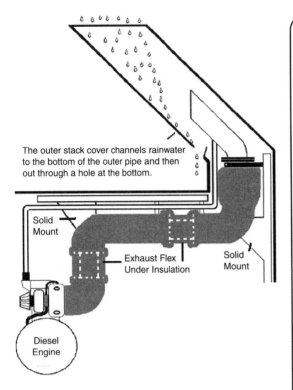

The outer stack cover channels rainwater to the bottom of the outer pipe and then out through a hole at the bottom.

Solid Mount

Exhaust Flex Under Insulation

Solid Mount

Diesel Engine

Fig. 8-5. Vertical exhaust system.

FOR THE WORKBOAT

Engine Silencing

Tony's marine 8V92 Detroit Diesel engine was too noisy, and he wanted to do something about it. He asked if we could put a better muffler on the engine exhaust system. The 8V92 Detroit is known for being loud, but after a little research we found that most of the noise was actually coming from the air-intake system.

There are at least two types of marine engines that have especially noisy air intakes: any two-stroke Detroit Diesel, and the 3208 Cat diesel. In the case of the Detroit, the engine's blower is responsible for supplying the cylinders with fresh air, and it's very noisy. In the case of the

Cat, the intake valves are so large and such a short distance from the intake manifold that they are tremendously loud.

What we did for Tony was buy a heavy blanket of sound-deadening material, like the kind found in the cabs of earthmovers. The material is called "barrier de-coupler," and it absorbs sound waves rather than reflecting them. This 1-inch-thick blanket was carefully fitted so it covered the top of the engine, and extended over the valve covers and exhaust manifolds and down both sides of the engine. Provision was made to ensure that the material was a safe distance from the jacketed exhaust manifolds and any other warm parts of the engine.

We also made an intake air system adapter lined with the same barrier de-coupler material shaped to allow air into the engine without letting much sound escape. It worked better than we had hoped. It was quite comfortable and quiet in the cabin while the boat was under way.

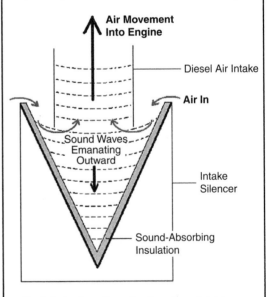

Air Movement Into Engine

Diesel Air Intake

Air In

Sound Waves Emanating Outward

Intake Silencer

Sound-Absorbing Insulation

Fig. 8-6. A schematic section through an air-intake silencer. The inverted cone inside the cylindrical silencer absorbs the sound waves.

(lengthening) of the steel pipe when it is heated, and contraction (shortening) when it cools. Consider a vessel with an exhaust system fifteen feet long. The steel pipe and the muffler (silencer) between the engine and the top of the pipe elongate up to 1 inch as the system reaches full operating temperature. The expansion is quite forceful and will damage the system. Pipe hangers that allow for changes in the length of the exhaust pipe, flex joints, and a combination of solid and flexible pipe mounts compensate for expansion and contraction.

Stanley Wolrich of Harbor Welding, in Kodiak, Alaska, warns against installing exhaust flexes in torsion. They can take expansion and contraction, but not a twisting force (Fig. 8-7). You should orient the flex joint athwartships, not fore and aft.

The solid brackets used to mount a dry exhaust pipe are always used in conjunction with flex joints and flexible brackets as shown in Fig. 8-5. Lengthening of the pipe between solid brackets is taken up by these flexible components as the system warms. Flexible mounts allow the exhaust pipe to slide in either direction as the system expands and contracts.

BACK-PRESSURE

Since the downstream end of the exhaust system is open to the atmosphere, hot gases should rise from the engine and exit at the top of the pipe, working much like a fireplace and chimney. However, sometimes restrictions hinder the upward flow of hot gases, which in turn causes high exhaust pressure at the engine end of the system. This is called back-pressure, and it was briefly discussed in Chapter 2. As mentioned in that chapter, back-pressure can lower an engine's power output. In older engines, it causes black smoke. Back-pressure can occur in wet or dry exhaust systems in gasoline and diesel engines.

Back-pressure is usually measured with a manometer, which works something like a barometer. Inside the manometer are parallel columns of water or elemental (liquid) mercury. Pressure coming in on one side of the manometer is going to move one column down and the other column up. Comparing the difference in height between the columns provides a pressure measurement, as discussed in Chapter 16. The resulting measurement will be in inches (or millimeters) of water or mercury, depending on the type of manometer.

Each engine manufacturer specifies the amount of exhaust back-pressure that is allowed, and it is generally in the range of 20 inches of water. Again, too much back-pressure will drastically lower any engine's available power.

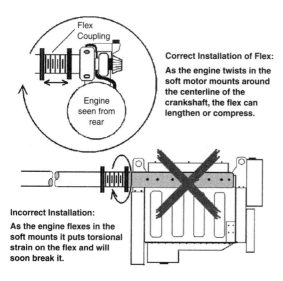

Fig. 8-7. Don't put an exhaust flex joint in torsion. Mount it athwartships on a propulsion engine.

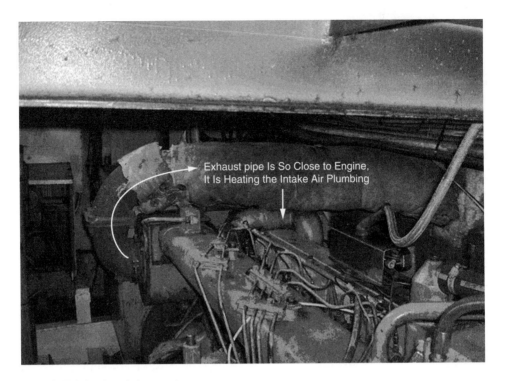

Exhaust pipe Is So Close to Engine, It Is Heating the Intake Air Plumbing

Fig. 8-8. Tight bends and close quarters.

Most exhaust systems have a small plug on a straight stretch of the exhaust pipe, within 24 inches of the turbocharger, if the engine is so equipped. Connect your manometer to the port with a section of copper tubing and run the engine at full power long enough to determine the amount of backpressure.

SILENCERS AND MUFFLERS

In boats, a steel muffler is called a silencer and a rubber muffler is called just that, a muffler. Steel exhaust silencers come in several grades, and grades delivering quiet performance cost more. Exhaust silencers trap sound waves and turn them back into heat without overly restricting the flow of gases.

Note: Don't be misled by the 3-inch diameter exhaust outlet on your turbocharger, if you have one! An engine with a 3-inch turbo outlet will often still need a 5- or 6-inch exhaust system, depending on the manufacturer's recommendations. The exhaust gases are superheated and easy to pump at the turbo. As they cool in the exhaust system, they get much harder to pump, and therefore need to make a transition to a much larger exhaust pipe diameter.

Sizing of silencers is a science. The following factors are involved:

+ the amount of exhaust gas coming out of the engine at full rated power and speed
+ the inside diameter and length of the steel exhaust pipe
+ the number of bends in the exhaust pipe; it also matters whether bends are 45, 90, or 180 degrees, as shown (Fig. 8-8)
+ the level of desired silencing

CHAPTER 9

RUDDERS AND STEERING

It is amazing how often recreational and even professional mariners neglect the steering systems on their boats. It is an out-of-sight, out-of-mind situation that can lead to calamity, or, at best, inconvenience and expensive repairs. From a safety standpoint, the steering system ranks close to the top of the list in terms of importance. If a vessel loses steerage at sea, it will drift at the mercy of wind and waves. If it loses steerage in a busy harbor or near rocks, quick action will be necessary to avoid serious trouble. Take the time to thoroughly understand your steering system and how it works, and schedule regular inspections and maintenance. This chapter will provide you with information about various steering systems and how they work in tandem with the rudder.

ALL ABOUT RUDDERS

Most conventional vessels are equipped with an aft-mounted rudder consisting of a single blade attached to a vertical metal shaft (Fig. 9-1).

Fig. 9-1. The rudder of this steel motoryacht is mounted on a vertical rudderpost, or shaft. A shoe extends aft from the keel to capture and support the post's bottom end.

The rudder typically swings up to 45 degrees either side of its centered position. At maximum angle, the rudder is said to be hard over with its largest surface area exposed to the flow of water. The greatest force is generated along its leading edge, and the force diminishes as the flow of water moves aft toward the trailing edge.

The earliest rudders were fastened by their leading edge to the transom, the sternpost, or the after end of a full keel—often with an aperture cut out for the propeller. This design shadows the leading edge and leaves the rudder unbalanced. Early rudders were not very effective, especially when made of wood.

Because the rudder is crucial to a vessel's safety and utility, serious thought should be given to its design. The most common catastrophic steering system failures usually involve the rudder shaft and its connections. While rubber-lined bearings—as in a stern tube—are sometimes used for the rudderpost, a solid brass or high-density plastic is a far better bearing material for this application.

The top of the rudderpost comes up through the hull by way of a stuffing box with a packing gland. The top of the rudderpost is keyed or squared off to allow the attachment of the tiller (lever arm). The steering cylinder

Fig. 9-2. A rudder hung from the after edge of the full keel on a traditional sailboat.

Fig. 9-3. This wooden rudder hung on the back of a keel looks like a jerry-built arrangement.

attaches to the tiller. Figure 9-4 shows the tiller detached during steering system repairs.

The steering system requires robust components to perform dependably. Resist the temptation to cut corners. The boat's steering system is a poor place to save a few dollars. Figure 9-5 is an example of an inefficient rudder design with a very small leading edge.

RUDDER SHAPES

Flat plate rudders: A powerboat rudder works in the turbulent environment behind the propeller and can be made of metal or any material durable enough to withstand heavy loads.

Foil rudders: According to Lowell Stambaugh of Deflector Marine Rudder, Naselle, Washington, foil shapes, such as those developed by the National Aeronautics and Space Administration (NASA), are far superior to plate rudders. Foils pass through air or water more easily than other shapes. The thicker forward section of the foil diminishes the buffeting effects of prop wash. Foil-shaped rudders work best for slower vessels.

Wedge rudders: In contrast to a foil, vessels cruising at speeds in excess of thirty knots require a sharp, wedge-shaped rudder.

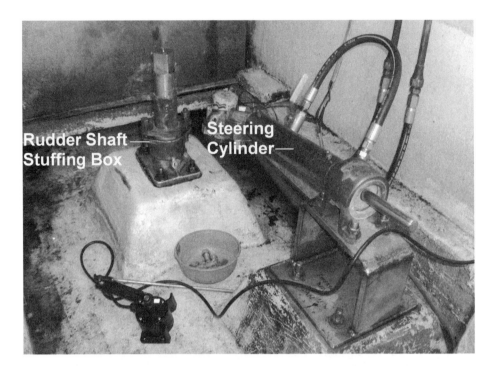

Fig. 9-4. The top of the rudderpost and a hydraulic steering cylinder are clearly visible in this photo. The rudder arm has been detached from the post so that the rudderpost stuffing box can be repacked. The arm is hanging from the far end of the cylinder and is not clearly visible.

Fig. 9-5. A small leading edge is inefficient.

Flap rudders: Rudders designed with an articulating hinged flap on the trailing edge are twice as effective as flat plate or wedge rudders. Such designs can reduce a vessel's minimum turning circle by 50 percent without increasing the size of the rudder.

Articulating or flap rudders (Fig. 9-6) are called high-lift rudders, in the sense that an aircraft wing with adjustable flaps is a high-lift wing. Incidentally, the underpinnings in the science of aerodynamics and hydrodynamics are essentially the same. The main difference between them is that water is 840 times denser than air.

Flap rudders share some things with their less elegant cousins in that the high pressure concentrates on the leading edge, and the pressure diminishes as the water moves aft along the rudder surface. But with flap rudders, sometimes referred to as deflector rudders, the angling out of the flap from the trailing edge creates a secondary high-pressure area to enhance steering ability.

While the trailing edge of the conventional rudder is loafing, the flap of the deflector rudder is doing double duty when the back of the rudder begins exerting force against the water flow. The balance area (leading edge) of this type of rudder—the portion of the total blade area ahead of the rudder shaft—can be made larger and more aggressive, with up to 38 percent of the total rudder area located forward of the leading edge. This makes the boat much easier to steer.

Plate, wedge, and flap rudders each have their own benefits and liabilities, and they share factors that influence performance regardless of rudder type. For example, let's take a brief look at how speed impacts steering ability. When a hull is moving at eight knots or more, the speed is sufficient to create enough force so that even a small rudder will work. However, most steering maneuvers occur at slower speeds. The water flow past the rudder is slower and exerts less force, requiring a larger rudder to compensate in terms of turning power.

There are many hull sizes and shapes, and rudders to fit each one. For a powerboat a proper rudder should be shaped to redirect prop wash. Proper rudder shape and placement facilitates this. The aspect ratio (the rudder's height compared to its width) of most rudders is typically 2:1. In other words, the rudder is usually twice as tall as its fore-and-aft dimension. (See Fig. 9-7.) For a very shallow boat the ratio will probably be closer to 1:1, or almost square.

The blade portion ahead of the rudder shaft (on the leading edge) is the balance area of the rudder (Fig. 9-8), described above. The size of this section determines whether a vessel is easy or hard to steer. For boats cruising in excess of twelve knots, the balance area on the leading edge of the rudder should be 15 or 20 percent of the total surface area of

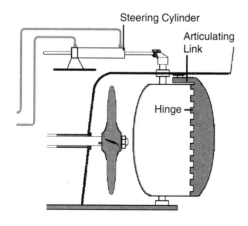

Fig. 9-6. Articulating (flap) rudder.

Fig. 9-7. Rudder with a 2:1 aspect ratio.

the blade. The rule is that slower boats need more balance area and faster boats need less. Displacement boats requiring excellent maneuvering ability can have a balance area as much as 25 percent of the total surface area of the blade.

Increased balance area reaches across the centerline of the boat and grabs more water. This is a great aid for maneuvers executed at low speeds. Proper balance area also diminishes the load at the tiller and therefore the helm.

Consider the relative pressures around a rudder to see why some rudders work better than others. Recall that for a given vessel

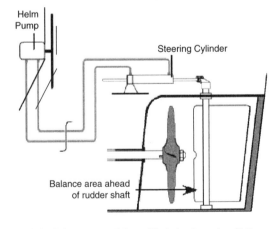

Fig. 9-8. Balance area of the rudder's leading edge. Notice too the helm pump, which is powered by the skipper's movement of the helm and sends oil to the hydraulic steering cylinder.

(displacement hull type) and rudder size, a rudder that is deeper in the water will be more resistant to stall. This is due to the greater water "head" pressure surrounding the rudder. Raise the same rudder three feet, on the same boat, and the rudder will tend to stall more often.

Again, this concept is similar to the stall speed of an aircraft. With the flaps down, stall is avoided at a lower airspeed.

When a hull resists turning for any reason, the conventional rudder begins to stall as the water in the low-pressure area behind the rudder becomes turbulent. This condition can progress to a full stall, and the rudder will temporarily lose its grip.

Notice that rudder A in Figure 9-9 has a vacuum (negative pressure), which indicates turbulence and a stall condition on the right side, while rudder B creates more positive pressure on the left side and avoids extremely low pressure on the right side of the rudder.

The rudder cavitates (pulls a pocket of air or a void in the water behind it) during a stall. A swift, temporary loss of steering is usually the result of a stalled rudder. If you think you're in a stall, ease the rudder angle. The rudder will bite into the water again.

A small or poorly designed rudder can stall at less than 12 degrees from the centered position.

Because of this possibility, many designers believe rudders should only be able to swing 30 degrees from the centerline of the boat, which will decrease the chances of a stall. However, the best rudder designs will provide for more rudder travel rather than less. An effective rudder that still resists stalling needs a total swing range of up to 90 degrees.

Rudder effectiveness is also important for tracking. Good tracking saves fuel, gets the boat to its destination faster, and makes for a more comfortable ride. When a hull veers off track, the boat may roll and present either its right or left side to the oncoming water. This results in drag and heeling. If the steering system is slow to react, you can actually lose control of the boat. It's a bit like a bicycle rider who is slow to react. He wobbles, and one wobble prompts another, until he tumbles.

STEERING ACTUATION
Most rudders move through force applied to a tiller (lever arm). The simplest steering system consists of a rudder with a tiller

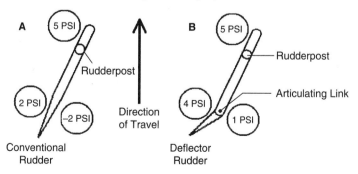

Fig. 9-9. The response of a conventional rudder (left) versus a deflector rudder in a difficult turn. The deflector rudder's articulating link helps prevent a stall.

attached to the rudderpost, and turning is accomplished by pushing the tiller right or left. Anyone who has ever sailed a small boat knows that the forces exerted on the rudder can be quite strong, requiring lots of muscle to control the tiller. On larger boats, the forces exerted on the rudder and transferred to the tiller or lever arm would easily overpower even a strong person. Mechanical advantage is needed, and sophisticated and powerful systems have been designed to provide it. Let's take a look at some of them.

Rack-and-pinion steering is common on small boats because it's designed for light-duty applications, making it less costly to manufacture. A steering wheel is attached to a pinion gear, which moves a rack bar attached to a cable extending to the tiller. The system usually includes a drag brake to allow you to temporarily set the helm on a certain heading.

Cable-and-sprocket systems often feature a cable quadrant (one-quarter of the diameter of a pulley), though there are many custom systems employing sprockets, rotating shafts, and even automotive worm gears. These systems are complicated and difficult and expensive to adapt for use with an autopilot. In contrast, hydraulic steering systems are simple, strong, and more easily coupled with an autopilot.

Rack-and-pinion mechanisms, rotary actuators, T-rams, and rotary vane actuators are good at transmitting steering force to turn the rudder shaft without causing extreme side loading on the rudderpost. Rotary vanes are the best solution out of these four systems, but they are costly.

The most common steering for vessels under fifty feet in length is manual hydraulic.

This type of system employs a manual pump that is turned by a steering wheel. Rotating the wheel sends oil to a ram (steering cylinder) attached to the tiller. Changing the diameter of the steering wheel can change the steering effort of these types of systems. Most of these fixed-displacement pumps move from $1^1/_2$ to 4 cubic inches of oil volume per revolution of the wheel.

There are also variable displacement steering pumps, which allow for adjustment of the steering effort. Whether fixed or variable, displacement steering pumps do not work well with autopilots. It is very strange that while the smallest automobiles have hydraulic power steering, the owners of 20-ton boats want manual steering!

Manual hydraulic steering systems do not work well on large vessels, where they fail to provide the optimal combination of mechanical advantage and quick steering. Big boats need power steering, and there are two types. The first includes an automotive-type hydraulic pump driven by a PTO from the main engine (Fig. 9-10). It is simple and economical, and parts for repairs can be generic, which means that several manufacturers supply them.

Steering pressures are usually limited to 1,000 psi to allow for pressure spikes. A cross-port pressure relief is usually provided and can be adjusted to lower pressure for manually steering with an emergency tiller. Another solution for emergency steering is valving configured so as to direct hydraulic fluid around the cross-port pressure relief, eliminating the need to make adjustments.

The second, more elaborate type of hydraulic steering uses an electrically driven power steering pump that works independently of

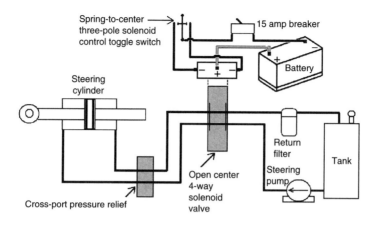

Fig. 9-10. Power-assisted hydraulic system.

the main engine. These are used on larger motoryachts and workboats, most often with a reversing motor to provide power assist to a manual-hydraulic steering system. The ability to reverse the pump eliminates the need for a DC four-way valve.

The power available from a DC-assisted system is limited, however, relegating it to light-duty applications. For heavy-duty steering there are two options: a pump driven by the main engine (as in Fig. 9-10) or an AC electric motor driving a non-reversing pump.

Non-reversing fixed-displacement systems work well when coupled to autopilots and are easy to adapt. They are suitable for vessels above sixty feet in length. A continuous source of AC power is required to run them. More elaborate variable-displacement pumps and AC reversing motors are available, but they are beyond the scope of this discussion.

RAMS

The most popular rams (steering cylinders) for boats under sixty feet are comprised of a balanced, spherical yoke-mounted cylinder. A balanced cylinder has the piston centered in the rod, with the rod protruding out both ends. This equalizes the volume on both sides of the piston. Otherwise, the system would require fewer turns, develop less power, and move faster in one direction than the other.

Steering rams for boats in this size range come with bores as small as $1\frac{1}{4}$ inches in diameter. However, the diameter can get to 3 inches in some applications. These cylinders tolerate poor alignment, especially when equipped with a spherical rod end. Spherical rod ends should be used because they eliminate lash or slack in the linkage. Clevises are inferior to a spherical rod end for this application.

Steering systems for larger boats use unbalanced cylinders in pairs, with one on each side of the tiller. This is better for geometrical reasons. When the tiller moves toward the extreme of its travel, the angle between the ram and the tiller becomes oblique. This transmits a large portion of the ram force as a side load on the rudderpost, and it is even worse in single cylinder applications.

The outboard end of a steering cylinder should be installed so as to be slightly forward

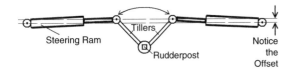

Fig. 9-11. Hydraulic steering ram configuration.

of its inboard end when the tiller arm is pointing directly aft. This will put the cylinder at right angles to the tiller arm when the rudder is hard over to port or starboard, which is when maximum leverage is needed (Fig. 9-11).

What type and size must steering components be? Only experience and a comparative analysis will tell. Properly specifying the displacement of the components and arranging them to work well will result in an effective system. When planning a steering system, boatowners should rely on the best information and professionals to do the design work. One needs to be well informed in the science and principles of steering to shop well. Many otherwise fine vessels are burdened with poor handling characteristics because of poor rudder design and poorly engineered steering systems.

AUTOPILOTS

Good crew at the helm see waves coming and anticipate the preemptive action required to keep the boat tracking well. The autopilot can't, and thus must wait for input from the compass after the boat is pushed off course, making it less responsive in adverse conditions.

Most modern autopilots consist of computer microprocessors that receive inputs from a compass for heading, and a tiller-mounted potentiometer that feeds back the rudder position. There is a common misconception that large boats need more autopilot capacity and small boats need less. However, the opposite is true. Small boats change their headings much more quickly and need more responsiveness from the autopilot, not less. Keeping a boat on track in any kind of seaway requires fast and powerful rudder responses. Windage (wind resistance) makes the autopilot's job more difficult, and it should be considered when sizing an autopilot for your boat.

Where fuel economy is concerned, it is vital to have the autopilot tuned to keep the vessel on the right heading. Many vessels zigzag their way home, actually traveling far more miles than needed. Every time the side of the boat is presented to the direction of travel, fuel economy suffers. The effect of even a large amount of rudder drag is very small compared to the excess drag involved with a poorly tracking boat. No matter what brand of autopilot is used, be sure yours has a very steady input compass and a high-quality rudder angle indicator (RAI).

PART 2: TROUBLESHOOTING

CHAPTER 10

ENGINE TROUBLESHOOTING BY SYMPTOM

Troubleshooting is problem solving. It's the process of reducing the number of *possible* causes of engine problems to the smallest number of *probable* causes. This chapter uses a conventional approach to troubleshooting quite similar to the way troubleshooting material is presented in engine service manuals; in Chapter 11 the methods used will be rather unconventional, employing the five senses.

BASIC TOOLS

It is important to carry basic tools with you so that you can dig in and find the problem. The photo on page 118 shows the tools I carry on every troubleshooting trip. The tools and toolbox weigh 36 pounds, a weight that is easy to manage one-handed while climbing aboard. The tools are listed below to help with identification.

1. Small and surprisingly powerful butane torch
2. White correction fluid—this paint works well to mark valves that have been adjusted during a tune-up
3. Electrical pliers for cutting, stripping wires, and crimping terminals
4. Stainless steel serrated knife
5. Long chisel
6. Medium ball-peen hammer
7. Channel-lock adjustable pliers
8. Extra hose clamps
9. Multi-tip screwdriver that works well for hose clamps—caution these tips *can and will* fall

into an engine—do not use this above an open engine!
10. Telescoping magnet
11. Variety of high-quality nylon zip-ties (note: cheap ones look identical but soon fail)
12. Ultra-gray silicone sealer
13. More white correction fluid
14. Hose clamp tightening driver that fits in No. 39
15. $3/8$" ratchet
16. Multimeter
17. Shallow and deep metric $3/8$" drive 6-point sockets
18. 3M-brand electrical tape
19. Red heat-shrink tubing
20. Adjustable wrench with jaws drilled to accept $1/8$" spanner dowels
21. Nylon pot webbing—very strong
22. Medium-sized Vise-Grip locking pliers
23. Side cutters—note how hinge pin was center punched three times to tighten the joint
24. Medium sheet-metal shear
25. Waterproof LED flashlight
26. Metric Allen wrench set
27. Thread locking compound
28. Fuel sightglass for finding air in the fuel in diesel engines
29. Short ruler in inches and millimeters
30. Standard angle screwdriver
31. Coarse point black marker
32. Feeler gauge
33. Very fine point black marker
34. Needle-nose pliers with wire cutter
35. Small Vise-Grip needle nose
36. Earplugs
37. Standard Allen wrench set
38. 8-foot tape measure
39. Multi-point screwdriver with locking tips that *cannot* fall into an engine
40. Metric and standard combination wrenches

Fig. 10-1. A basic tool collection (see page 117).

The following pages cover general troubleshooting for diesel and gasoline engines, with discussions on low-power issues, hard starts, and engine teardowns. Outboards and vacuum testing four-stroke gasoline engines will also be addressed.

In this chapter we will be pulling and prodding the engine's wires, belts, and hoses and really looking things over. We'll be watching for things that look great on the outside, but are faulty, such as the coolant hose in Figure 10-2. This hose was very close to failure, having been destroyed by electrical activity in the coolant, but someone happened to look inside and catch it in time. It's important to change the coolant regularly and add conditioner to stop electrical activity in the coolant.

DIESEL ENGINES

The following section lists specific problems you may encounter when operating a diesel engine and identifies probable causes. For details on how to proceed after narrowing down the probable cause, see the index of this book or refer to the appropriate section in your engine service manual.

ENGINE MISSES
Probable causes:
- Air in the fuel
- Water in the fuel
- Faulty valve seat
- Faulty injector
- Faulty injection pump

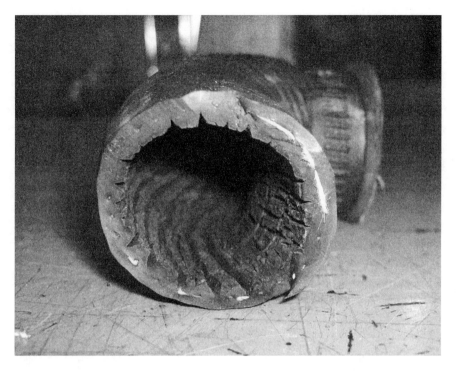

Fig. 10-2. Faulty coolant will destroy hoses. (Courtesy MER Equipment, Seattle, Washington)

ENGINE KNOCKS

Probable causes:

+ Spun connecting rod bearing
+ Wrong fuel injection timing
+ Injector tip, glow-plug end, valve head, or other object in the cylinder intake, or exhaust valve stuck open and piston striking it
+ Severely worn engine bearings
+ Extreme crankshaft end play
+ Extreme clearance between cylinder wall and piston

ENGINE LOCKED UP, OR CRANKSHAFT WILL TURN JUST A LITTLE

Probable causes:

+ Hydraulic lock with coolant, water, or fuel on top of a piston
+ Object on top of a piston

+ Piston rings and cylinder walls severely rusted due to water in the cylinder (see Fig. 10-3)
+ Too long a bolt or fastener inserted too deeply into the engine or timing gears hindering crankshaft movement

ENGINE LOW ON POWER (SEE ALSO SECTION BELOW)

Probable causes:

+ Air filter restricted or plugged with dust and soot
+ Collapsed muffler (silencer) or exhaust pipe
+ Wrong fuel in engine
+ Air in the fuel
+ Water in the fuel
+ Plugged fuel filter or restricted fuel lines on the suction side, pressure side, or return side of fuel system

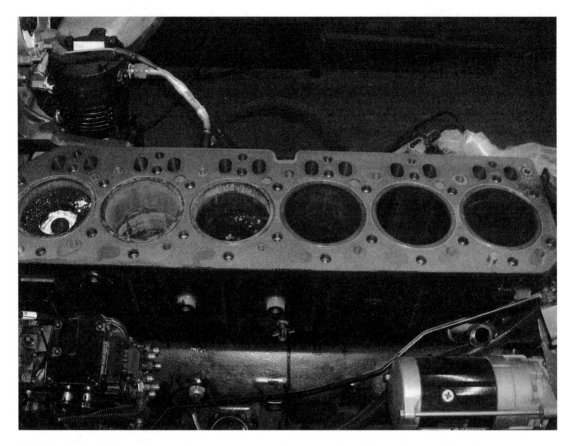

Fig. 10-3. Rust in cylinder walls caused by rainwater entering through an exhaust stack. (Courtesy Wilkies Equipment, Anchorage, Alaska)

- Faulty fuel injection timing, injection pump, or injector, or faulty adjustment of injection pump or injector
- Faulty turbocharger
- Low compression due to cylinder damage
- Valve clearance too much or too little, adjustment is set too loose or too tight
- Faulty throttle linkage doesn't pull governor lever to full fuel flow

ENGINE STARTS HARD

Probable causes:

- Low battery charge causes slow cranking speed
- Poor ground between engine and battery
- Low or no fuel, wrong fuel type, air in fuel, or fuel filter plugged
- Injection pump faulty or water damaged
- Fuel injection timing wrong, low injection pump pressure, or poor atomizing of fuel by injectors
- Low compression due to piston ring and cylinder wear
- Exhaust pipe covered or blocked
- Injection pump shutdown linkage stuck in the off position
- Valve clearance setting too tight or too loose

EXCESSIVE BLACK EXHAUST

Probable causes:

+ Plugged air filter
+ Excessive fuel delivery by pump or injectors
+ Insufficient atomization of fuel by the injector
+ Engine overloaded and lugging
+ Exhaust system restricted due to a collapsed muffler, or pipes with too small a diameter or too many tight bends

EXCESSIVE BLUE EXHAUST

Probable causes:

+ Piston rings and cylinders extremely worn
+ Extremely worn valve guides and seals
+ Faulty oil seals in turbocharger
+ Engine overfilled with oil

EXCESSIVE WHITE EXHAUST

Probable causes:

+ Low compression
+ Late injection timing
+ Water in the fuel or poor fuel quality

EXHAUST WHITE, BUT HAS A SLIGHT YELLOW CAST

Probable cause: Antifreeze entering the cylinder as engine runs, due to a faulty cylinder head gasket or broken casting

COOLANT TEMPERATURE TOO HIGH, LOW COOLANT FLOW

Probable causes:

+ Coolant pump not turning, loose water pump belt if so equipped
+ Pump impeller slipping on shaft, broken, or reduced in size by corrosion

COOLANT TEMPERATURE TOO HIGH, LOW COOLANT LEVEL

Probable causes:

+ Thermostat faulty and not opening
+ Keel cooler plugged internally, kinked, or bent
+ Heat exchanger core plugged, or water inlet plugged

ENGINE OVERHEATING, YET COOLANT TEMPERATURE READS NORMAL OR LOW

Probable causes:

+ Faulty gauge
+ Cooling system has large amount of air in it, displacing coolant

LOW OIL PRESSURE

Probable causes:

+ Low oil level or no oil in crankcase
+ Wrong viscosity of oil or oil diluted with fuel
+ Oil pump pressure relief valve stuck open
+ Crankshaft bearings extremely worn
+ Faulty gauge gives wrong reading when oil pressure is actually OK

HIGH OIL CONSUMPTION

Probable causes:

+ Worn cylinder, pistons, and rings
+ Faulty turbocharger oil seals
+ Worn valve guides and valve stem seals
+ Incorrect lubricating oil
+ Plugged oil drain-back holes in cylinder head causing valve guide oil leakage
+ Engine overfilled with oil

POOR FUEL ECONOMY

Probable causes:

+ Restricted air filter or exhaust flow
+ Wrong fuel injection timing setting

+ Either too much or too little pitch or diameter on the propeller
+ Cylinder pressure abnormally low
+ Fuel leaking into bilge (easy to smell)
+ Engine in a poor state of tune; valve adjustments too loose or tight, or fuel injection timing is wrong

WORK-AROUND SOLUTION—ENGINES WITH MECHANICAL LIFTERS

Adjusting Valves on the Exchange of Rocker Arms One Cylinder at a Time

There are a number of ways to adjust engine valves on gasoline or diesel engines. The first, of course, is the one you'll find in the engine manual. The manual will suggest adjusting the valves after a certain number of engine hours and will provide the required valve adjustment specifications as well as instructions. You will need a feeler gauge, screwdriver, and a locknut wrench for the adjusting screw.

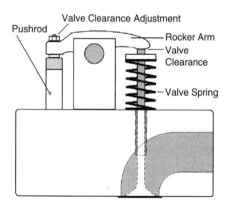

Fig. 10-4. Cylinder head and valve components.

Sometimes the engine manual is not available. When this is the case, there is a method that will work on all engines with mechanical

rather than hydraulic lifters and screw-thread adjusters. Measure, or closely estimate, the length of the valve pushrods and use the following method to assign temporary valve adjustment specifications to your engine. The valve pushrods on the intake and exhaust valve mechanisms are usually the same length. Multiply the length (in inches) of the intake valve pushrod by two to get the valve clearance in thousandths of an inch. For example, the intake valve clearance for a 10-inch-long pushrod would be the following: $10 \times 2 = 20$, or 0.020 (20 thousandths of an inch).

Since the exhaust side of the engine runs hotter than the intake side, the valve mechanism elongates due to the heat, and the valve clearance must be greater. Therefore, we will use a multiplier of 2.5 for the exhaust valve adjustment specification: $10 \times 2.5 = 25$, or 0.025 (25 thousandths of an inch).

Setting the valve clearances a little loose (excess clearance) won't damage the engine. Setting them too tightly, though, with insufficient clearance, will harm the valve seats. The above method is liberal enough with clearance to serve on a temporary basis, but you don't want to run that way for long. As soon as you can, adjust the clearance to factory specifications.

When a feeler gauge can't be found, there is another way to determine and set the clearance. Take a ruler or tape measure and count the number of threads per inch on the valve adjustment screw. For example, on a screw with 20 threads per inch, one turn will advance the screw 0.050 inch (50 thousandths of an inch). Therefore, adjusting the screw one-half turn would equal 0.025 inch (25 thousandths of an inch). Likewise, one-quarter turn will advance the screw 0.0125 inch (12.5 thousandths of an inch).

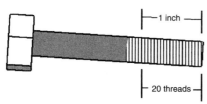

1 inch = 1,000 thousands of an inch.
This screw has 20 threads per inch.
1 inch divided by 20 = .050" per turn.
Therefore, each turn of the screw advances it .050" (50 thousands of an inch).

Fig. 10-5. Calculating travel per turn of the screw.

To use this method with the specifications above, the exhaust valve adjusting screw would be turned clockwise enough to eliminate all slack or clearance from the mechanism (known as zero lash), and then the screw would be backed off *almost* one-half turn for a clearance of 0.020 inch. The intake valve adjusting screw, on the other hand, would be backed off *slightly more* than one-quarter turn from zero lash to get a running clearance of 0.015 inch.

Now, to begin the adjustment procedure, consider a four-cylinder diesel engine. Start by disconnecting the negative battery cable to prevent the starter from being energized while the valves are adjusted. Then find a way to bar the engine over before removing the valve cover; you will need to gently rotate the crankshaft as you observe rocker arm travel. Wipe the oil from the rocker arms so that paint marks will later adhere. Identify the rocker arms and mark them with an "I" for intake or an "E" for exhaust so appropriate adjustments can be made. The engine manual will show which are intake and exhaust.

If no manual is available, look to see how and where the intake and exhaust manifold ports connect to the cylinder head. Then visualize how the ports must be routed in the

cylinder head to each valve on each cylinder. Make a list to help keep track of the arrangement. For example, from front to rear, the valves on the four-cylinder engine may be arranged with the intake all on one side and the exhaust on the other, or they may alternate. As you mark the rocker arms, you may see the pattern is IE, IE, IE, IE, or you may see it alternate to look like IE, EI, IE, EI. It all depends on the design of a particular engine. Do not proceed any further until you can positively identify intakes versus exhaust valves. It may take a call to your engine dealer.

After identifying and marking the valve rockers, begin at the first valve at the front of the engine. Remember, the flywheel is at the rear of the engine and the cooling pump is generally in the front. Turn the engine to rotate the crankshaft until the tip of the first rocker arm touching the valve stem rocks downward to the bottom of its travel.

To summarize the exchange method: On any cylinder of any four-stroke engine, be it gasoline or diesel, when one valve rocker is all the way to the bottom of its travel, it is safe to adjust the other rocker's valve clearance on the same cylinder. The method works by adjusting the valves one cylinder at a time.

INSUFFICIENT POWER

Fuel Supply

Low fuel level: When engines develop lows power problems, check the fuel level first. How much fuel is in the tank? Is the fuel level in the tank below the suction side of the engine's fuel system? Fill the tank and start the engine, putting it in gear to see if the low power issue has been resolved. If the engine runs normally, then the problem was related to the fuel supply. Lack of fuel can also cause hard starts, which will be covered later in this chapter.

If the engine was recently worked on, then it is important to consider that as a plausible reason for low power. It is possible that critical wiring or fuel lines were accidentally disturbed during the repair. If that isn't it, there are plenty of other potential suspects to consider.

Suction leaks in fittings and water in fuel: When low power accompanies a low fuel level, it may be a sign of suction leaks allowing air into the fuel system on the suction side of the system. Air enters the system through loose fuel fittings or pipe fitting threads that have not been properly sealed with pipe joint compound. Pipe threads are designed to require joint compound to seal them.

To correct problems with pipe thread leaks, begin resealing each joint in the incoming fuel line between the fuel tank and the engine. Use pipe dope instead of Teflon tape on fuel line plumbing to avoid getting strands of Teflon tape in the fuel system.

If there is no fuel gauge or the existing one is questionable, dip the tank with a clean dowel or broom handle that will reach the bottom. This can be impossible on many boats, but if it can be done, it should be. It's always good to dab the end of the dowel or broom handle with paste designed to change color if water is present in the fuel at the bottom of the tank. The paste is available at most fuel docks.

If the fuel level is satisfactory and there is no water in the fuel, then move on to the filters. When water is present, it will settle to the bottom of a fuel-water separator type filter.

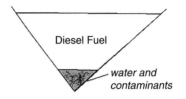

Fig. 10-6. Use a plastic bag to test fuel for water.

Just open the drain cock and pour a little fuel into a cup or even a plastic bag (Fig. 10-6), and water will be easy to spot.

Water in the fuel filter indicates water in the tank, and it must be removed. An hour of your marine mechanic's time will go a long way toward solving or preventing water problems in the fuel system. *Note: Don't disperse water in diesel fuel with chemical fuel treatments. The water will pass through the fuel injection system, which you don't want.*

Fuel line sizing: The inner diameter (ID) of fuel lines, if too small for a given engine, can cause low power problems. Some older boats, for example, might have a $1/2$-inch ID fuel pipe coming into the engine room. This line may have been enough to feed the original engines when the boat was built.

However, over the years, after a boat is repowered or a generator is added there may be times when one or more of the engines surge or seem sluggish. In the case of a generator, the lights may occasionally dim, which indicates the generator engine has lost rpm, or the lights may dim when the main engine is also running because there isn't enough fuel to supply them both. If this happens, it is time to upgrade the fuel supply lines to what the factory specifies for each engine, and then go up one pipe size.

To figure out the correct sizing for fuel lines, first calculate the cross-sectional area of the ID of all fuel lines and add them together. After getting the area of cross section needed to feed them all, go up to the next higher sized pipe to allow for an adequate supply of fuel for all the engines. Always inspect the fuel return lines and consider upgrading them to a larger size as well.

Engines with Stanadyne diesel fuel injection systems will not run with a plugged or valved-off fuel return line. Most vessels do have a valve on the return line, so check and make sure that the return line valve is definitely open, or the engine will not start.

Wrong fuel type: Fuel tanks can also be accidentally filled with the wrong fuel. No. 1 diesel fuel is sometimes put in, when the boat really needs No. 2. This will reduce engine power because there is less energy in a gallon of No. 1 fuel than in a gallon of No. 2 diesel fuel.

Diesel-powered boats have been filled with gasoline as well. Unlike gasoline fuel systems, diesel fuel systems have internal parts fitted at almost unimaginably small running clearances, and they depend on the lubricity of the diesel fuel to lubricate (and cool) the system. Gasoline has zero lubricating ability and will quickly destroy a diesel engine's close-tolerance fuel injection equipment.

Air in fuel: Air in the fuel, as mentioned earlier in relation to it entering the system through leaky fittings, will cause an engine to lose power. Air should not be allowed to get into fuel lines. When any gets in, bleeding the lines usually ejects it. However, if the air just keeps coming, it indicates that the fuel system is pulling air into the fuel on the suction side of the fuel transfer pump. Examine all fuel lines, hoses, fittings, and clamps between the engine and its fuel supply.

Consider installing a sight glass in the fuel system, before the fuel injection pump. A sight glass helps spot air in the fuel, a big help when troubleshooting low power problems. The place to install one is between the low-pressure fuel transfer (lift pump) and the high-pressure pump or unit injectors, depending on the type of injection system on the engine. Be sure to check the pressure that the transfer pump produces, and be sure that the sight glass is rated to handle it. Most major engine manufacturers can supply a suitable sight glass through their parts sales organization.

After the sight glass is installed and the fuel system is primed according to the engine manual, you should see no air passing through the sight glass if the fuel system is sound.

If, however, you have run the engine for at least fifteen minutes and you see even one bubble of air, there is a problem with the system that must be solved. That bubble means that there is at least a 5 percent mixture of air in the fuel.

Electronic fuel system governors have a hard time stabilizing engine speed when there is air in the fuel. This is especially true for generator engines, which require extremely precise speed control. When there is air in the fuel, the engine speed drops too low and the governor responds to increase the engine speed. If a slug of fuel does happen to get through, the engine speed will suddenly increase, and then the governor reacts by reducing speed. This is very bad for engines.

Note: If an engine suddenly develops a starting problem, and the fuel filters have recently been changed, check for air (Fig. 10-7) in the engine's fuel pump and injector lines. Air may have entered the system during the filter change.

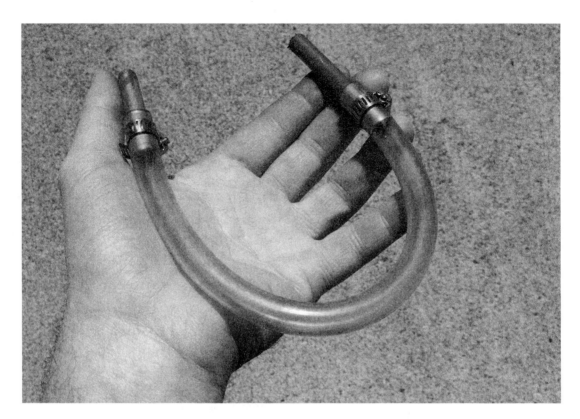

Fig. 10-7. Use a see-through hose to check for air in the fuel.

As previously mentioned, a sight glass installed on the suction side of the fuel system works nicely for checking fuel for air. Some diesel injection systems are self-bleeding, but most are not. Read your engine service manual or work with a local expert to learn the best way to bleed the engine's fuel system before you need to! Knowing this procedure should be considered a safety precaution.

Other Areas to Check

Governors: The governor control lever on the engine must move to full fuel when the engine speed control in the wheelhouse is pulled into the full throttle position. If it doesn't, the engine will appear to suffer from low power problems.

To check for trouble with linkage, station a helper at the engine while you are in the wheelhouse. Now, with the engine off, pull the engine speed control to full throttle and have your helper pull the engine linkage to see if the governor lever on the engine moves farther toward full fuel. If it does, then the throttle control must be repaired or adjusted.

Mufflers and air filters: A collapsed muffler (silencer) will reduce engine power by restricting airflow through the engine, which will result in excessive back-pressure. Check the back-pressure on the engine exhaust system every two years. Adequate airflow into and through the engine must not be hindered in any way. Many engines have a filter restriction gauge on the intake air system that shows red

THE TOO LONG BOLT

Some time ago, I was called north to Prudhoe Bay to troubleshoot a Caterpillar 3412, a V-12 engine with very low power. I traveled from Kodiak to Anchorage to Prudhoe Bay by air, arriving at 10:00 a.m. in total darkness. Lining up to wait for the bus, I found myself in the company of approximately sixty men in a zombie state, all keeping silently to themselves without making eye contact with anyone. They worked in the dark for weeks at a time on Alaska's North Slope. Once on the bus I felt as though I might as well have been riding to a funeral.

After the bus ride, I rode in a pickup to a remote oil rig. Upon arriving at the rig, where morale was better, I found that a bolt $\frac{1}{4}$-inch too long had been installed in a governor housing. The excess length protruded into the governor housing and prevented a piece of internal linkage from moving far enough to give the engine full power.

It took just a few minutes to install a shorter bolt, which let the engine reach full power. That was a long, expensive trip to make for such a minor fix.

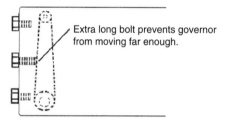

Fig. 10-8. Beware of fasteners that are too long and may interfere with vital components of a system, like a governor.

Fig. 10-9. Bolts that are too long can exert great force and damage the engine. The dimple in this camshaft thrust bearing was made by an overly long bolt. In this case it did not cause an engine failure, but it could have.

FOR THE WORKBOAT

Transmission Slippage

On workboats, don't forget the trolling valve. The trolling valve control linkage must be adjusted to remain fully closed when the boat is getting under way for cruising. If it should hang even partially open while the boat is moving, the trolling valve will cause clutch slippage and the boat will appear to lose power. This slippage will destroy the clutch discs in just a few minutes of running time at high engine speeds.

---

when the air filter should be serviced; air filters get loaded with dust and grime. Always check the condition of your air filter to avoid potential problems with low engine power.

Line in the propeller: Like driving a car with the emergency brake on, line wrapped around the propeller or propeller shaft will make it appear as though the engine has a low power problem. The best thing to do is to recall how much effort it takes to turn the propeller shaft with a pipe wrench, or even by hand, when the propeller is free of obstructions. You'll immediately notice a difference if the prop is fouled because it will take much more effort to turn the shaft, if you can turn it at all.

Checking the cylinders: In a low power situation, it's easy to assume there is big trouble in the engine cylinders. However, unless the engine is smoking badly, the cylinders may well be fine. They are difficult for the average person to inspect. However, when it is time to check them, there are several ways to do it. The first way is known as shorting out an injector. The procedure will help you identify faulty cylinders.

Fuel injectors on older engines with lower pressure fuel systems are easy to short out. Just start the engine and let it idle slowly. Next, using gloves and eye protection, carefully and slowly loosen the fuel line nut to each cylinder one at a time. Place a clean rag over each line nut before you loosen it.

While working through all of the injectors, it will be obvious that the engine rpm drops suddenly on strong cylinders when the fuel line nut is loosened. However, loosening the fuel line nut on a faulty cylinder will cause little difference in engine rpm. If a tachometer is available, the exact amount of speed loss for each cylinder can be recorded as each injector is shorted out. You can then compare the speeds to get a better idea of which cylinders need attention.

Caution: It is important to stay away from the stream of fuel that leaks out past the loosened fitting and also have your skin well covered. High-pressure fuel systems can produce a stream of fuel that will cut through skin! Serious blood poisoning can occur from fuel injection under the skin. If the engine's fuel system produces more than 2,500 psi, leave this test to a professional. Consult the engine manual to find your engine's maximum fuel injection pressure.

Mechanical unit injectors, like Detroit Diesel injectors, require a different method to short them out. Remove the valve cover to provide access. With the engine running at low idle, push a screwdriver down on the injector's plunger to hold it seated in the body of the injector. As each injector is shorted out, you will hear the engine slow down slightly if the cylinders are functioning properly. If the engine speed remains constant when an injector is shorted out, then the cylinder in which that injector resides is weak. An alternate method is to pry sideways slightly on the plunger spring retainer to prevent the plunger from popping back up after the rocker arm depresses it.

Electronic unit injectors also require their own testing method. Check these injectors using the engine manufacturer's electronic code reader and let the system tell you which cylinder is weak. *Caution: Never detach the power wire from an electronic injector because many of the newer systems use over 90 volts DC. Electrical shock with high levels of DC voltage is more dangerous than the same level of AC voltage. Also, since the injection pressures are so high, never hold down an electronic injector plunger!*

All this testing brings us to the next hurdle. If a cylinder is weak, the question is why. Is it weak because of a bad injector, faulty piston, or even one of the valves? To answer the question, try swapping an injector from a bad cylinder into a good one. Shorting out the injector will tell the tale. You will be listening for a *miss*, which is an irregular chugging sound that tells you the engine is not running smoothly as you troubleshoot. Often a vibration can accompany a miss.

If you switch injectors into a seemingly good cylinder and it suddenly starts to miss, or appears weak, then the injector is bad. If the cylinder works fine, then the injector is good and the cylinder from which it came is bad. Before condemning it, though, double-check the valve adjustment, just in case the valve adjustments are set too tightly. A valve set too tight mimics a faulty valve, and a cylinder with a valve set too tight will not build full pressure.

The other extreme is when valves are set far too loose. A loose intake valve will not open long enough to let in fresh combustion air. An extremely loose exhaust valve also limits the amount of fresh air that can enter the cylinder by hindering the escape of exhaust gases. If the exhaust gases can't exit, then the cylinder can't get a full charge of fresh air for combustion. Without the ability to develop its rated cylinder pressure, no diesel engine will run properly. There are several types of compression tests to check cylinder pressure.

Dynamic compression testers provide a reading of cylinder pressure while the engine is cranking using its starter. This type of test uses a fitting that threads into the injector hole, or a glow-plug hole, if so equipped, in the cylinder head. When the fitting is installed and connected to the pressure gauge with a flexible hose, the test may proceed. The test consists of cranking the engine with the starter while observing the pressure reading on the gauge. Most diesel engines need a minimum pressure of 400 psi to start properly.

When a cylinder has low pressure, and you're not sure why, you can do what the old-timers did and give it the *wet test*. To perform a wet test, just squirt a little motor oil in the cylinder before reattaching the compression tester, and see if the pressure increases. If it does, you know the piston rings are badly worn.

Note: Some engines have such a small combustion chamber volume that a wet compression test can severely over-pressure the cylinder. Consult the engine service manual to be sure the wet test is permissible on your engine. See page 29 for an illustration comparing combustion chambers in gasoline and diesel engines.

Recording compression testers are a variation on the tester described above and are widely used in Europe. The recording tester connects the same way as the compression tester and does the same type of pressure test. The difference is that the recording tester graphs the pressure of all the cylinders for easy comparison.

Leak-down testers have two pressure gauges and are often used by aircraft mechanics with the engine shut off. This test puts a certain amount of compressed air through the cylinder each minute. The air pressure coming in is regulated at 40 psi and is displayed on one of the two pressure gauges. If the engine cylinder leaks so much that the second gauge pressure can't reach 80 percent of the reading on the first gauge, then the cylinder is faulty. The good thing about this test is that you can listen in the crankcase for leakage past the piston rings; you can listen in the exhaust pipe for leakage past an exhaust valve; or you can listen at the air filter for a leak past an intake valve.

Note: Putting air pressure to one cylinder can move the piston and turn the crankshaft. It may be necessary to hold the crankshaft unless it is possible to put the piston on the cylinder to be tested very near top-dead-center (TDC) on the compression stroke.

The *bore scope* lets the troubleshooter look inside almost any diesel cylinder. Access to the cylinder can be gained through the injector hole or through an open valve. Better-quality bore scopes have a light source that illuminates the engine cylinder and allows you to see whatever damage is there. The bore scope can also help detect coolant leaks into the cylinder, if the cooling system is pressurized while the bore scope is in the cylinder. Many bore scopes enable the user to photograph the inner parts of the engine.

GASOLINE ENGINES

The following section provides the probable causes for specific problems you may encounter when operating a gasoline engine. For details on how to proceed after narrowing down the probable causes, see the index for further guidance or refer to the appropriate section in your engine service manual.

ENGINE MISSES
Probable causes:
+ Air or water in fuel
+ Faulty valve seat, spark plug, ignition system, or distributor

ENGINE KNOCKS
Probable causes:
+ Spun connecting rod bearing
+ Wrong ignition timing
+ Valve head or other object in cylinder
+ Valve stuck open and piston striking it
+ Severely worn engine bearings
+ Extreme clearance between cylinder wall and piston (piston slap)

ENGINE LOCKED UP, OR CRANKSHAFT WILL TURN JUST A LITTLE
Probable causes:
+ Hydraulic lock with coolant, water, or gasoline on top of piston
+ Object on top of piston
+ Piston rings and cylinder walls severely rusted due to water in cylinder
+ Too long a bolt or fastener inserted too deeply into the engine or timing gears

ENGINE LOW ON POWER
Probable causes:
+ Air filter restricted or plugged with dust and soot

+ Collapsed muffler or exhaust pipe
+ Wrong fuel or water in fuel; fuel mixture set too rich
+ Plugged fuel filter or restricted fuel lines on the suction or pressure side of fuel system
+ Wrong ignition timing or faulty ignition system
+ Low compression due to cylinder damage
+ Valve clearance insufficient, or adjustment set too loose or tight
+ Faulty throttle linkage won't pull governor lever to full fuel

ENGINE STARTS HARD
Probable causes:

+ Low battery causes slow cranking speed
+ Poor ground between engine and battery
+ Low or no fuel, wrong fuel, or fuel filter plugged
+ Ignition system damaged or ignition timing wrong
+ Fuel pressure low
+ Poor atomizing of fuel by fuel injectors, if so equipped
+ Low compression due to worn cylinders
+ Exhaust pipe covered or blocked
+ Valve adjustment excessively loose or tight

ENGINE WON'T READILY SHUT OFF WITH THE KEY
Probable cause: Rust holding fuel system governor lever in the run position

EXCESSIVE BLACK EXHAUST
Probable causes:

+ Plugged air filter
+ Fuel mixture too rich

EXCESSIVE BLUE EXHAUST
Probable causes:

+ Cylinder extremely worn
+ Piston or rings worn
+ Extremely worn valve guides and seals
+ Faulty oil seals inside turbocharger
+ Engine overfilled with oil

EXCESSIVE WHITE EXHAUST
Probable causes:

+ Water in fuel
+ Salt or fresh water entering cylinder when engine is running

EXHAUST WHITE, BUT HAS SLIGHT YELLOW CAST
Probable cause: Antifreeze entering the cylinder as the engine runs, due to a faulty cylinder head gasket or broken casting

COOLANT TEMPERATURE TOO HIGH
Probable causes:

+ Coolant pump not turning or coolant level low
+ Thermostat faulty and not opening
+ Keel cooler plugged internally, kinked, or bent
+ Heat exchanger core or cooling water inlet plugged

LOW OIL PRESSURE
Probable causes:

+ Low oil level or no oil in crankcase
+ Wrong viscosity of oil or fuel dilution of oil
+ Oil pump excessively worn or oil pump pressure relief valve stuck open
+ Crankshaft bearings extremely worn
+ Faulty gauge gives wrong reading when oil pressure is OK

HIGH OIL CONSUMPTION

Probable causes:

- Worn cylinder, pistons, and rings
- Faulty turbocharger oil seals
- Worn valve guides and valve stem seals
- Incorrect lubricating oil
- Plugged oil drain-back holes in cylinder head causing valve guide oil leakage
- Engine overfilled with oil

POOR FUEL ECONOMY

Probable causes:

- Restricted flow through air filter or exhaust
- Wrong ignition timing setting
- Too little pitch or diameter on the propeller, or too much
- Cylinder pressure abnormally low
- Fuel leaking into bilge (easy to smell)

INSUFFICIENT POWER

Fuel Supply

Low fuel level and water in fuel: There are similarities between gasoline and diesel engines when it comes to low power (and starting) problems and the way they are tested. As with a diesel, when a gasoline engine has reduced low power, check the fuel level first. Filling the tank may solve the problem.

If there is no fuel gauge or the existing one is questionable, dip the tank with a clean dowel or broom stick that will reach the bottom. This can be impossible on many boats, but if it can be done, it should be. It's always good to dab the end of the dowel or broom handle with paste designed to change color if water is present in the fuel at the bottom of the tank. The paste is available at most fuel docks. If there is water in the tank, it must be removed. It may be necessary to call a marine mechanic to get an idea of the best way to remove water from the gasoline tank and to prevent the water contamination from happening again.

After the cause of the water in the tank has been found and addressed, and the tank has been emptied and refilled, gasoline fuel conditioner may be used to disperse any remaining water in the fuel. Dispersants carry water through the engine's carburetor or fuel injectors with the fuel. While this is fine with a gasoline engine, it's not for a diesel.

Fuel filters: The next check involves the fuel filters. If they are clogged, reduced power can result. Also, if water is found in the separator bowl, you will have an indication that water is in the tank. Change the filters and remove the water from the tank as described above.

Fuel line sizing: If the boat has been recently repowered with more powerful engines, take a careful look at the fuel lines. If they weren't replaced when the new engines were installed, they may not have sufficient inner diameters to carry enough fuel. Poor fuel flow will make an engine appear to have less power than it should. Checking fuel pressure with the engine producing full power will reveal any existing problem. The fuel pressure to the engine fuel system will drop below the engine manufacturer's specifications if fuel lines are inadequate.

Wrong fuel type: Boats with gasoline engines have been mistakenly filled with diesel fuel. While the engine won't run with diesel fuel in the tank, it doesn't usually harm the engine. Replacing all the diesel fuel with gasoline is time-consuming, but it is a simple fix.

Other Areas to Check

Carburetor and fuel injection control levers: The control lever on the engine must move to full fuel when the engine speed control in the wheelhouse is pulled into the full speed position. If it doesn't, the engine will appear to suffer from low power problems. To check for trouble with linkage, station a helper at the engine while you are in the wheelhouse. With the engine off, pull the engine speed control to the full speed position and have your helper pull the engine linkage to see if the control lever on the engine moves farther toward full fuel. If it does, then the throttle control must be repaired or adjusted.

Mufflers and air filters: A collapsed muffler (silencer) will reduce engine power by restricting airflow through the engine, which will result in excessive back-pressure. Check the back-pressure on the engine exhaust system every two years.

Adequate airflow into and through the engine must not be hindered in any way.

Many engines have a filter restriction gauge on the intake air system that shows red when the air filter should be serviced; air filters get loaded with dust and grime. Always check the condition of your air filter to avoid potential low power problems.

Line in the propeller: Like driving a car with the emergency brake on, line wrapped around the propeller or propeller shaft will make it appear as though the engine has a low power problem. The best thing to do is to recall how much effort it takes to turn the propeller shaft with a pipe wrench, or even by hand, when the propeller is free of obstructions. You'll immediately notice a difference if the propeller is fouled because it will take much more effort to turn the shaft, if you can turn it at all.

Checking the cylinders: Engine cylinders are difficult for the average person to inspect. But for those who are inclined to check them when the need arises there are some indirect ways to learn what is happening in the heart of the engine. Auto repair shops use engine analyzers to check gasoline cylinder condition by turning off the spark to one cylinder at a time and then measuring the amount the engine speed drops. Engine speed drops the most when cylinders that are carrying their share of the load are shorted out (see below). However, when weak cylinders are shorted out the engine speed changes very little.

The engine analyzer turns off the spark to each cylinder in turn by putting the spark to ground. If this isn't done, the test may damage the ignition system insulation. Once the spark plug wire is charged with tens of thousands of volts from the ignition system, the current must go somewhere! If it doesn't go to ground, it'll try to fry the insulation. You might ask, "Can't I just pull off the spark plug wire to each cylinder, one at a time, and listen to the change in speed?" The short answer is yes. Sometimes mechanics do just that. But it really shouldn't be done because it is hard on the electrical system.

In an emergency, go ahead in spite of the hazards, if you must know which cylinder is misfiring to make a repair. The higher the ignition system voltage is, the harder it is on the system to pull off a plug wire with the engine running. One good strategy for checking to see if there is spark is to make a test

Fig. 10-10. Ignition testing spark plug.

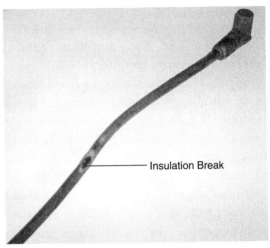

Fig. 10-11. Examine the insulation on spark plug wires if misfiring is a problem.

plug as shown (Fig. 10-10). By grounding the test plug and attaching a spark plug wire to it, you will easily see if there is spark in the test plug when the engine is started. Using this tester will not harm the system.

If a cylinder is weak, the question is why. Is it weak because of a bad spark plug, or is a piston or one of the valves damaged? Try swapping a spark plug, and even the spark plug wire, from a known good cylinder into the bad cylinder. The problem may be a faulty plug or bad insulation on the spark plug wire (Fig. 10-11).

If the miss (weak cylinder) moves to the other cylinder when spark plugs and then the wires are switched, then the plug or wire is bad. If the miss doesn't move to the new cylinder, then the missing cylinder is damaged. However, before condemning it, double-check the valve adjustment, in case the valve adjustments are set too tight. A valve set too tight mimics a faulty valve. A valve set too loose will hinder the cylinder's efficiency, too. However, it will make such a loud clicking noise that the sound will give it away.

A simple compression test for a gasoline engines consists of removing the spark plugs as each cylinder is tested, inserting the compression tester into the spark plug hole, and then energizing the starter motor to build pressure in the cylinder. Inexpensive compression testers are available at auto parts stores. Simply record the pressure of each cylinder and then compare pressures at the end of the test. The pressure on most engines will be 100 psi or greater, with no more than 10 psi variation between cylinders.

More variation than this indicates bad rings, valves, or both.

Note: I do not recommend removing all of the spark plugs first and then moving the tester from cylinder to the next, cranking the engine each time. This method works, but can allow extra dust and airborne abrasives into the cylinder.

TROUBLESHOOTING HARD STARTS—DIESEL AND GAS ENGINES

In spite of the differences between them, diesel and gasoline engines share many features, including many of the problems you may encounter regarding hard starts. For example, a squealing alternator belt will result from the same causes regardless of engine type. Hard start issues share many common factors in both types of engines, so the information that follows should be construed to apply to both unless otherwise noted.

Of course, as previously mentioned, the first thing to do if faced with a hard start regardless of what type of engine you have is to check the fuel level and fuel filters. These are the most likely culprits. Failing that, there are plenty of other probable causes. Below you will find a detailed troubleshooting list to help you resolve hard start problems.

CRANKSHAFT WON'T TURN WHEN STARTER ENGAGED, NO SOUND OF STARTER MOTOR TRYING TO WORK

Probable causes: Faulty or discharged battery, or battery low on electrolyte

+ Corroded battery terminals, corroded or partially cut cables, damaged battery posts
+ Alternator output low or nonexistent, belt slipping, excessively worn pulley
+ Faulty starter switch, low voltage to switch
+ Bad starter solenoid

Suggested actions:

Batteries: Check battery voltage with a multimeter. You should get a reading of 12 volts or better. If you don't have a multimeter, turn on the lights powered by the DC electrical system. If lights are dim, your batteries are low and lack the power to energize the starter.

Check the electrolyte in lead-acid batteries and fill with distilled water if the levels in each cell are low (rainwater, tap water, or even electrolyte from an old battery are also options, though not as good as distilled water, which is free of minerals that can damage the battery).

Check for corroded terminals or cut battery cables, which will cause an open circuit. Replace any damaged or cut cables. In a pinch, you can scavenge cables from an arc welder, if you happen to have one on board. *Note: Severe voltage drop at the positive post of the starter, when trying to crank the engine, indicates that there is severe corrosion between the cable and the inside of the cable terminal, or that the cable is cut nearly all the way through somewhere between the battery and the starter.*

After these checks, charge the batteries with an AC charger. If no charger is available, jump the discharged batteries from a fully charged battery. When a jumper battery isn't available and a DC arc welder is, use the welder as the power source to energize the starter (through the battery) and turn the engine. Since many DC "stick" welding machines operate at 24 volts, make sure to put it on a lower amp setting. Connect the welding leads in the right polarity with very good, tight connections, and try it. If the engine is warm it may start.

Alternator: After checking the batteries, look for alternator belt slippage. Tighten or replace the belt if necessary. If no belt is available, make one from a length of Push-Loc hose rated for 300 psi. See page 55 for a detailed illustration on this type of repair. As a last resort, you can fashion a belt from a nylon stocking. Check the alternator pulley and replace it if it's worn.

Overcharging will eventually boil lead-acid batteries until the electrolyte level drops too low for them to function properly. When you check the electrolyte level and find it low, check the alternator charge rate after refilling the batteries. Assuming you have found a way to start it, make note of the alternator charging system voltage *before* starting up the engine. It should be 10.5 to 12 volts, or twice that for a 24-volt system. Now, start the engine, take another reading, and compare it with the previous one. The voltage after the engine is started should be 13.5 to 14.2 volts for a 12-volt system or twice that for a 24-volt system.

Note: If alternator diodes are faulty, current can leak from the system through the alternator when the engine is at rest. This will sometimes make the alternator warm even when the engine is off.

Starter switch and solenoid: The next component to check is the starter switch in the wheelhouse. Using a voltmeter (black lead to ground and red lead to the wire supplying the switch and then to the wire leaving the switch), verify that current is reaching the switch and verify the voltage output when the switch is operated. If current isn't reaching the switch or the voltage output is weak, you have found the root of the problem. You can try jumping the starter as shown in Fig. 11-3. But if all is well, move on to the next step.

Check the starter motor solenoid. It is possible to bypass the solenoid altogether by creating a temporary connection from the solenoid's main positive terminal direct to the starter field post. Using eye protection and leather gloves, momentarily span these two terminals with a stout screwdriver or pry bar. *Caution: There will be some arcing.* If the starter motor spins when the solenoid is bypassed, then the solenoid is faulty and must be replaced.

If no replacement solenoid is available, it is possible to remove the solenoid and engage the starter drive gear manually with the flywheel, using a pry bar. When the starter drive is engaged with the flywheel, you can energize the starter motor directly by touching the positive cable from the battery to the starter's high-amperage positive post. *But I do not recommend this. There will be tremendous arcing from the battery cable to the starter terminal or to any other ground the cable touches. This is an extreme emergency measure.*

If the starter is faulty, it will not spin even if the solenoid is bypassed, and it must be replaced. If no new starter is available, get a used starter from another engine. Alternatively, in an emergency, you may use a starter with a lower voltage rating. For example, if your workboat engine has a 32-volt starter, a 24-volt or even a 12-volt starter will work in an emergency. This is a temporary fix. Install the right starter for the engine as soon as possible.

CAN HEAR THE STARTER TRYING TO TURN CRANKSHAFT, BUT ENGINE WON'T TURN FAST ENOUGH TO START

Probable cause: Possible low voltage

Suggested action: See previous actions related to charging or jumping batteries.

CAN HEAR DRIVE "CLUNK" INTO FLYWHEEL TEETH, BUT DOESN'T SPIN CRANKSHAFT

Probable cause: The starter windings may be an open circuit

Suggested action: Replace the starter or take steps as previously explained.

THE STARTER MAKES GRINDING SOUND DUE TO DAMAGED FLYWHEEL RING GEAR TEETH

Probable cause: Faulty starter ring gear
Suggested actions:

If a new ring gear is not available, remove the existing one from the flywheel and flip it to expose undamaged teeth to the starter. Then reinstall the ring gear to the flywheel and the flywheel to the engine.

If the gear tooth contour isn't compatible with flipping over, then remove the ring gear and change its clock orientation to the flywheel. Rotate the ring gear slightly and reinstall it. For example, on a four-cylinder engine (Fig. 10-12),

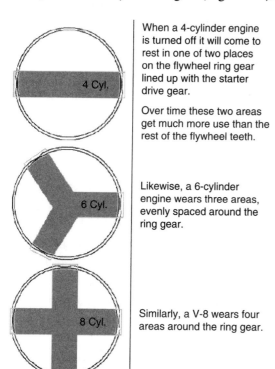

When a 4-cylinder engine is turned off it will come to rest in one of two places on the flywheel ring gear lined up with the starter drive gear.

Over time these two areas get much more use than the rest of the flywheel teeth.

Likewise, a 6-cylinder engine wears three areas, evenly spaced around the ring gear.

Similarly, a V-8 wears four areas around the ring gear.

Fig. 10-12. Areas of wear on a flywheel ring.

mark and move the ring gear one-quarter turn from its original position. Rotate the ring gear one-sixth of a turn on a six-cylinder engine, and one-eighth of a turn on an eight-cylinder engine.

THE STARTER MOTOR CAN BE HEARD OVER-REVVING BUT NOT ENGAGING WITH THE FLYWHEEL

Probable cause: Starter drive (also known as the Bendix) may be bad
Suggested actions: The starter drive will need to be replaced.

CRANKSHAFT TURNS A LITTLE BUT THEN LOCKS UP BEFORE MAKING A FULL REVOLUTION

Probable causes:
  • Hydraulic lock (fluid on top of a piston)
  • Mechanical lock

Suggested actions:

Hydraulic lock: Remove the injectors or glow plugs (diesels) or spark plugs (gas engines) to allow barring over the engine by hand. On a diesel, if injectors or glow plugs can't be removed, rotate the adjusting screws on all exhaust valves one-half turn to tighten them past zero-lash. (Zero lash is an absence of clearance between the rocker-arm tip and the end of the valve stem.) This will hold all exhaust valves open and enable the engine to be barred over. The fluid will be pumped out of the cylinders and into the exhaust manifold. After the fluid is gone, the valves must be readjusted.

Note: Always err on the side of caution and be sure the cylinders are clear before energizing the starter! Bar the engine over, by hand, two complete revolutions to clear fluid from above the piston rings. Be sure to find out where the fluid is coming from and stop it.

Mechanical lock: The lock may be due to recent repairs in which a bolt was threaded in too far, causing interference with some moving internal engine part. Loose internal parts may have jammed inside the engine, or the lock may be due to a severe engine failure. Cut open the oil filter and check for metal particles (glitter) lodged in filter media paper. If you find any, you're seeing evidence of metal-to-metal contact, and that almost always means the engine is damaged. Remove the valve cover and inspect for damaged valves and for valves that have contacted a piston.

CRANKSHAFT TOTALLY LOCKED UP
 Probable causes:
   ◆ Rusted cylinders
   ◆ Mechanical lock

Suggested actions: Rusted cylinders will seize up. Water may have come down the stack of a dry, vertical exhaust system, or it may have entered the engine from excessive bilge water splash. If the boat has been refloated after sinking, then you know exactly how the water got in! Check the cylinders for rust or see previous problem for information about mechanical locks.

ENGINE TURNS BUT WILL NOT START
 Probable causes:
   ◆ Engine not getting fuel
   ◆ Low compression in cylinders
   ◆ Fuel injection timing out of specification

Suggested actions:

Fuel doesn't reach engine: If no smoke comes from the exhaust pipe during cranking, then no fuel is entering the cylinders. Find out why by bleeding the high-pressure fuel fittings on the pressure side of the fuel system. Follow the directions in your engine service manual for bleeding the fuel system.

On a diesel engine only, if you determine that fuel is reaching the cylinders (there is smoke coming out of the exhaust pipe), but the engine will not fire, try ether starting fluid to see if it helps. See the accompanying sidebar for proper use of ether. *Note: Some engines such as Volvo-Penta diesels are equipped with a certain type of keystone piston rings that don't respond to ether starting aids. See Fig. 2-14 for a detailed comparison of keystone and square-cut rings.*

Low compression and fuel injection timing: Verify that there is at least 350 psi of compression in the cylinders (see above for more on compression tests). If the engine still won't start, refer to your engine service manual for directions on checking fuel injection timing.

You may never have thought of this, but a trick of the trade is to heat the oil. This won't work well on boats with large engines, but if your engine is fairly small, consider draining the oil as soon as you shut the engine off. Store the oil in a warm place, and when you're ready to go, pour the warm oil back into the engine. Start the engine immediately. Believe it or not, this has worked well more than once! These techniques are good for diesel and gasoline engines.

TROUBLESPOTS TO LOOK FOR WHEN DISMANTLING AN ENGINE

Professional mechanics develop a heightened ability to detect important clues during the

USING STARTING FLUID ON A DIESEL ENGINE

The starting fluid sold in auto supply stores is pressurized ether, a highly explosive gas that is misused most of the time. Starting fluid is a lot like a sledgehammer. Skillfully applied, it does its job better than any substitute, but if not used carefully, it will do expensive damage quickly.

You should not use starting fluid on gasoline engines, because they have light-duty connecting rods and pistons that are easily damaged. What's more, gasoline is nearly as explosive as ether, and if you have a spark and good spark timing, compression, and fuel, the engine will start when it turns fast enough. When a gasoline engine won't start, check each of the items in the preceding sentence.

Ether starting fluid is useful for balky diesel engines, however, especially for very cold starts. If used properly, it will not hurt your engine.

Begin by charging the batteries and warming the engine. Even a small electric heater blowing warm air onto the engine for an hour is helpful. While warming up the engine, make sure there is fuel in the tank and fuel to the engine. Next remove the air filter and have someone energize the starter to get the crankshaft turning.

Here is the important part: *After the engine is spinning,* squirt a small "puff" of ether into the air filter. Wait two seconds, then squirt another quick puff. Wait two seconds more and squirt another.

While the engine is cranking, keep watching for smoke out of the exhaust pipe. Black smoke proves that fuel is entering the cylinders and starting to ignite. An absence of smoke means that the engine isn't getting fuel in the cylinders.

Ether can destroy an engine if you spray a liquid stream into the air filter before you start turning over the engine. The ether gets into the cylinder and explodes so violently that it temporarily locks the engine. This is called an *ether lock,* and it will break the piston rings. After an ether lock, the engine will need ether to start every time because the rings won't hold pressure in the cylinders. The engine is then said to be addicted to ether.

TIPS FOR COLD WEATHER STARTS

One major consideration when discussing hard starts in diesel and gasoline engines is older diesel engines often require warming to facilitate the starting process, especially in cold weather. While gasoline engines start better in the cold, a modern diesel is less prone to hard starts in cold weather because injection pressures are now much higher for good starting. However, larger diesel-powered vessels still often have electric forced-air heat plumbed into the engine room to make starting in cold weather easier.

On a smaller boat, you can use a hairdryer, a hot-air popcorn popper, or even a lightbulb to warm the engine compartment. Never use an open flame. Direct the heat toward the oil pan for best results.

Warming the battery will also help. Ideally, you would warm the battery along with the engine. But you could remove the battery, if it's not too heavy, and put it inside a warm cabin. Alternatively, you could place the battery in a container of heated water. Keep the top dry to preserve the integrity of the electrolyte in a lead-acid battery.

disassembly of an engine. They don't merely take an engine apart to rebuild it. They view the exercise as an ideal way to identify potential areas of trouble that may have caused a breakdown or threatened to in the future. As they work, they are extremely careful not to introduce problems, such as not allowing dirt, fasteners, tools, or even small shop cloths to fall unnoticed into vital oil, fuel, coolant, or air passages. They cap, plug, tape, or cover all openings as they remove components from the engine.

Whenever possible, professional mechanics also avoid doing engine jobs where there is going to be a lot of foot traffic in the work area, like in a shed where major structural repairs are being done on the boat. Dust and metal grinding near an engine rebuild is just asking for trouble. It's better to do the engine rebuild either before or after the other boat work that must be done. This is a safety consideration as much as anything else.

When a marine engine fails, lives are on the line, much as they are when an aircraft engine suddenly stops working. While certainly not as deadly, engine failure on the water is dangerous, especially in bad weather or near rocks. To lose power in a boat will often be life-threatening.

In a truck or piece of heavy equipment it's not hard to "swing" (change) a new engine in a day's time. However, on a boat it's no simple matter to replace or rebuild an engine. Hatch covers and bulkheads must be opened, removed, unbolted, or even cut to pass large and heavy engines, or pieces of an engine, through to the top deck and then back to the engine room after repairs are made. What follows is a point-by-point troubleshooting tour of an engine as it is taken apart, prior to rebuilding.

Is the engine paint burned or darker in some areas due to overheating of the engine or some part of the engine? If the head and upper engine are discolored, watch for signs of internal overheating damage. This damage will include things like cracked heads or a damaged cylinder block.

How does the exterior of the engine look? Are aluminum pieces corroded and iron pieces rusted? If so, the engine may have been wet often or even submerged in water. Does the oil pan or even the cylinder block have a high-water mark that indicates swamping?

Is the exterior of the engine dented or scuffed, or are there bent or broken parts? If so, it has had rough handling.

Are there streaks of leaking oil running down the side? This indicates an oil leak.

Are there streaks of white mineral residue running down the side? This indicates a coolant leak with poorly maintained coolant containing high levels of dissolved solids (Fig. 10-13).

When the oil pan drain plug is loosened, what appears first, water or oil? If water

Fig. 10-13. White streaks on the side of this engine indicate the presence of dissolved solids in leaking antifreeze coolant.

THE CRANKCASE VENT

The boatowner on the other end of a scratchy sounding phone asked me to charter a plane from Kodiak, Alaska, to Port Moller, which is several hundred miles west of Kodiak. He said to bring the 1,200 pounds of parts that it would take to rebuild his Cat D353. He said he had blown a piston and the engine was down. Then he added that the engine kept blowing the dipstick from its hole because the engine had terrible blowby (high crankcase pressure).

When I arrived and checked the engine, I found the crankcase vent tube kinked, which was causing the high crankcase pressure. I assured the skipper that his engine was just fine, and that we needed to plumb his vent system as shown in Figure 10-14.

As this drawing reveals, the pipe inserted in the exhaust stream causes a swirling low-pressure area at the end of the small pipe. This actually acts like a vacuum cleaner to draw the crankcase gases from the crankcase. This is known as the venturi effect.

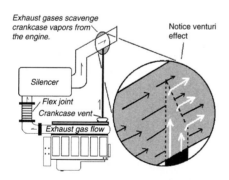

Fig. 10-14. A proper marine crankcase vent system.

The skipper didn't believe that the problem was fixed after we properly vented the crankcase, and he insisted on doing an eight-hour sea trial during a storm. Soon after we left our anchorage I became really seasick. The skipper told me it would help if I went on deck and got some fresh air.

The boat was pitching and rolling so violently I had to stand with my feet far apart just to remain upright. The cover of the crab tank, which was six feet square, was up on the edge of the tank, apparently left that way so just one person could slide it open.

Suddenly, a wave swept over the deck from the port side and carried me over the rail on the starboard side of the boat. I flailed and caught the rail as I went over and hung on, then quickly climbed back on deck. As soon as I got my balance again, the boat pitched violently and the cover of the dry crab tank slid open, seemingly to receive me as I started to fall in!

Totally panicked, I grabbed the edge of the tank as I fell through the opening and hung there with the boat rolling. Giving it everything I had, I was able to swing and climb back out of the tank, fearing all the while that the tank cover would slide closed on my arms. Getting back to my feet, I lunged through the door and back into the galley.

Slowly regaining my composure, I realized I had been totally cured of the seasickness by my stark terror out on deck. The skipper calmly informed me that the engine seemed to be doing just fine.

shows first, then there is water (or coolant) in the oil pan. As the disassembly progresses, it is vital to find the source of this water.

After cutting open a fuel filter, is it full of rust, algae, or even water? These are signs of water in the fuel. Finding water in the fuel can turn what was supposed to be a quick "in-frame" overhaul into a more costly job because the injection pump and injectors will need to be replaced.

After cutting open the oil filter and inspecting the pleats of filter media for contamination, is aluminum present? This is piston material. Are there a lot of black soot particles? This shows excessive piston ring blowby, too much time between oil changes, or poor maintenance.

Before removing the water pump and alternator belts, did they allow slippage and are they glazed? Are the belt pulleys badly worn? These are signs of belts slipping. If the engine overheated, it is possible it overheated because the coolant pump was not turning as fast as it should have.

Collect and test the antifreeze for freezing protection and also do a pH test. Many drugstores sell inexpensive pH tape for the testing of water-based fluids. The coolant must be slightly alkaline in pH to prevent galvanic corrosion from attacking dissimilar metals inside the engine. Acidic coolant means the engine you are reconditioning may be going back into a boat where the cooling system needs cleaning and flushing.

How does the valve cover gasket look? Is the gasket crushed from overtightening of the cover bolts? Overtightening of these bolts, using excessive silicone sealer on a valve cover gasket, or using sealer instead of a gasket are all signs of a novice. Cat green (contact cement) or 3M weather-stripping adhesive on the valve cover side of the gasket are signs of a pro.

Do the engine's gasketed surfaces show signs of someone having previously scraped an old gasket off during a previous rebuild? If so, the engine has been rebuilt. If not, it may be that you are rebuilding the engine for the first time since it was new. Are the scraped surfaces gouged or scratched? If so, you are not the first to repair the engine.

Inspect fasteners as they are removed. Are the fasteners you are removing all similar and of the type the manufacturer used when the engine was new? Or does the engine have a mixture of some factory and some aftermarket fasteners? To tell the difference, just look at the markings on the bolt heads. These are more clues to help you learn if the engine has been previously repaired, and if the job was done well.

Is the bottom wear surface on the rocker shaft excessively worn? This will show the engine has a high amount of hours on it. If so, new rocker arms will need to be ordered.

Check the valve settings with a feeler gauge before you remove the rocker arms. Are they loose or overly tight? This can tell you what state of tune the engine was in. If the valves are overly tight, watch for a burned valve seat when you get the head disassembled.

Loosen the valve adjustment locknuts and back off the valve lash before removing the rocker arms. This will help you avoid bolting the rocker arms back onto the engine with insufficient valve clearance later. This is important because the cylinder head valves and seats will be machined during the rebuild, and the valve stems may protrude upward through the valve guides a little higher after the heads are done. Bolting the rocker arms back in with insufficient valve lash settings could cause a valve to hit a piston and bend as the crankshaft is being turned during the rebuilding process.

Note: Before removing the head bolts, be sure to remove the injectors, because the injectors sometimes take a little force to remove. Injectors are easier to remove while the heads are bolted securely to the engine. Injector tips also often protrude through the cylinder head and will be damaged if the head is set on a workbench, so remove the injectors to prevent injector tip damage.

Be sure to notice the level of head bolt tightness as the bolts are removed. Are they uniformly tight? If not, they may not have been torqued properly, or one may have been missed during the tightening procedure. If you find one that was not tight, notice which cylinder it was near. Then, once the head is off, make note of any places the head gasket may have blown out. These places will show darkening or actual destruction of the head gasket.

Any engine will have a certain number of head bolts under the valve cover, protected from the elements. These inside bolts will have no paint on their heads. There will also be a certain number of outside head bolts. However, these bolts will have painted (and possibly rusty too) heads from when the engine was painted.

As you disassemble the engine, make note if any painted bolt heads are found under the valve cover. Likewise, notice if any of the unpainted bolts were used as outside bolts. If any irregularity is found here, it will prove previous service work was done. It will also indicate that the work was unprofessional.

Head bolt threads must be lubricated during assembly, according to the manufacturer's directions, which usually call for engine oil on the threads of the bolts and under the head of the bolt. Never-Seez compound, also known as anti-seize compound, is a thick paste often containing minute flakes of graphite, copper, nickel, molybdenum, and grease. The compound works great, but it should not be used on bolts inside the valve cover or crankcase because the residue will contaminate any oil analysis sampling that is done on the engine.

As the head bolts are removed, smell the oil on the bolts. If the engine has been overheated, the oil will have a very strong burned smell.

Can you wiggle the valve stems much? Put a dial indicator on the stem and measure the movement. How does this amount of movement compare with the service manual specifications? If the guides are far out of specification, the engine, or at least the heads, will have a lot of running time.

When removing the pushrods, keep them in order. As the pushrods are removed, check to see if they can be rolled smoothly on a flat surface. If so, they are straight. If not, they are bent. A bent valve-actuating pushrod tells you that a valve contacted a piston. Can you see a mark on any of the pistons that will verify that contact was made?

Another important check for hollow tubular pushrods, like those used in older Cummins engines with PT fuel systems: Hold them up by one end and tap them gently with a hammer to make sure each rings with the same resonance. This indicates they are not filled with oil. When one has a different tone than the others, then it does have oil inside and must be replaced.

Inspect the head gasket surfaces on the head and block immediately after removing the head. Watch for discolored areas where coolant or compression may have been poorly contained.

Similarly, watch for a deep scratch or gouge under a critical area of the head gasket. Scratches will let fluids pass under gaskets, preventing them from holding pressure.

Watch for mismatched, wrong length, or bolts of various strength ratings, and bolts with painted heads inside of the engine covers. This includes the flywheel housing, the timing gear cover, and the oil pan and the valve cover. Mismatched bolts are signs of poor or sloppy workmanship.

When inspecting the heads further, look for cracks between the exhaust valve (often the smaller diameter valve in each cylinder) and the injector hole. Cracks here prove overheating occurred.

Are there gouges on surfaces where gaskets have been scraped? Is the head straight and true according to a straightedge? If not, it has been overheated.

As the exhaust manifold is removed, is there any trace of red (rust) in the intake or exhaust ports of the head or the passages of the exhaust manifold? If there is, this is a sign of water in the corresponding cylinder.

Looking into the exhaust ports of the head, are all of them flat black in color and tone? This is good. It shows that the cylinders were in good shape and that each was probably doing its share of the work of keeping the crankshaft turning. On the other hand, is one or more of the exhaust ports a shiny wet-looking black color? If so, this indicates the possibility of weak cylinders, and especially cylinders that are low on compression and not completely burning the fuel.

Do the exterior (out of the crankcase) bolts have Never-Seez on them? Good! This is a sign of craftsmanship. However, if interior bolts have Never-Seez on them, this is not good, and is the sign of a novice at work. As mentioned above, Never-Seez compound inside the crankcase will cause faulty oil sample results. Never-Seez compound will make

an oil sample from a sound engine appear as though it is self-destructing.

After the cylinder head (or heads) is removed, it is time to check the tops of the pistons for evidence of contact between a valve and piston. Often the contact is more subtle than shown in Figures 10-15 and 10-16.

Fig. 10-15. Broken valve head embedded in a piston.

Fig. 10-16. Debris embedded in a piston.

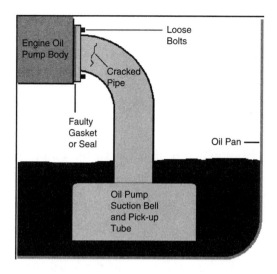

Fig. 10-17. Poor oil suction.

rust

Fig. 10-18. Rust in the injection pump.

Are the O-rings on the lube oil pump suction tube hardened? This could explain damage to the crankshaft bearings even when there is no fuel in the oil. Hard O-ring seals on the suction side of the lube oil pump will aerate the oil, as will faulty suction pipe gaskets and loose bolts on the pipe (Fig. 10-17).

What is the condition of the main and rod bearings that are farthest from the oil pump? If the engine runs low on oil, these will be damaged first.

Are the oil pump gears scratched? They are supposed to be soft, so that hard particles will embed rather than lock the pump gears. Scratches, though, indicate contaminants in the lube oil system.

What is the condition of the water pump impeller? If it is missing a blade, the missing blade may be trapped in the cooling system. It also means the engine may have been running hot.

Is the crankshaft rear main bearing sloppy? This indicates extreme crankshaft wear and poor maintenance.

Are all locating dowels present on the front and rear cover and on the top of block? Note: Locating dowels protrude upward from the cylinder block, and they are what aligns the head gasket and the head to the cylinder block.

Take the lid off of the injection pump (if it has one) and look for rust in the pump. If there is rust in the pump (Fig. 10-18), the injectors and injector lines must be replaced.

OUTBOARD ENGINE TROUBLESHOOTING

A good share of maintaining an outboard depends on strong troubleshooting techniques. It also helps to have impressions about how your particular outboard starts, runs, sounds, smells, and steers, and the temperature on different parts of the engine after it warms up. If you observe and recall how the engine acts when it is running well, you'll notice immediately if it begins to misbehave.

Take temperatures, for example. Since the hottest object a person can hold onto with a bare hand is 140°F (60°C), this natural thermometer in your hands can be a real help if overheating becomes a problem. Learn the normal temperatures of the different parts of your equipment, and if you find any part is too hot to touch, you'll know you've got a problem.

Did you ever notice that a small stream of bypassed cooling water runs out of your outboard when your engine is moving through the water? This stream is a clue that the cooling system is doing its job. If the water stops, it is time to stop, tilt the outboard, and check for blockage of the water inlet on the lower unit. If the inlet is clear, then the water pump may have failed. Also, in very cold weather in saltwater applications, ice can build up and block the water outlet opening above the waterline.

When an outboard engine fails to start, it's a good idea to check fuel flow first. Simply unhook the fuel line where it enters the carburetor or fuel injector housing and see if fuel flows into a jar when you crank the engine. If there is fuel flow, then hold the jar up and look for water lying below the fuel. If there is no fuel flow, then check the fuel level in the tank and squeeze the bulb. Pump the bulb a few times and see what happens. No fuel means there is a problem in the fuel pump, fuel line, or the tank itself. Also, a plugged fuel screen can certainly make you late for the barbecue! To check it, remove the fasteners on the cover of the fuel screen that are close to the carburetor or fuel injector.

When an engine cranks but will not start, check for spark using a good spare spark plug. Instead of removing the engine's spark plugs, use an extra plug and connect the spark plug wire to it and ground it on the cylinder head while cranking the engine (see Fig. 10-10). Leaving the spark plugs in their respective cylinders for the time being will keep debris out of the cylinders that could scratch the cylinder walls.

It is important never to try to start an engine with a spark plug wire ungrounded. The reason for this is that an ignition system with an ungrounded plug wire is something like a hydraulic pump that has its outlet opening plugged; if you turn the pump on, something will break. The newer outboard ignition systems are powerful! When a spark plug wire is unhooked, there is no easy ground path for the high voltage. The high voltage must go somewhere, and if it goes to ground through the wrong part of the ignition system, it can fry something. If there is no spark, then be sure there are 12 volts available to the ignition system.

Turning the engine flywheel by hand allows you to feel the pistons come up on the compression stroke. If compression isn't evident, there may be a hole in a piston. It will pay to remove the spark plugs at this point and look in each cylinder for a clue.

On four-stroke engines, a failed camshaft timing belt will make it impossible to start the engine. It's an easy visual check. Also, a cog belt that is close to failure will be cracked on the inside of the belt next to the cog. The neutral safety switch can be a source of starting problems if it gets sticky, because it is in the circuit between the starter switch and the starter.

Of course, you could have a dead battery or corroded battery posts. A bad battery cannot take or hold a full charge. The most basic alternator test is to check the battery voltage before starting the engine. After it starts, check the voltage again. If the alternator is working, voltage should increase by one to three volts.

LOW POWER PROBLEMS

The all-time winner for low power complaints on any type of engine-driven equipment is the lowly throttle linkage. If there isn't full travel of the throttle at the engine when the throttle lever is at its full power position, then low power will result. The way to check this is to pull the throttle control to full throttle (with the engine off) and then look and see if you can pull any more travel at the engine.

Another problem on four-stroke outboards is a timing belt that is one cog off the correct setting. Usually, a cog belt gets that way because it was improperly installed. A piece of line in the propeller can be another troublemaker, but fortunately that is easy to check!

OUTBOARD MAINTENANCE

There is a lot of dust over water, even over the ocean. Regular air filter service is important. Regular changes of the lube oil and filter as well as fuel filters, if so equipped, are vital to four-strokes. Also, two-stroke engines require either oil mixed with the fuel in older engines or the oil level maintained in the oil injection tank.

Change lower unit oil regularly to keep water out of the gear lube in the lower unit. Because *all* outboard lower units are vented to the atmosphere from the top of the unit, there will always be condensed moisture coming in. Oil changes are the only way to keep water out of a lower unit.

Fuel injection is used on higher horsepower engines while smaller ones use carburetors. Fuel conditioner should be used for long-term storage to prevent gum deposits. The gum is actually a microorganism that develops in old gasoline, and it is the outboard motor's biggest problem. When gasoline is bad, it smells like turpentine. If it sits for longer than one month, the best prevention for gum deposit problems is to drain the float bowls.

Check valve lash every 200 hours on four-stroke engines or at the interval recommended in the service manual. Four-stroke engines need regular valve adjustments for long engine life and best performance. There are plastic and stainless steel feeler gauges available to do this job. Regular ferrous metal feeler gauges won't last around the water. There is easily a 3 to 5 hp penalty for a sloppy valve adjustment on a 100 hp outboard.

If the need arises to remove the cylinder head from your outboard—for example to check the pistons for holes and the cylinder walls for scratches—be sure to remove the cylinder head bolts in the order specified by the service manual. This can prevent warping a cylinder head. Before reinstalling the head, clean the boltholes and remove all oil, coolant, or foreign matter. Visually inspect each bolthole for cracks or weak threads before reinstalling the head.

FOUR-STROKE GASOLINE ENGINES

Interpretation of vacuum gauge readings: Before the engine is vacuum tested, all obvious causes of vacuum leaks must be repaired and the engine must be warmed up. Vacuum testing is one of the best troubleshooting techniques for inboard/outboard (IO) engines and outboard motors. Before beginning the test, set the engine's idle speed to the factory specification.

The place on the engine where vacuum testing (Fig. 10-19) takes place is on the intake manifold. The intake manifold is the area between the throttle plates and the upstream side of the intake valves. Inside this space

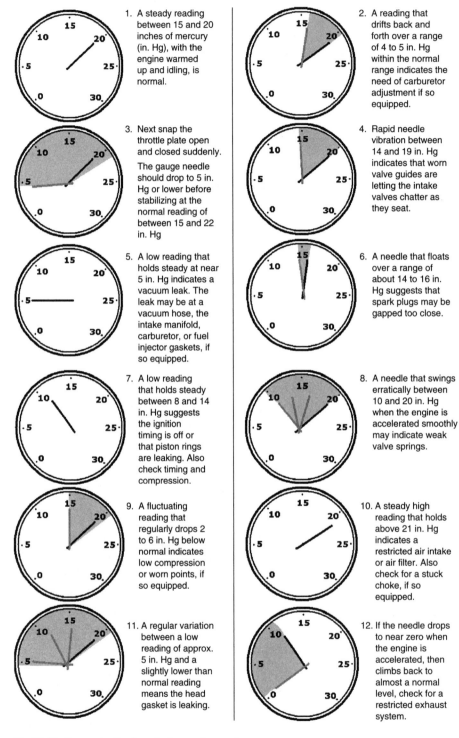

1. A steady reading between 15 and 20 inches of mercury (in. Hg), with the engine warmed up and idling, is normal.

2. A reading that drifts back and forth over a range of 4 to 5 in. Hg within the normal range indicates the need of carburetor adjustment if so equipped.

3. Next snap the throttle plate open and closed suddenly. The gauge needle should drop to 5 in. Hg or lower before stabilizing at the normal reading of between 15 and 22 in. Hg

4. Rapid needle vibration between 14 and 19 in. Hg indicates that worn valve guides are letting the intake valves chatter as they seat.

5. A low reading that holds steady at near 5 in. Hg indicates a vacuum leak. The leak may be at a vacuum hose, the intake manifold, carburetor, or fuel injector gaskets, if so equipped.

6. A needle that floats over a range of about 14 to 16 in. Hg suggests that spark plugs may be gapped too close.

7. A low reading that holds steady between 8 and 14 in. Hg suggests the ignition timing is off or that piston rings are leaking. Also check timing and compression.

8. A needle that swings erratically between 10 and 20 in. Hg when the engine is accelerated smoothly may indicate weak valve springs.

9. A fluctuating reading that regularly drops 2 to 6 in. Hg below normal indicates low compression or worn points, if so equipped.

10. A steady high reading that holds above 21 in. Hg indicates a restricted air intake or air filter. Also check for a stuck choke, if so equipped.

11. A regular variation between a low reading of approx. 5 in. Hg and a slightly lower than normal reading means the head gasket is leaking.

12. If the needle drops to near zero when the engine is accelerated, then climbs back to almost a normal level, check for a restricted exhaust system.

Fig. 10-19. **Vacuum testing four-stroke gasoline engines.**

within the engine there is only filtered air and fuel, at least when all is well. *(Note: This kind of vacuum testing will not work on a diesel engine. Because marine diesels do not have throttle plates, there is seldom a vacuum in the diesel's intake manifold. Be sure to check all of the information in the troubleshooting section in the engine service manual for your particular engine.)*

SURVEYING MARINE ENGINES AND TRANSMISSIONS

When buying a used boat, a careful inspection can reveal potential problems. You should never rely on your own expertise, even if you think you are qualified. Always hire a professional surveyor. However, it is very helpful to understand what to look for in a boat's engine and transmission *before* paying for an expensive professional survey. The following information will point out some of the more important things to check.

Oil filter: After you've done your homework about what kind of engine is in the boat, arrive for the inspection with a new oil filter for the engine and a filter wrench. If the seller is on the level, there will be no problem about taking his existing oil filter home so you can cut it open to look for signs of trouble. Turn the filter upside down and let it drain overnight. Then cut it open (Fig. 10-20) and inspect the filter media for aluminum, iron, or excess soot.

Fluid levels: Check the oil levels in the engine and transmission, and the coolant level too.

Oil color: Open the oil filler cap and shine a bright light in the opening. Make note of any cream-colored oil that has water emulsified in it. This will tell you the engine might have a little coolant in the oil.

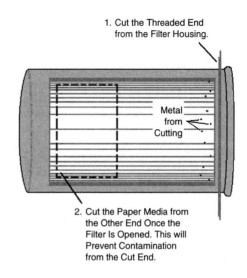

1. Cut the Threaded End from the Filter Housing.

Metal from Cutting

2. Cut the Paper Media from the Other End Once the Filter Is Opened. This will Prevent Contamination from the Cut End.

Fig. 10-20. Cut open the oil filter to learn the engine's condition.

Water in oil: Loosen the oil drain plug and turn it outward only one full turn; don't take it all the way out. Now notice what comes into view. There should be no water present, only oil. If, however, water is the first thing that drips out of the threads, then the engine has water in the oil and you should consider the engine only a rebuildable core, not a functional engine.

Crankshaft: Turn the engine crankshaft two complete revolutions by hand. Feel for tight spots in the movements and verify that the engine will indeed turn two revolutions. This proves the engine is ready to start.

Intake manifold plug: If the engine is turbocharged, find a plug on the intake manifold downstream of the turbocharger and remove it. Look at the end of the plug to check its condition. It should be clean and bone-dry, and it should have no oil on it. An oily intake plug indicates oil leaking from the center section of the turbocharger into the cold side (intake side) of the turbocharger. Next, even if the intake plug is dry and clean, shine a light into the manifold and verify that it is also clean and dry.

Engine mounts: Check for loose engine mount bolts and shims under the mounting feet. If mounts or shims are loose, there may be a soft foot (see Chapter 17).

Antifreeze: Check the antifreeze with a tester to get an idea if the engine has been well maintained.

Air filter: Check the air filter for evidence of a lot of black soot. A soot-plugged air filter indicates an exhaust leak. If the engine has been operated with a plugged air filter, there may be a lot of fuel in the oil. An oil analysis will show if there is fuel in the oil.

Oil test: If the engine is operational, warm it up and take an oil sample to send to an oil lab.

Watch the engine smoke when it is running. White smoke indicates low compression, and black smoke indicates a plugged air filter or sluggish turbocharger. Notice the oil pressure when the engine is cold and hot. Be sure the pressure is no less than 25 psi at low idle when the engine is warm, or check the engine manufacturer's specification.

Oil pan: Notice if there is a watermark on the oil pan (inside or out), which will show the bilge water has been deep for some reason.

Transmission wear metal: Check the transmission screen, which is on the suction side of the oil pump. You may need to read the transmission service manual to find the screen. A slight amount of wear metal is normal for a transmission with under 1,000 hours on it or one that was just rebuilt. More than just a few small pieces of wear metal indicate a problem and reduces the transmission to rebuildable core status.

CHAPTER 11

TROUBLESHOOTING WITH THE FIVE SENSES: DIESEL ENGINES

Most of us are familiar with traditional methods of troubleshooting onboard systems, as discussed in the previous chapter. When something goes wrong, it becomes painfully obvious. There is a horrifying noise, a burning smell, a mysterious appearance of water in the bilge. All you want to know at that moment is what happened and how to fix the problem. Yet, there is far more to good troubleshooting than a gut-level reactive response, and, for that matter, there is far more to good boat maintenance as well.

Professional marine mechanics prevent problems using their five senses. They look, listen, sniff, taste, and touch, hovering over a system like a hunter stalking prey. One or more of the five senses can tell the mechanic quite a lot about what may or may not be happening with a given system, and knowing the signs of impending problems goes a long way in heading them off at the proverbial pass. When something does go wrong, in spite of the mechanic's vigilance, the five senses play an important role in helping to diagnose the problem.

The following five chapters will take you through a unique approach to troubleshooting and maintenance by showing you how you can put your five senses to work. The same terms and vocabulary you will find in service manuals and hear when discussing problems and remedies with mechanics have been included deliberately. Professionals will recognize the terms and vocabulary, but recreational mariners may not and will need to know both in order to communicate effectively when calling a mechanic.

This chapter provides a lengthy and detailed look at diesel engines; Chapter 12 covers gasoline engines; Chapter 13 addresses systems in the cabin and engine room; Chapter 14 deals with transmissions and power-take-offs; and Chapter 15 takes you through steering as well as engine speed and transmission controls. In short, you will have all the information you need to prevent or respond to problems like a professional. In fact, these chapters are almost like having a seasoned professional on board with you as you puzzle through the sometimes baffling situations that come up on every boat, be it large or small.

These chapters have been crafted to make it as easy as possible for you to access the information. For example, this chapter is all about using your five senses to troubleshoot your diesel engine. The chapter is broken down into parts, each dedicated to a particular subsystem related to your diesel. Under each of these you will find a series of *symptoms* organized according to which of the five senses you would use to identify a problem or potential problem. If you see black smoke billowing out the exhaust pipe, naturally that symptom would fall under troubleshooting by sight. Following the symptoms are sub-headings that will tell you how *urgent* the problem is, what *suggested actions* you should take to address it, and *background* material on what may have caused it.

ENGINE PERFORMANCE

WHAT YOU SEE

ENGINE TAKES LONGER THAN NORMAL TO REACH FULL SPEED IN GEAR

Urgency: Not urgent, but should be monitored

Suggested actions:

1. Check for a plugged air or fuel filter.
2. Check for line or other obstruction on the propeller.
3. Check the engine service manual for recommendations.
4. Check the bottom of the boat for fouling.
5. If there were recent repairs, contact your marine mechanic.

The problem may also result from insufficient throttle travel due to a faulty governor control linkage, a poorly adjusted throttle control, or even something like a bolt that's too long and causes a restriction of the governor control at the engine. A propeller of incorrect size is another possibility.

ENGINE HEATS UP FASTER THAN USUAL, THEN OVERHEATS

Urgency: Requires immediate attention
Suggested actions:

1. Shut the engine down. When it cools, be sure the cooling system is full and the belts on the belt-driven water pump are tight.

2. Look for any possible restriction of coolant or raw-water flow.
3. Check the engine service manual for cooling system troubleshooting information.

Other causes include a faulty thermostat, the water pump not turning at full speed (belt slipping), or the coolant pump's metal impeller slipping on the pump shaft.

ENGINE TAKES LONGER THAN NORMAL TO WARM UP

Urgency: Not urgent, but should be monitored

Suggested actions:

1. Conduct a stovetop test on the thermostat. As previously mentioned, simply place the thermostat in a saucepan full of water, heat the water, and use a meat thermometer to verify that the thermostat opens at the correct water temperature.
2. Replace the thermostat if necessary.

The thermostat's opening temperature will be stamped on it. To see if the thermostat opens, watch its center section for a slight gap that opens and grows wider as the temperature increases. If the thermostat opens late (at a higher temperature than its rating), replace it.

ENGINE QUICKLY GOES TO FULL SPEED WHEN PUT IN GEAR AND FULL THROTTLE IS APPLIED, BUT THE BOAT IS SLOW TO ACCELERATE

Urgency: Not urgent, but should be monitored

Suggested actions:

1. Double-check the pitch and diameter of the prop.
2. If the boat has an extremely shallow draft, it may need a cupped-out four-blade propeller.

The problem is most likely with the propeller, particularly if it happens after a propeller change. There may not be enough wheel pitch and/or diameter. If the boat has always behaved this way, then it may have never had the correct propeller. Check with your local propeller shop for recommendations.

WORK-AROUND SOLUTION

Stopping a Runaway Diesel Engine

When an engine races beyond its normal governed top speed to the point where it will destroy itself, it's called a runaway. A runaway engine can fly apart and seriously injure anyone nearby. The pistons will hit the valves, often breaking them, and seconds later the connecting rods are likely to break apart too.

Take precautions against a runaway diesel engine any time fuel system governor work has been done. Before starting the engine after repairs, act as though you know it's going to become a runaway. Have strategies in mind so you can respond immediately. Here are some helpful tips to help you deal with a runaway engine:

1. Shut off the intake air supply. Never try to block an intake air passage with any part of your body! However, it may be possible to block the air filter inlet pipe with a piece of wood or the bottom of a plastic oil bucket. Even some heavy cardboard can help.

The best solution is to fabricate a shut-down paddle in advance to be ready for just such an emergency. Make it from aluminum or steel to cover the air intake on the engine. To be prepared in case you need to use it, wipe all dust away from around the engine's air intake where the air filter is attached. Remove the air filter before starting the engine to expose the end of a pipe that the paddle can seal against to positively stop the airflow if needed.

2. Shut off the fuel supply to the injection pump by breaking off the main fuel suction fitting going to the engine. Identify this fitting before you need to know where it is! Lay a two-pound hammer near the fitting in case the fitting must be broken.
3. Put a load on the engine to reduce engine speed. In some cases, it is possible to engage the power-take-off and the transmission at the same time. Doing this may buy some time. However, this option won't be much help if you have a runaway diesel generator.

Remember to stand more in front of the engine or behind it in case you cannot stop it! Internal pieces (shrapnel) of the engine will break out through both sides of the block and fly through the engine room. These pieces of engine will hurt you. If the engine can't be stopped, get away from it!

ENGINE RAPIDLY ACCELERATES OUT OF CONTROL, WITH AN INCREASING ROAR OF ENGINE SOUND

Urgency: Requires immediate attention
Suggested actions:

1. Using a shut-down paddle, shut off the air to the intake side of the engine.
2. Break off the most critical fuel fitting with the largest diameter in the fuel system.

Note: You've got to identify the correct fitting before you encounter this problem!

Runaway engines, also called overspeeds, occur most often because of rust inside the fuel injection pump, which causes the governor linkage to lock up in the full fuel position when the engine is shut off. When this happens, it becomes impossible to pull the throttle to low idle/or even to turn off the engine. The quickest way to stop a runaway engine is to place a shut-down paddle over the engine's air intake.

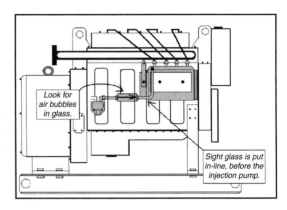

Look for air bubbles in glass.

Sight glass is put in-line, before the injection pump.

Fig. 11-1. Insert a sight glass before the injection pump.

ENGINE "HUNTS" OR THE SPEED SURGES AT HIGHER RPM

Urgency: Attend to as soon as convenient
Suggested actions:

1. For two-stroke diesels this is often a tune-up issue that is resolved by adjusting the fuel system according to the engine manual.
2. Four-stroke engines will do this when the fuel filter is becoming plugged or the system is pulling air in with the fuel.

A faulty governor may be another cause.

ENGINE "HUNTS" OR THE SPEED SURGES AT LOWER RPM

Urgency: Attend to as soon as convenient
Suggested action: See previous symptom.

ENGINE CRANKS, BUT TAKES A VERY LONG TIME TO START

Urgency: Requires immediate attention
Suggested actions:

1. Check for air in the fuel system by plumbing a suitable temporary sight glass between the transfer pump

and the injection pump as shown in Figure 11-1.
2. Check the engine service manual troubleshooting section to learn more about the causes of hard starting.

Cold ambient temperatures or a weak starter are other likely suspects.

ENGINE RELUCTANT TO TURN OFF OR WON'T STOP AT ALL

Urgency: Requires immediate attention
Suggested action: Rust makes the mechanical fuel injection system hard to control. Suspect water in the fuel and follow up with the engine manual to troubleshoot this problem. *Diesel fuel injection systems with internal, spring-loaded electric shutoff solenoids may not shut off if the mechanical linkage between the solenoid and the pump gets rusty. Check the engine manual to determine how the engine is configured.*

RUST IS APPARENT ON THE OUTSIDE OF ENGINE AND TRANSMISSION

Urgency: Not urgent, but should be monitored

Suggested action: Watch for sources of water in the engine room.

Unpainted iron and steel will rust in the marine environment, but it will be much worse if the metal is exposed to salt spray. When an engine is positioned low in the bilge, bilge water can splash it in rough seas.

CORROSION VISIBLE ON ALUMINUM ENGINE COMPONENTS

Urgency: Not urgent, but should be monitored

Suggested action: Watch for sources of water in the engine room.

Exposing aluminum to salt spray or strong detergents will cause corrosion. Aluminum can be polished or cleaned with a very mild rotating abrasive pad to remove corrosion, or it can be sprayed with a cleaner such as Zep-a-lume. There are marine grades of aluminum that resist corrosion better than others. For best results, coat new aluminum, or aluminum that has been cleaned, with zinc chromate primer before painting.

VISIBLE WEAR ON EDGES OF A DRIVE BELT

Urgency: Not urgent, but should be monitored

Suggested actions:

1. Obtain a new belt and a spare, and change it when convenient.
2. Check belt idlers and belt-driven units like the alternator for proper belt tension and alignment.

Wear on the edge of a belt means either that the pulleys are misaligned or that something is rubbing on the side of the belt. When replacing a serpentine belt, be sure to diagram the layout of the belt first, noting where pulleys engage the rib side and the flat side of the belt.

WHAT YOU HEAR
ENGINE HAS DULL KNOCK

Urgency: Requires immediate attention
Suggested actions:

1. Have the engine oil analyzed routinely. It will help you spot trouble early.
2. Cut open the oil filter and inspect as previously described.
3. If metal is present in the filter, the oil pan must be removed to allow inspection of the connecting rods.

Bad rod bearings are noisy as they start to fail. They start out sounding dull, and the sound becomes sharper as the piston begins to travel farther upward in the cylinder and contacts the valves. A very loose (excess clearance) bearing can even let the piston slap the cylinder head.

ENGINE BEGINS KNOCKING SEVERELY

Urgency: Requires immediate attention
Suggested actions:

1. Stop the engine.
2. Cut open an oil filter to inspect for aluminum or iron in the oil.

When a foreign object gets on top of a piston, the engine will make a knocking noise. Also, overheated pistons expand to seize in the cylinder wall, and something has to give. What gives is usually the connecting rod or connecting rod bolts. After the rod breaks, the broken end swings around on the crankshaft and begins to behave like an out-of-control jackhammer. The side of the cylinder block can be broken out by this action, ejecting pieces with great force—sometimes great enough to injure or kill a person or to damage the other engine in a twin-engine installation. *Note: It is a good safety practice to avoid standing beside a running engine whenever possible. Should an engine blow up, it is better to be standing in front of or behind it.*

WHEN ATTEMPTING TO START THE ENGINE, THE ENGINE GOES "CLUNK" AND COMES UP HARD AGAINST SOMETHING, AND WILL NOT TURN ANY FARTHER

Urgency: Requires immediate attention
Suggested actions:

1. Unless recent repairs have been done, this will most likely be a hydraulic lock problem.
2. Use the engine service manual and the lists below to determine if there is a hydraulic lock and figure out how to clear it.

When fluid rises over the top of a piston (Fig. 11-2), the engine is said to have a hydraulic lock, and this will stop crankshaft movement until the fluid is removed. There are three ways to address this:

1. Remove all injectors and bar the engine over by hand, turning it two full revolutions of the crankshaft. This will pump out any fluid in the cylinders. (See Fig. 2-15 and the accompanying sidebar for information on barring an engine over.) *Note: The cylinders on all*

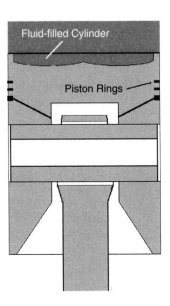

Fig. 11-2. Fluid over the top of a piston is known as a hydraulic lock.

four-stroke marine engines come up on a compression stroke within two revolutions of the crankshaft. Use caution because the fluid forcefully squirts out through the cylinder head injector holes!

2. If the engine is equipped with glow plugs, it is easier to remove them instead of the injectors and bar the engine over. This allows the fluid to be purged from the cylinder.
3. Another method is to make the exhaust valves leak temporarily, so the fluid is pumped out to the exhaust manifold when the engine is barred over. Remove the valve cover and identify the exhaust valve for each cylinder. Tighten the valve lash adjustment on each exhaust valve so that the valves are held open just a little (even when they're off-the-cam just a few thousandths of an inch). Now bar over the engine and the excess fluid will flow

out into the exhaust manifold through each cylinder's exhaust valve. **Caution:** Be sure to readjust the valve lash when the fluid is pumped from the cylinders. *Note: If the starter motor were used to turn the engine with fluid on top of a piston, severe damage could follow. This damage could include a bent connecting rod or a bent or cracked crankshaft.*

SHARP, METALLIC-SOUNDING NOISE WHEN STARTING COLD, DISAPPEARS WHEN WARM

Urgency: Attend to as soon as convenient
Suggested actions:

1. Cut open an oil filter and look for metal debris, the sign of a failure.
2. Consult the engine service manual and listen to similar engines in other boats.

If the sound goes away when the engine is warm, then it may be normal. Older engines with precombustion chambers will make a terrific clattering sound that is actually normal. Newer direct injection engines can also do this if air is coming in with the fuel. A seeming metallic knock can also be an injector that is atomizing poorly.

Every boat has a unique acoustical environment. The material the boat's hull is made of will greatly influence the sound of an engine. Older, heavy wooden hulls absorb mechanical noise, a metal hull reflects and even amplifies noise, and fiberglass hulls fall somewhere between these two extremes.

SHARP METALLIC KNOCK, ALL THE TIME

Urgency: Requires immediate attention

Suggested actions:

1. Stop the engine and cut open a filter. If there is metal in the filter, avoid starting the engine until repairs are made.
2. Remove the valve cover and look for a valve stem that stays lower than the rest. This is the sign of a bent valve.

The knock is probably due to a faulty rod bearing or something in the cylinder. After a faulty rod bearing gets enough slack in it, the piston on that cylinder will begin hitting the valves first and the head itself later on.

ENGINE HAS METALLIC CLICK

Urgency: Attend to as soon as convenient
Suggested action: Stop the engine and adjust the valve lash according to the engine manual specifications.

Loose valve adjustment may also be the problem.

HEAR CLICKING NOISE WHEN TRYING TO START ENGINE, BUT IT WILL NOT START

Urgency: Requires immediate attention
Suggested actions:

1. Check the DC electrical system's voltage. If it's a 12-volt system, the gauge should show 12 volts.
2. If voltage is low, check for a loose belt on the alternator.
3. Turn off the battery switch and clean both ends of all battery cables.
4. Try jumping the starter on the engine. Jumping means temporarily connecting the starter solenoid pull-in, or energizing, terminal to the positive battery

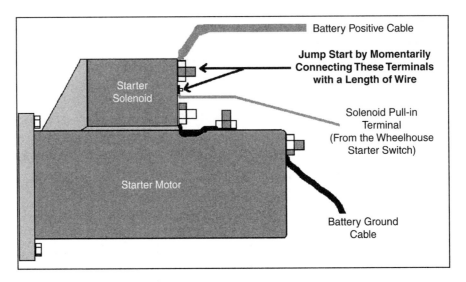

Battery Positive Cable

**Jump Start by Momentarily
Connecting These Terminals
with a Length of Wire**

Starter
Solenoid

Solenoid Pull-in
Terminal
(From the Wheelhouse
Starter Switch)

Starter Motor

Battery Ground
Cable

Fig. 11-3. Bypassing the starter switch.

cable lug on the solenoid as shown in Figure 11-3.

5. If all else fails, have the starter solenoid and starter motor bench-tested at an auto parts store, or replace them both.

Clicking without the engine starting usually means there is low voltage to the starter motor or battery terminal connections are dirty. A dirty battery case can drain the battery between the posts. Be sure to keep the battery clean!

ENGINE HAS HIGH-PITCHED SQUEAL

Urgency: Requires immediate attention

Suggested action: Stop the engine and tighten all intake manifold and exhaust system bolts to specifications.

Steel shim gaskets in either the intake or exhaust system can work like the reed in a clarinet. Tighten all fasteners on both the intake and exhaust sides of the cylinder head.

SLIGHT BUT DEFINITE CHANGE IN SOUND OF ENGINE, TRANSMISSION, OR GENERATOR

Urgency: Attend to as soon as convenient

Suggested actions:

1. Cut open filters from the engine and the transmission and inspect. Again, metal means damage.
2. Generator: Inspect the bearing (known as the single bearing).
3. Tighten the coupling bolts between the engine and generator.

Fuel in the oil can also cause this problem, as can a turbocharger impeller contacting its housing. The impeller should not touch the housing.

STARTER MOTOR SOUNDS LIKE GEARS STRIPPING

Urgency: Requires immediate attention

Suggested actions:

1. Replace the starter as soon as possible.
2. To get the engine to start one more time, turn the crankshaft one-quarter turn and see if the starter drive will engage enough teeth to start the engine.
3. Remove the starter to inspect the flywheel and starter drive teeth.

The starter drive may not be engaging the flywheel due to bad teeth on the starter drive or on the flywheel ring gear.

ENGINE HAS "RAPPING" NOISE NEAR THE FRONT, BUT DOWN LOW

Urgency: Requires immediate attention
Suggested actions:

1. Cut open the oil filter and inspect. This may be a timing gear failure.
2. Check the tightness of the front crankshaft damper bolts.
3. Listen to the alternator and water pump to hear if the noise is coming from a faulty bearing inside these components.
4. Check the engine service manual to see how the front of the engine is constructed, and what might be causing noise there.

Be mindful of the position of the engine's timing gear and of the end of the engine where the oil pump is driven. Noise low on the front of the engine can be associated with these two components. Other potential sources of noise from this location are the crankshaft damper and pulley, where they are connected to the crankshaft, and also something loose in a front-mounted power-take-off arrangement.

SQUEALING AT FRONT OF ENGINE

Urgency: Requires immediate attention
Suggested action: Stop the engine and check all drive belts for adequate tightness.

A slipping alternator belt or an alternator that is beginning to fail, or has failed, can cause this kind of noise, especially if the alternator has a locked-up bearing. As mentioned above, a shim-type intake or exhaust side gasket on the cylinder head can also make a terrible racket.

LOUD RUMBLING NOISE NEAR ENGINE STARTER

Urgency: Requires immediate attention
Suggested actions:

1. The noise may be the starter drive staying engaged with the flywheel. Stop the engine, turn off the battery power to the starter, and remove the starter to inspect the starter drive gear. Check to see if the gear or the flywheel ring gear teeth show signs of extreme wear.
2. If the starter is fine, check the tightness of the flywheel bolts.

When the starter drive (also known as the Bendix) stays engaged in the flywheel, it will cause an ominous rumbling.

"BELCHING" NOISE INSIDE THE ENGINE AFTER RUNNING FOR A SHORT TIME, THEN STOPS

Urgency: Not urgent
Suggested action: None.

This kind of noise is normal on some engines. It happens when freshly pumped lube oil is pumped into the lubrication system after an engine starts. The oil displaces the air pockets that formed as cavities in the lube oil system the last time the engine was turned off.

ENGINE LETS OUT A LOUD "SQUAWK" AND THEN LOCKS UP (STOPS TURNING)

Urgency: Requires immediate attention
Suggested action: Severe overheating or a mechanical failure inside the engine will cause this sound. Follow engine manual suggestions.

Piston, rod bearing, or main bearing seizure will suddenly stop an engine. Cut open the oil filter and check for metal fragments. Engine seizures like this usually require the cylinder head or heads to be removed as part of the troubleshooting procedure.

WHEN THE ENGINE IS PLACED IN GEAR, IT SOUNDS LIKE IT LUGS BADLY AND THEN DIES WITHOUT TURNING THE PROPELLER SHAFT

Urgency: Requires immediate attention
Suggested actions:

1. Check for line in the propeller by attempting to turn the propeller shaft with a pipe wrench.
2. Check the transmission filter for the presence of metal, which indicates a failure.

Shaft brake problems, if so equipped, line in the wheel, or broken gear teeth in the transmission can stop an engine. However, the engine may have just run out of fuel as it was put in gear. Check the fuel level and try it again.

ENGINE SOUNDS LIKE IT IS SPINNING WELL, BUT THERE IS NO SOUND OF IT TRYING TO START

Urgency: Requires immediate attention
Suggested actions:

1. Verify the shutoff lever, if so equipped, is in the run position.
2. Verify the energize-to-run feature, if so equipped, of electronic injection pumps is energized.
3. Verify all fuel valves are open and the engine is getting fuel.
4. Fully prime and bleed the air from the fuel system according to the engine manual instructions.
5. Check the engine manual for troubleshooting hard starting.

A mechanical fuel shutoff or compression release lever that is not returning to the run position will make it impossible for the engine to start. Find the mechanical shutoff lever, if so equipped, and check its movement. Make sure it is in the run position.

ENGINE WITH STANADYNE DB2 OR DB4 FUEL SYSTEM STARTS, THEN IMMEDIATELY DIES, OR WON'T START AT ALL

Urgency: Requires immediate attention
Suggested action: Check for pressure on the return side of the fuel system.

These Stanadyne fuel injection systems will shut off the engine if pressure develops on the return side of the system. One of the most important things to check in either a DB2 or

DB4 configuration is the fuel return line. If the fuel line is blocked or obstructed in any way, the engine will not run. Check the energize-to-run solenoid, or determine if the injection pump uses an energize-to-stop solenoid.

SQUEAKY SERPENTINE BELT, SQUEAK GOES AWAY WHEN BELT IS SPRAYED WITH STARTING FLUID OR WATER

Urgency: Not urgent, but should be monitored

Suggested action: Replace the serpentine belt and idlers. This should stop the belt from squeaking.

According to belt manufacturers, all belt idlers should be replaced with the belt.

TROUBLESHOOTING BY TOUCH

A NEW ENGINE VIBRATION IS NOTICED

Urgency: Requires immediate attention

Suggested actions:

1. Hold a glass of water on a flat spot on both the front and rear of the engine while it is running. On a big engine, the ripples will be more pronounced where the vibrations are the most intense. (On a small engine the vibrations are more general.) Run the engine at slow and high speeds to see which throttle setting causes the worst vibrations.
2. Ascertain whether the vibration is present only when the transmission is engaged. If so, the transmission is the likely source of the vibration. If this is the case, determine whether the vibration is worse in forward or reverse gear.
3. Check for loose mounting bolts and fasteners on the engine and transmission, especially around the propeller shaft coupling to the transmission.
4. Check the front crankshaft vibration damper pulley and any other pulleys for slack, and if any is found consult the service manual.

Loose mounting bolts can allow movement and vibrations. A soft engine mounting foot (Fig. 11-4), one that is bearing less than its intended share of engine weight, will also cause vibration problems and can even cause engine failure if one corner of the engine and transmission mounting system is lower or higher than the others. A soft foot should be shimmed, not tightened. When all four mounting bolts are tightened in response to vibrations caused by a soft foot, the engine casting bends, which also bends the bore in which the crankshaft turns. When the bending of the bore gets too severe, vibration will occur. If any engine mount foot seems to spring upward when its bolt is loosened, it is a soft foot. Have a marine mechanic check it.

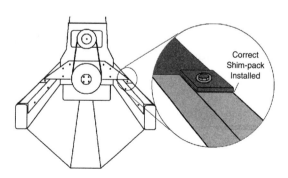

Fig. 11-4. A soft foot will need to be shimmed with off-the-shelf or fabricated sheet-metal shims stacked to the needed thickness.

ON ENGINE VIBRATIONS

Some engines will normally vibrate at a certain speed. For example, an engine may vibrate near 1,150 rpm, but as the speed increases the engine settles down and runs smoothly. Therefore, not all engine vibrations indicate a problem. However, a change in any engine's vibration pattern may indicate trouble. If you notice a change, the first thing to do is cut open the oil filter and look for metal particles.

WHEN YOU HOLD A GLASS OF WATER ON A FLAT SPOT ON THE TRANSMIS-SION OR REAR OF ENGINE, RIPPLES ON THE WATER SHOW THAT REAR OF ENGINE SHAKES MUCH MORE THAN THE FRONT

Urgency: Requires immediate attention
Suggested actions:

1. Perform the checks discussed with the preceding symptom. (On a small engine, the vibrations are more general and harder to localize.)
2. Watch for any visible wobble in the propeller shaft as it turns. There should be none.
3. If there is any wobble in the shaft, vibrations should occur only when the transmission is engaged. Check engine and shaft alignment.
4. Check the transmission suction screen.
5. If the problem persists, remove the starter motor and pry gently on the flywheel to verify that it is tightly fastened to the crankshaft. If the fly-wheel is loose in its housing, it must be removed and repaired according to the engine service manual.

If recent work has been done in the area, it should be rechecked. Be sure to check all engine mounting bolts for tightness and for proper flywheel installation.

VIBRATION AT THE FRONT OF THE ENGINE

Urgency: Attend to as soon as convenient
Suggested actions:

1. If applicable, check the engine's front-mounted power-take-off for vibration and for tightness of the fasteners.
2. Check the front crankshaft pulley hub and vibration damper as well as all retaining bolts and fasteners.
3. Check the front engine mounts and the power-take-off mounts, if so equipped.

Vibration at the front of the engine may indicate looming problems. Do not wait too long to investigate.

WHEN CHECKING FOR VIBRATIONS, ENGINE'S FRONT POWER-TAKE-OFF (PTO), IF SO EQUIPPED, SHAKES MORE THAN THE TRANSMISSION

Urgency: Not urgent, but should be monitored
Suggested actions:

1. Check that the front motor mount bolts are tight. Tighten if needed. *Note: Most engine manuals provide a bolt-tightening table based on the diameter and grade of the bolt.*
2. Verify that the crankshaft vibration damper pulley is tight and running true on the crankshaft or hub.
3. Read the engine service manual and consult a marine mechanic if needed.

FLYWHEEL TIGHTENING PROCEDURE

When the mating surfaces between the crankshaft and flywheel are damaged or dirty, misalignment will occur. Misalignment will cause the flywheel to wobble and vibrate.

Similarly, when flywheel housings are installed off-center or cannot seat perfectly flat on the cylinder block, there will be misalignment that may damage the transmission or an engine-mounted generator.

Flywheel wobble can also occur when the flywheel is bolted improperly to the crankshaft—when the bolts are not tightened alternately with increasing torque. This can cause imbalance even though the mating surfaces are clean and flat when bolted. When installing a flywheel or flywheel housing, verify that you are using the proper bolts and gently file the mating surfaces totally flat. Start tightening the bolts with very little torque, alternating across the bolt pattern until the bolts are tightened to full torque (see illustration). Use the manufacturer's suggested tightening pattern if it is available. *Note: Some manufacturers require new flywheel bolts every time the bolts are removed.*

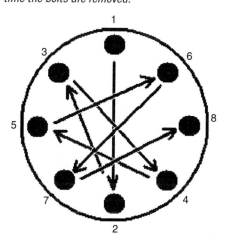

Fig. 11-5. **Suggested pattern for tightening flywheel bolts.**

If you have done everything by the book and the flywheel still has too much wobble (according to your service manual), loosen the bolts. If you kept track of the first bolt you tightened, you can start by tightening the opposite bolt in the bolt circle first. This will often cure a wobble and the resulting vibration. If all such efforts fail, consult the engine manual for directions on checking for a bent crankshaft.

A PTO is any place on the engine where a pulley or some other arrangement is turning to power an accessory. Often, the boat's steering pump is powered by an engine PTO. A PTO that has excessive run-out (appears to wobble off-center) or that is out of balance will vibrate.

ENGINE VIBRATION AT LOW SPEED
Urgency: Attend to as soon as convenient
Suggested actions:

1. Check to see if the starter is still engaged in the flywheel (it should not be), and that the flywheel is tightly mounted to the crankshaft (it should be). See also Figure 11-6.
2. Confirm that the transmission drive adapter is attached properly to the flywheel and that the elastomer drive member is intact and properly attached. The elastomer drive is a synthetic drive cushion that some propulsion engines have between the engine flywheel and the transmission. The cushion protects the transmission from engine vibrations.
3. Check for a loose front crankshaft damper or pulley. Tighten the bolts as needed.

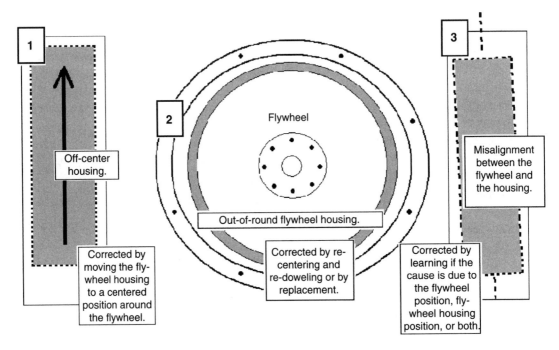

Fig. 11-6. Flywheel housing and possible problems.

4. Check engine mounts to make sure they are intact and that all bolts are tight.

One or more cylinders misfiring or not firing at all will also cause engine vibration.

ENGINE VIBRATION AT MEDIUM SPEED
Urgency: Attend to as soon as convenient
Suggested action: See previous symptom.

A starter that stays engaged in the flywheel will damage both the starter and the ring gear. The flywheel ring gear will eventually fail because of where the engine tends to come to rest when turned off. If the engine was recently repaired or rebuilt, confirm that the correct pistons, rods, and wrist pins were used.

ENGINE VIBRATION AT HIGH SPEED
Urgency: Attend to as soon as convenient
Suggested action: See the last two symptoms.

PULLEYS OR HUBS APPEAR TO WOBBLE AND DON'T SEEM TO RUN TRUE
Urgency: Attend to as soon as convenient
Suggested actions:

1. If a vibration accompanies the visible wobbling of a pulley or hub, stop the engine immediately and investigate by gently prying on the part in question. Obvious slack indicates loose bearings.
2. If bearings are loose, consult the service manual or a mechanic.
3. Check for an oil leak in the area where the piece is wobbling. If oil is leaking,

FLYWHEEL AND FLYWHEEL HOUSING PROBLEMS, RING GEAR DAMAGE

Flywheel ring gear wear takes place over time as the starter drive jumps out and wrenches the engine to life during starting. Wear patterns will differ depending on the number of cylinders in the engine. See Figure 10-12.

On a four-cylinder engine, for example, every time the engine is turned off it is likely that the flywheel will come to rest with one of two possible areas directly in front of the starter drive gear. Therefore, a four-cylinder engine will have two spots of high wear opposite each other on the ring gear. A six-cylinder engine will have three areas of high wear, and a V-8 engine will have four. In time, this worn area will shorten the life of the starter drive gear. If you find yourself frequently installing new starters on your engine, it is time to inspect the flywheel ring gear and take action if wear is detected.

To correct ring gear wear, first remove the flywheel and put it on a block of wood before driving the old starter ring gear off with a hammer and chisel. To install the new ring gear, locate the front face of the ring gear before the installation. Then heat the gear to 350°F and drop it in place on the flywheel. Heating the ring gear expands it enough to allow it to drop into position without any hammering. When the ring gear cools to the same temperature as the flywheel, an interference fit will hold it in place.

When a new ring gear is not available, I have seen old-timers remove the damaged ring gear, turn it 20 degrees, and reinstall it on the flywheel. This gives the teeth on the starter drive gear a new area to engage. This solution will usually work until a new ring gear can be obtained.

the bearings and possibly the shaft must be repaired when the seal is replaced.

4. If there is no vibration or oil leak, continue to run the equipment until a mechanic can check it.

Sometimes castings, like a rotating crankshaft pulley, may have a rough (unmachined) portion that may appear lopsided when there is really nothing wrong. Also, the pulley may appear to have excess run-out, when in fact there is no problem. Run-out is defined as a piece of machinery rotating off-center.

OIL AND FUEL SYSTEMS

WHAT YOU SEE
ENGINE OIL IS BLACK AND VERY THICK (MORE VISCOUS THAN NORMAL)

Urgency: Attend to as soon as convenient
Suggested action:

Change the oil and filter when convenient and shorten the oil change interval by 50 hours.

Thick, black engine oil indicates either that the oil change interval is too long or that the piston rings' sealing ability has been degraded. Poor ring sealing can result from a number of causes:

1. Installing the piston rings on the pistons by hand during an engine rebuild can slightly bend the ring so that it is not round in the cylinder. A mechanic should always use a piston ring installer to uniformly expand the piston rings during a rebuild. An

even better practice is to install cylinder kits that come with the piston and rings preloaded in the cylinder liner.

2. Not breaking in the engine according to the engine manufacturer's directions can cause ring seating problems. For example, sometimes the engine must run the first few hundred hours with special break-in oil in the crankcase. Break-in oil allows a little more friction between the piston rings and the cylinder liner surface so that the surfaces of the rings mate properly with the inside of the cylinder liner.

3. Another cause of poor ring seating is the ingestion of abrasive dust due to a faulty air filter or a suction leak between the air filter and the turbocharger.

AIR-INTAKE PLUMBING LEAKS

There is an easy way to test the intake air system plumbing between the air filter and the engine for good seal integrity. Begin by starting the engine and letting it idle, then lightly spray all the joints in the air plumbing with starting fluid and see if the engine speed suddenly changes. A joint is any place in the intake air plumbing that has a gasket or an O-ring seal. Engine speed will fluctuate if the engine gets a whiff of the starting fluid. This indicates a leak that will allow dust to get into the cylinder and damage it. Dust can also enter the engine during repairs if openings aren't covered.

OIL IS BLACK, BUT APPEARS THIN AND DRIPS RAPIDLY FROM DIPSTICK

Urgency: Requires immediate attention
Suggested actions:

1. Change the oil and filter immediately, and shorten your oil change interval by 50 hours.
2. Cut the filter open and look for shards or flecks of metal. If any are found, it usually means extensive repairs are needed.

This condition suggests that soot or unburned fuel is getting past the piston rings and into the oil. When the oil is thinned by fuel, the oil film strength breaks down, causing severe metal-to-metal wear. Metal-to-metal wear puts metal particles in the lubricating oil. A portable viscosity tester (such as the model offered by the Exxon Mobil Corporation) can be used to check for soot or fuel contamination of the oil as described in the accompanying sidebar. If this test suggests fuel in the oil, look for the cause. The sources will vary based on engine construction, and the engine manual must be consulted.

ENGINE OIL REMAINS HONEY-COLORED EVEN WITH MANY HOURS ON THE OIL

Urgency: Attend to as soon as convenient
Suggested action: Verify at oil change time that the proper oil is used in the engine.

Honey-colored oil may be a reason to double-check the detergent level in the oil you are using. For non-synthetic diesel engine oil, it is usually a good sign when the oil blackens immediately after changing. This proves that the detergent level is high enough to keep soot and other

USING A PORTABLE VISCOSITY TESTER

To use the tester shown (Fig. 11-7), lay it flat on a level surface and fill the used oil reservoir with a sample of oil from the engine. Fill the new oil reservoir with the same brand and weight of oil as the used oil. *The next point is critical: Both oils must be precisely the same temperature.* The easiest way to do this is to let containers of the new and used oil sit in the same place for several hours before testing.

Overfill each reservoir slightly and let the excess flow through the small overflow passage into the overflow containers at the end of each reservoir. This ensures that both test reservoirs are holding precisely the same amount of oil.

Now tip the tester up on its beveled end and watch the oil flow down the grooves. When the new oil gets to the midpoint shown in the illustration, the used oil should be somewhere between points A and B. If the used oil is uphill of point A when the new oil is at the midpoint, there is too much soot in the oil, and the oil change interval must be shortened by 50 hours. At the end of this shortened interval, the oil should be retested. If the used oil has flowed all the way downhill past point B, there is fuel in the oil. Shorten the oil change interval by 50 hours and locate the source of the fuel contamination.

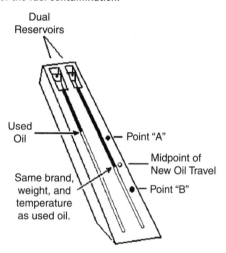

Fig. 11-7. The Exxon Mobil Corporation portable oil viscosity tester.

impurities suspended in the oil stream flowing through the oil filter. Too low a detergent level, as is typical of a cheap brand of oil meant for gasoline engines, may allow sludge to build up and cling to internal engine surfaces rather than being carried to the filter. There are several oil filtering options, as shown in Figure 11-8. See Chapter 5 for further discussion.

On the other hand, it is also possible, if your engine is fitted with superior aftermarket bypass (partial-flow) filtration, that this is a normal condition due to very clean engine oil. Synthetic oil stays clean much longer by resisting the heat and chemical breakdown that affects petroleum-based lube oil.

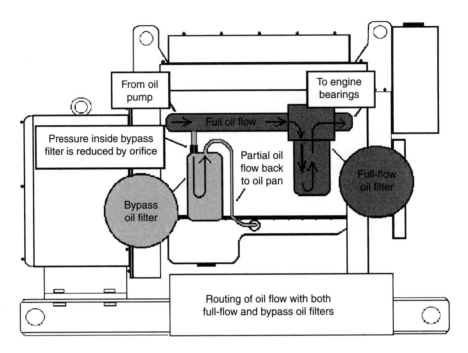

From oil pump

To engine bearings

Full oil flow

Pressure inside bypass filter is reduced by orifice

Partial oil flow back to oil pan

Full-flow oil filter

Bypass oil filter

Routing of oil flow with both full-flow and bypass oil filters

Fig. 11-8. Bypass and full-flow filtration.

DARK OIL DRIPS (LEAKS) SLOWLY FROM ENGINE

Urgency: Attend to as soon as convenient
Suggested actions:

1. Find the general location of the leak by narrowing it down to the left or right side, front or rear, or even the top or bottom of the engine.
2. After finding the general location, trace the leak to a gasket, fitting, or crack, then check your engine manual for instructions.

Dark oil leaking from an engine indicates a lube oil leak, but it's important to be careful on this point because it is also possible for fuel leaks to wash down the side of the block. If the fluid is thick, it's engine oil, but if it is very thin, it is fuel. (Refer to wet stacking under the following symptom.) In either case, pinpoint the source of the leak and make repairs.

CLEAR, THIN, OILY SUBSTANCE (FUEL) LEAKING FROM ENGINE

Urgency: Requires immediate attention
Suggested actions:

1. To avoid a fire hazard, immediately shut off the engine and see if the leakage slows or stops.
2. Wipe the area dry and then start the engine to pinpoint the location of the leak so that repairs can be made.

The path of the fuel running down the side of the engine will appear to shimmer when a light is held up to it, thus making it easier to spot. The source of a fuel leak can be a loose filter, loose fitting, a faulty gasket or seal, a crack in some part of the fuel system, or a fuel line that has cracked or rubbed through.

LIGHT BROWN OIL LEAKING FROM ENGINE OR TRANSMISSION

Urgency: Attend to as soon as convenient
Suggested actions:

1. Stop the engine and check the transmission oil level.
2. Follow the oil lines that run back and forth between the transmission and the oil cooler. This will help you pinpoint leaks so they can be repaired.
3. Check the opening in the bottom of the flywheel housing to see if the oil leak is coming from this area, indicating a leak from the front transmission oil seal.

Lighter-colored oil, as opposed to black oil, is from the transmission and may be an indication of a leak in an engine-mounted oil cooler. Oil leaking from the front oil seal requires removing the transmission to gain access to the seal.

BLACK OIL LEAKING FROM BETWEEN THE CYLINDER HEAD AND BLOCK

Urgency: Attend to as soon as convenient
Suggested actions:

1. Keep the oil level up in the engine until repairs can be made.
2. Check the service manual for instructions.

This leak could be from the oil supply port to the cylinder head valve mechanism, but there may also be a leak of oil that has circulated through the valve train and is draining through the cylinder head on its return to the oil pan. Replacement of the head gasket is often required to stop a leak like this.

BLACK OIL LEAKING FROM THE BOTTOM OF FLYWHEEL HOUSING

Urgency: Requires immediate attention
Suggested actions:

1. Keep the engine oil level up until repairs can be made.
2. The flywheel must be removed to permit inspection of the possible sources of the leak (Fig. 11-9).

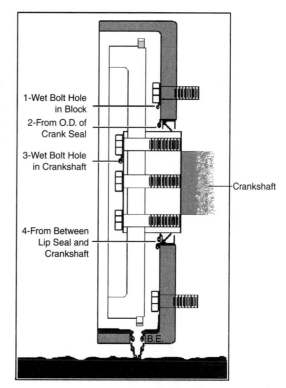

1-Wet Bolt Hole in Block

2-From O.D. of Crank Seal

3-Wet Bolt Hole in Crankshaft

Crankshaft

4-From Between Lip Seal and Crankshaft

Fig. 11-9. Potential sources of engine oil leaks in the flywheel housing.

The bottom of the flywheel housing can potentially leak either black oil (from the engine crankcase) or light brown oil (from the transmission). The source of black oil is most often the rear crankshaft oil seal (on the engine side of the flywheel). If crankcase pressure gets too high (above two pounds psi) due to a plugged or restricted engine crankcase vent, both the front and rear seals of the crankshaft may fail.

On the other hand, a generator engine can only leak dark oil from the flywheel housing because there is no oil in the generator side of the flywheel. This is one important area where a generator engine differs from a propulsion engine. Figure 7-18 (page 94) shows the flywheel housing and crankshaft seal arrangement used on every type of engine, regardless of whether the application is for propulsion or for generating electricity.

BROWN OR LIGHT-COLORED OIL LEAKING FROM BOTTOM OF FLY-WHEEL HOUSING

Urgency: Requires immediate attention
Suggested actions:

1. Check for a low oil level in the transmission and keep it full until repairs can be made.
2. Consult the transmission service manual for specific instructions.

For engines that power transmissions (as opposed to generators), a lighter-colored oil leaking from the flywheel housing indicates a transmission oil leak. The source is the transmission input shaft oil seal (Fig. 11-10) located on the transmission side of the flywheel.

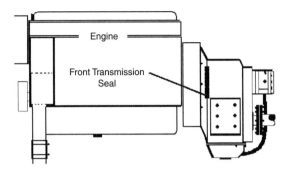

Fig. 11-10. The transmission input shaft oil seal on the front of the transmission.

OIL LEAK AT FRONT OF ENGINE, BEHIND CRANKSHAFT PULLEY OR AN ACCESSORY DRIVESHAFT PULLEY

Urgency: Attend to as soon as convenient
Suggested action: Keep the engine full of oil until repairs can be made.

The front crankshaft oil seal can leak, especially if crankcase pressure is high due to a plugged crankcase breather. Use a slide hammer to replace the seal (see Figure 7-19), or follow the service manual instructions.

METALLIC PARTICLES (GLITTER) IN ENGINE, HYDRAULIC SYSTEM, TRANSMISSION, OR THE OIL FILTER MEDIA PAPER

Urgency: Requires immediate attention
Suggested actions:

1. This is most likely a mechanical failure in progress. Consult the equipment manual and call a marine mechanic if possible.
2. If the engine must be run, operate it at the lowest possible speed.
3. If the sound of the engine changes, a failure is imminent. Remove the valve cover and inspect the valve train, looking for obvious damage.

Cutting open an oil filter is one of the best ways to learn the condition of an engine, transmission, or hydraulic system. The filter media shown in Figure 11-11 are from two different engines. Both engines were brand new (not rebuilt), with three hours of operating time. The filter paper on the right shows a normal amount of metal for a new engine that is still breaking in. Notice, though, that the paper on the left has more metal and is darker. The dark particles are rust from rain entering the exhaust pipe of the engine while it was stored. Two cylinders were badly rusted, and the engine was in the process of failing. The engine represented by the paper on the right would have had no more metal visible in the filter after the second oil change.

When flecks of metal are discovered in a filter after you cut it open, try to determine what type of metal it is. Brass or copper from crankshaft thrust bearings, on engines equipped with them, will be golden or yellow. Metal from aluminum (pistons on most engines) will be dull white. Metal from

abnormally high amount
of rust and metal

normal amount
of metal

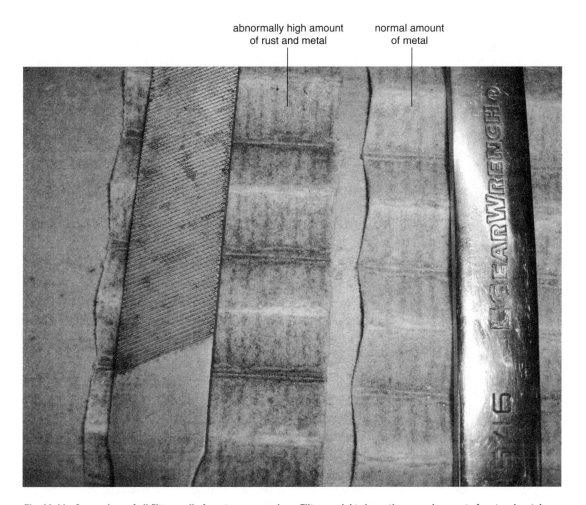

Fig. 11-11. Comparison of oil filter media from two new engines. Filter on right shows the normal amount of rust and metal.

chromium (piston rings) will be bright and shiny, while cast iron or steel from crankshaft, cylinder, or even cylinder block wear will be dull gray. Passing a clean magnet over the filter paper (media) will pick up flecks of ferrous (iron-containing) metal and flag your attention to potential problems. Be alert when the magnet attracts iron and steel particles, because some engines have either cast-iron or steel pistons. Reduction shafts, gears, and bearings are made of steel, and hydraulic pump gears are made of soft steel. A file will easily scratch gears made of soft steel.

FUEL TEST RESULTS PRINTOUT SHOWS LUBRICITY OF FUEL IS POOR

Urgency: Not urgent, but should be monitored

Suggested actions:

1. Add diesel fuel conditioner to the fuel and retest the fuel at the time of the next refill.
2. If the lubricity isn't up to specifications, find a new fuel supplier.

Modern diesel fuel is sometimes too "dry" for older diesel fuel injection systems designed for fuel lubrication. In the past, diesel fuel had much better lubricating qualities. When there is damage and wear in a fuel system from lack of lubrication, ultrafine metal particles will contaminate the diesel fuel tanks in small boats. If the engine's fuel injection pumps keep failing, it may be necessary to put a 2 micron fuel filter on the return line of the fuel system to keep the wear particles from circulating through a new fuel system. When there has been a failure such as this, it is important to install a new pump, new high-pressure fuel lines (if so equipped), and new injectors.

One major U.S. auto manufacturer recently came up with a fix for one of their diesel engines that was experiencing chronic fuel injection pump failures due to the low lubricity of the newer diesel fuel formulation. The fix included replacement of the injection pump, all eight injectors, and all eight high-pressure fuel lines to the injectors. The fuel tank also had to be removed and steam-cleaned. They also suggested motorists use Stanadyne diesel fuel conditioner in the fuel.

BLACK (SOOT) OR DARK (RUST) PARTICLES SEEN IN ENGINE OR TRANSMISSION LUBE OIL FILTER MEDIA WHEN THE FILTER IS CUT OPEN

Urgency: Not urgent, but should be monitored

Suggested actions:

1. For soot problems, shorten the oil change interval until the accumulation clears up.
2. For rust, examine the engine or transmission for water or coolant intrusion.

As previously mentioned, passing a very clean magnet over filter paper laid out flat after you cut open the filter will determine whether iron or steel particles are present. The best way to clean the tip of a magnet is with a blast of high-pressure compressed air.

Ferrous metals (iron or steel) often look dark or even black in the filter and will be drawn to the magnet. Black particles that are not attracted to the magnet are soot. The presence of large amounts of soot in the engine oil filter can indicate poor maintenance or faulty cylinder kits (pistons, rings, and liners).

CREAM-COLORED SLUDGE NOTICED INSIDE ENGINE OR TRANSMISSION OIL FILL CAP

Urgency: Attend to as soon as convenient
Suggested actions:

1. What you are seeing is an emulsification, or mixture, of oil and water. Keep track of how often the cooling system needs filling in case coolant is leaking into the engine crankcase lube oil.
2. Also check for coolant or water in the oil by loosening the oil drain plug as outlined earlier. Coolant or water will leak out first.
3. If coolant is leaking into the oil, take such measures as are outlined in the equipment's service manual.

The causes and consequences of coolant leaking into oil are covered in detail in Chapter 3. See also Figure 11-12.

ENGINE OIL LEVEL ON DIPSTICK SLOWLY RISES OVER TIME

Urgency: Not urgent, but should be monitored
Suggested actions:

1. Stop the engine, let it cool for thirty minutes, then loosen the oil drain plug and check for water in the oil. If water (coolant) is present, the source of the leak into the oil pan must be found.
2. Fuel leaking into the oil will also cause the oil level to rise. The vital clue that fuel is leaking into the oil is that the oil pressure gauge will read lower than normal for a given coolant temperature. For example, the oil level might rise and

the oil pressure might drop to 40 psi at a coolant temperature of 180°F, whereas the normal oil pressure at that temperature is 45 psi. Changing the oil and filter will restore the oil pressure to normal until more fuel leaks into the oil.

Fuel leaking into the crankcase oil will cause the oil level to slowly rise. In an even worse scenario, an engine that is burning oil, the fuel can enter at the same rate as the oil is burned, making the problem difficult to spot. The oil thins out, losing its lubricating properties, until suddenly there is an engine failure!

ENGINE OIL LEVEL ON DIPSTICK SLOWLY RISES OVER TIME AND OIL BECOMES MILKY

Urgency: Requires immediate attention
Suggested actions:

1. A milky color to the oil indicates water (coolant) in the oil.
2. Verify the presence of water in the oil by stopping the engine and letting it stand for thirty minutes before loosening the oil pan drain plug. If water or coolant is present, it will be the first liquid to drip out.
3. Change the oil immediately and consult the service manual or a marine mechanic to find the source of the leak.

Water (coolant) entering and emulsifying with the oil causes milky oil. The cause might be a faulty head gasket, cracked head, faulty liner seal, cracked or pitted liner, cracked water-cooled exhaust manifold (due to overheating), or failed oil cooler core or associated seals. Coolant in the oil will quickly destroy an engine.

ENGINE OIL LEVEL RISES DRAMATI-CALLY, IMMEDIATELY AFTER ENGINE IS TURNED OFF

Urgency: Requires immediate attention

Suggested action: Drain the oil and watch to see if coolant comes out first. If any coolant is seen, there is a severe coolant leak into the oil pan that will need to be found. Call a marine mechanic.

Symptoms like this indicate a huge coolant leak that may quickly cause a hydraulic lock in one or more of the engine cylinders. A broken marine water-cooled exhaust manifold or a water-cooled turbo exhaust housing that has cracked while the engine is running will pump a lot of coolant into the oil system and will continue to do so until the coolant expansion tank empties or the engine is shut off. When the engine is turned off, all water above the head gasket will leak into the cylinders through open exhaust valves. Those cylinders that have both valves open when the engine comes to rest will be flooded, with the excess then flowing out through the intake valve, into the intake manifold, and into any other cylinder that has an intake valve open.

ENGINE OIL LEVEL SUDDENLY VERY HIGH WITH THE ENGINE RUNNING

Urgency: Requires immediate attention

Suggested actions:

1. Stop the engine.
2. Drain the oil and determine whether it is fuel or coolant that is causing the level to rise. This is done by watching to see what comes out of the drain plug first. If water comes out first, then the problem is coolant in the oil. If not, the problem is likely fuel in the oil.
3. Call a marine mechanic.

Coolant can rapidly fill the crankcase if the O-ring liner seals at the bottom of the liners fail, whether the engine is running or not. Likewise, pitting and pinholes in the cylinder liners due to galvanic corrosion will permit coolant to leak into the crankcase. Adding a conditioner to the cooling system will prevent galvanic corrosion. If pitting problems persist, have an electrician test both the AC and DC electrical systems for ground faults. A failed engine oil cooler will also allow coolant into the oil.

ENGINE OIL LEVEL RISES SLOWLY WHEN ENGINE IS OFF, EVEN AS THE EXPANSION TANK COOLANT LEVEL DROPS

Urgency: Requires immediate attention

Suggested actions:

1. This symptom is coolant leaking into the oil. If possible, remove the oil pan to find out where the coolant leaks into the crankcase.
2. After the source of the leak is found, consult the service manual to learn the best way to deal with the leak.

Some imported copies of Caterpillar heads will only leak when hot and when they are torqued down on the engine because of their very poor casting quality.

ENGINE OIL LEVEL SUDDENLY VERY LOW

Urgency: Requires immediate attention

Suggested actions:

1. The first clue that this is happening, when the engine is running, is a reduction in oil pressure on the pressure

FOR THE WORKBOAT

Coolant in the Lube Oil

The customer reported that the main engine's coolant was apparently leaking into the oil pan. We took the starboard inspection plates from the Caterpillar D353 and could see water trickling down the inside of the third cylinder.

It seemed straightforward enough to remove the forward cylinder head and look for the source of the leak.

When we pulled the head, we found no visual evidence of a head gasket failure. Looking closely at the head showed no apparent cracks either. We took the head to the machine shop, where it was subjected to a Magnaflux test. (Magnaflux is a brand name for a practice called magnetic particle testing to reveal surface and subsurface flaws in ferrous metals.) The test identified no problems. Next, we filled a tank with hot water and did an air pressure test with the head submerged, and this showed no problem.

After these two tests, we reasoned that the problem must have been with the head gasket after all. We reinstalled the head, and we decided to do a pressure test on the engine. We found that it leaked exactly as it had the day before! Pulling the intake manifold, we looked in the head's intake air port for the third cylinder (see illustration), and there we saw the crack! The head would only leak when it was torqued down on the engine.

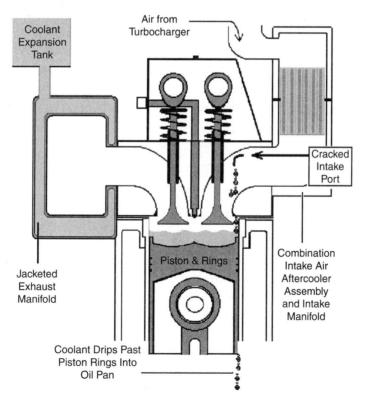

Fig. 11-12. Coolant leaking from a cracked intake port.

gauge. Stop the engine and inspect the engine for an oil leak.

2. If nothing obvious is found, refill the crankcase and inspect under the engine. If the oil pan has rusted through, replace the pan or use a temporary fiberglass patch to stop the leak until a new pan can be obtained.

3. If there are no obvious oil leaks, check for oil in the cooling system and pressure-test the engine oil cooler. Replace if needed.

Cracks or rust holes in the oil pan will allow lube oil to leak into the bilge. It's easy to spot oil in the bilge because it floats on the surface of the bilge water. Oil can also quickly transfer into the cooling system through a split engine oil cooler. Thus, when oil pressure drops quickly, you should also check the cooling system for the presence of oil.

COOLANT (WATER) FOUND IN TRANS-MISSION OIL FILL OPENING OR ON DIPSTICK

Urgency: Requires immediate attention
Suggested actions:

1. Check the engine coolant level. If it is low, refill as needed.

2. Determine whether the water came in from the oil cooler or leaked into the transmission from a high level of bilge water. The best way to do this is to pressure-test the oil cooler.

3. Replace the oil cooler if it is defective.

4. Change the transmission oil and filter.

Failure of a transmission oil cooler can allow engine coolant to enter the oil cooler after the engine is turned off. Pressure on the water (coolant) side of the oil cooler is higher than the pressure on the oil side, causing coolant to travel to the oil side. As previously explained, leaks in the cooler core will cause liquids to travel to either side, the oil or water side, because of pressure differences.

WATER OR COOLANT SQUIRTS OUT ENGINE'S DIPSTICK HOLE WHEN DIP-STICK IS REMOVED

Urgency: Requires immediate attention
Suggested actions:

1. This happens after a swamping or a severe internal coolant leak such as from a leaking oil cooler. Drain the water from the engine oil pan.

2. The source of the leak must be found before starting the engine. Check the service manual for recommendations or call a marine mechanic.

3. After the leak is repaired, bar the engine over manually (two complete revolutions; see the sidebar on page 36) to check for a hydraulic lock. Most engine manufacturers now sell an engine turning tool for use in turning the engine by hand when service work is done. As previously discussed, a hydraulic lock occurs when there is fluid above a piston that prevents the engine from turning. If the engine won't turn two complete revolutions, a hydraulic lock probably exists. If there is no hydraulic lock, start the engine.

Water can enter the crankcase if the engine room is flooded due to a leaking stuffing box, a crack or leak in the hull, a leaking through-hull fitting, or a leaking bow thruster. Tasting the fluid will reveal whether it is fresh water, salt water, or antifreeze coolant. Coolant has a sweet taste.

LIGHT OIL RUNS OUT DIPSTICK HOLE WHEN STICK IS REMOVED

Urgency: Requires immediate action
Suggested actions:

1. Change the engine oil and filter and monitor the oil level while investigating the problem.
2. Use the engine only for emergencies until the problem is solved.

This can only be diesel fuel. Each engine has its own peculiar route or routes for fuel to enter the crankcase. The engine service manual will help you ascertain how the engine's fuel system is constructed and the most likely pathway fuel will take when entering the engine oil.

OILY VAPOR, IN LARGE AMOUNTS, BLOWS OUT OF ENGINE'S CRANKCASE VENT OR DIPSTICK TUBE

Urgency: Not urgent, but should be monitored
Suggested actions:

1. Check that the crankcase vent tube is unobstructed.
2. Cut open an oil filter to check for the presence of piston material, which, if found, indicates that an engine failure is occurring.

Inside the engine, combustion gases that leak past the rings into the crankcase will build a harmful level of pressure in the crankcase. Engine crankcase vents carry these blowby gases out of the engine. In many boats, the gases are vented into the engine room! When an engine is nearing rebuild time or is failing altogether, it will begin to produce much larger amounts of blowby. This is a vital clue that the engine cylinders are weak and the piston rings are excessively worn. A plugged crankcase vent will cause these same symptoms. To check the crankcase vent, look for drooping or kinked crankcase vent hoses. Further, disconnect the vent line at the engine to see if excess pressure still comes out of the dipstick hole when the dipstick is removed. If it doesn't, you have found the problem: The vent line is obstructed. If removing the vent line doesn't help, the engine probably needs a rebuild.

CRANKCASE PRESSURE BLOWS DIPSTICK FROM DIPSTICK TUBE

Urgency: Requires immediate attention
Suggested actions:

1. Verify that the crankcase vent tube is clear and that crankcase fumes are free to vent. If the vent is obstructed, clear it.
2. If the vent is working as it should, the engine may be tired or recently damaged and should be checked for cylinder wear.

High crankcase pressure resulting from one or more failed pistons will overwhelm the crankcase vent and cause the pressure to blow the dipstick from its tube. On some engines, this condition can even blow lubricating oil from the dipstick tube.

ENGINE OIL PRESSURE READS LOW WHEN ENGINE IS WARM

Urgency: Requires immediate attention
Suggested actions:

1. Change oil and see if the pressure increases. If so, fuel is getting into the oil. Consult the engine manual for instructions.
2. If changing the oil doesn't help, verify the low oil pressure with a good test gauge.

Possible causes include a faulty oil pressure gauge, faulty oil line to a mechanical oil pressure gauge, faulty pressure sender or wiring, low oil level, a pressure relief valve stuck open, weak or broken pressure relief valve spring, contamination plugging the oil suction strainer in the oil pan, fuel in the oil, plugged oil filter (some systems), or a worn oil pump.

NO OIL PRESSURE AT ALL

Urgency: Requires immediate attention
Suggested actions:

1. Make sure there is oil in the engine.
2. Install a mechanical pressure gauge (a great thing to have on any boat) and start the engine to check the pressure.
3. Refer to the engine service manual to learn how to check the oil pump drive mechanism, then check that the oil pump is turning.
4. Check the engine manual regarding the location of the lube system pressure relief valve. Be sure the valve is operating freely and not stuck open.

The drain plug in the oil pan may not have been replaced after a change. Also, oil pans do leak due to rust, corrosion, or cracking. Something can also hit an oil pan and split or dent it. A severely dented oil pan not only reduces the volume of the pan, but it may break off the oil pump pickup. Try not to damage the oil pan. On most boats it's pretty inaccessible and hard to remove for repairs.

ENGINE OIL PRESSURE HIGHER THAN SPECIFIED WHEN ENGINE IS WARM

Urgency: Attend to as soon as convenient
Suggested action: Check for a faulty electrical gauge or sender.

While a faulty electrical oil pressure gauge or a faulty pressure sender (if the gauge is electric) are the likely suspects, other considerations include a sender incompatible with the engine, oil with viscosity too high for the engine, or even very cold oil.

ENGINE OIL PRESSURE READS HIGH WHEN AIR TEMPERATURE IS EXTREMELY COLD

Urgency: Not urgent, but should be monitored
Suggested action: This is normal in frigid weather, especially if heavy (30 weight) oil is used in an engine.

It's important to follow the engine manufacturer's instructions for using lube oil that is the correct weight, based on the usual outdoor temperature where the boat is operated. Many boat operators neglect this, which can lead to problems in the lube oil system.

ENGINE OIL PRESSURE READS LOW ONLY WHEN ENGINE IS COLD

Urgency: Requires immediate attention
Suggested action: Check the oil pickup tube (see Figure 10-17).

Oil that is so cold and thick that the pump can't easily move it, or a faulty seal or gasket where the tube attaches to the oil pump, will cause low oil pressure readings.

FUEL PRESSURE READINGS, WHEN CHECKED WITH A TEST GAUGE, ARE LOWER THAN SPECIFICATIONS

Urgency: Not urgent, but should be monitored

Suggested actions:

1. Most often this will be a partially plugged fuel filter.
2. Follow the engine manual directions for filling and bleeding the system.

There are several probable causes: a plugged fuel filter, low fuel level in the tank, faulty fuel pump or fuel pump gauge, faulty electric sender, or an unrestricted fuel-return fitting, if so equipped. (Older two-stroke Detroit Diesels, for example, require a restricted fuel return in order to build sufficient fuel pressure.)

FUEL PRESSURE READINGS HIGHER THAN SPECIFICATIONS

Urgency: Attend to as soon as convenient
Suggested actions:

1. Check for a faulty gauge or sender.
2. Check the engine service manual for further suggestions.

A sticky fuel pump pressure relief valve or a kinked fuel-return line may also be causing the higher readings.

TACHOMETER READS LOW, ENGINE WON'T SEEM TO GO TO FULL SPEED

Urgency: Attend to as soon as convenient
Suggested actions:

1. Before starting to troubleshoot a tachometer problem, determine if your tachometer is a mechanical or an electronic unit.
2. Try to verify or disprove the reading with a test tachometer.
3. If the engine has a mechanical tachometer, verify that the spinning drive cable (like a speedometer cable) is spinning at the tachometer gauge end. If not, replace the cable; otherwise suspect the gauge.
4. If the engine has an electronic tachometer with a magnetic pickup mounted on the flywheel housing, check the fuse, the magnetic pickup adjustment, the magnetic pickup, and the gauge, in this order. Consult the manual for the procedure to reset the dip switches in the gauge, if so equipped.

Mechanical tachometers work like an old magnetic speedometer, that is, the engine drives a spinning magnet that attracts and moves a lever arm behind the gauge face. If it's a mechanical tachometer, it may have the wrong drive gear ratio, or the cable drive may be worn or slipping. The electronic tachometer may be calibrated improperly, or the boat may have an improperly sized propeller.

TACHOMETER READING WAVERS, WITH ENGINE SOUND CONSTANT

Urgency: Attend to as soon as convenient
Suggested action: See previous symptom.

NO READING ON TACHOMETER AT ALL

Urgency: Attend to as soon as convenient
Suggested action: See previous symptom (tachometer reads low).

WHAT YOU TASTE

NO TASTE TO WATER FOUND IN ENGINE OIL PAN

Urgency: Requires immediate attention
Suggested actions:

1. This is fresh or rainwater, and the source of the leak into the oil pan must be found. If you have a vertical, dry exhaust system, check it to ensure that rain isn't getting in through the stack.
2. Look for evidence of swamping in the engine room, such as a high-water mark on the side of the engine or nearby equipment.

When an engine is turned off, it always comes to rest with a few intake and exhaust valves open. Rainwater coming down the inside of a dry exhaust stack will flow through an open valve and into the cylinder. In the cylinder, the water will slowly trickle down through the piston ring gaps and into the oil pan.

WATER IN ENGINE OIL PAN TASTES SWEET

Urgency: Requires immediate attention
Suggested actions:

1. After noting that the color of the liquid dripping from the oil pan drain plug appears to match the color of the antifreeze coolant in the engine, confirm by tasting a tiny amount. Coolant will taste sweet even when contaminated with oil.

2. Pressure-test the engine cooling system to learn how coolant is getting into the oil pan.
3. Check the engine oil cooler, liner seals, cylinder head, and head gasket.

Coolant entering the lube oil in the engine may indicate a serious problem.

WATER IN ENGINE OIL PAN IS SALTY (BOAT IS OPERATED IN SALT WATER)

Urgency: Requires immediate attention
Suggested actions:

1. Find the possible routes of salt water into the bilge and then check the bilge pumps and switches to see if they are allowing the bilge water to get too high.
2. For boats with horizontal saltwater-cooled exhaust systems, check the system to see if salt water is entering the engine through an exhaust valve port.

The engine may have been swamped or bilge water may have gotten high enough to enter the engine through the rear crankshaft main seal.

COOLING SYSTEM

WHAT YOU SEE

ENGINE PAINT TURNS DARKER THAN ORIGINAL COLOR AFTER AN APPARENT ENGINE OVERHEATING

Urgency: Requires immediate attention
Suggested actions:

1. Let engine cool a few hours.
2. Check engine oil and coolant levels.
3. Refill cooling system if low.
4. If the oil level is higher than normal or higher than before the overheating

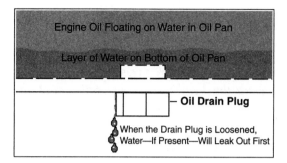

Fig. 11-13. Notice what type of liquid comes out first when opening the oil drain plug.

incident, loosen the oil drain plug in the oil pan and note what leaks out first (Fig. 11-13). If coolant or water leaks out before oil, there is coolant in the oil, and the engine has been severely damaged.

If the engine died when hot, remove the oil filter and use a filter cutter or hacksaw to cut it open on the threaded end. Remove a piece of the filter media paper and inspect it for the presence of metal. Shards or flecks of metal in the oil filter usually indicate piston seizure and the need for extensive repairs. (See Figure 10-20.)

If the engine temperature gauge was reading higher than normal or the engine space seemed hotter than usual, this indicates engine overheating. The engine may have even stopped running due to the extreme heat, though it is possible that the engine will start again after cooling for an hour. Engines die when overheating because the pistons expand and become too large for the cylinder bores. When this happens, friction between the pistons and the cylinder walls stops the pistons' up-and-down movement, and the crankshaft stops turning.

Overheating of an engine or even a transmission to temperatures above 270°F will cause the paint on the unit to darken. Overheating of this magnitude usually requires extensive repairs and the services of a marine mechanic. What if the engine appears to overheat (darkened paint; hot engine space) without it registering on the temperature gauge? Such an occurrence is possible if all the coolant has suddenly leaked away, because few engine temperature gauges will register overheating unless coolant is touching the sender.

Engine mechanics keep track of engine paint color during disassembly, especially when an engine of unknown history is brought into the shop for a rebuild. (See Chapter 10 for more information on what to look for during an engine rebuild.) Decisions about testing or replacement of components are sometimes based on changes of paint color.

During overheating, the upper half of the engine, including the cylinder heads and the water-cooled exhaust manifold, if so equipped, will get *much* hotter than the lower parts of the engine. This is because the fuel burns in the upper third of the engine, and even a small diesel engine must manage millions of British thermal units (Btu) of heat production every hour! As a point of reference, note that a three-bedroom home can easily be heated in the winter by a 100,000 Btu furnace. After any change in paint color, even if the engine appears normal after the immediate cause of overheating is addressed, check the engine oil level carefully and monitor it closely. Use the engine cautiously for a few days to be sure it is OK.

As mentioned above, coolant in the oil means that the engine has been severely damaged. Coolant can enter the oil through any of the following routes, depending on how the engine is configured:

1. Cracked cylinder head
2. Cracked water-cooled exhaust manifold
3. Cracked jacketed turbocharger (into cylinder, then down past piston rings)
4. Leaking gaskets between the parts of the jacketed exhaust system
5. Failed head gasket
6. Failed cylinder liner seals, if so equipped
7. Cracks or pinholes in the cylinder liner, if so equipped
8. Via the crankcase through the drive end of a gear-driven (as opposed to belt-driven) coolant pump

If the pressure-tested (Fig. 11-14) components, such as oil coolers, exhaust manifolds, or oil filter housings, fail the test and leak, further disassembly and more specific testing of each piece is needed until the source or sources of the leak is found. *Note: A pressure test can also be performed on the cooling system pressure cap itself, if it begins to leak. However, when huge amounts of steam and water gush from the pressure cap, it usually means the head gasket has failed and the engine is damaged.*

ENGINE OVERHEATS SEVERELY. TEMPERATURE GAUGE READS OVER 210°F, STEAM IN ENGINE ROOM, AND ENGINE RADIATES FAR MORE HEAT THAN NORMAL

Urgency: Requires immediate action
Suggested actions:

1. Stop the engine and let it cool for an hour.
2. Check the oil level; it will be high if coolant is entering the oil.
3. If the oil level is high, drain the water from the oil pan and find a marine mechanic familiar with your equipment.
4. If the oil level was not out of the ordinary, refill the cooling system and bar the engine over two complete turns.

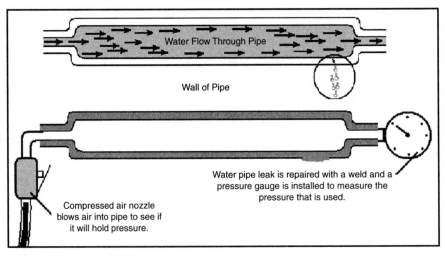

Fig. 11-14. Basic pressure testing.

5. If it bars over smoothly, start the engine and watch carefully for an external leak.
6. If no leak is found, there may be a faulty water pump or some other reason why coolant is not circulating through the engine. Consult the engine manual for more specific information on your system.

Careful observation of all the gauges is important at all times, but especially during overheating. See the previous symptom. Fluid can flow either way in a leaky oil cooler, as the next symptom shows.

BLACK OR BROWN OIL FOUND IN ENGINE COOLING SYSTEM
Urgency: Requires immediate attention
Suggested actions:

1. Black oil comes from the engine, and brown oil comes from the transmission. Verify the source of the oil.
2. Oil entering the engine's cooling system will most likely do so through a leaky oil cooler. If the oil is black, pressure-test the engine oil cooler.
3. If the oil is brown, pressure test the transmission oil cooler.
4. Follow the service manual instructions for replacing the part of the system that is responsible for the leak, and for flushing the oil from the cooling system.

This is the opposite of the preceding symptom, in that oil is traveling into the coolant side of the oil cooler and thereby contaminating the cooling system. Boatowners will sometimes mix no-suds electric dishwasher detergent with water and pour it into the cooling system to break down the oil. This practice is not recommended, because dishwasher detergent contains sodium that will cause corrosion in the cooling system. If dishwashing detergent is used, the cooling system must be flushed until all sodium is gone. Only a coolant sample sent to a lab will tell for sure that all of the oil is gone and that the sodium level in the cooling system is low enough to run the engine safely. Contact the engine manufacturer for instructions.

LIGHTER-COLORED OIL FOUND IN ENGINE COOLING SYSTEM
Urgency: Requires immediate attention
Suggested actions:

1. Check the transmission oil level and refill if needed. If the oil is low, it is likely that it is entering the cooling system through the transmission oil cooler, if so equipped.
2. Pressure-test and replace the oil cooler as needed (Fig. 11-15).

This oil cooler has its bottom opening (on the oil side) plugged for a pressure test. A pressure gauge is teed into the other opening. If the cooler can't hold 50 psi of test pressure on the oil side, there's an internal leak that could let coolant into the oil (engine off) or oil into the coolant (engine on).

CLEAR WATER LEAKING FROM ENGINE
Urgency: Attend to as soon as convenient
Suggested actions:

1. Check the cooling system coolant level and refill if needed.

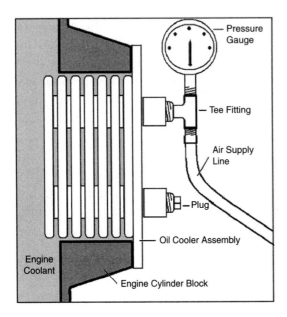

Fig. 11-15. **Testing an engine or transmission oil cooler.**

2. Start the engine and bring it up to operating temperature. Because cooling systems are pressurized and the pressure increases as the engine warms, leaks will be worse (more apparent) when the engine is hot.

3. When the leak is found, determine if the problem is a gasket, O-ring seal, faulty hose, loose hose clamp, faulty fitting, or a crack.

This symptom usually indicates one of the following: 1) water is leaking from the cooling system itself; 2) water is flowing from the cooling system overflow; or 3) there is no antifreeze protection in the cooling system. If there were, the leaking fluid would be the color of the antifreeze in the engine.

When resealing a faulty gasket, a thin coat of silicone sealer is often helpful. If the leak is high up toward the front of the engine, the cause may be a pinhole in a thermostat housing caused by galvanic corrosion. (The front of the engine is the end with the coolant pump, and the rear of the engine is the end with the flywheel.) Galvanic corrosion can be prevented by keeping the antifreeze coolant mixture slightly alkaline in pH, rather than acidic. Coolant test kits and coolant additives are available at fuel docks and most auto parts stores.

Note: To test the level of the cooling system conditioner in the field, turn your multimeter onto the "Volts" function and ground the black lead probe. Next, submerge the tip of the red probe and observe the voltage in the coolant. If the voltage is more than one or two volts, add conditioner. If the voltage is a lot higher, then there is stray electrical current that must be found by your marine electrician.

COLORED WATER (COOLANT MIXTURE) LEAKING FROM ENGINE

Urgency: Attend to as soon as convenient
Suggested actions:

1. Shut off the engine and refill coolant if the level is low.
2. Pressurize the cooling system by replacing the pressure cap and bringing the engine to normal operating temperature.
3. When the engine is warm, turn it off, and look for the leak with a good light source.
4. Consult your service manual for instructions on repairing the leak.

Antifreeze coolant is often red, blue, orange, green, or yellow, so a leak tinged with these colors indicates coolant.

COOLANT (SOMETIMES AIR BUBBLES TOO) LEAKING FROM BETWEEN THE CYLINDER HEAD AND THE CYLINDER BLOCK

Urgency: Attend to as soon as convenient
Suggested actions:

1. Keep the cooling system full until repairs can be made.
2. Consult the service manual for instructions.

This type of leak indicates that coolant is flowing past or near the head gasket. Bubbles usually indicate a slight compression leak. The head will normally need to be removed to fix this type of leak.

WATER IS OVERFLOWING FROM COOLING SYSTEM EXPANSION TANK

Urgency: Requires immediate action
Suggested actions:

1. Stop the engine and let it cool. Do not loosen the pressure cap (if so equipped) until the engine is cool enough to touch with a bare hand (about 140°F).
2. Refill the cooling system and watch for obvious leaks. Check the oil level to learn if coolant is now going into the oil pan as a result of overheating from coolant loss.
3. Obstructed coolant flow will cause loss of coolant. Check that the engine coolant pump is indeed free to turn. If it is, remove it and make sure the impeller is tightly attached to the impeller shaft.
4. If your system includes a keel cooler, visually inspect it to verify that it is free

from crushing or kinking, which will reduce coolant flow.
5. If you have a freshwater-cooled system with a heat exchanger, be sure that raw water is flowing by looking overboard at the raw-water outlet. (If your boat has wet exhaust, the used raw water is injected into the exhaust and exits through the exhaust pipe.)
6. If you see no raw-water flow, be sure the raw-water pump is working. If the impeller in the pump disintegrates or a blade breaks off, the pump won't move water and cool the engine. Also check the raw-water strainer for plugging from seaweed or trash.
7. To test for combustion gases in the cooling system, attach a pressure gauge to the cooling system and start the engine. If combustion gases are entering the cooling system, the pressure will increase beyond the system's pressure cap rating within two or three minutes. When this happens, the cylinder head must be removed to allow checking the head for cracks and to replace the cylinder head gasket.

The simplest and most common reason that an expansion tank overflows is that it has been overfilled. When the engine and coolant get up to temperature, the excess coolant has to go somewhere. An expansion tank overflow might also mean that the engine has overheated and combustion gases are entering the cooling system by way of a bad head gasket.

COOLANT SLOWLY VANISHES WHEN ENGINE SITS IDLE FOR LONG TIME

Urgency: Attend to as soon as convenient

Suggested actions:

1. Tighten all hose clamps. Most often the problem is a slow leak on one of the coolant hoses.
2. If the problem persists, ask a marine mechanic to pressure-test the cooling system. This will help determine if there is internal leakage in the engine, and, if so, where it is happening.

When coolant is lost from an idle engine, these are the usual suspects: 1) leaking fittings or hoses between the engine and a keel cooler (if so equipped); 2) leaking from a keel cooler into water surrounding the hull; 3) leaking fittings or hoses between a heat exchanger (if so equipped) and the engine; 4) leaking fittings or hoses between the expansion tank and the engine; 5) leaking from the heat exchanger core (if so equipped) into water surrounding the hull; 6) leaking from pinholes in the thermostat housing due to galvanic corrosion (which will also allow slow leakage of coolant into the bilge); 7) leaking from a cracked cylinder head or block, or any other water-jacketed part such as a turbocharger or exhaust manifold; 8) leaking from a faulty head gasket, a cracked cylinder liner, or a faulty O-ring seal.

COOLANT SLOWLY VANISHES WHEN ENGINE RUNS

Urgency: Requires immediate action
Suggested action: Same as above.

A cracked cylinder head or a crack in a jacketed exhaust manifold can also cause an engine to burn coolant (turn it into steam) and expel it through the cylinder or the exhaust stream.

A FINGER WIPED INSIDE COOLING SYSTEM FILLER NECK (UNDER THE COOLANT PRESSURE CAP) COMES AWAY COATED WITH OILY SCUM

Urgency: Requires immediate attention
Suggested actions:

1. Check the engine oil level and refill if needed. If the oil is low, it is likely that engine oil is entering the cooling system through the oil cooler.
2. Pressure-test and replace the engine oil cooler as needed.

When oil enters the engine's cooling system, it emulsifies with the coolant and reduces the coolant's ability to transfer heat. As the oil transfers into the cooling system, levels drop in the lube oil system. Soon the engine (or the transmission; see following symptom) runs out of oil, locks up, and is permanently damaged.

The source of the oil is either the engine or the transmission oil cooler. If you see black, oily film in the coolant, it's the engine oil cooler, and if you see lighter-colored oil (the same color as the transmission oil), it's the transmission oil cooler. A pressure test of the offending oil cooler is the next step. Oil in the cooling system makes it very likely that coolant is also getting into the engine or transmission oil. *Note: Small sailboat transmissions do not have oil coolers. However, as a general rule, it is safe to say that most transmissions used on engines over 50 hp will have an oil cooler.*

COOLANT TEMPERATURE READS LOWER THAN USUAL WHEN WARM

Urgency: Attend to as soon as convenient

Suggested actions:

1. Begin by reading the engine service manual cooling system troubleshooting section.
2. Plug a spare gauge into the panel to verify the accuracy of the low reading.
3. If no change is detected, install a new sender to further verify that the low reading is accurate.
4. If you confirm that the temperature is indeed low, replace the thermostat.

A faulty electric gauge or gauge sender will incorrectly provide low coolant temperature readouts. Another cause may be low coolant level. Low levels of coolant won't reach the sender probe consistently and will prompt erroneous temperature readings (coolant must touch the sender probe at all times). A thermostat that won't close could also be the root of the problem, or, on boats with small engines equipped with oversize keel coolers, a cooling system shunt line may bypass too much and trigger low coolant temperature readings.

COOLANT TEMPERATURE READS HIGH

Urgency: Requires immediate attention
Suggested actions:

1. It is safest to always assume the worst and proceed as if the engine is overheating. Shut off the engine, and after it cools check the coolant level and the coolant pump to be sure it is working.
2. Read the engine service manual to get specific troubleshooting information.

The source of the problem may be a faulty gauge or electric sender, a sender incorrect for the engine, or a thermostat stuck closed, or the water pump may not be turning fast enough to move coolant through the cooling system. Check for a slipping belt on belt-driven pumps and also check the impeller; it may be slipping on the shaft or a blade may be missing. If the boat is equipped with a keel cooler, the plumbing may be obstructed or flattened, and if operating in freezing temperatures, the coolant may be frozen somewhere in the keel cooler, preventing adequate flow.

COOLANT TEMPERATURE GAUGE DOESN'T REGISTER ANY RISE IN TEMPERATURE

Urgency: Requires immediate attention
Suggested actions:

1. This may be a result of coolant leaking out of the system. Most gauges will not register temperature on steam (the absence of water). Check the engine to see if it is overheating. Shut it off and go below. Carefully touch the surface of the engine. If it feels too hot to touch, then it has overheated and you must take appropriate action.
2. If the engine isn't too hot to touch, chances are you've got a less serious problem with the gauge, sender, or the wiring between the two.

If the problem is with the gauge or sender, it is easiest to replace the sender first, before moving on to the gauge.

COOLANT HOSES BULGED OR BLISTERED

Urgency: Attend to as soon as convenient
Suggested action: Replace as soon as possible.

Bulging or blistering indicates that the hose is weak or is being subjected to more pressure and temperature than it can handle. Perhaps the hose is of the wrong kind for the application. Blistering can also result from chemicals attacking the rubber compound on the hose exterior. It is possible that the rubber compound isn't compatible with cleaning compounds that are used to clean the engine room. Avoid putting strong detergent on the hoses.

WHAT YOU FEEL

RAW-WATER COOLING SYSTEM PLUMBING COLD

Urgency: Not urgent, but should be monitored

Suggested action: This is normal and a good check to make several times during the day when operating the engine.

Cold pipes prove the raw-water side of the cooling system is working well.

RAW-WATER COOLING SYSTEM PLUMBING HOT

Urgency: Requires immediate attention
Suggested actions:

1. Shut off the engine and check for obstructions on the outside of the raw-water strainer that could block water flow.
2. Check inside the raw-water strainer for debris that could block water flow.
3. Check the condition of the raw-water pump impeller and be sure it is turning.
4. Consult the engine manual for further instructions.

This is a serious problem because a freshwater-cooled engine depends on the raw-water pump for cooling and will soon overheat and fail unless the engine is immediately turned off. The cause is usually a clogged raw-water inlet. It may be that the raw-water pump belts are slipping or the raw-water pump impeller has disintegrated.

OUTLET OF RAW-WATER HOSE ON HEAT EXCHANGER WARM

Urgency: Not urgent, but should be monitored

Suggested action: None. This is normal.

The raw water is carrying heat away from the engine cooling system, so it's a good sign when the outlet plumbing is warm.

INLET TO COOLANT PUMP TOO HOT TO TOUCH FOR LONG

Urgency: Requires immediate attention
Suggested actions:

1. Stop the engine and check for any possible restriction of coolant flow.
2. Be sure the coolant pump is turning.
3. Verify that the thermostat is opening or replace it.
4. Consult the engine service manual for troubleshooting suggestions.

The excessive heat indicates that coolant is not circulating through the keel cooler or heat exchanger, depending on how the engine is equipped. The keel cooler tubes may be pinched or badly bent.

OIL, COOLANT, FUEL HOSES HARD

Urgency: Attend to as soon as convenient
Suggested actions:

1. Replace the hoses.
2. Avoid overtightening hose clamps.

Old hoses with high hours of operation, or those that have been used in very hot conditions, will get hard and should be replaced.

ENDS OF COOLANT HOSES SOFT

Urgency: Attend to as soon as convenient
Suggested action: Replace the hoses.

Galvanic corrosion occurring in coolant hoses will soften hose ends where they connect to the engine or cooling system fittings.

SURFACE OF O-RING SEALS ROUGH, OR SEAL HARD

Urgency: Requires immediate attention
Suggested action: Replace any rough or brittle O-ring seals.

Do not use any O-ring that doesn't have a smooth surface, because it will not seal properly. It is really handy to string O-rings on a wire for easy access; however, over time, the wire can wear a flat spot on the seals and ruin them. It's best to store extra O-rings in sealed plastic bags.

WATER PUMP AND ALTERNATOR BELTS TOO TIGHT

Urgency: Requires immediate attention
Suggested action: Loosen belts immediately.

Belts that are tighter than needed will reduce water pump and alternator bearing life. They should be tightened according to manufacturer's specifications.

WATER PUMP AND ALTERNATOR BELTS TOO LOOSE

Urgency: Attend to as soon as convenient
Suggested action: Tighten belts when convenient.

Belts that are too loose will slip, causing noise, wear, and possible loss of efficiency in belt-driven components.

EXHAUST SYSTEM

WHAT YOU SEE
WHITE EXHAUST SMOKE ON STARTING COLD

Urgency: Not urgent, but should be monitored
Suggested actions:

1. If the white smoke clears up when the engine is warm, it may be normal. Compare your engine smoke to other similarly equipped boats.
2. If the smoke does not seem normal, check the fuel injection timing and the cylinder cranking pressure.

So-called cold smoke occurs when fuel is not completely burned in one or more of the cylinders. For some low-compression-ratio diesel engines, this is normal. Low-compression diesel engines, those with compression ratios below 16:1, are designed so that turbocharging raises the cylinder pressure once the engine is warm. However, if white smoke persists beyond five minutes after starting an engine with a compression ratio above 16:1, the engine will need to be checked for low compression. Possible causes include low compression or late fuel injection timing. Low compression can be caused by too tight a valve adjustment, scored pistons and liners, broken rings, valve and valve seat damage, or even a camshaft that was installed out of time.

WHITE EXHAUST, ENGINE WARM

Urgency: Requires immediate attention
Suggested actions:

1. Check for the presence of fuel in the oil with the Exxon Mobil Corporation's portable viscosity tester (see Fig. 11-7).

2. Check the engine manual for model-specific information.

White smoke with the engine warm suggests low compression or late injection timing. If white smoke persists after an engine is warm or if the engine starts smoking white very suddenly, especially after overheating, then severe engine damage is possible. There may be a hole in a piston or a bent or damaged valve.

WHITE EXHAUST WITH YELLOW TINGE, ENGINE WARM
Urgency: Requires immediate attention
Suggested actions:

1. The engine may have antifreeze coolant entering one of the cylinders or the exhaust stream. Check the coolant level.
2. If coolant is low, it is likely that coolant is leaking internally. See Chapter 16 for more details.
3. Consult the engine manual.

When coolant enters the cylinder or the exhaust manifold and is exposed to intense heat, it produces a very dense, off-white to yellow smoke.

BLUE EXHAUST
Urgency: Not urgent, but should be monitored
Suggested actions:

1. Monitor engine oil consumption.
2. Check the cold side of the turbocharger for an oil leak. Remove the pipe that takes the pressurized air to the cylinder head and inspect it for the presence of oil. Any amount of oil

indicates a leak and the need for turbocharger repair.
3. If no oil is found on the cold side of the turbocharger, check the hot side with the engine stopped. See if the bearings are loose enough to let the turbocharger shaft wobble significantly, and if they are, you may have to try replacing the turbocharger to see if that stops the blue smoke.
4. Finally, if all else fails, check the condition of the cylinders. Because there are so many cylinder configurations, it's important to start by consulting the engine service manual. A cylinder leak-down test or a compression test is usually done at this time. See Chapter 16 for more details on engine testing procedures.

Blue smoke indicates that oil is either passing by the piston rings or valve guides or is passing from one or both of the turbocharger seals, if the boat is so equipped. While it seldom occurs, adding too much of some kinds of fuel conditioner to the fuel will cause an engine to produce blue smoke. Blue smoke is usually a sign of a worn turbocharger or engine.

BLACK EXHAUST, BOAT IDLING AT DOCK
Urgency: Attend to as soon as convenient
Suggested actions:

1. Replace the air filter first.
2. Check the valve adjustment dimension next. It is possible that extremely loose valve adjustments will keep the cylinder from filling with enough air to burn all the fuel.

3. A marine mechanic can test the exhaust system back-pressure. Back-pressure that is too high indicates a collapsed muffler or other restriction in the exhaust system.

4. If nothing else is found, suspect poorly atomized fuel, a result of tired fuel injectors.

Sometimes an injector will seize inside the cylinder head, requiring its removal or removal of the copper sleeve that holds the injector to address the problem.

However, it is possible to test injectors while they are still in the head. Just take the injector tester to the engine and do a pop test to get an idea of how the injectors perform. If it pops well, then keep operating the engine, and remove the head later at a more convenient time. *Note: When injectors are working well, they suddenly open and spray or pop at a preset pressure. If there is no pop, they are faulty.*

BLACK EXHAUST, BOAT UNDER WAY

Urgency: Not urgent, but should be monitored

Suggested action: Follow the steps in the previous symptom.

Causes of black smoke while the engine is under load include a plugged air filter, a collapsed muffler, a stuck or hindered turbocharger unable to spin freely, restricted airflow to the engine room, an overheated engine room, or too much propeller pitch.

PERIODIC BLACK PUFFS, BOAT UNDER WAY

Urgency: Not urgent, but should be monitored

Suggested action: Remove and test the injectors.

Worn mechanical fuel injection system governors can cause erratic fuel system action, such as erratic rpm levels, also known as surging.

NO SMOKE AND LOW POWER

Urgency: Attend to as soon as convenient
Suggested actions:

1. For older engines with aneroid or air-fuel-ratio controls, check the settings of the controls.

2. For electronic engines, go into limp-home mode when there is a fault. Consult the service manual to learn how to check and clear fault codes, and for other advice no matter what type of engine you have.

For older engines this can actually indicate an aneroid or fuel-ratio control is set too lean, thereby reducing engine power.

ENGINE BLOWS WHITE SMOKE RINGS FOR A COUPLE OF MINUTES AFTER STARTING UP COLD

Urgency: Not urgent, but should be monitored

Suggested action: Ignore them. They don't seem to cause any harm.

Smoke rings might be related to low-compression marine diesel engines that rely on heavy turbocharging once the boat is under way.

ENGINE EXHAUST TEMPERATURE TEST GAUGE (PYROMETER) READS HIGH

Urgency: Requires immediate attention

Suggested actions:

1. Slow the engine immediately to protect it until the condition is remedied.
2. If this is a propulsion engine, check to see if there is too much pitch or diameter in the propeller, which will cause too much load on the engine. While you can't easily determine the pitch or diameter of a propeller when under way, a lugging condition, with the engine unable to reach its full specified rpm, is quite obvious.

Most small recreational boats don't have instruments to measure the temperature of exhaust. However, many large motoryachts and workboats do have such instruments (pyrometers). If the boat is so equipped, know that pyrometers rarely fail and read high. However, the pyrometer might have faulty calibration of the gauge to accommodate the length of the run of the thermocouple wires (contact your supplier for instructions on this). The thermocouple may be faulty, or it may even be the wrong one for the particular system. The engine may also be lugging, or the boat may have too much propeller.

Note: The hot end of the pyrometer system is the replaceable thermocouple end, with the calibrated length of high-resistance wire between the gauge and the thermocouple. The weakest part of the system is the replaceable thermocouple.

ENGINE EXHAUST TEMPERATURE READS LOW

Urgency: Attend to as soon as convenient
Suggested action: Verify the pyrometer readings before replacing the thermocouple.

See above symptom. Also, check for a faulty throttle linkage that does not provide full travel of the governor control on the engine.

ENGINE EXHAUST TEMPERATURE GAUGE SHOWS NO READING

Urgency: Attend to as soon as convenient
Suggested actions:

1. Replace the thermocouple (hot end).
2. Use the engine conservatively until you repair the system.

See the previous two symptoms.

DARK OR BLACK SUBSTANCE LEAKING FROM EXHAUST MANIFOLD JOINTS

Urgency: Not urgent, but should be monitored
Suggested action: Idle the engine far less and work the engine harder.

The source liquid is not lube oil. It is soot-laden, incompletely burned fuel leaving the cylinder with the exhaust gases. This problem is known as wet stacking and is a result of light loading, very low compression, or a tired diesel engine that has low cylinder pressure and poorly atomized fuel. Long periods of idling an engine will also cause wet stacking, which is why it is bad if you run your diesel in idle to charge the batteries while at anchor. You're slowly killing your engine if you do that.

Light loading is cured by putting more load on the engine. Increasing the load makes the engine work hard enough to increase the cylinder pressure, and this helps force the piston rings against the cylinder walls. Wet stacking while idling an engine is reduced if you don't let it run for long periods below

1,000 rpm, but you don't want to run in high idle for long periods while charging batteries! Find another way to charge your batteries that doesn't require running the engine in idle or under light loads.

WHAT YOU HEAR

EXHAUST TONE ROUGH AND IRREGULAR

Urgency: Not urgent, but should be monitored

Suggested actions:

1. Consider a tune-up that includes an injector change.
2. Learn what the engine manual says about this problem.
3. If the problem proves hard to solve, try checking for air in the fuel.

An engine miss due to a faulty cylinder, a poorly atomizing injector, or air in the fuel can make the engine sound irregular while the boat is under way.

EXHAUST TONE HAS STEADY POPPING SOUND

Urgency: Requires immediate attention
Suggested actions:

1. Check the valve adjustment according to the engine manual.
2. If adjustment does not help, remove the valve cover and check visually for an exhaust valve that is not closing. This is done by sighting down the row of valve stems and finding one that is low and has a lot of extra valve lash when the rocker arm comes off it. The engine will need to be turned (barred

over) by hand a few times to check them all.

It's important to check *any* popping noise, because a sticking valve can cause it. A sticking valve can result in a broken connecting rod. A bad exhaust valve face or seat can also result in a popping sound. Perform a compression test to check cylinder pressure.

EXHAUST TONE HAS INTERMITTENT POPPING SOUND

Urgency: Requires immediate attention
Suggested actions:

1. Check fuel injection timing according to the engine manual and adjust as needed.
2. Check for a valve that hangs open by removing the valve cover and doing a visual inspection as mentioned above.

See above symptom. Also, faulty injection timing and exhaust valves that hang open can cause an intermittent popping noise.

BACKFIRING OR POPPING AUDIBLY TRACED TO INTAKE SIDE (INTAKE VALVES) OF ENGINE

Urgency: Requires immediate attention
Suggested actions:

1. Check the intake valve adjustment.
2. Visually check the valve stems to be sure all valves are closing when needed.

Bad valve seats or valves that are slow to close, or even sticking open, will cause this problem. Remove the valve cover and inspect the valve lash to make sure no valves are adjusted too tight (insufficient valve lash).

MECHANICAL/ELECTRICAL INTERFACE

WHAT YOU SEE

ELECTRICAL CIRCUIT BREAKERS KEEP TRIPPING

Urgency: Attend to as soon as convenient
Suggested actions:

1. First, be doubly sure the power is turned off before inspecting an electrical system.
2. Check that the load is powered by the breaker power and make sure it is functioning properly and not a dead short. This may require a marine electrician.
3. Inspect the wiring between the load and the breaker.
4. Be sure the breaker is the right capacity to protect the circuit.
5. Consult a marine electrician as needed.

There may be an excessive load, such as a faulty electric motor, on the breaker. There may be a short circuit, or you may have a bad circuit breaker or one of the wrong capacity.

CORROSION VISIBLE ON ELECTRICAL TERMINALS

Urgency: Attend to as soon as convenient
Suggested actions:

1. Disconnect the power from the circuit and detach the terminal. Brush the terminal and post to clean it, then reattach the terminal.
2. Protect all electrical components from water spray and detergents.

Electrical wiring and terminals will corrode much more when components are subjected to salt spray or sprayed with strong detergents. Replace corroded terminals with higher-quality connectors with a shrink-fit boot incorporated onto the connectors. Check to see whether corrosion has crept up into the wire under the insulation. If it has, replace the wire.

BLACK OIL LEAKS FROM FAN HOUSING AT ENGINE END OF GENERATOR

Urgency: Attend to as soon as convenient. This could coat the generator windings and cause them to overheat.
Suggested actions:

1. Oil leaks in this area are usually due to a failed rear crankshaft oil seal. Replace the seal.
2. If you can't immediately replace the seal, monitor the engine oil level and keep it up to a safe range.

An engine rear crankshaft oil seal will leak oil into this area, and the generator fan will pick it up and blow it all over the engine room.

GENERATOR FREQUENCY METER READS LOW, HIGH, OR NOT AT ALL

Urgency: Requires immediate attention
Suggested actions:

1. For a low reading, raise engine rpm.
2. For a high reading, lower engine rpm.
3. For no reading, replace the frequency meter (cycle meter).

For alternating current (AC) electrical systems to work properly, the cycles per second,

k ... z, must be
... S., the
... ond,
... orld
... the
... eter,
... ator
... ower
... era-
... atio
... ency
... oove
... quals
... eter
... , the
... f the
specified 1,800 rpm. A frequency meter can be calibrated using a test tachometer. All it takes is to first adjust the engine governor to run at exactly 1,800 rpm. When this is done, adjust the screw on the face of the frequency meter to exactly 60 cycles. For more specific information, call a marine electrician. Unfortunately, this subject is not well covered in most repair manuals.

VOLTMETER READS LOW OR NO READING

Urgency: Requires immediate attention
Suggested actions:

1. If the engine is on, do not turn it off until you find another battery to use as a backup. The engine may not start again with low voltage.
2. With the engine at rest, check the electrolyte level in the batteries.
3. Look for obviously loose alternator belts with the engine running. The

---

AN EMERGENCY FREQUENCY METER

David Pflaum of Ketchikan, Alaska, found that he could check both the rpm of a generator and the accuracy of a frequency meter with a 120-volt clock with a second hand and his wristwatch. He plugged the clock into the circuit powered by the generator and coordinated its second hand with the seconds on his wristwatch. Next, he watched for three minutes to see if the generator-powered second hand ran faster or slower than the second hand on his wristwatch. He then adjusted the generator engine speed until the second hand of the 120-volt clock matched the one on his wristwatch. When that was accomplished, he adjusted the generator frequency meter to read 60 cycles per second.

slack side of the belt will be flexing back and forth two inches or so if the belt is loose.
4. It's dangerous to tighten a belt with the engine running. Turn off the engine and tighten the alternator belt.
5. If the voltage doesn't increase, check the alternator, the batteries, and all connections between the two.
6. Check the system voltage by using a test gauge such as a Fluke voltmeter to verify readings; otherwise, check the electrical connections in the system.

The 12-volt system on a generator or marine propulsion engine is often regulated a little lower (13.2 as opposed to 14.2 volts) than on engines used in trucks, cars, and other land-based applications. This is the case because engines on the water tend to idle far less. *Note: Batteries produce extremely flammable hydrogen gas, both when charging and discharging! Wear rain gear, rubber gloves, boots, and a complete face shield when working near batteries.*

VOLTMETER READS HIGH

Urgency: Requires immediate attention
Suggested actions:

1. Verify the voltage with a test meter and then stop the engine.
2. Consult the engine service manual to learn if the alternator is adjustable; some are. Replace the alternator if it is not adjustable.
3. To get home with an overcharging alternator, identify, disconnect, and tape the alternator field wire as identified by the service manual.

The gauge may be faulty or the alternator's regulator may be causing an overcharge. Overcharging will quickly damage any battery.

VOLTMETER READING WAVERS

Urgency: Not urgent, but should be monitored
Suggested actions:

1. Stop the engine and check the wiring connections to the voltmeter.
2. The regulator may require replacement. Since many alternators have internal regulators, the alternator is often replaced.

Check the connections to the gauge. The load may actually be fluctuating, or the voltage regulator may be faulty.

MULTIMETER SHOWS VOLTAGE READING WHEN CONNECTION IS MADE BETWEEN EITHER BATTERY POST AND THE SURFACE OF BATTERY

Urgency: Not urgent, but should be monitored
Suggested action: Clean the exterior of the batteries with brush, soap, and water.

This indicates a dirty battery discharging between the posts. Simply wash it and brush it before rinsing it off with water

WHAT YOU FEEL

AFTER SHUTTING OFF ENGINE, ALTERNATOR PULLEY CAN BE TURNED INSIDE OF THE BELT BY HAND

Urgency: Requires immediate attention
Suggested action: Tighten the belt. If you can still turn it by hand after tightening, then the pulley must be replaced.

This results from slippage between the pulley and the belt. To repair, tighten the belts. If it takes a huge amount of belt tension, suspect that the width and contour of the belt and/or pulley may be wrong.

PULLING SIDEWAYS ON LARGE STUDS ON STARTER SOLENOID RESULTS IN STUD WOBBLING

Urgency: Requires immediate attention
Suggested action: Replace the solenoid.

Loose starter studs show an electrical component is damaged or failing and needs to be replaced.

PULLING SIDEWAYS ON ALTERNATOR OUTPUT STUD RESULTS IN WOBBLING

Urgency: Attend to as soon as convenient
Suggested action: Replace the alternator.

A loose stud on the alternator shows it needs to be replaced.

BATTERY CABLES WARM TO THE TOUCH

Urgency: Attend to as soon as convenient
Suggested action: The engine is cranking or starting too hard, or the cables are too small for the application. Find out what can be done to make the engine start more easily or increase the cable size.

High current draw, such as during the starting of a tired engine, can cause the battery cables to get warm. Heat is generated by repeatedly cranking an engine that is reluctant to start, or by high resistance in the battery cable ends.

BATTERY CABLES HOT TO THE TOUCH AFTER STARTING ENGINE

Urgency: Requires immediate attention
Suggested action: See previous symptom.

Hot battery cables mean the amp draw is too high and the engine is taking too much cranking to start. The cables may also be sized too small, or the starter motor current draw may be too high, indicating a faulty starter possibly in the process of failing.

STARTER MOTOR WARM TO THE TOUCH

Urgency: Attend to as soon as convenient
Suggested actions:

1. If this happens regularly it will shorten the starter's life. Tune the engine and do anything you can to aid quick starting.
2. While it is expensive, using the largest battery and starter cables you can will help the system last longer.

The action of a starter motor, when everything is right, is that of a controlled dead short. Heat harms starters by breaking down the insulation of the windings. Barely perceptible heat in the starter motor is acceptable.

STARTER MOTOR IS HOT TO THE TOUCH

Urgency: Requires immediate attention
Suggested actions:

1. A hot starter will soon fail. Get a new one and keep it on board.
2. Increasing the cable size will help.
3. Check the engine manual for troubleshooting hard starting.

Heat at the starter motor indicates that the insulation has overheated, and this will cause a short circuit.

WHAT YOU HEAR
NOISE COMING FROM ALTERNATOR

Urgency: Attend to as soon as convenient
Suggested actions:

1. Remove the alternator drive belt and run the engine momentarily to see if the noise stops. (This may not work on some boats because the alternator belt also drives the raw-water pump.) *Note: Water pump noise can sometimes be checked this way too.*
2. Replace the alternator if needed.

As alternator bearings begin to fail, the bearings can begin to make noise. Also, when the bearing clearance becomes excessive, the drive belt tension will pull the armature off-center. The spinning armature will begin to contact the side of the bore in the field windings, making even more noise. Normally, however, long before things get this bad, someone will notice that the alternator isn't working.

WHAT YOU SMELL

STRONG ODOR OF BURNING RUBBER

Urgency: Requires immediate attention

Suggested actions:

1. Stop the engine and track down the smell to make sure there is no fire hazard.
2. Check the belts.
3. Turn off all AC and DC electrical power and check for hot electrical wiring by quickly running your hands over all of the accessible wiring harnesses and cables on the boat. *Make absolutely certain before doing this that no AC power source is connected.*

The smell of burning rubber indicates a drive belt is probably slipping and overheating on the pulley. Electrical problems, as mentioned above, are also possible causes.

ODOR OF SULFUR (SMELLS LIKE ROTTEN EGGS) IN ENGINE ROOM

Urgency: Not urgent, but should be monitored

Suggested action: Overcharging batteries smell like this. Check the alternator charging voltage. It should be no more than 14.2 volts.

A smell like sulfur can be overcharging batteries.

CHAPTER 12

TROUBLESHOOTING WITH THE FIVE SENSES: GASOLINE ENGINES

Refer to the introduction to Chapter 11 for an explanation of how Chapters 11 through 15, Troubleshooting with the Five Senses, are intended to work. This chapter provides a detailed look at gasoline engines.

Compared with diesel engines, fewer specialized and expensive tools are required to troubleshoot gas engines. For example, compression-testing tools for gas engines cost a lot less because they need only measure half the pressure that diesel cylinders develop. Likewise, diesel fuel-system pressures can be as much as one or two thousand times higher (no, this is not a misprint!) than those in a gas engine, and therefore the fuel pressure–testing equipment for a gas engine costs much less than that for a diesel.

As with diesel engines, gas engine troubleshooting frequently focuses on starting problems and low power. So the ability to raise full pressure in the cylinders is important, as is timing of valve openings and closings. Gasoline engines require a timed spark to ignite the fuel in the cylinder, so a spark tester and a timing light are needed.

While easier in some respects, working on gasoline engines requires greater caution than working on diesels, because gasoline fumes are terribly explosive in a confined space like a boat's interior. If you should create a spark before the blower fan clears the engine space of fumes, the boat will be gone, and you with it.

ENGINE PERFORMANCE

WHAT YOU SEE

ENGINE TAKES LONGER THAN NORMAL TO REACH FULL SPEED IN GEAR

Urgency: Not urgent, but should be monitored

Suggested actions:

1. Check for a plugged air filter or fuel filter.
2. Check for line in the propeller.
3. Check the engine service manual for recommendations.
4. If there were recent repairs, contact your marine mechanic.
5. Check the bottom of the boat for fouling.

This problem can also result from insufficient throttle travel due to a faulty throttle control linkage.

ENGINE GETS HOT MORE QUICKLY THAN USUAL, THEN OVERHEATS

Urgency: Requires immediate attention

Suggested actions:

1. After the engine cools, be sure the cooling system is full and the water pump belts, if so equipped, are tight.

2. Look for any possible restriction of coolant or raw-water flow, depending on the type of cooling system.
3. Check the engine service manual for cooling system troubleshooting information.

This symptom may be the result of a faulty thermostat, a water pump not turning at full speed (belt slipping), or the coolant pump's metal impeller slipping on the pump shaft.

ENGINE OVERHEATS SEVERELY, TEMPERATURE GAUGE READS OVER 210°F, STEAM IN ENGINE ROOM, AND ENGINE RADIATES FAR MORE HEAT THAN NORMAL

Urgency: Requires immediate attention
Suggested actions:
Note: There are so many ways to build a cooling system that it's important to start with the engine and boat service manuals to learn how the boat is equipped. Then follow the directions below that apply to the equipment on your boat.

1. Let the engine cool until it can be touched with a bare hand, and then fill the cooling system.
2. Find and repair any damage causing an obstruction to the coolant plumbing and hoses.
3. Verify that the coolant pump (and raw-water pump, if so equipped) is turning.
4. If the engine is raw-water cooled, check the raw-water strainer and the ball valve on the through-hull fitting for obstructions.
5. Check the engine oil level to see if coolant is going into the oil. If so, serious damage has occurred.

6. If no coolant has gone into the oil, watch for external leaks and repair them if possible.
7. Pressure-test the cooling system.
8. After pressure-testing the engine, bar it over two complete revolutions of the crankshaft. (See the sidebar on page 36 for information on barring over an engine.)
9. Cut open the oil filter and check for metal, the sure sign of an impending engine failure. The presence of metal shows that damage has been done. If there is little or no metal in the filter, continue to the next action.
10. If the cooling system holds pressure with no decrease for one hour, start the engine and warm it up. If no overheating or leaks occur, run the engine at a low power setting to see if it's safe to use.

After overheating, O-ring seals throughout the system will harden, allowing coolant to leak into the oil pan. The cylinder head and even the cylinder block can crack, any of which can cause serious damage. Heated head bolts seem to elongate during severe overheating. This could relax the tension on the head gasket and thereby cause head gasket failure.

ENGINE TAKES LONGER THAN NORMAL TO WARM UP

Urgency: Not urgent, but should be monitored
Suggested actions:

1. Test the thermostat to make sure it opens at the rated temperature.
2. Replace the thermostat as needed.

The thermostat may not be closing when the engine cools down. To test the thermostat, heat water in a saucepan with the thermostat totally submerged. If no test thermometer is available, use a meat thermometer. The thermostat's opening temperature will be stamped on it. When the thermometer approaches the stamped temperature, watch the center section of the thermostat for a slight gap that opens and grows wider as the temperature increases. If the thermostat opens late (at a higher temperature than its rating), replace it.

ENGINE QUICKLY GOES TO FULL SPEED IN GEAR, BUT WHEN FULL THROTTLE IS APPLIED THE BOAT IS SLOW TO ACCELERATE

Urgency: Not urgent, but should be monitored

Suggested actions:

1. Double-check the pitch and diameter of the propeller to ensure that it is right for the boat.
2. If the boat has an extremely shallow draft, it may need a cupped-out four-blade propeller.

If the problem happens after a propeller change, suspect that there is not enough wheel pitch or diameter. If the boat has always behaved this way, then it may never have had the correct propeller. Check with your local propeller shop for recommendations.

Some high-speed outboard drive propellers have rubber vibration isolators built into the hubs. These units can fail and will let the drive slip rather than turning the propeller at full speed.

ENGINE CRANKS BUT TAKES A VERY LONG TIME TO START

Urgency: Requires immediate attention
Suggested actions:

1. Check for a plugged fuel filter or faulty anti-drain-back check valve in the fuel lift pump.
2. Read the engine service manual troubleshooting section for hard starting.
3. Check for a weak starter that doesn't provide full cranking speed.

Gasoline engines that take lots of cranking to start often have a weak check valve in the fuel transfer pump, which allows the fuel line just before the carburetor to fill with air that can only be purged by cranking. To see if this is the problem, just pour $1/4$ cup of gasoline down the carburetor opening before cranking. Then try to start the engine. If the engine starts immediately, you know the fuel is draining back and the check valve in the transfer pump is faulty.

ENGINE DIESELS, IS SLOW TO TURN OFF, OR WON'T STOP AT ALL

Urgency: Requires immediate attention
Suggested actions:

1. Lower engine speed.
2. Retard the ignition.
3. Remove deposits from the combustion chamber.

Dieseling is a problem with older gasoline engines that idle too fast and have glowing phosphorus deposits that keep igniting whatever fuel arrives in the cylinder. The engine idle speed may be set too high. Engines with phosphorus deposits in the combustion chamber can continue to run with the ignition turned off because the phosphorus apparently gets hot and glows, thereby continuing to light the incoming gasoline.

Take these steps to eliminate the deposits without removing the cylinder head: With the engine at operating temperature, bring the engine speed to approximately 1,500 rpm while pouring a steady stream of water down the carburetor (or through the throttle body on fuel-injected engines). Be sure to pour enough water in the opening to almost stall the engine, but not quite. Apparently the steaming action helps loosen the deposits.

ENGINE TAKES A VERY LONG TIME TO START

Urgency: Attend to as soon as convenient
Suggested actions:

1. For gasoline engines, a lengthy start process is usually caused by lack of fuel, so replace the fuel filter first.
2. Next, consider installing a new mechanical fuel pump, if so equipped, because check valves in the pump can weaken and let the pump lose its prime when the engine is turned off and sits unused for six or eight hours.

If the fuel tank is lower than the engine, gasoline can drain from the engine back to the tank through the lift pump check valve in carbureted fuel systems. To test for this, use Vise-Grips to clamp any two flat objects on both sides of the rubber fuel supply hose leading from the tank to the lift pump. This improvised clamp will close the hose. You must do this immediately after the engine is shut off. Wait a day, and, immediately before starting the engine, remove the clamp. If the engine starts well, then you have proven that the pump check valves are bad. Proceed by replacing the fuel lift pump.

DISTRIBUTOR ROTOR WON'T TURN WITH ENGINE CRANKSHAFT

Urgency: Requires immediate attention
Suggested action: Remove the distributor and look down the distributor hole to see if the end of the camshaft is turning. If it is not, the cam drive (timing) chain is broken.

The power to turn the ignition distributor and the oil pump of most gasoline engines comes through the engine's camshaft. Therefore, if the timing chain between the crankshaft and the camshaft breaks, the camshaft won't turn and neither will the distributor and oil pump. For overhead camshaft engines that have a cam driven by a cog belt, a broken belt can be handled differently. Other potential problems with distributors include carbon tracking (Fig. 12-1). When present, carbon tracking looks like a pencil line drawn from one of the posts in the cap to another post, or down the side of the cap. The current then flows along the track to ground, rather than traveling to the spark plug.

WORK-AROUND SOLUTION

Stripped Cam Belts
The cam belts that power most overhead cams in gasoline engines should be replaced after 1,500 hours of use. If your belt snaps before you can replace it and you can't get a new one, you can use the technique shown in Chapter 4 to get home.

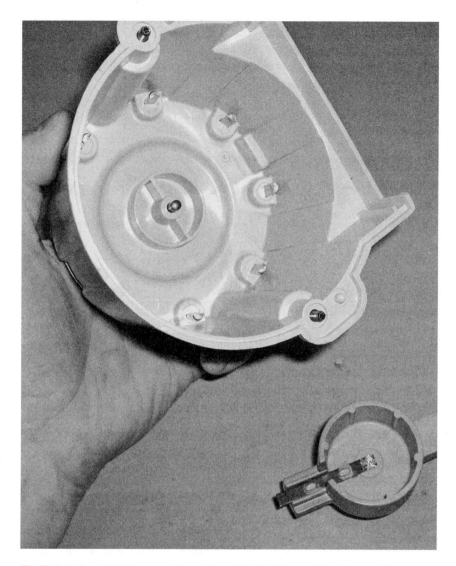

Fig. 12-1. A clean distributor cap—if yours has what looks like pencil lines, you may have a carbon tracking problem.

GASOLINE CLOUDY OR FUEL FILTERS PLUG WITH DARK MATERIAL

Urgency: Attend to as soon as convenient
Suggested actions:

1. Drain the fuel tank and refill.
2. Replace all fuel filters.

Water in the fuel encourages the growth of microorganisms known as algae, which can form a type of gum in the fuel. Fuel stabilizer additives stop algae and gum from contaminating gasoline. Keeping the tanks full of fuel will help reduce condensation in the fuel tanks, which results from temperature changes and provides an ideal environment for algae.

VISIBLE WEAR ON EDGES OF DRIVE BELT

Urgency: Not urgent, but should be monitored

Suggested action: Replace the belt and any associated idlers.

Wear on the edge of a belt means that either the pulleys are misaligned or that something is rubbing on the side of the belt. When replacing a serpentine belt, be sure to diagram the layout of the belt and where pulleys engage the rib side and the flat side of the belt. See the photo on page 54.

WHAT YOU HEAR

WHEN YOU ATTEMPT TO START THE ENGINE, IT GOES "CLUNK," COMES UP HARD AGAINST SOMETHING, AND WILL NOT TURN

Urgency: Requires immediate attention
Suggested actions:

1. First, determine if the problem is mechanical or hydraulic by removing the spark plugs to see if the engine will turn with the cylinders open. If the engine is still locked after removing the spark plugs, the problem is mechanical.
2. To track down the mechanical lock, remove the valve covers and inspect the valve mechanism for one valve that stays open even when the cam is down.
3. Next, consult the engine manual for ideas, and consider removing the cylinder heads to investigate further.

When there is water or fuel on top of a piston, it stops crankshaft movement until

---

CLEARING A HYDRAULICALLY LOCKED GASOLINE ENGINE

Remove all spark plugs and, using the method outlined in the sidebar on page 36, bar the engine over by hand, turning it two full revolutions of the crankshaft. Caution is needed, because the fluid really squirts out through the spark plug holes!

If the starter motor were used to turn the engine with fluid on top of a piston, severe damage could occur. This damage could include a bent connecting rod or a bent or cracked crankshaft.

---

the liquid is removed. *Note: A hydraulic lock sounds like a mechanical lock.*

ENGINE HAS DULL KNOCK

Urgency: Requires immediate attention

Suggested action: Oil analysis is a great tool to help spot trouble early. Of course, there is always the old standby, cutting open a filter for inspection to detect the presence of metal particles that indicate damage.

Bad rod bearings are noisy. A very loose (excess clearance) bearing can even let the piston slap the cylinder head at the top of its upward travel. Cut open the oil filter and check for bearing material in the pleats of the filter media. If metal is present in the filter, the oil pan must be removed for a visual inspection of the connecting rods.

SHARP METALLIC KNOCK, ALL THE TIME

Urgency: Requires immediate attention

Suggested actions:

1. Stop the engine and cut open a filter. If there is metal in the filter, avoid starting the engine until repairs are made.
2. Remove the valve cover and look for a valve stem that stays lower than the rest. This is a sign of a bent valve.

Possible causes of this sound include a faulty rod bearing or a valve hitting a piston.

SHARP METALLIC-SOUNDING "RAP" WHEN STARTING COLD, DISAPPEARS WHEN WARM

Urgency: Requires immediate attention
Suggested actions:

1. Cut open an oil filter with at least twenty-four hours of running time on it and look for the presence of aluminum.
2. Consult the engine service manual and listen to similar engines in other boats.
3. Send the oil for analysis at a lab.

A piston with too much cylinder wall clearance will make this sound when cold. As the piston warms up, it expands and the noise ceases. If large amounts of aluminum are detected when inspecting the oil filter, replace the pistons.

ENGINE HAS METALLIC CLICK

Urgency: Attend to as soon as convenient
Suggested actions:

1. Remove the valve cover and inspect the valve train.
2. Check the engine service manual for clues.

3. If nothing is apparently wrong, cut open an oil filter and also do an oil analysis.

This sound may result from loose valve adjustments or a faulty valve mechanism. If you remove the pushrods, if so equipped, roll them on a flat surface to check for straightness. If they are bent, replace them. Solid pushrods, however, can be hammered straight for a temporary fix.

HIGH-PITCHED SQUEAL

Urgency: Attend to as soon as convenient
Suggested action: Check for alternator or water pump belt slippage.

A slipping alternator, power steering pump, or water pump belt will cause a squealing noise. For engines with serpentine belts, do the following check. With the engine idling, use a spray bottle with water in it and spray the back of the serpentine belt to see if the noise goes away. If it does, the belt idle may be faulty or misaligned. *Note: Many gasoline engines use two idlers, and one is down low on the front of the engine where it is easy to miss.*

SLIGHT BUT DEFINITE CHANGE IN SOUND OF ENGINE THAT PUZZLES YOU

Urgency: Attend to as soon as convenient
Suggested actions:

1. Cut open the oil filter to check for metal in the oil, the sign of ongoing engine destruction.
2. Follow up with an oil analysis.

If no metal is present in the oil filter and the oil analysis comes back clean, then monitor the oil pressure and water temperature gauges for any changes from the norm.

LOUD RUMBLING NOISE NEAR ENGINE STARTER

Urgency: Requires immediate attention

Suggested action: Remove the starter and check for drive gear damage.

When the starter drive (also called the Bendix, see Fig. 12-2) stays engaged in the flywheel, it will cause an ominous rumbling. The Bendix is the part of the starter that carries the gear that engages with the flywheel teeth. When the starter is engaged,

the drive gear jumps out and meshes with the flywheel teeth. To check this further, remove the starter motor (with the engine shut off, of course) and inspect both the starter drive gear teeth and the flywheel teeth for excessive wear. The best sign of excess wear is the presence of metal filings in the hole where the nose of the starter resides. If there is a lot of metal present, replace the starter.

ENGINE SOUNDS LIKE IT IS RAPIDLY ACCELERATING OUT OF CONTROL

Urgency: Requires immediate attention

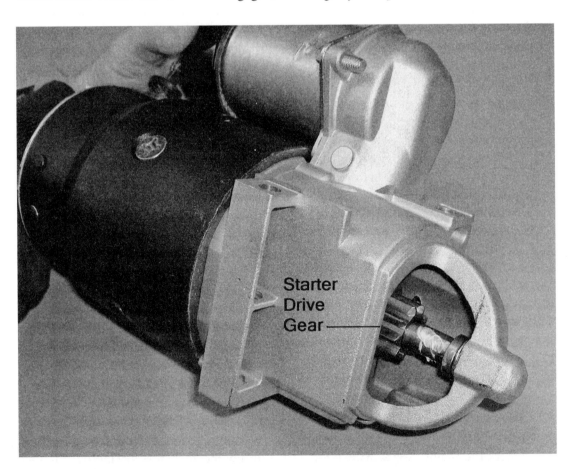

Fig. 12-2. The Bendix—hidden here inside the starter motor housing—carries the starter gear that is visible at right.

Suggested actions:

1. Quickly find a way to pull back the throttle or turn off the ignition system.
2. Check the throttle linkage to see if it's held in the top speed position.

The throttle linkage may be disconnected, or the throttle return spring may have broken.

ENGINE SPUTTERS OR STUMBLES WHEN STARTING TO ACCELERATE
Urgency: Attend to as soon as convenient
Suggested action: Consult the engine service manual to learn how to repair the fuel system's acceleration circuit.

Every carburetor or fuel injection system is designed to supply extra fuel during acceleration. If this function of the system is not working, the engine will stumble on acceleration.

WHEN YOU PLACE AN ENGINE IN GEAR, IT SOUNDS AS IF IT LUGS BADLY AND THEN DIES WITHOUT TURNING THE PROPELLER SHAFT
Urgency: Requires immediate attention
Suggested action: Check to see if there is something fouled in the propeller.

This may be a line in the wheel or broken gear teeth in the propulsion drivetrain.

ENGINE SEEMS TO CRANK WELL (CRANKSHAFT IS SPINNING), BUT THERE IS NO SOUND OF IT TRYING TO START
Urgency: Requires immediate attention
Suggested actions:

1. Verify that there is a spark by plugging in a spare spark plug to a plug wire and cranking the engine to see if the spark jumps the gap in the test plug.
2. If there is no spark, verify that there is 12-volt power to the primary side of the ignition system. The ignition system has two sides—the primary, which is battery voltage, and the secondary, which is the much higher voltage that makes the spark. On the primary side, possible problems are a cut wire, a corroded electrical terminal, or even a faulty ignition resistor.
3. Check the engine service manual for ignition troubleshooting instructions.
4. To check fuel delivery to a carbureted or throttle body fuel-injected engine, remove the air filter and, viewing from slightly above and to the side of the carburetor, check to see if there is incoming fuel when the engine is cranked. *Caution:* When checking for the presence of fuel, beware of backfiring! Wear a face shield and glasses when doing a visual check for gasoline, and remember to look down the carburetor or throttle body from the side rather than from directly above the unit.
5. Another possibility is severe flooding. Remove a spark plug to see if it is drenched with fuel.
6. If the engine is flooded, remove all spark plugs for one hour to let the excess fuel dissipate.

A weak ignition spark, a restriction of the fuel supply, or severe flooding with fuel are likely causes. Also, the secondary side of the ignition system may have a failed ignition coil or a failed coil wire to the center of the distributor cap. It may also be a faulty rotor in the distributor cap, if so equipped, or a faulty distributor cap.

Remove the air filter and look down the carburetor or throttle body while someone cranks the engine. No fuel in this area means there is a fuel supply problem, and that it's time to change the fuel filter or the fuel pump, or even put some fuel in the tank.

ENGINE BACKFIRES

Urgency: Requires immediate attention

Suggested action: Check ignition timing, the distributor cap, and rotor.

A more severe cause could be the failure of the timing belt or the chain that turns the distributor.

BACKFIRING

A backfire is defined as unexpected popping or even an explosion of fuel and air, usually coming from the engine intake manifold. In other words, the air and gasoline mixture is traveling backward and coming back out of the intake manifold.

When a loud explosion comes from the exhaust pipe it would seem that it should be called a front fire, but it isn't. Exhaust explosions are still called a backfire. It is true that the gases are flowing in the right direction. However, the air and fuel are making a severe increase in pressure in the wrong place (in the exhaust system, rather than in the cylinder). A mechanic would describe these two types of backfiring as "backfiring from the intake" or "backfiring from the exhaust."

ENGINE SOUNDS LIKE IT ALMOST STARTS, BUT THE STARTER'S DRIVE KICKS OUT FIRST

Urgency: Requires immediate attention

Suggested actions:

1. Use a timing light as directed by the engine repair manual to verify that the ignition timing is correct.
2. Older engines with a burned-out ignition resistor will run as long as the starter motor is cranking; however, when you let off on the key, the engine stops. Replace the starter motor.

Suspect the starter drive mechanism in the starter. If possible, try installing another starter motor assembly.

ENGINE SOUNDS LIKE IT'S RUNNING ROUGH AT LOW IDLE

Urgency: Attend to as soon as convenient

Suggested actions:

1. Check spark plug wires for insulation damage.
2. Check spark plugs and replace as needed.
3. Check the distributor cap.

Rough running could be spark related, due to faulty spark plug wire insulation or even a faulty distributor cap or rotor. This could also be a faulty cylinder, due to damage of valves or even a hole in a piston crown.

ENGINE MISSES AT HIGH SPEED

Urgency: Attend to as soon as convenient

Suggested action: See previous symptom.

ENGINE MAKES "PINGING" SOUND
Urgency: Requires immediate attention
Suggested actions:

1. Use premium-grade gasoline.
2. Set the ignition timing to specifications.

Pinging is caused by the premature detonation of the air-fuel mixture in gasoline engines. It happens before the piston travels to the top of the cylinder on the compression stroke when the spark timing is set too early. This can even happen from the heat of compression, especially when high-compression engines are fueled with low-octane gasoline.

ENGINE VIBRATES AT LOW RPM
Urgency: Attend to as soon as convenient
Suggested actions:

1. First cut open the oil filter and look for metal particles that indicate damage. If there is no metal in the filter, the engine can be safely run for additional checking.

GASOLINE ENGINE VIBRATIONS

All gasoline engines (except four-cylinder) are normally vibration free, though some will have a small amount of vibration at a certain speed. It is important to pay attention to your engine's usual pattern of vibration, if it has one. As you get to know a new engine, make a mental note of how it sounds through the full range of throttle settings. A change in any engine's vibration pattern is something to check out immediately, because it could be the first sign of a problem.

2. Remove the starter to see if the drive gears are damaged by staying engaged after the engine starts.
3. Check for one or more cylinders misfiring or not firing at all.
4. Check for a loose front crankshaft damper or pulley.
5. Check engine mounts to make sure they are intact and tight.
6. Check the flywheel to ensure that it is installed tight to the crankshaft.
7. Confirm that the transmission drive adapter is attached properly to the flywheel and that the elastomeric (rubber-like material) drive member is intact and properly attached.
8. Confirm that the flywheel housing is centered on the flywheel and is not egg-shaped, off-center, or otherwise misaligned. (See Figure 11-6.)

If the starter stays engaged, it will produce a noisy rumble because the gear ratio between the starter and the flywheel is greater than 10:1. For example, when the starter stays engaged, it will spin at least 10,000 rpm if the engine is running at 1,000 rpm. Check the starter drive visually by removing the starter and looking for shiny shards of metal or damage to gear and flywheel teeth. If the engine has had recent repairs or a rebuild, confirm that the correct pistons, rods, and wrist pins were used.

ENGINE VIBRATES AT MEDIUM RPM, WITH LOUD RUMBLING
Urgency: Attend to as soon as convenient
Suggested action: See previous symptom.
As in the previous symptom, a starter that stays engaged in the flywheel will damage

both the starter and the ring gear. The fly-wheel ring gear will fail in time because of where the engine tends to come to rest when turned off. To see whether the starter is remaining engaged in the flywheel after the engine starts, remove the starter and look for bright (recent) wear on the flywheel teeth. The starter drive gear will also show extra wear and the presence of metal filings throughout the starter drive cavity, which is the hole the starter plugs into.

Also check for one or more cylinders mis-firing or not firing at all. Check for a loose front crankshaft damper or pulley. Check engine mounts to make sure they are intact and tight. If the engine was recently repaired or rebuilt, confirm that the correct pistons, rods, and wrist pins were used. Confirm that the flywheel is installed tight to the crank-shaft. Ensure that the transmission drive adapter is attached properly to the flywheel and that the elastomeric (rubber-like) drive member is intact and properly attached.

ENGINE VIBRATES AT HIGH RPM
Urgency: Attend to as soon as convenient
Suggested action: See previous two symptoms.

INBOARD/OUTBOARD (IO) APPLICA-TIONS: ENGINE VIBRATION IS NO-TICEABLE AND IS WORST AT THE REAR OF ENGINE
Urgency: Attend to as soon as convenient
Suggested action: Check alignment of the engine to the outdrive according to the ser-vice manual.

Faulty engine mounting can allow move-ment and vibration when there are loose mounting bolts. A soft foot differs from a soft (flexible) engine mount. Many inboard gas engines have soft mounts as shown in Figure 12-3. A soft foot is when one corner

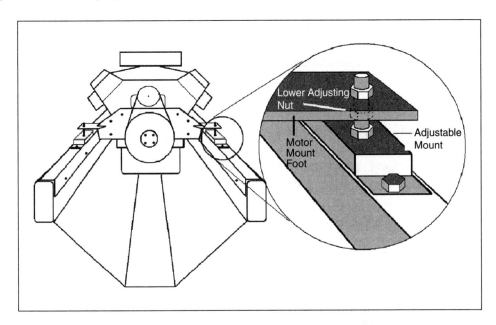

Fig. 12-3. Most small diesels (such as those on pleasure boats) and gasoline engines can be installed with adjustable mounts, as shown here. If, when you back off the top nut on both sides, one side or the other springs up, you have a soft foot and will have to adjust the mount to meet it.

of the engine and transmission mounting system is on a different plane than the other mounting feet. When all the mounting bolts are tightened in a soft foot situation, it can bend the exterior of the engine, especially large engines mounted on strong steel rails in steel boats.

To check for a soft foot, loosen both front mounting bolts to see if the shim pack on either front mount can be easily slid out of place. If the shim pack is loose, you have found a soft foot that must be shimmed up so that it carries the same amount of weight as the other front foot.

Inboard/outboard (IO) applications require the engine to be mounted and aligned according to the manufacturer's directions. These instructions usually come in an installation manual, rather than in the service manual. Many IO engine systems are a package that consists of an engine, the transom support for the rear of the engine, and the outdrive. Often the engine and outdrive are manufactured by different companies and married together in a package. Factory technical support is terrible for many of these packages after the sale.

WHAT YOU SMELL
GASOLINE ODOR
Urgency: Requires immediate attention
Suggested action: Use extreme caution and check for a visible fuel leak on the pressure side of the engine fuel system. Remember, if gasoline smells strongly it is potentially explosive!

Sources of gasoline leaks include hoses, fittings, flooding of the engine intake and cylinders with gasoline, or an overfilled fuel tank.

OIL AND FUEL SYSTEMS

WHAT YOU SEE
ENGINE OIL BLACK AND VERY THICK (VISCOUS)
Urgency: Attend to as soon as convenient

Suggested actions:

1. Verify that the proper oil is being used.
2. Change both oil and filter and shorten the oil change interval.
3. Monitor the oil color, and send a sample to an oil lab to troubleshoot this problem.

Thick, black oil in a gasoline engine shows that the oil change interval is too long. Over time, badly worn piston rings and scored cylinder walls causing gaps between rings and cylinder walls will also contribute to black oil. Another cause of poor ring seating is the ingestion of abrasive dust due to a faulty air filter or even due to dust entering the engine during repairs. Poor break-in of gasoline engines, which results in excessive blowby, is almost unheard of.

OIL VERY THIN AND DRIPS RAPIDLY FROM DIPSTICK
Urgency: Requires immediate attention
Suggested actions:

1. Change the oil and filter.
2. Investigate the possibility of a choke that is stuck closed on a carbureted engine.

Oil in this condition means that there is raw gasoline going past the rings. This can be due to a choke set too rich on a carbureted engine, or it can also be caused by cranking the engine with the throttle open when attempting to start it.

ENGINE OIL REMAINS HONEY-COLORED EVEN WITH MANY HOURS ON IT
Urgency: Not urgent, but should be monitored

FLOODING THE ENGINE WITH GASOLINE

The word "flooding" means delivering far too much raw (wet) fuel to the intake manifold and the cylinders. Fuel-injected gasoline engines are easy to flood. Generally, manufacturers recommend not opening the throttle at all before starting one.

Once a fuel-injected gasoline engine is flooded, the best thing to do is turn off the boat's battery switches to avoid any possibility of sparking, and then remove the air filter. Next, select a clean and slender object, like a long screw or screwdriver, that is too large to fall through the throttle plates. Gently open the throttle, and slide the screwdriver tip past the throttle plates to hold them open. This will allow pooled-up gasoline in the intake manifold to evaporate.

Pooled gasoline prevents the engine from starting. It typically can be found in the intake manifold and in the engine cylinders. When an engine comes to rest after the ignition is turned off, some of the intake valves and some of the exhaust valves remain open until the engine is cranked again. Blocking the throttle plate open and waiting for one-half hour in warm weather, or an hour in cooler weather, will allow most of the excess gasoline to evaporate.

If you try this procedure and the engine still won't start, remove the air filter again and block the throttle plate open. This time, go one step further and remove all the spark plugs and wait for two hours. When you're ready to try starting the engine, withdraw the screwdriver from the throttle plate and reinstall the air filter.

Note: Before trying to start the engine after the waiting period, be sure to run the vessel's ventilation fan until the engine compartment is clear of all gasoline fumes. To be on the safe side, continue running the fan for five minutes after you can no longer smell fumes.

Suggested action: This is probably normal. However, verify the correct weight and grade of the engine oil.

For gasoline engines, this is a normal condition due to clean engine oil. Also, synthetic oil stays clean much longer than petroleum-based oil because it resists breaking down from engine heat.

There are two kinds of oil filters: the full-flow filter that all engines come with from the factory, and the optional partial-flow filter (also called a bypass filter). The full-flow unit filters all oil going to the engine from the oil pump as long as it doesn't exceed its capacity to hold solids. After the filter pleats clog with solids, or when the filter pores become restricted, the filter capacity is reached and a small spring-loaded bypass (pressure relief) valve opens as a stopgap measure to lubricate the engine. When this happens, the filter is in bypass mode and none of the engine oil is filtered. Good maintenance will prevent this problem.

The partial-flow filter is supplied by aftermarket companies as an add-on. This unit supplements the action of the full-flow filter by continuously taking a small amount of pressurized oil from the engine's oil pump flow and super-cleaning it. The partial-flow filter will clean up a dirty engine in a few days of operation.

OIL LEAKING FROM ENGINE
   Urgency: Attend to as soon as convenient
   Suggested actions:

1. Keep the engine oil level full until repairs can be made.
2. Find the source of the leak by narrowing it down to the left or right side, front or rear, or top or bottom of the engine.

3. After finding the source of the leak, further classify it as either a faulty gasket or fitting or a crack. Then check the engine manual for instructions.

To zero in on the source of an engine oil leak, check the engine oil level. If it is high, the leak may be coming from a front or rear oil seal. Find out if it is the front or rear seal that is leaking, and if the leak appears to be high or low on the engine. It may be on the left or right side of the engine. The leak may also not even be a leak, but rather the result of someone having spilled oil when it was last added to the engine. Engines with a banjo fitting to the dipstick tube can also leak (Fig. 12-4).

OIL LEAKING FROM BOTTOM OF BELL HOUSING OR FROM FRONT CRANK-SHAFT SEAL

Urgency: Attend to as soon as convenient
Suggested actions:

1. Keep the oil level full until the leak is repaired.

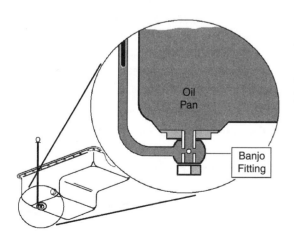

Fig. 12-4. One possible source of an oil leak is the banjo fitting at the bottom of the dipstick tube.

2. If it's the front crankshaft seal, then the vibration damper must be removed and the seal replaced according to engine service manual directions.
3. If it's the rear seal, the engine will need to be removed and pulled forward to allow replacement of the seal. Check the engine manual to learn the best way to do this.
4. If the engine must be used before the seal is replaced, one strategy is to maintain the oil level right at the low-level mark on the dipstick. This will sometimes slow the rate of oil leakage.

The bottom of the bell housing can leak oil. The source of this type of leak is the engine's rear crankshaft oil seal. If crankcase pressure gets too high due to a plugged or restricted engine crankcase vent, the front and/or rear crankshaft seals may fail. Use a slide hammer to remove the old seal. See page 95 for more details on leaky crankshaft seals.

Gasoline engines are also prone to leaks from the timing chain cover in the front of the engine. The fix for this involves removing the front crankshaft pulley and vibration damper first and then the engine front timing gear cover before replacing the gasket.

OIL LEAK AT EITHER SIDE, NEAR FRONT OF ENGINE

Urgency: Attend to as soon as convenient
Suggested actions:

1. Tighten the valve cover bolts to see if this repairs the leak.
2. If not, replace the valve cover gaskets.

Faulty valve cover gaskets will cause oil to leak down either side or down both sides of an engine. Leaks low on either side of the engine will come from an oil pan gasket.

Note: When resealing a valve cover gasket, never use silicone sealer on both sides because it acts like a lubricant and will let the gasket slip out of place when the cover bolts are tightened. Instead, glue one side of the valve cover gasket to the cover with contact cement. Do this while keeping the boltholes in the gasket lined up with the boltholes in the cover, and let it dry. Then, just before assembly, put a light coat of silicone sealer on the other side (surface that will seal against the cylinder head). When clamped, the gasket will stay in place.

METALLIC PARTICLES (GLITTER) VISIBLE IN ENGINE OR TRANSMISSION OIL OR IN FILTER MEDIA PAPER

Urgency: Requires immediate attention
Suggested actions:

1. Listen for new and worrisome noise that accompanies the metal particles.
2. Remove the valve cover and check for valve train damage as it is described in the engine manual troubleshooting section.
3. Consult a marine mechanic if the source of the damage isn't apparent.

Where there is glitter, there is mechanical damage. Changing the oil and filter and cutting open a second filter after repairs are made will tell if a situation is under control. In the case of an outboard or outdrive that has no filter, simply draining the oil and comparing new and used oil will visually reveal the presence of metal.

When filters are cut open and there is metal present, try to determine what type of metal it is. For example, brass or copper will be golden or yellow, which may be material from a crankshaft thrust bearing. The presence of aluminum (pistons on most engines) will be dull white, chromium (piston rings) will be bright and shiny, and cast iron or steel will be harder to locate visually. Passing a clean magnet over the media paper should attract cast-iron or steel particles, making them easier to identify.

CREAM-COLORED SLUDGE SEEN INSIDE ENGINE OIL FILL CAP

Urgency: Attend to as soon as convenient
Suggested actions:

1. Change oil and filter and start monitoring the cooling system for coolant loss.
2. If coolant seems to be leaking into the oil, consult your engine manual and also see Chapter 16.

When water or coolant leaks into the engine crankcase, it goes to the bottom of the oil pan because it is heavier than the engine's lube oil. It will stay on the bottom until the engine is started. When the engine is running, the water is pulled from the bottom of the pan into the engine oil pump. From there it is sent throughout the lubricating system. As the engine warms up, the oil and the coolant emulsify into a foamy, oily consistency that cannot properly lubricate the engine.

The source of coolant entering the crankcase may be an oil cooler, if so equipped, or a head gasket. The test for either one is the pressurization of the cooling system. If the system will not hold 20 psi, there is a leak somewhere. Check the oil cooler, if so equipped. If the oil cooler is good, then it is time to remove the oil pan if there is room, and if not, to remove the cylinder heads to inspect the head gaskets for signs of obvious damage (bending) or discoloration.

It's best to learn about head gasket failures before you need the information. Visit a repair shop and ask to see faulty head gaskets. The second best scenario is to buy a new set of head gaskets for your engine and examine them with an experienced mechanic.

Water in the oil often occurs after overheating from plugged coolant passages (Fig. 12-5).

If no damage is found, then each head must be pressure-tested. If no pressure tester is available, with the engine cold, remove the pressure system cap from the reservoir and top off the tank with fresh water (salt water will damage the engine). Now, start the engine and watch for bubbles going up through the reservoir. Constant bubbles coming up through the reservoir indicate combustion gases leaking into the cooling system through a cracked head or a faulty head gasket. *Note: A faulty oil cooler will not make bubbles in the reservoir, but it will transfer oil into the cooling system.*

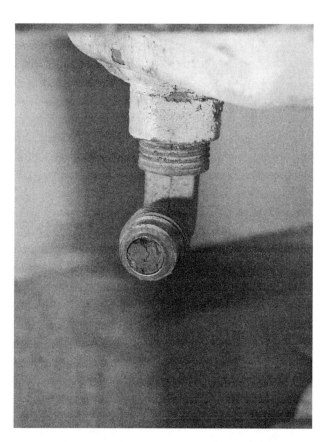

Fig. 12-5. This plugged coolant passage could have been avoided by regular changing of the coolant. (Courtesy MER Equipment, Seattle, Washington)

Engine oil can also enter a cooling system through the oil cooler when an internal leak develops in the tubes inside the unit. To test the oil cooler, remove both oil lines and plug one of them. Pressurize the cooler through the other passage to 40 psi to verify that it is sound. If it will not hold pressure, replace it.

Boatowners have been known to mix no-suds dishwasher detergent with water and

---

REPAIRING AN ENGINE THAT SANK WHILE RUNNING

When a running marine engine is inverted or sunk in a boating accident, water soon enters the intake manifold. When the water enters the next cylinder of the firing order that is on the intake stroke, the engine takes a deep "breath" of water. However, when the intake valve on that cylinder closes and the flywheel tries to carry the crankshaft motion through, the piston comes up against the water in the cylinder because the exhaust valve is closed. Water is incompressible, forcing the engine to stop very suddenly.

The sudden stop will usually bend *only* one connecting rod: the rod on the cylinder that first took in water. To restore the engine, remove the cylinder head and the oil pan and measure the full extent of the height of each piston in the cylinder with a dial indicator. One of the pistons will be a little lower in its cylinder than the rest. Change the rod, piston, and rings on the cylinder with the piston not at its full height.

If the engine is completely dismantled, have a machine shop check the crankshaft for cracks. If, however, the engine must be used as is for a while, over time any cracks may increase in length. The check for measuring maximum piston height is the same for gasoline and diesel engines.

---

pour it into the cooling system to break down the oil and thereby clean the system. If this is done, the system will need to be flushed with fresh water several times, because many dishwasher detergents contain salt. Contact the engine manufacturer or your marine mechanic for instructions.

ENGINE OIL LEVEL ON DIPSTICK RISES SLOWLY OVER TIME, AND OIL BECOMES MILKY

Urgency: Attend to as soon as convenient
Suggested actions:

1. Change the oil and filter and monitor the coolant level to see if coolant is slowly leaking into the crankcase.
2. If the engine is using coolant, perform a pressure test as covered in Chapter 16 or consult the engine repair manual.

Water (coolant) entering the oil and emulsifying with the oil will cause this milky appearance.

WATER SQUIRTS OUT ENGINE DIPSTICK HOLE WHEN DIPSTICK IS REMOVED

Urgency: Requires immediate attention
Suggested actions:

1. Change oil and filter.
2. See if the cooling system is low on coolant, and if so, pressure-test the cooling system to pinpoint the leak.
3. If the coolant level is OK, the water must have come from an external source.

Tasting the water will prove if the water is fresh, salt, or antifreeze coolant.

This will help track down the source of the water. After the taste test, proceed according to the configuration of your vessel's cooling system. Consult Chapters 3 and 10 for more cooling-system information.

OILY VAPOR IN LARGE AMOUNTS BLOWS OUT ENGINE CRANKCASE VENT OR DIPSTICK TUBE

Urgency: Requires immediate attention
Suggested actions:

1. Disconnect the crankcase vent at the engine to see if this reduces the pressure in the crankcase.
2. If not, the engine has a blowby problem, which means at least one of the pistons is severely scuffed or has a hole in it.
3. Cutting open the oil filter will reveal metal in the filter if a piston is damaged to the point of requiring replacement.
4. Consult the service manual to learn the engine manufacturer's suggestions for repairing the internal engine damage that is causing the blowby.

After engines seize up hard from overheating, they will sometimes start again, but will have excessive blowby of combustion gases past the rings because the pistons, rings, and cylinder walls have been severely damaged. Excess combustion gases that leak past the rings into the crankcase will build pressure in the crankcase that will eventually overwhelm the crankshaft seals. Engine crankcase vents are designed to carry the normal amount of these gases out of the engine, and, in many boats, they are vented into the engine room! However, when an engine is damaged by overheating, is nearing rebuild time, or is failing, it will begin to produce large amounts of crankcase gases. This is a sign that the engine cylinders are weak. *Note: A plugged crankcase vent will cause these same symptoms.*

ENGINE OIL LEVEL CHANGES ERRATICALLY, SOMETIMES READING HIGH, SOMETIMES LOW

Urgency: Requires immediate attention
Suggested actions:

1. Change the oil and filter, taking care to use the amount of oil specified by the manufacturer.
2. If the oil level continues to fluctuate rapidly, check the bottom of the external oil dipstick tube, if so equipped, for blockage.

Erratic changes in oil level can easily happen when an engine has an external dipstick tube that goes to the bottom of the oil pan as shown in Figure 12-6. Even new engines with few hours on them can have a surprising amount of debris in the oil pan during the break-in period. While the break-in period (also called *run-in*) for a new diesel engine can be as much as 500 hours of operation, gasoline engines are considered run-in at 100 hours.

The fix for erratic dipstick readings in a case like this is to remove the banjo fitting bolt and clean it. If the debris appears to be a metallic chip, then the decision must be made whether or not to keep running the engine or to tear it down and find the source of the contamination that plugged the tube.

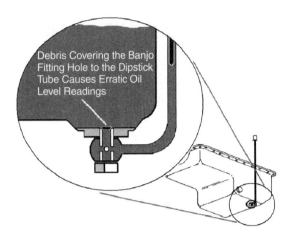

Debris Covering the Banjo Fitting Hole to the Dipstick Tube Causes Erratic Oil Level Readings

Fig. 12-6. Erratic dipstick readings can be caused by debris clogging the banjo fitting hole.

ENGINE OIL LEVEL SUDDENLY VERY LOW

Urgency: Requires immediate attention
Suggested actions:

1. Change the oil and filter so there is a known quantity of oil in the engine and then proceed to troubleshoot by checking the bilge for oil floating on the bilge water.
2. If there is oil leaking from the engine, determine the source of the leak and proceed as needed.
3. If no leak is found, the engine may be burning a lot of oil or leaking oil into the cooling system.

Cracks in the oil pan, or a pan that has rusted through, will quickly dump the lube oil. Oil can also quickly transfer into the cooling system through a split (or leaking) engine oil cooler. When the oil level quickly drops, it is time to check the cooling system for the presence of oil in the coolant reservoir. If there is also oil in the coolant, then the oil

cooler must be pressure-tested by capping off one of the oil openings and putting 20 psi to the other opening. If the oil cooler will not hold pressure, then it must be replaced.

WHAT YOU TASTE

WATER IS FOUND IN OIL PAN AND HAS NO TASTE

Urgency: Requires immediate attention
Suggested actions:

1. This is fresh water or rainwater. Change the oil and filter and watch for the source.
2. Water may have entered the engine through the horizontal exhaust system, if so equipped.
3. Check for evidence of engine room swamping.

Another possible cause may be specific to boats operating in fresh water. The source of the water might be from waves getting past the flap at the exhaust pipe on the transom and traveling into the engine via open exhaust valves.

WATER IN ENGINE OIL PAN TASTES SWEET

Urgency: Requires immediate attention
Suggested actions:

1. This indicates antifreeze coolant is leaking into the oil pan. Pressure-test the cooling system to find the leak.
2. Check the engine oil cooler that interfaces with engine coolant.

When the engine is off, the pressure on the coolant side of the oil cooler is often higher, and coolant may travel into the oil. When the engine is running, pressure is greater on the oil side of the system, and oil will travel into the coolant.

WATER IN ENGINE OIL PAN TASTES SALTY

Urgency: Requires immediate attention

Suggested action: Find out where bilge water is getting into the engine.

The engine may have been swamped, or bilge water may have gotten high enough to enter the engine through the crankshaft rear main seal.

COOLING SYSTEM

WHAT YOU SEE

ENGINE PAINT TURNS DARKER THAN ORIGINAL COLOR

Urgency: Requires immediate attention

Suggested actions:

1. Let engine cool for one hour.
2. Check engine oil and coolant levels.
3. Refill cooling system if low.
4. If the oil level is higher than normal or higher than before the overheating incident, loosen the oil drain plug in the oil pan and note what leaks out first. If coolant or water leaks out before oil, there is coolant in the oil and the engine has been severely damaged.
5. If the engine died (stalled or quit running) when hot, remove the oil filter and use a filter cutter or hacksaw to cut it open on the threaded end. Remove a piece of the filter media paper and inspect it for the presence of metal. Shards or flecks of metal in the oil filter usually indicate piston

seizure and the need for extensive repairs. If the pistons have seized, aluminum will be found in the oil filter.

Severe overheating of an engine or transmission causes the paint to change color. At a temperature of just over 270°F, engine paint begins to darken. The upper half of the engine, including the cylinder heads, will get hotter than any other external area of the engine. Keeping track of engine paint color during disassembly is a great troubleshooting tool. This will help with decisions about testing or replacement of components. See Chapter 10 for more information on what to look for when rebuilding an engine.

Contamination of the cooling system degrades coolant flow and results in severe overheating.

Extreme overheating most often results in engine seizure because the aluminum pistons in gasoline engines expand greatly and then act as brakes against the cylinder walls. This braking action scuffs the cylinder wall and the piston. It also welds aluminum to the cylinder wall. The engine can often be started after it cools, but the engine will burn oil until it is repaired.

When there is a change in paint color, pressure-test the engine cooling system to 20 psi. See Chapter 16 for more detailed information. It is also important to test individual engine components, like the jacketed marine exhaust manifold. If the individual pressure-tested components won't hold pressure, then replacement is required. See Chapter 3 and Figure 3-15 for more details on severe overheating.

CLEAR WATER LEAKING FROM THE ENGINE

Urgency: Attend to as soon as convenient
Suggested actions:

1. Keep the coolant level full while finding the source of the leak.
2. Bring the engine up to temperature. Because cooling systems are pressurized and the pressure increases as the engine warms, leaks will be worse (more apparent) when the engine is hot.
3. When the leak is found, determine if the problem is a gasket, O-ring seal, faulty hose, loose hose clamp, a faulty fitting, or a crack.

A leak like this usually comes from the cooling system itself or simply from the cooling system overflow, but it might also indicate a lack of antifreeze protection in the cooling system. If the antifreeze is sufficient, the leaking fluid should show the antifreeze color, as in the next symptom.

COLORED WATER (COOLANT MIXTURE) LEAKING FROM ENGINE

Urgency: Attend to as soon as convenient
Suggested actions:

1. Shut off the engine and refill coolant if the level is low.
2. Pressurize the cooling system by replacing the pressure cap and warming up the engine to normal operating temperature.
3. When the engine is warm, turn it off and look for the leak with a good light source.

4. Consult the service manual for instructions on the procedure for repairing the leak.

Antifreeze coolant is often red, blue, green, orange, or yellow, so a leak of one of these colors indicates a coolant leak. Use the same method mentioned in the previous symptom to pinpoint the leak by narrowing down its location.

WIPING A FINGER INSIDE ENGINE COOLING SYSTEM FILLER NECK REVEALS AN OILY SCUM UNDER COOLANT PRESSURE CAP

Urgency: Requires immediate attention
Suggested actions:

1. Pressure-test the engine oil cooler, if so equipped. Replace if needed.
2. Drain the cooling system.
3. Obtain a no-suds detergent recommended by the manufacturer and mix with hot water. Pour this mixture into the cooling system and operate the engine until the engine comes up to operating temperature.
4. Drain the cooling system again and refill with the recommended mixture of antifreeze and water.

When oil enters the engine cooling system, it emulsifies with the coolant and reduces the heat transfer of the coolant. No matter what size the engine, oil in the cooling system is a valuable clue that some system will soon run out of vital lubricating oil, and bearing damage will soon occur (Fig. 12-7).

The source of the oily scum is often either the engine or the transmission

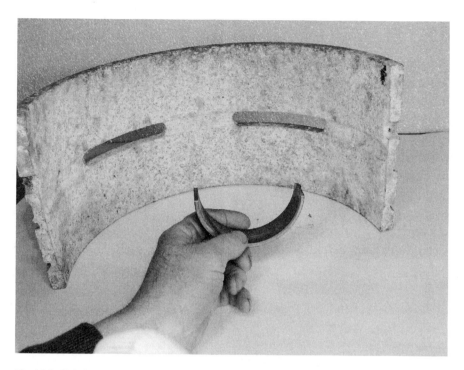

Fig. 12-7. Main bearings come in all sizes. The bearing in the hand is from a modern engine. The bearing is the background is from an ancient 100 hp diesel.

oil cooler. Black oily film in the coolant indicates that it is the engine oil cooler, while lighter-colored oil (the same color as the transmission oil) indicates that it is the transmission cooler. A pressure test of the offending oil cooler is the next step in solving the problem.

WATER OVERFLOWING FROM ENGINE COOLING SYSTEM EXPANSION TANK

Urgency: Requires immediate attention
Suggested actions:

1. Stop the engine and check for any problem that is restricting coolant flow, such as a pinched coolant hose or dented keel cooler, if so equipped.

2. If nothing is found, check the water pump drive belt for adequate tightness.

3. At this point, after no apparent cause is found, it is time to suspect a faulty head gasket.

4. Pressure-test the cooling system. If it will not hold pressure, the head gasket is suspect and must be replaced according to the engine manufacturer's directions.

After an expansion tank is overfilled, it will overflow as the engine and coolant get up to temperature. However, if an engine has overheated and combustion gases are entering the cooling system by way of a bad head gasket, this too can make the expansion tank overflow.

COOLANT SLOWLY VANISHES WHEN ENGINE IS IDLING

Urgency: Attend to as soon as convenient
Suggested actions:

1. Check all hose clamps on the cooling system for adequate tightness.
2. Check the bilge for evidence of antifreeze.
3. Follow up by pressure-testing the cooling system.
4. Check for leaking fittings or hoses between the engine and the heat exchanger.
5. Examine all fittings or hoses between the engine and the expansion tank.

Coolant might be leaking from the heat exchanger into water surrounding the hull. The heat exchanger can also leak into the bilge after it is damaged by vibration (Fig. 12-8).

COOLANT SLOWLY DISAPPEARS, BUT ONLY WHEN ENGINE RUNS

Urgency: Requires immediate attention
Suggested action: Remove the exhaust manifold and check for a slightly rusted exhaust port in the cylinder head (Fig. 12-9).

Severe Leak Caused By Vibration Against Framework

Fig. 12-8. A coolant leak into the bilge can be caused by excessive vibration of the heat exchanger. Here a mechanic has pulled the heat exchanger away from its point of contact with the engine bed. (Courtesy MER Equipment, Seattle, Washington)

Fig. 12-9. The exhaust ports shown in this section of exhaust manifold were badly rusted. Rainwater had invaded the cylinders through a vertical stack.

The engine can is probably "burning" coolant (sending it out the exhaust pipe as steam), and a corroded exhaust port is a likely result. You might have a cracked cylinder or faulty head gasket, or coolant might be entering a cylinder or the exhaust stream by way of a crack in a jacketed exhaust manifold.

COOLANT HOSES BULGED OR BLISTERED

Urgency: Requires immediate attention

Suggested action: Replace the hoses as soon as possible. Take care not to overtighten the hose clamps. It's important to always have spares on the boat.

Bulged or blistered hoses can result from chemicals attacking the rubber compound on the outside of the hose. It might be that the rubber compound isn't compatible with cleaning agents that are used to clean the engine room. According to the Gates Rubber Company, many hose failures that occur at or near the end of a hose are due to electrical activity. This happens especially if the coolant is slightly acidic and then becomes the electrolyte in a galvanic cell, a sort of battery at the hose end.

WHEN REPLACING SEALS, YOU NOTICE THE SURFACE OF O-RING SEALS ARE ROUGH

Urgency: Requires immediate attention

Suggested action: Replace the O-ring seals.

Do not use any O-ring (Fig. 12-10) seal that isn't pliable or doesn't have a smooth surface.

WHAT YOU HEAR

NOISE COMING FROM WATER (COOLANT) PUMP

Urgency: Requires immediate attention

Suggested action: If the belts feel rough, replace the pump.

Faulty water pump bearings will cause the water pump (Fig. 12-11) to get noisy. Excessive belt tension first reduces the life of the water pump bearings and then the seal.

WHAT YOU FEEL

WATER PUMP OR ALTERNATOR PULLEYS ARE HOT, IMMEDIATELY AFTER THE ENGINE IS SHUT DOWN

Urgency: Not urgent, but should be monitored

Suggested action: Increase belt tension.

A slipping belt will cause a warm or even hot pulley. Tighten the belts and see if the

Fig. 12-10. Inspect O-ring seals carefully—they should be pliable and have smooth surfaces.

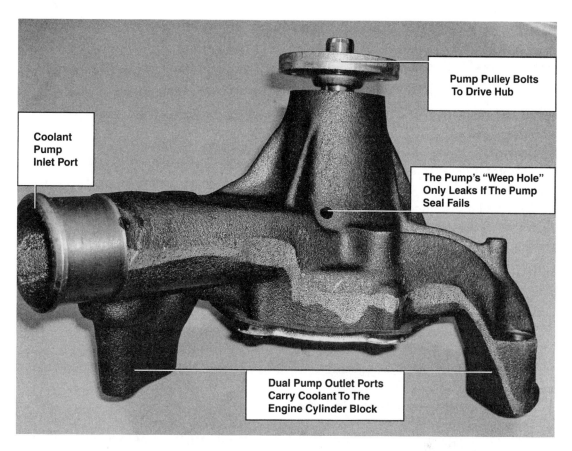

Pump Pulley Bolts To Drive Hub

Coolant Pump Inlet Port

The Pump's "Weep Hole" Only Leaks If The Pump Seal Fails

Dual Pump Outlet Ports Carry Coolant To The Engine Cylinder Block

Fig. 12-11. A belt-driven coolant pump for a gasoline inboard engine, shown with the pulley removed from the shaft at top. When a pump like this fails, water drips from the weep hole.

pulley still gets hot. If it does, it is because the belts are worn, the V-groove in the pulley is worn beyond specifications, or both causes may be in play. When changing serpentine belts, draw a diagram to help correctly reinstall the belt.

COVER OF RAW-WATER PUMP COLD
Urgency: Not urgent
Suggested action: None. This is normal.

A cold raw-water pump cover is a good sign and is proof that cold water is indeed being pumped through the cooling system to cool the engine.

COVER OF RAW-WATER PUMP HOT
Urgency: Requires immediate attention
Suggested actions:

1. Clear the raw-water opening outside the hull.
2. Clean the raw-water suction screen inside the hull.
3. Remove the cover of the raw-water pump and inspect the neoprene (rubber-like) impeller for damage.

A hot raw-water pump cover means that no raw water is passing through the engine to cool it. Check the raw-water strainer. If it is clear, the through-hull to the raw-water pump is probably clogged.

RAW-WATER COOLING SYSTEM PLUMBING COLD

Urgency: No action needed

Suggested action: This is normal and very desirable.

The plumbing is supposed to be cold when the engine is running.

RAW-WATER COOLING SYSTEM PLUMBING HOT

Urgency: Requires immediate attention

Suggested actions:

1. Clear the raw-water inlet opening outside the hull.
2. Clear the raw-water strainer inside the hull.
3. Verify that the raw-water pump is turning and that the impeller is intact.

Hot raw-water plumbing is a serious problem. A freshwater-cooled engine that depends on the raw-water pump for cooling will soon overheat and fail unless the engine is immediately turned off. The usual cause is a blocked through-hull that cuts off water flowing to the raw-water pump.

OUTLET PLUMBING OF RAW-WATER HEAT EXCHANGER IS WARM

Urgency: No action is needed.

Suggested action: This is normal.

The raw water is carrying heat away from the engine cooling system (Fig. 12-12).

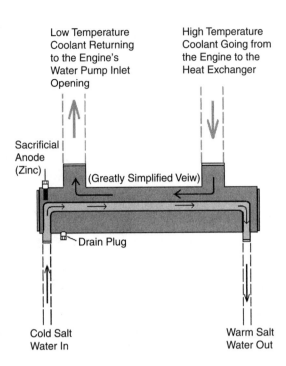

Fig. 12-12. The heat exchanger sends excess engine heat overboard.

INLET OPENING TO ENGINE COOLANT PUMP TOO HOT TO HOLD WITH BARE HAND

Urgency: Requires immediate attention

Suggested actions:

1. If so equipped, check for crimps, kinks, or other damage to the keel cooler plumbing inside or outside the boat. A frozen keel cooler will stop coolant circulation.
2. Check the belt tension on the coolant pump, if so equipped, to be sure the pump is turning.
3. Replace the thermostat.
4. Heat exchanger problems can also cause the coolant pump to warm up if the raw water is not flowing through

the heat exchanger system. Check the heat exchanger and raw-water and coolant lines.

Lack of coolant circulation through the keel cooler or heat exchanger will cause excessive heat.

OIL, COOLANT, FUEL HOSES HARD

Urgency: Attend to as soon as convenient

Suggested action: Replace hoses as soon as possible.

Old hoses or those that have been used in very hot conditions will get hard and should be replaced.

ENDS OF COOLANT HOSES VERY SOFT; ALMOST GUMMY IN CONSISTENCY

Urgency: Attend to as soon as convenient

Suggested action: Replace hoses as soon as possible.

Hoses attacked on the exterior by strong chemicals, fuel, or oil will soften and fail. Galvanic corrosion in coolant hoses can also soften hose ends.

WATER PUMP AND ALTERNATOR BELTS SEEM EXCESSIVELY TIGHT

Urgency: Attend to as soon as convenient

Suggested action: Loosen the belts.

Excessive belt tension will wear pump bearings.

WATER PUMP AND ALTERNATOR BELTS TOO LOOSE

Urgency: Attend to as soon as convenient

Suggested action: Tighten the belts.

Loose belts will slip on the pulley, limiting the available power to the driven member while shortening belt and pulley life.

EXHAUST SYSTEM

WHAT YOU SEE

ENGINE PRODUCES BLUE SMOKE

Urgency: Not urgent, but should be monitored

Suggested actions:

1. Remove the valve covers and carefully inspect the inner part of the valve springs. Watch for small pieces of black neoprene (rubber) that are the sign of degraded valve stem oil seals.
2. If the valve stem seals are good, then the piston rings may be worn or damaged.
3. The next step is to consult the engine repair manual for directions on performing a cylinder compression test. See Chapter 16.

Blue smoke indicates oil consumption that is going by the piston rings or valve guides. While it seldom occurs, adding too much of some kinds of fuel conditioner to the gasoline will cause an engine to produce blue smoke. Blue smoke is usually the sign of a worn engine.

ENGINE PRODUCES BLACK SMOKE

Urgency: Not urgent, but should be monitored

Suggested actions:

1. Black smoke indicates either too much fuel or too little air in the cylinder. First, change the air filter.
2. Next, consider adjusting the choke on carbureted engines, or even installing a manual choke.

3. For fuel-injected engines, consult the engine repair manual.

The problem may be that the choke is set too rich or stuck closed (on a carbureted gasoline engine), an air filter may be clogged, or there may be restrictions in the exhaust system. Black smoke from a gasoline engine with fuel injection likewise indicates the air-fuel ratio is too rich with gasoline. However, since most fuel-injected engines are computer controlled, the engine will require scanning for trouble codes from the computer.

WHAT YOU HEAR

EXHAUST TONE NOT SMOOTH, RATHER IRREGULAR

Urgency: Attend to as soon as convenient
Suggested action: Check for sparking coming from the spark plug wires. Replace any that spark, if not the whole set.

An engine miss due to a faulty cylinder or ignition system problem can make the engine sound irregular while the boat is under way.

EXHAUST TONE HAS INTERMITTENT POPPING SOUND

Urgency: Attend to as soon as convenient
Suggested action: Crossed spark plug wires will sound like a pop. Verify that the plug wires and plugs are wired in the correct firing order and in the correct rotation.

A sticky exhaust valve that hangs open can also cause an intermittent popping noise.

BACKFIRING OR POPPING NOISE COMING FROM ENGINE AIR-INTAKE OR EXHAUST PIPE

Urgency: Requires immediate attention
Suggested actions:

1. Check the distributor cap for carbon tracking. Carbon tracking looks like a pencil line drawn inside the cap. The carbon in the track lets the high voltage current flow to ground rather than jumping the gap at the spark plugs.
2. Rewire the spark plug wires to the distributor cap.

This type of sound can be due to a faulty intake valve or seat, or spark plug wires placed in the wrong order on the distributor cap (Fig. 12-13). Consult the engine manual for the correct firing order. Ignition spark timing must also be checked. If nothing else is found, the engine timing chain may be so loose that the spark timing has slipped (jumped time). The chain drives not only the camshaft and oil pump on many gasoline engines, but also the ignition distributor. Notice the numbered firing order labeled on the cap for each wire and also the distributor's direction of rotation in Fig. 12-13.

MECHANICAL/ELECTRICAL INTERFACE

WHAT YOU SEE

SPARKING COMES OFF IGNITION WIRES

Urgency: Not urgent, but should be monitored
Suggested actions:

1. At the least, replace any wires that are sparking.
2. Consider replacing the wires as a set and upgrading to a premium type of insulation and a larger diameter wire.
3. Route the wires away from areas of heat and chafing.

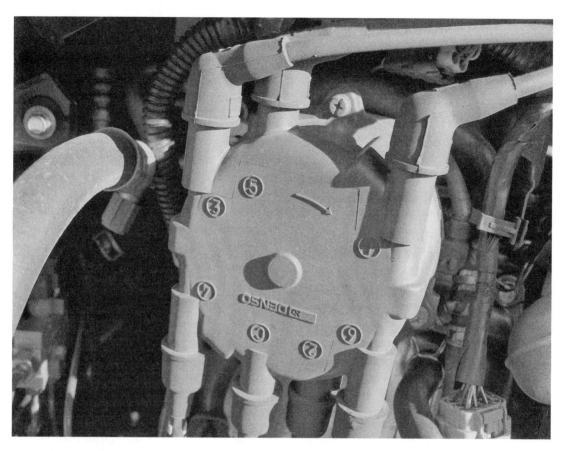

Fig. 12-13. Make certain the spark plugs that connect to the numbered terminals on the distributor cap fire in the correct order.

When spark plug wires age, are physically damaged, or are exposed to excessive heat, the insulation will break down and the spark will go to ground before reaching the spark plug. When this happens, replacement is required.

Note: To positively check an ignition system for faulty insulation, watch the engine run at night. The short circuits are easy to spot in the dark. The wires can be rerouted until new ones are obtained. An air gap is a good insulator for even a bare wire, if the wire can be kept suspended and away from grounds. Wires can be temporarily insulated with almost any plastic or rubber-like material. Newer gasoline engines have very high voltage to the spark plugs and will require thicker insulation.

WHAT YOU HEAR

NOISE COMING FROM ALTERNATOR

Urgency: Requires immediate attention

Suggested action: Remove the alternator belt and turn the alternator by hand to see if it sounds or feels rough. If it does, replace the alternator. Note: Always disconnect the battery when changing alternators.

As alternator bearings begin to fail, they can make noise. When the bearing clearance becomes excessive, the tension of the drive belt will pull the armature off-center and the spinning armature will begin to contact the side of the bore in the field windings, making even more noise. Normally, however, long before things get this bad, someone will notice that the alternator isn't working.

WHAT YOU FEEL

BATTERY CABLES WARM TO THE TOUCH

Urgency: Attend to as soon as convenient
Suggested action: Consult the engine service manual to learn how to do a starter amperage draw test.

High current draw, such as overcranking while starting a tired engine, can cause the battery cables to get warm. High resistance in the battery cable ends or cables of too small a gauge or that are too long are other possible causes.

BATTERY CABLES HOT TO THE TOUCH

Urgency: Requires immediate attention
Suggested action: Perform a starter amperage draw test and prepare to replace the starter and possibly the cables.

Hot battery cables are a bad sign because it means that the electrical current (amperage draw) is too high, and the engine requires too much cranking to start. The starter motor may be failing.

STARTER MOTOR WARM TO THE TOUCH

Urgency: Attend to as soon as convenient
Suggested action: Slight heat at the starter motor is OK, although it is true that a starter on an engine that starts well will never get warm.

The action of a starter motor, when everything is right with the electrical system, is that of a scarcely controlled dead short. Excessive heat harms starters by breaking down the insulation of the windings and eventually melts conductors inside the starter.

STARTER MOTOR HOT TO THE TOUCH

Urgency: Requires immediate attention
Suggested action: Check the tune of the engine and its general condition.

Heat at the starter motor indicates the insulation has overheated. This will eventually cause a short circuit. For the best dependability, consider replacing the starter, or at least getting a new spare as soon as possible.

AFTER SHUTTING OFF ENGINE, ALTERNATOR OR WATER PUMP PULLEY CAN BE TURNED INSIDE THE BELT BY HAND

Urgency: Attend to as soon as convenient
Suggested action: Increase belt tension.

If it takes a huge amount of belt tension to stop the slippage, suspect that the width and contour of the belt or pulley may be wrong.

LOOSE STUDS ON ELECTRICAL CONNECTIONS ON STARTER, STARTER SOLENOID, OR ALTERNATOR RESULTS IN STUD WOBBLING

Urgency: Requires immediate attention
Suggested action: Replace components that have loose studs.

Loose studs show that an electrical component is failing and requires replacement. This often results from the stud being struck or bumped, or from the electrical component being severely overheated.

WHAT YOU SMELL
ODOR OF BURNING RUBBER OR PLASTIC

Urgency: Requires immediate attention
Suggested actions:

1. Check for a slipping alternator belt or a locked-up alternator or water pump.
2. See if something like raingear is leaning against a hot part of the engine.
3. Turn off all AC and DC electrical power and check for hot electrical wiring by quickly running your hands over all of the accessible wiring harnesses and cables on the boat. *Be certain that no AC power source is active before you do this.*

The odor could mean there is a fire on board. Use extreme caution in this situation.

ODOR OF SULFUR (SMELLS LIKE ROTTEN EGGS)

Urgency: Requires immediate attention
Suggested actions:

1. Turn off the engine and the power to any battery chargers on the boat, and fill the batteries with distilled water.
2. Start the engine and check the alternator charging voltage and be sure it is within specifications. If it's not, the alternator or the voltage regulator requires repairs.

An overcharging battery or one that is boiling dry of electrolyte will produce a sulfur smell.

CHAPTER 13

TROUBLESHOOTING WITH THE FIVE SENSES: CABIN AND ENGINE ROOM

The cabin and engine room are both important locations on board. The crew must have a safe and comfortable place to eat, sleep, and relax while the boat is at rest or under way. The engine room is obviously important because it houses the boat's propulsion system, and it is where many connecting systems join together. Freshwater pumps, bilge pumps, refrigeration systems, battery chargers, inverters, generators (Fig. 13-1), and myriad hoses and electrical cables all can generally be found in an engine room.

Fig. 13-1. Larger boats often have generator sets. (Courtesy MER Equipment, Seattle, Washington)

When something goes wrong in the cabin or engine room, knowing what to look for and how to address what you find is essential. This chapter will provide you with a series of symptoms that may become apparent in engine room systems, as well as a detailed checklist highlighting the level of urgency and suggested actions you should take to troubleshoot the problem. The more in-depth background material will help you determine what caused the problem. As in the previous chapters dealing with diesel and gasoline engines, this one is organized by each of the five senses you will use in the troubleshooting process. The remaining two troubleshooting chapters also share this format.

WHAT YOU SEE
STEAM IN CABIN OR ENGINE ROOM
Urgency: Requires immediate attention
Suggested actions:

1. Turn off the engine and check the engine temperature gauge for an excessive reading (over 180°F).
2. While the engine cools, check for coolant leaks, especially for any that might spray hot engine surfaces.
3. When the engine is cool enough to touch (below 140°F), check the coolant level. Low coolant is further proof of a coolant leak.
4. Consult the engine manual and consider performing a cooling system pressure test.

Steam in the engine room that lacks a sweet smell indicates that it derived from straight water, or at least from water with very little antifreeze coolant mixed in. The steam resulted from possible overheating or a leak, which is probably at the pressure relief built into the pressure cap on the cooling system expansion tank.

HAZE WITH EXHAUST ODOR HANGS IN CABIN OR ENGINE ROOM
Urgency: Requires immediate attention
Suggested actions:

1. Check the engine air filter. It will be black if there is an exhaust leak.
2. Check all joints in the exhaust plumbing for the accumulation of black soot, which shows there is an exhaust leak in the area.
3. If soot has accumulated on a bolted joint, try tightening the bolts around the exhaust flange.
4. Look for failed gaskets and cracked exhaust tubing (Fig. 13-2).

New gaskets can be cut from high-temperature gasket material and installed after removing the bolts from the exhaust flange. Tap out the new gasket as shown in Figure 13-3, by laying the gasket paper over the flange and then tapping with the hammer

---

HUNTING EXHAUST LEAKS

To find the exact location of a leak, trace along the exhaust system's outer insulation wrap and look for black areas. Another way to find an exhaust leak is to start the engine and let it idle in neutral. Next, turn off the engine room lights and turn on a flashlight. Now, while still in neutral, give the engine some throttle. The leak will gush and be easy to see with the flashlight. Even very small exhaust leaks are made worse by high back-pressure in the exhaust system.

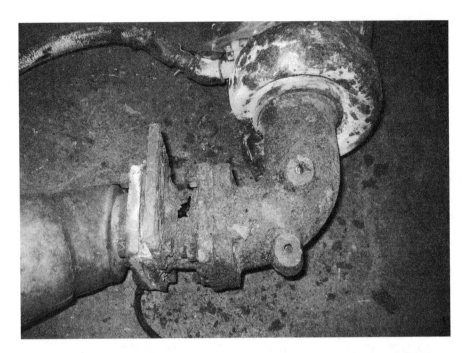

Fig. 13-2. Check the exhaust system tubing for holes. This section of exhaust pipe rusted through from the outside.

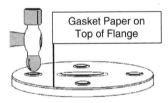

Fig. 13-3. Tapping out a new gasket. Here a gasket paper blank has been laid over an exhaust flange, and now we're tapping out the fastener holes.

to cut the needed holes and outline. Coat the bolt threads with anti-seize thread lubricant before installation. This will enable future removal of the bolts rather than having to cut them off when the threads gall. (Galling is the seizure of threaded nuts on bolt threads.)

HAZE WITH SWEET SMELL

Urgency: Requires immediate attention

Suggested action: See first symptom, the one related to steam in the engine room.

Hot antifreeze coolant dripping or spraying on a hot surface on the engine, such as the exhaust manifold, will vaporize and cause a haze that a person can smell or taste.

HAZE WITH SULFUR SMELL

Urgency: Requires immediate attention

Suggested actions:

1. Turn off the battery charger or check the alternator for overcharging due to a faulty voltage regulator.
2. Turn off the battery switch and fill the batteries with distilled water to the mark inside the fill opening.

Severely overcharging batteries will put a haze in the air that smells like sulfur. Turning off the alternator or battery charger will allow you to safely fill lead-acid batteries. To locate the source of the overcharging, first run the alternator, then the battery charger. Measure the voltage each time you do this. If the voltage is more than 3 volts over the electrical system's rating, then the alternator regulator must be replaced or a certified marine electrician must be called to troubleshoot the battery charger. *Note: Many alternators have internal regulators. In a case like this, the alternator would need to be replaced.*

VAPOR OR STEAM COMING FROM TRANSMISSION VENT

Urgency: Requires immediate attention
Suggested actions:

1. Turn off the engine and let the transmission cool for one hour or until it can be touched.
2. Check the transmission oil level and fill it to the mark if low. If the level is high, drain the transmission and change the oil because engine coolant may be present.
3. If there is coolant in the transmission, replace the oil cooler.

Failure of the transmission oil cooler core will allow engine coolant to enter the rear of the unit when the engine is turned off. When the engine and transmission are used again, coolant will vent from the transmission as water vapor or steam, indicating that further checking must be done.

CRACKS INSIDE DRIVE BELTS

Urgency: Attend to as soon as convenient
Suggested action: Replace the belts.
Cracks on the traction side of a belt mean either that the belt has many hours on it or that the engine compartment is too hot.

Engine compartment temperature must be kept between 40° and 70°F.

BLACK POWDER COATING FRONT OF ENGINE NEAR A V-BELT

Urgency: Attend to as soon as convenient
Suggested actions:

1. Tighten belts to stop slippage.
2. Replace the belts if they are badly worn.

A slipping belt will "throw rubber"—that is, small particles of belt material (Fig. 13-4). This will lead to slippage of the alternator belt on the pulley, and can even result in water pump belt slippage. Water pump belt slippage can result in engine overheating.

BATTERY POSTS MELTED AND ERODED AWAY BY ARCING, MAKING IT IMPOSSIBLE TO CONNECT BATTERY CABLE

Urgency: Requires immediate attention
Suggested action: Replace the battery or, in an emergency, pour a temporary battery post.
Damaged battery posts can be temporarily restored. See Chapter 7 and Fig. 7-16 for more details.

ALTERNATING CURRENT (AC) LIGHT BROWNOUTS

Urgency: Attend to as soon as convenient
Suggested actions:

1. Replace the generator fuel filters and check for low fuel levels.
2. Check the air filter for partial plugging.
3. Check for air in the fuel (refer to generator service manual).

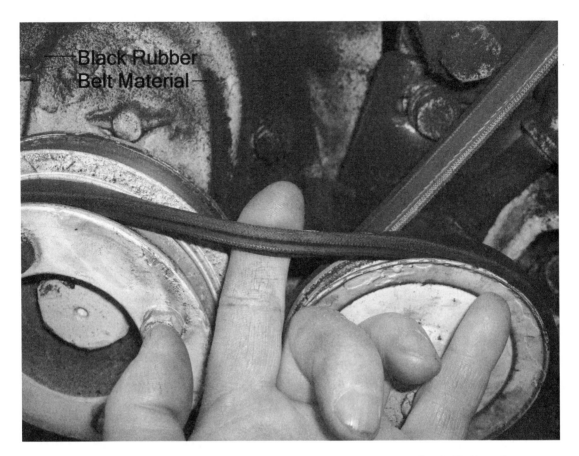

Fig. 13-4. Replace belts that are giving off rubber or have slipped. (Courtesy MER Equipment, Seattle, Washington)

A "brownout" indicates a lowering of voltage to the lights and other electrically powered equipment, often the result of a loss of engine speed when additional load is added to the system. When the generator size is marginal for the application, or when new electrical equipment capable of using more electricity has been installed in the boat, sequential switching of loads may be needed. Sequential loading means that the largest loads are put on the generator first, and then smaller and smaller loads are added until the generator is loaded to its maximum capacity.

Air in diesel fuel can cause brownouts. The air trapped in the generator fuel system triggers irregular fuel delivery that in turn makes the engine run faster or slower in short intervals of time. The end result is a power surge or power drop. When generator engine speed drops, the lights dim. Use a sight glass in-line in the fuel system to spot air bubbles. A sight glass can be made from clear plastic tubing for use on fuel systems with less than 7 psi of fuel transfer pump (fuel lift pump) pressure. Consult the engine service manual to learn the pressure of your system.

DIRECT CURRENT (DC) LIGHTS BROWNOUT

Urgency: Requires immediate attention

Suggested action: Brownouts in DC systems often result from dirty electrical connections. Turn off your battery charger, disconnect the AC shore power cord, and begin troubleshooting by cleaning the battery cable terminals.

A DC brownout is caused by low voltage. A gradual dimming is normal as batteries discharge. However, a sudden dimming of the DC lights is a sign of trouble, and the reason must be found immediately. Start by turning off any battery chargers and also all loads before looking at the batteries and the battery connections. Check the electrolyte level in the batteries, unless they are maintenance-free AGM or gel types. Watch for wires or cables with faulty insulation or those that are warm.

INSTRUMENT PANEL GLOW-PLUG INDICATOR BURNS OUT

Urgency: Attend to as soon as convenient

Suggested action: Order the part from the factory and replace the indicator, or try the following tip.

For diesel engines equipped with glow plugs, it is important that the glowing hot wire indicator in the instrument panel works. The purpose of the indicator is to show when to crank the engine, so that the glow plugs are not energized for too long. If left on too long, the tips of the glow plugs will burn off and fall into the cylinder on top of the piston, and this will destroy the engine. To make your own glow-plug indicator, fabricate a small metal tube and install an extra glow plug in it behind the instrument panel. See Chapter 7 and Fig. 7-17.

Note: If a good indicator fails to glow, you may have at least one burned-out glow

plug in the system. Check each glow plug for continuity. The indicators are rated for the draw the system has; therefore, a 3-cylinder indicator will not work properly on an engine with more cylinders (glow plugs).

WATER SLOWLY ENTERS BOAT NEAR PROPELLER SHAFT

Urgency: Attend to as soon as convenient

Suggested actions:

1. Check the stuffing box packing and shaft gland for soft hose.
2. Tightening the packing nut will reduce the water flow. If adjustments don't help, replace the packing.

Check the engine manufacturer's recommendations regarding stuffing box flow rates. Water dripping out so fast (Fig. 13-5) that you can't easily count drops per minutes is excessive. Newer boats are often equipped with dripless shaft seals. Be sure you know whether your boat has one or if it has a traditional stuffing box.

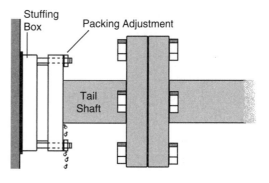

Fig. 13-5. Monitor stuffing box water flow. The steady drip rate shown here is probably about right.

WATER SLOWLY ENTERS BOAT
BEHIND PROPELLER SHAFT PACKING
GLAND, WHERE STUFFING BOX
ATTACHES TO REAR OF SHAFT ALLEY

Urgency: Attend to as soon as convenient
Suggested action: Tighten the bolts that attach the body of the stuffing box to the end of the shaft alley.

The boat must be hauled or careened to repair seals behind the stuffing box. The stuffing box can then be unbolted and pulled far out enough to be resealed with the appropriate gasket, sealant, or both.

HOLE IN HULL ALLOWS WATER
INTO BOAT

Urgency: Requires immediate attention
Suggested action: Obviously, plug the hole by any means possible.

In a pinch, grab a pillow or mattress and wedge it into the hole to slow the water. When bilge pumps fail and the leak is small, replumb the engine heat exchanger pump, if so equipped, to draw water out of the bilge through the engine freshwater cooling system. Figure 13-6 shows commonsense mounting of the pump. The pump switch is on the right, and the level alarm switch is next to the pump. The block of wood is well attached to the metal angle iron, and the pump and switches are mounted on the wood.

WHAT YOU HEAR

HEAR RAPID *TICK, TICK, TICK* SOUND
IN CABIN

Urgency: Attend to as soon as convenient
Suggested actions:

1. Check the oil stove fuel lift pump, if so equipped.

WATER ENTERING THROUGH THE EXHAUST SYSTEM

A horizontal exhaust system needs a periodic replacement of the rubber flap outside the transom where the exhaust exits the boat. It may also need changes to improve the water exclusion. Such changes could include installing the exhaust system with a steeper downward grade from the engine to the exhaust outlet, or the installation of a neoprene water trap muffler in the system.

---

2. Check the fuel level in the tank and check the stove for a fuel leak. A fuel leak should be easy to smell.
3. Check the water level in potable water tanks to detect any possible leaks.
4. Check the bilge for a high water level.

The ticking may be coming from the electric galley stove oil pump working or running out of fuel. It may also be a potable water pump working or running out of water.

WHAT YOU SMELL

AMMONIA ODOR IN ENGINE ROOM
OR CABIN

Urgency: Attend to as soon as convenient
Suggested actions:

1. Check pressure of ammonia refrigeration system, if so equipped.
2. Check the bilge and clean it if needed.

The odor may be coming from an ammonia refrigeration system leak, if so equipped. This can also be decomposing fish in the bilges of fishing vessels.

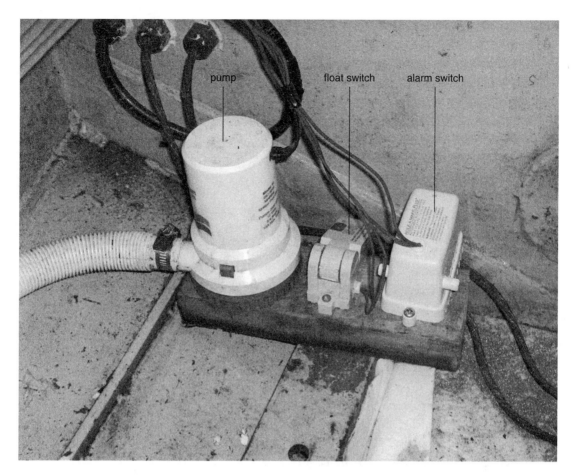

Fig. 13-6. A good bilge pump installation on a steel sailboat. A piece of hardwood fastened to the engine bed is the base for the components. The pump is low in the bilge, and the float switch and alarm are submersible.

BURNING OIL ODOR IN ENGINE ROOM OR CABIN

Urgency: Requires immediate attention
Suggested actions:

1. Check for a valve cover leak on the engine that may allow oil to drip on a hot surface, such as an exhaust manifold.
2. Monitor the engine for unusual oil consumption.

Oil leaking on a hot surface will make obnoxious smoke and may eventually burn. The source of such a leak is easy to find by following your nose.

DECOMPOSING FISH ODOR IN ENGINE ROOM

Urgency: Attend to as soon as convenient
Suggested action: Clean the bilge with a bristle brush and bleach dissolved in water.

Rotting fish in the bilge should be cleaned out because it outgases into the engine room. The gas from decomposing fish is toxic, not to mention highly offensive.

EXHAUST ODOR IN ENGINE ROOM, WITH VISIBLE HAZE

Urgency: Requires immediate attention

Suggested action: Check all the joints in the exhaust system for black soot, a sure sign of a leak. Repair the leak.

Exhaust leaks will cause a haze in the engine room that will plug every engine's air filter. When exhaust flexes are installed incorrectly, they will soon fatigue, causing a leak.

PEOPLE GET SICK SUDDENLY OR CONSISTENTLY WHEN WORKING IN BOAT'S ENGINE ROOM

Urgency: Requires immediate attention

Suggested action: Monitor the fire suppression system and the refrigeration system, if so equipped, for slow leaks. If any are detected, repair them. If you can't find anything unusual, have a professional look at the boat.

Toxic gases in the engine room must be eliminated. The engine room and the cabin must both have a carbon monoxide alarm installed. If people get sick or even fail to feel their best when boating, the air in the boat must tested to determine the percentage of oxygen in a variety of situations:

1) when the boat is under way; 2) when the boat is closed up at night for sleeping and the heat is on; 3) when the boat is idling at the dock.

ODOR OF BURNING PLASTIC OR ELECTRICAL WIRE INSULATION

Urgency: Requires immediate attention

Suggested actions:

1. Check the wires coming out of the breaker panel for warmth. **Caution:** If there is any doubt in your mind whether you have the knowledge to do this effectively, don't mess with the wiring. Simply shut off the electricity and look for signs of fire. Safety requires the use of an infrared thermometer when testing for heat in wiring, in case there is bare insulation. If you don't have an infrared thermometer, stay away from the wiring in this situation!
2. Check the electrical breakers (fuses) for radiated heat with the infrared thermometer.

A yearly survey of the boat's electrical system by a marine electrician is a good preventive measure. Sure, it costs money, but the potential trouble you'll avoid, such as a fire, is well worth the expense.

CHAPTER 14

TROUBLESHOOTING WITH THE FIVE SENSES: TRANSMISSIONS AND POWER-TAKE-OFFS

The transmission is as important as your boat's engine. It transfers engine power to the propeller shaft at controlled speeds and allows you to shift gears to make the boat go in forward and reverse. If something goes wrong, you need to know what to do to address the problem. This chapter will provide some guidance on how you can use your five senses in the troubleshooting process, just as in Chapters 11 through 13.

In this chapter, you will find information on transmissions with hydraulically applied internal clutches since these are most common on motoryachts and commercial vessels. When troubleshooting older transmissions with mechanically applied clutches, you will need to consult the manufacturer's repair manual. However, the information provided in these pages will still be helpful to you. Details on troubleshooting outboards and outdrives will also be included.

WHAT YOU SEE
LIGHT BROWN OIL LEAKS FROM TRANSMISSION WHILE UNIT IS TURNED OFF

Urgency: Attend to as soon as convenient

Suggested Action: Replace the oil pan gasket, if so equipped.

Oil can also leak from the transmission pump suction hose when the engine is off. If there is a leak, even a small one, the pump can draw air into the oil when the engine is running. Aerated oil will quickly cause severe damage to the pump. It is possible for the suction hose to let air into the stream of oil, with no visible evidence of oil leaking to the outside of the hose when the unit is turned off. It's a very good preventive measure to replace the suction hose yearly or when it begins to harden.

LIGHT-COLORED OIL LEAKS FROM FLYWHEEL HOUSING

Urgency: Requires immediate attention

Suggested action: Replace the transmission front seal, which is located under the drive coupling (Fig. 14-1).

For engines that power transmissions, such as a BorgWarner Velvet Drive, Hurth, Twin Disc, or ZF, to name just a few, a lighter-colored oil leaking from the flywheel housing indicates an oil leak in the front seal. It is coming from the transmission's input shaft oil seal located between the engine's flywheel and the front of the transmission housing. The transmission must be removed to gain access to the seal.

LIGHT BROWN OIL LEAKS FROM ENGINE-MOUNTED TRANSMISSION OIL COOLER

Urgency: Requires immediate attention

Fig. 14-1. The front transmission seal is under this drive coupling.

Suggested action: Check for loose or faulty fittings or a faulty hose.

An oil leak in the oil cooler can lead to damage. Make repairs immediately.

PROPELLER SHAFT CREEPS SLOWLY IN NEUTRAL BEFORE TRANSMISSION WARMS UP

Urgency: Not urgent, but should be monitored

Suggested action: This can be normal if high-viscosity oil is used in a cold climate. Follow up by checking the transmission filter for the presence of wear metals or brass-colored clutch material. If a lot of metal is present, call a marine mechanic.

It is normal for some older transmissions to creep in forward or reverse when they are cold. This condition is sometimes referred to as gear creep, which is defined as a slow turning of the output shaft (and therefore the propeller) when the engine is running in neutral. Creep usually turns the propeller in the direction of forward travel, because it is often the forward clutches that get the most use and finally warp. Warped clutch discs cannot fully disengage.

Taking great care for safety's sake, grasp the shaft with a gloved hand and try stopping the motion of the propeller. If you can, there is no cause for alarm. Just check periodically to see if the creep worsens. If you can't stop the output shaft, then there is clutch disc damage inside the transmission. When the shaft tries to propel the boat forward, the discs in the forward clutch pack are warped. The same applies to reverse. When the shaft wants to back down, the discs in the reverse clutch pack are warped. Warped discs must be replaced. Consult the transmission service manual for instructions on making repairs.

PROPELLER SHAFT CREEPS SLOWLY IN FORWARD OR REVERSE DIRECTION WHEN TRANSMISSION AND OIL ARE UP TO TEMPERATURE

Urgency: Attend to as soon as convenient

Suggested action: Check to be sure that the transmission control lever is centered in the neutral position (Fig. 14-2). A control or control valve that is partially in gear when the control handle in the wheelhouse is in neutral will cause creep.

If the control is centered and the shaft still creeps, the cause is likely warped clutch discs. If clutch material (brass-colored metal) is found in the oil, consult a marine mechanic about clutch replacement.

Fig. 14-2. Center the transmission control to neutral.

After a transmission clutch assembly has slipped under power, whether it is the forward or reverse clutch pack, the clutch discs warp. The sign of warped discs is pretty simple to identify: The shaft still creeps in neutral even when the transmission is up to temperature. When this is the case, the propeller shaft is difficult or impossible to stop by hand. Creep indicates the clutch pack is on the way out, because the forward clutch discs have warped and can never truly disengage; they will continue to overheat and degenerate.

PROPELLER WON'T SPIN WITH TRANSMISSION CONTROL IN FORWARD OR REVERSE

Urgency: Requires immediate attention
Suggested actions:

1. Consult the repair manual to identify the correct hydraulic pressure when the transmission is in neutral and in gear. Also, refer to the troubleshooting section.
2. If the pressure is low or nonexistent, check the transmission oil level.
3. If the boat is a fishing vessel equipped with a trolling valve, make sure the control is in the disengaged position.

Although rare on recreational boats, trolling valves are often fitted to fishing boat transmissions. The trolling valve permits the skipper to reduce the propeller speed even lower than it would be with the engine at low idle. If the trolling valve is fully activated, it will sometimes stop the propeller from turning even though the transmission is in forward or reverse. This will make it appear as though the transmission is not working.

A broken internal shaft inside the transmission, a broken input coupling, or a failed clutch will stop the propeller from spinning. Transmissions will also slip if the oil leaks away. A broken transmission control can make you think the engine is in gear when in fact it is not.

Note: Some transmissions provide the option of a manual clutch application in forward, which is called the come-home feature (Fig. 14-3). With it, the forward clutch mechanism can be locked (applied) even though the clutch pack has failed. Your service manual will say if your gear is so equipped. Engagement of the come-home screws is done with the engine turned off. See Chapter 6 for more details on the come-home feature.

OBJECTS FORWARD IN BOAT SHAKE MORE THAN THOSE AFT

Urgency: Not urgent, but should be monitored
Suggested actions:

1. Check the tightness of all fasteners on the front motor mounts.
2. Tighten fasteners on the front crankshaft pulley; these are especially important.
3. Check the engine repair manual for troubleshooting ideas.

Faulty front power-take-offs are a likely cause of vibration toward the front of a boat. A defective front crankshaft pulley or vibration damper can also cause severe vibration. Always identify the engine speed at which the vibration is the most noticeable and whether the vibration is related to boat speed while under way.

Fig. 14-3. Accessing the come-home screws, both of which are circled.

To learn if the front PTO is the source of the vibration, turn off the engine and unbolt the PTO drive coupling, if so equipped. Next, run the engine (and the boat, if needed) at the speed that resulted in the most vibration.

OBJECTS AFT IN BOAT SHAKE MORE THAN THOSE FORWARD

Urgency: Not urgent, but should be monitored

Suggested actions:

1. Check all fasteners on the propeller shaft for tightness.
2. See Chapter 17 for more on shaft alignment.

Propeller shaft misalignment, a damaged propeller, or intermediate shaft pillow block bearing damage are likely causes for this sort of vibration problem.

PROPELLER SHAFT SPINS WITH ENGINE OFF

Urgency: Not urgent

Suggested action: None. A propeller will spin when the engine is turned off under certain circumstances: a sailboat under sail, a powerboat tied to a dock in swift current, or a boat under tow.

A freewheeling propeller does not represent a problem for a hydraulic transmission that is rated to allow turning of the output shaft with the engine off (see your service manual for rating). If yours isn't so rated, hang a pipe wrench on the shaft (with an old leather glove in the wrench jaws to protect the shaft) wherever it is accessible to stop the spinning. The teeth of the pipe wrench will grab the shaft and the handle will come to rest on the bottom of the boat, locking the shaft. Most small diesel engines use mechanical transmissions, which are lubricated even when freewheeling. It is common practice to leave these transmissions in neutral when under sail.

METALLIC PARTICLES (GLITTER) IN TRANSMISSION OIL OR IN OIL FILTER MEDIA

Urgency: Requires immediate attention
Suggested actions:

1. This is most likely a mechanical failure in progress. Consult the transmission service manual and call a marine mechanic.
2. If the engine must be run, operate it at the lowest possible speed to nurse the transmission until repairs can be made, which should be done quickly.

Dull gray shards of metal in the filter media indicate steel. This results from metal-to-metal contact inside the transmission, a sure sign of damage. A forward clutch pack may be excessively worn and failing to fully disengage.

CREAM-COLORED SLUDGE INSIDE TRANSMISSION OIL FILL CAP OR ON THE DIPSTICK (FIG. 14-4).

Urgency: Requires immediate attention

Suggested action: Pressure-test the transmission oil cooler. If you have determined that the engine is also losing coolant, replace the oil cooler.

When water or coolant leaks into the transmission through a faulty oil cooler, it travels to the bottom of the oil pan because it is heavier than the lube oil. It will stay on the bottom until the engine is started. When the engine is running, water or coolant is pulled from the bottom of the oil pan into the transmission oil pump. From there, it is sent throughout the transmission lubrication system. As the oil and coolant warm up, emulsification occurs, creating a foamy, oily substance that cannot provide proper lubrication.

TRANSMISSION OIL PRESSURE LOW

Urgency: Requires immediate attention
Suggested actions:

1. Check the oil level.
2. Verify the accuracy of the gauge.
3. Consult the repair manual for troubleshooting strategy.

Low oil pressure could be the result of a faulty gauge, sender, or pressure control valve. There could be an oil suction leak on the oil supply pump, or the oil pump may not be pumping to capacity.

TRANSMISSION OIL PRESSURE HIGH WHEN WARM

Urgency: Attend to as soon as convenient
Suggested actions:

1. Verify the existing gauge is correct.
2. Consult the repair manual to learn how to check the pressure relief valve (pressure control valve).

See previous symptom.

Use The Dipstick To Check For Emulsified Oil And Water.

Fig. 14-4. The dipstick on this brand-new hydraulic transmission (not yet installed) is clearly visible. Transmissions like this are common in fishing vessels and motoryachts.

TRANSMISSION OIL PRESSURE NEVER COMES UP ON GAUGE, BUT TRANSMISSION WORKS JUST FINE

Urgency: Attend to as soon as convenient

Suggested action: Replace the pressure gauge or the sender.

See previous two symptoms.

VIBRATION AT REAR OF ENGINE

Urgency: Attend to as soon as convenient

Suggested actions:

1. Check the transmission suction screen and ensure that it's clear of wear metals.

2. Check the output shaft bolts for tightness.

3. Verify that the front propeller shaft coupling is tight on the propeller shaft.

4. Remove the starter motor and pry on the flywheel to see if it is loose on the crankshaft. If so, the transmission must be removed to enable removal of the flywheel.

5. Check the transmission-to-engine flywheel coupling bolts.

If the transmission suction screen contains over one-quarter teaspoon of debris, then transmission or bearing failure is likely.

COOLANT RUNS OUT TRANSMISSION DIPSTICK HOLE WHEN DIPSTICK IS REMOVED

Urgency: Requires immediate attention

Suggested action: Replace the transmission oil cooler.

A split or damaged oil cooler will allow engine coolant to flow into the transmission.

TRANSMISSION SLOW TO ENGAGE

Urgency: Not urgent, but should be monitored

Suggested actions:

1. Check the oil level.
2. Consult the repair manual to learn how to check the directional control valve.

If the oil is low, the gear will engage slowly. A faulty suction hose on the suction side of the oil pump will also cause slow engagement, as will a weak oil pump or plugged oil filter (screen). Check the service manual to learn if the pressure is too low, and then follow the directions to address the problem.

WATER SQUIRTS OUT TRANSMISSION DIPSTICK HOLE WHEN DIPSTICK IS REMOVED

Urgency: Requires immediate attention

Suggested actions:

1. If the transmission has been swamped, drain and refill it with the correct oil and run it for two hours at the dock, periodically shifting from neutral to forward and back to neutral. Shut off the engine and change the oil and filter again.

2. If, however, the unit is full of antifreeze coolant from a faulty oil cooler, replace the cooler.

When the oil cooler core is leaking, it will allow coolant into the transmission oil and transmission oil into the engine cooling system. To test for this, first drain the engine coolant and then pressure-test the oil side of the transmission oil cooler by disconnecting both oil lines. Next, plug one oil cooler opening and apply under 30 psi to the other opening by whatever means is available. If the cooler core holds pressure, it is fine, but if not, it must be replaced.

If there is no replacement cooler available, the ends of the oil cooler hoses may be coupled together after disconnecting both lines from the oil cooler. This will allow the boat to limp home at very low engine rpm. But remember: Marine transmission oil coolers are not optional like transmission oil coolers are on a car or truck. Without one, the marine transmission won't last more than a few minutes at full power.

WHAT YOU HEAR

TRANSMISSION MAKES LOUD CLUNKING NOISE WHEN SHIFTED INTO GEAR

Urgency: Requires immediate attention

Suggested actions:

1. Make sure the propeller is tight on the shaft.
2. Tighten all shaft coupling bolts.
3. Check the transmission screen or filter for wear metal.

Extra-high idle speed will cause shifting noise even when all else is fine. Verify that the engine idle speed is within the manufacturer's specifications. Reduce the idle speed accordingly. Never adjust idle speed lower than specified, because the engine may die when shifted from forward to reverse during docking. If the idle speed is fine, check the transmission suction screen for debris. Debris in the screen or filter suggests that the transmission is failing.

Loose couplings on the propeller shaft, a bad keyway between the shaft and coupling, loose coupling bolts between couplings, or even a loose propeller will all make noise. When there is room for the propeller and shaft to move forward a few inches, the forward end of the shaft can be cut off, if the keyway is long enough and a new coupling and key can be installed. (Note: The coupling shown in Fig. 14-5 has yet to be bored for the shaft it will fit.) This new coupling comes with bolts and self-locking nuts. Each piece of the system must be visually checked. Extreme wear in the transmission can also be very noisy during and after engagement.

SLIGHT BUT DEFINITE CHANGE IN SOUND OF TRANSMISSION, OUTBOARD, OR OUTDRIVE

Urgency: Not urgent, but should be monitored

Fig. 14-5. New couplings are made with self-locking nuts. This coupling has yet to be bored for the shaft it will fit. (Courtesy MER Equipment, Seattle, Washington)

Suggested actions:

1. Check the transmission screen or cut open the oil filter to check for glitter that indicates damage or accelerated wear.
2. Send a sample of the oil to an oil analysis lab.

Changes in the way an engine or a transmission sounds should be promptly investigated.

HEAR STEADY RUMBLE IN TRANSMISSION OR OUTDRIVE

Urgency: Requires immediate attention
Suggested action: See previous symptom.
Oil filled with small particles of wear metal indicates transmission or clutch pack failure.

WHAT YOU FEEL
VIBRATIONS IN MIDDLE OF BOAT

Urgency: Not urgent, but should be monitored
Suggested actions:

1. Check the forward end of the propeller shaft and coupling for tightness on the shaft, as well as the rear transmission coupling.
2. Check the screen on the transmission suction side for glitter (metallic particles).
3. Check that the propeller is properly installed on the shaft taper and that the key is in position.

Glitter indicates the transmission is failing. When you find it, the source of the vibration is not far away.

BOAT'S RIGGING VIBRATES MORE THAN USUAL

Urgency: Not urgent, but should be monitored
Suggested actions:

1. Start by checking to see if the vibration is related to engine speed. Proceed by bringing the engine up to operating temperature and placing the transmission in neutral. Now, slowly bring the engine up to 75 percent of maximum speed and pay close attention to the level of vibration in the boat. This test will not harm the engine. If there is a certain engine speed that produces vibration every time, then the engine is the problem and you may proceed by troubleshooting the engine vibration according to the engine service manual.
2. If the vibration seems worse under way, even if it happens at a certain engine speed according to the tachometer, then it is probably related to propeller speed and not the engine.
3. Check the propeller for damage and take it to a prop shop if needed.
4. Check the screen on the transmission suction hose for glitter (metal particles). If any is found, the transmission is failing.
5. If there is no glitter in the screen, then check for a bent shaft by watching the shaft turning slowly with the engine in gear. A wobble indicates a bent shaft.

Excessive vibration is a general clue that there may be propeller damage, misalignment, or a transmission failure. It can also be the beginning of a shafting or bearing failure.

If the propeller and shaft are straight, then the shaft and engine alignment must be checked. For more detailed information on this see Chapter 17.

VIBRATION FELT IN BOAT
Urgency: Attend to as soon as convenient
Suggested actions:

1. Check the crankshaft vibration damper for wobbling or an oil leak if it is a viscous damper.
2. When the engine's front power-take-off (PTO) shakes more than the transmission, check to see if any part of the PTO has excess run-out (visible wobble). Often, an out-of-balance condition will accompany run-out.
3. Make note of any recent problems the boat may have had, such as line caught in the propeller. If the line had to be cut out, then the snag was serious enough to bend the propeller shaft.

To begin tracking down vibrations, it helps to make note of when and under which conditions the vibration is worst and of whatever reduces it. Boat vibrations are related to *when*, in relation to engine rpm, and *where* the vibration is most noticeable. It may be at the front of the boat, and this may be related to a front-mounted PTO. The vibration may be in the middle of the boat, and this may be engine or engine alignment related, or it may have to do with a rear-mounted PTO. Vibrations at the rear of the boat are usually related to bent shafting or misalignment of the shaft and engine.

WHAT YOU TASTE
WATER IN THE TRANSMISSION IS SALTY
Urgency: Requires immediate attention
Suggested action: Check to see if bilge water is getting into the transmission.

The transmission may have been swamped, or bilge water may have gotten high enough to enter it through the output shaft oil seal.

WATER IN TRANSMISSION TASTES SWEET
Urgency: Requires immediate attention
Suggested action: Check the engine and transmission manuals to locate the transmission oil cooler and then follow up by pressure-testing it as shown in Chapter 16.

Coolant tastes sweet and can enter the transmission through the oil cooler that interfaces with engine coolant.

NO TASTE TO WATER IN TRANSMISSION
Urgency: Requires immediate attention
Suggested action: Check for a way that rainwater could be getting into the transmission.

In boats with dry, vertical exhaust systems, rainwater could be dribbling down the outside of the stack and dripping into the transmission vent. If the stack is vertical, it may need a rain exclusion method installed.

OUTBOARDS AND OUTDRIVES
WHAT YOU SEE
OUTBOARD OR OUTDRIVE WON'T ENGAGE
Urgency: Requires immediate attention
Suggested action: Perform a visual check of the control cables and the controls (Fig. 14-6).

Fig. 14-6. Check the outboard throttle and shift controls for signs of breakage and for full range of movement. Shown here is a combination throttle and shift control. (The two functions are often separated.)

If the cables are fine, the unit may need to be opened up for a visual inspection.

ENGINE DIES WHEN PUT IN GEAR

Urgency: Requires immediate attention

Suggested action: Adjust the spark interrupt feature to factory specifications according to the repair manual.

The spark interrupt device is located on the shift linkage and works by interrupting the ignition power to the coil for just an instant to avoid gear clash in the leg (the leg is the propeller drive in the water). The gears that shift from forward to neutral to reverse are located in the leg. Also, the unit may have failed and be locked up internally. Draining the oil will allow a visual check for the presence of glitter (metal particles indicating a mechanical failure).

WHEN DRAINED, OIL IN LOWER UNIT OF OUTBOARD OR OUTDRIVE HAS METALLIC LUSTER

Urgency: Requires immediate attention

Suggested action: Consult a marine mechanic immediately. Metal in the oil is always a sign of internal destruction.

A very slight amount of metal in the oil is normal in new machinery with a low number of operating hours. If excessive glitter is detected and is accompanied by a new and alarming noise, then a failure is in process.

WHEN YOU DRAIN OIL FROM AN OUTBOARD LOWER UNIT OR AN OUTDRIVE, OVER ONE CUP OF WATER COMES OUT BEFORE ANY OIL IS SEEN

Urgency: Requires immediate attention
Suggested actions:

1. Drain the water from the outdrive.

2. Overfill the unit by one quart, and, with the boat on a trailer, watch for leaks throughout the day.
3. When the leak is found, follow the repair manual instructions for repairing the leak.
4. When finished, drain the excess oil from the unit.

The presence of this much water at the drain opening (Fig. 14-7) indicates that water is leaking into the leg, either through the output shaft (propeller shaft) seal or through a hole or joint in the case.

Fig. 14-7. The lower unit's drain plug.

WHEN YOU DRAIN OIL FROM AN
OUTBOARD LOWER UNIT OR AN
OUTDRIVE, ONLY ONE TEASPOON OF
WATER COMES OUT BEFORE ANY OIL
IS SEEN

Urgency: Not urgent, but should be monitored

Suggested action: Change the oil frequently as directed by the service manual.

This small amount of water is normal, because it is impossible to keep all water out of the vented drive housing.

OUTDRIVE OR OUTBOARD WON'T
TILT, WON'T HOLD TILT ADJUSTMENT,
OR FLIPS UP WHEN SHIFTED INTO
REVERSE

Urgency: Requires immediate attention

Suggested action: Many outboards and outdrives require periodic greasing (Fig. 14-8) to keep the tilt and breakaway mechanisms working well. Grease according to the repair manual.

Electrohydraulic trim and tilt systems also require power and an adequate supply of oil to work. Consult the service manual for your unit.

WHAT YOU SMELL
THICK, BROWN, STRONG-SMELLING
OIL LEAKS FROM LOWER UNIT

Urgency: Requires immediate attention

Suggested action: Note whether the leak is at the lower shaft seal or coming from joints

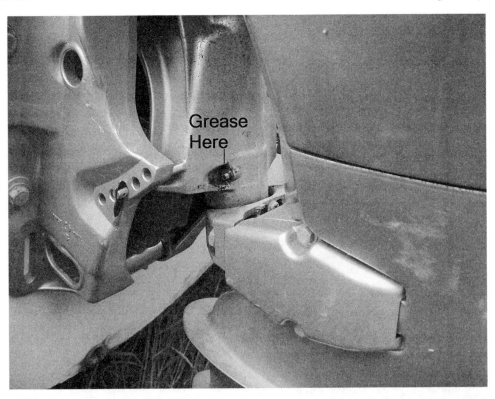

Fig. 14-8. Grease the steering pivot (using the zerk fitting shown here) and the tilt mechanism to ensure smooth operation.

in the lower unit where one section is bolted to another. Consult the service manual for your engine.

Mineral-based AW 80W-90 gear lube has a strong odor and is brown in color.

THICK, CLEAR OIL WITH NO STRONG SMELL LEAKS FROM LOWER UNIT

Urgency: Requires immediate attention

Suggested action: See previous symptom. Synthetic gear lube has no odor and is clear.

CHAPTER 15

TROUBLESHOOTING WITH THE FIVE SENSES: STEERING AND ENGINE CONTROLS

Steering systems and engine controls are critical to the safety of your vessel and crew. You must be able to move the rudder as needed and to operate the engine throttle and transmission controls to safely maneuver the boat. Anything that interferes with these vital functions can quickly lead to trouble. Fortunately, these systems are especially friendly to troubleshooting with the five senses.

Every time you manipulate the helm, you gain a feel for how it should respond. Thus you will quickly know if something is amiss. Likewise, every time you use the throttle to manage engine speed or the transmission control to shift gears, you can sense from the response of the control whether or not there is something wrong. This chapter will guide you through the process of troubleshooting these essential systems. Everything from stubborn steering or engine control cables to what to do if your outdrive starts making ominous noises will be covered.

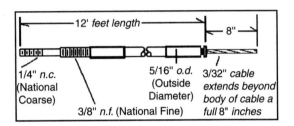

Fig. 15-1. Diagram the length and type of cable you need before ordering—and preferably before you are in dire need! The example shown here is SAE (non-metric), but metric sizes are also available. The thread designation "n.c." means "National Coarse," and "n.f." means "National Fine."

old one to a marine supply store or measure it for proper length. If possible, draw a diagram (Fig. 15-1) or photograph the ends of the cable to ensure that you get the right configuration.

WHAT YOU SEE

STEERING OR CONTROL CABLES APPEAR CHAFED OR DAMAGED

Urgency: Attend to as soon as convenient
Suggested action: Replace the cable.

Cables require protection from chafing damage. Cover the cable with chafing gear to protect it. You can buy chafing gear, or you can make it by splitting a hose lengthwise and attaching it with nylon cable ties. When replacing a cable, take the

CONTROL CABLES HANG HAPHAZARDLY

Urgency: Attend to as soon as convenient
Suggested action: Route cables out of the way and tie them securely to protect them.

Control cables will quickly wear through if not properly secured.

HYDRAULIC STEERING FLUID LEAKS FROM PART OF SYSTEM

Urgency: Requires immediate attention
Suggested action: Identify the leak and check with a marine mechanic about the best way to repair it.

There is very little standardization of steering systems on boats, and often there is no repair manual available. The various hydraulic steering systems use a number of fluids. These systems also use hose or tubing material, fittings, and even bleeding procedures that are specific for each type. Many pleasure boats have hydraulic steering systems plumbed with pipe and pipe-threaded fittings that are notorious for leaks. A far better practice is to use JIC or Boss O-ring connections.

WHAT YOU HEAR
OUTBOARD OR OUTDRIVE MAKES LOUD CLUNKING NOISE WHEN PUT IN GEAR

Urgency: Attend to as soon as convenient
Suggested actions:

1. If possible, lower idle speed slightly.
2. Adjust the spark interrupt mechanism to the manufacturer's specifications.

Some noise is normal when these are engaged. However, excessive noise is a sign of engine idle set too high or mechanical damage. Compare your engine to a similar unit. You will know if the noise is excessive by listening to the similar engine as the gears are shifted. Next, check for metal in the oil, which is a sure sign of trouble that will require repair. If there is a clunk but no metal (glitter) in the oil, then continue running the engine and keep an eye on it.

WHAT YOU FEEL
THROTTLE OR TRANSMISSION LINKAGE VERY STIFF
Urgency: Attend to as soon as convenient

Suggested actions:

1. Check for corrosion in the control housing as well as in any linkage. Remove linkage pins and clean all rust from the pins and the bores. Lubricate the pins and reinstall them.
2. Check the condition of control cables, if so equipped. Cables (Fig. 15-2) that have chafed through will rust and lose their internal lubrication.
3. For chain controls, check the chain, pulleys, and bushings to see if they are jammed and in need of lubrication.

Metal fittings rust without cleaning and lubrication. A brass wire brush and penetrating oil will often help clean and free up controls.

ENGINE SPEED (THROTTLE) OR TRANSMISSION RESPONDS INCONSISTENTLY TO CONTROL SETTINGS
Urgency: Attend to as soon as convenient
Suggested action: Check for broken cables or linkage at the engine and transmission.

The linkage may need lubrication, or there may be something pressing against the linkage in a way that hinders movement.

THROTTLE WON'T TAKE ENGINE TO FULL SPEED
Urgency: Attend to as soon as convenient
Suggested action: Check the adjustment of the throttle linkage and also the ratio between the actuator and the control valve.

The linkage may be bent, broken, or out of adjustment. The ratio of linkages may need to

Control Cable

Fig. 15-2. Inspect the throttle control cable for signs of wear.

be changed to get more speed control movement (Fig. 15-3). *Note: This condition may be more of a low power problem than a control problem.*

THROTTLE CONTROL LEVER WON'T HOLD FULL SPEED

Urgency: Attend to as soon as convenient

Suggested action: The friction surfaces in some controls can be adjusted to help hold the throttle setting better. If the control cannot be adjusted to hold the throttle at full speed, it must be replaced.

Hydraulic controls, such as those from Hyanautic (Fig. 15-4), need to be bled according to the manufacturer's instructions when they will not hold. Be sure to use Hyanautic's fluid in the system and keep the separate Hyanautic air pressure reservoir in the 50 to 70 psi range, or as specified.

THROTTLE REDUCES ENGINE SPEED TOO MUCH WHEN SUDDENLY THROTTLED BACK ALL THE WAY, ENGINE DIES

Urgency: Requires immediate attention

Suggested action: Adjust the engine idle speed upward.

When the idle speed is set too low on a gasoline or diesel engine, the engine will die as

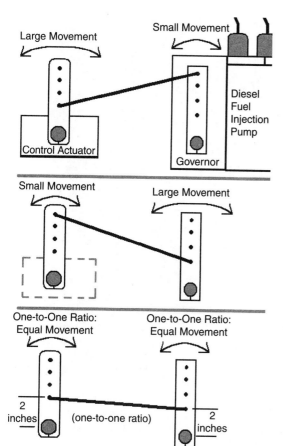

Fig. 15-3. Some controls, like the hydraulic controls shown here, require adjustment of the movement ratios to ensure that full throttle in the wheelhouse corresponds to full throttle on the governor, and that idle speed in the wheelhouse corresponds to idle on the governor. Adjust the linkages as in these three scenarios until you find the ideal. Shift linkages are adjusted in the same fashion.

the throttle is pulled back suddenly or when changing from forward to reverse (or the opposite).

THROTTLE LEVERS ON TWIN
ENGINES DON'T MATCH POSITION,
YET TACHOMETER SHOWS EQUAL
ENGINE SPEEDS AND BOAT STEERS
STRAIGHT

Urgency: Not urgent, but should be monitored

Suggested action: Check to see if the control levers can be adjusted to matching positions.

Again, the control ratios may require adjusting as shown above in Figure 15-3.

THROTTLE LEVERS ON TWIN
ENGINES MATCH VISUALLY, RUDDER
ANGLE INDICATOR SHOWS BOTH
RUDDERS APPARENTLY STRAIGHT,
AND THE ENGINE SPEEDS ARE EQUAL,
YET BOAT WANTS TO VEER ONE WAY
OR THE OTHER

Urgency: Not urgent, but should be monitored

Suggested actions:

1. Have the rudder angle indicator calibration checked, because it might be off.
2. Verify that both propellers have the same pitch and diameter.

Propeller diameters or pitch may differ from one another if work has recently been done on them. Also, one engine's tachometer may be inaccurate.

TRANSMISSION GEARSHIFT CONTROL
TAKES TOO MUCH EFFORT TO SHIFT
INTO OR OUT OF FORWARD OR
REVERSE

Urgency: Not urgent, but should be monitored

Suggested action: Disconnect the shift linkage at the transmission to see if the control valve is hard to turn manually. If so, the valve must be repaired. If not, there is a cable

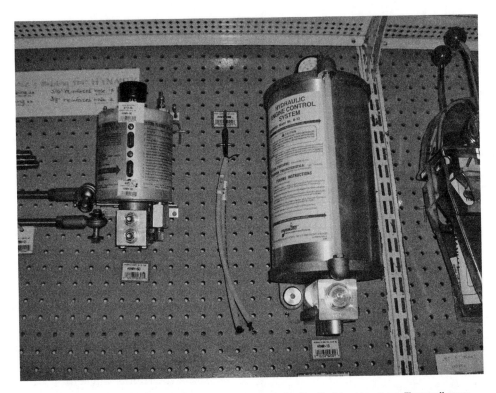

Fig. 15-4. Hydraulic throttle and shift controls require reservoirs like the two shown here. The smaller one at left is for single helm-station controls. The larger one at right is for multiple-station controls. These reservoirs need refilling and pressurizing after repairs and before the controls are bled. The bleeding isn't easy. Consult your manual, and use the fluid specified there.

or linkage problem between the control and the transmission.

Binding linkage or cables or a faulty transmission control valve will cause stiff controls.

STEERING REQUIRES EXTRA EFFORT

Urgency: Not urgent, but should be monitored

Suggested actions:

1. With an outboard or outdrive, it may only take greasing the unit's outer hinge point to correct hard steering.

2. For larger boats with a rudder, check all mechanical parts of the steering system.

Possible causes include a bent steering cylinder rod. Visually inspect every part of the system.

MOVING HELM HAS NO EFFECT ON STEERING BOAT

Urgency: Requires immediate attention

Suggested actions:

1. Check the oil level in the hydraulic steering system, and fill the helm pump (Fig. 15-5), if so equipped, according to manufacturer's directions.

Fig. 15-5. A hydraulic helm pump viewed from behind the bulkhead where it's mounted. There are many potential sources of steering-fluid leaks throughout the system.

FOR THE WORKBOAT

Emergency Steering Improvised

Many years ago, Kodiak logger Paul Hansen was crab fishing with his dad twenty miles east of Old Harbor, Alaska, off Kodiak Island. All was well until something gave way in the steering system, and suddenly control of the boat was lost. Looking in the lazarette, Paul and his dad found that a vital piece of the steering mechanism had broken and required welding. With no welding machine on board, they knew they had to get to Old Harbor to make the repairs.

With the broken steering, the boat would only go in big circles, always turning the same direction. To compensate, Mr. Hansen had the crew tie a line from the capstan (in the middle of the deck) to a 6-foot by 6-foot crab pot and ease the pot over the stern. They adjusted the line length so that the crab pot was barely under water.

When the boat was put in gear, the crew muscled the line from the port side of the stern to starboard and back, as needed, to keep the boat headed for Old Harbor. They arrived safely, having steered for twenty miles with a crab pot.

2. Check all parts of the steering mechanisms in the boat, including the steering linkage.
3. Check the key and keyway on the rudderpost, if so equipped.

When checking steering mechanisms, have someone move the helm back and forth while you follow the system to the rear of the boat. This approach will help you find out where the steering system stops working properly. If all else fails, you will have to check the rudder by diving on the boat or scheduling a haulout.

PART 3: THE RESOURCEFUL
BOAT MECHANIC

CHAPTER 16

DETECTION OF CRACKS, LEAKS, AND OTHER DEFECTS IN VITAL PARTS

Finding defects in critical parts is a major priority for every mechanical technician, with no exceptions. For boaters, it is a seemingly endless effort as parts of a boat corrode, wear, or fail. In this chapter, nondestructive testing methods will be discussed. These methods include pressure testing, dye penetrant testing, and the Magnaflux process, a brand name for testing ferrous (containing iron) metals for flaws.

When beginning to test metal objects, we soon learn that even brand-new, unused metals can have defects or cracks. Unfortunately, no method is completely accurate in identifying them. Visual inspection in good light is the starting point, and this includes the use of a magnifying glass. More advanced techniques, such as pressure, dye penetrant, and Magnaflux, extend and multiply the tester's senses.

When a mechanic is weary from long hours and overwork, he or she can start seeing hairline cracks all over a work piece—or, just as serious, can be looking directly at an obvious defect and miss it! So, in a life-or-death situation or one of huge financial importance, remember to check the part in question with a couple of different methods before condemning it or using it. Whenever possible, verify visual findings with a dye penetrant or pressure test.

PRESSURE TESTS

Pressure testing is the process of learning whether a device that should hold pressure or stop flow will actually do so. There is also flow testing. With flow testing (Fig. 16-1), it is possible to see if a device that is supposed to allow flow does indeed let the flow through. Figure 16-1 shows a coolant passage, but a qualitative check for presence or absence of flow also works for oil, fuel, and air passages. Pressure and flow tests allow you to check areas in systems where visual inspection is impossible.

There are devices aboard boats that must always hold pressure, must sometimes hold pressure, must always allow flow, or must sometimes allow flow. For example, the engine's water pump forces coolant through the cooling passages of the engine. The engine coolant thermostat must open and close at the right temperatures to either recirculate the coolant in the engine or to send it out to a heat exchanger for cooling. As previously mentioned, a flow test is simply verification that there is flow where it is needed. Compressed air, fuel, water, and coolant can all be used to

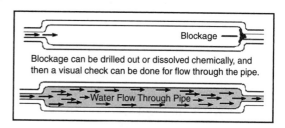

Fig. 16-1. Flow testing is one way to determine the source of blockages. In the upper schematic view of a coolant passage, no flow is getting through.

verify flow visually. Sometimes leaking fluid will leave a trail that you can track back to the source.

One reason engines overheat is plugging of the cooling passages with precipitated solids, which prevents coolant flow. After an engine overheats, cracks develop in the engine castings, and the coolant goes places it shouldn't go. For example, coolant will flow from a cracked head or faulty head gasket into the engine cylinders, causing a hydraulic lock. Eventually, the coolant will reach the oil pan. It can also leak to the outside of the engine.

One simple pressure test involves blowing into a hollow fitting while plugging the other end with your thumb. If air leaks out from somewhere it shouldn't, you've used a rudimentary form of pressure testing to locate the defect. This will work for testing many things, one example being engine vacuum controls. Marine gasoline engines have a vacuum advance diaphragm on the distributor that is easily tested with the mouth by pulling a vacuum on the diaphragm to see if it will hold a vacuum. You can also see if it will move the distributor linkage. When it's important to keep away from the work piece for safety reasons, connect a piece of new or clean vacuum hose to the device you are testing. Most pressure testing is simply a variation of this method.

Next, consider a pressure leak. A car tire with a slow leak may first be checked audibly, because leaks can often be heard. Stooping down by the tire and listening carefully may help locate the leak. If not, use a squirt bottle filled with diluted dish detergent to spray the tire, and watch for foam over the leak. If these methods don't find the leak, the people at the tire shop will take it to the next level and place the tire in a tank of water and simply watch

for bubbles. The same simple pressure tests used on a leaking tire will serve the boater well when a leak must be found.

TOOLS FOR TESTING

The pressure gauge and the manometer are two of the most common pressure-testing tools. Both take skill to use and read accurately. The range of pressure gauges varies widely. This is because a gauge that is used to check pressures in the 5,000 psi range won't be sensitive enough for use in the range of 5 psi. Therefore, mechanics use whatever range of pressure gauge is right for the application. When testing for 5,000 psi, a gauge of higher capacity would be used. A gauge with a range from zero to 6,000 psi would be used to provide a safety margin in case of an unexpected pressure spike. Likewise, to measure 5 psi, a 10 psi gauge would be suitable, or, as we'll see, a manometer will very accurately measure low pressures, including vacuum readings.

Note: When pressure testing, be careful to standardize the way you look at the pressure gauge (Fig. 16-2). It also helps to close one eye and center the line-of-sight so that readings taken over time are consistent.

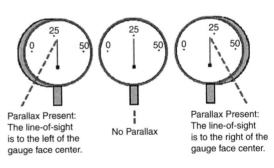

Parallax Present: The line-of-sight is to the left of the gauge face center.

No Parallax

Parallax Present: The line-of-sight is to the right of the gauge face center.

Fig. 16-2. When reading pressure gauges, maintain a consistent viewing angle so readings are not influenced by your changing line-of-sight.

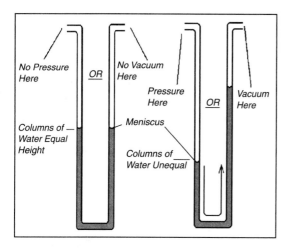

Fig. 16-3. A manometer is an instrument that measures changes in pressure.

Manometers are made of transparent tubing and work something like a barometer. They register changes in pressure by the movement of a column of liquid contained inside the transparent tubing. The advantage of the manometer is extreme accuracy. The pressure readings are taken in inches of water or inches of mercury. Both of these readings are easy to convert directly to psi or the metric unit of pressure, kilopascals (kPa). Manometers filled with water display a curve shaped (in cross section) like a smile (called a meniscus) at the top of the water column (Fig. 16-3). A mercury-filled manometer, on the other hand, displays a meniscus that is just the opposite, like a frown.

CYLINDER PRESSURE TESTING

The engine cylinder compression test is one of the most common. It uses a pressure gauge to register the maximum pressure that a cylinder will develop when the engine is cranked with the starter motor. The test pressure gauge is installed in each cylinder, one at a time, and then the cylinder pressures are compared.

The more uniform the cylinder pressures are, the better the engine will run.

When a cylinder's maximum pressure is less than 90 percent of the highest cylinder pressures, it is time to find the cause for the low cylinder's pressure reading. Considering the way piston engines are built, the most common reasons for low cylinder pressure are a valve seat leak, a piston ring leak, or a hole in a piston. This testing method can leave the user with some uncertainty as to the cause of the low pressure.

However, if the spark plug (gasoline engine) is fouled, it is safe to say the engine is burning a lot of oil and that the rings are involved. If the plug is not fouled and the engine does not burn much oil, then the compression may be leaking away through a valve seat. Often, an intake valve seat leak can be checked audibly by listening in the air intake while the engine is running. Likewise, an exhaust leak can be checked by listening near the outlet of the exhaust pipe.

There is a better test for cylinder condition that takes a little more time, skill, and equipment. It is called the cylinder leak-down test.

Cylinder Leak-Down Testing. Often used on aircraft engines, this method is very good for determining cylinder and valve condition. The testing is done after attaching the test apparatus to the spark plug hole (gasoline engine) or in the injector hole (diesel engine). This test must be done with the batteries disconnected to prevent accidental cranking of the engine. The leak-down test (Fig. 16-4) works by comparing the leakage rate of any cylinder against a known pressure and volume of air that is plumbed into the cylinder through the leak-down tester.

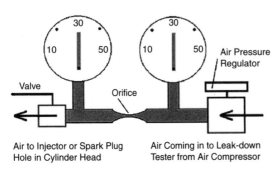

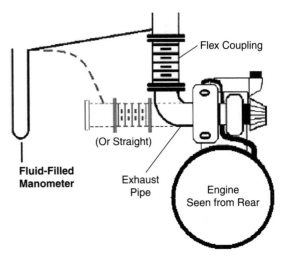

Fig. 16-4. The cylinder leak-down tester works by comparing the readings on the two gauges. The closer the readings are to one another, the better the condition of the cylinder. If the downstream gauge registers a lower pressure, the cylinder is losing pressure. This test is done with the engine off.

Fig. 16-5. There are two ways to connect a manometer to the exhaust system—one for a vertical exhaust and one for a horizontal one. In either case the manometer should be attached to a straight section of pipe. If you do not find a plugged hole, you will have to drill and tap one. The test is done with the engine running under full power.

Exhaust Back-Pressure Testing. Exhaust back-pressure testing measures excessive exhaust flow restriction. Engines run better with low back-pressure in the exhaust system. Generally speaking, exhaust back-pressure on gasoline and diesel engines must be less than four inches of mercury (1.5 psi) as measured with a manometer. The manometer must be connected (Fig. 16-5) only in a straight section of pipe at least a foot away from the nearest bend in the exhaust plumbing. When there is no place to connect the manometer to the exhaust system, a small hole may be drilled that is suitable for tapping to a $^1/_8$-inch NPT (National Pipe Tap) pipe fitting size. This hole is plugged with a pipe plug after the test.

It is not enough to run the engine up to full speed in neutral to check for back-pressure. The engine must be used at full power under sea trial conditions for accurate results. Check the exhaust pressure you see against the engine manufacturer's specs. *Note: Because elemental mercury is so much heavier than water, a manometer filled with mercury is capable of measuring much higher pressures than one filled with water.*

A manometer is also used for measuring the intake manifold pressure, and it's likewise good for testing turbochargers. The manometer works well for testing crankcase pressure too, and the test results are a good indication of the cylinder and piston condition. One sign of poor piston ring sealing is excessive blowby of combustion gases past the piston rings. When the engine crankcase pressure gets too high, the engine will tend to leak oil. High crankcase pressure will also cause the front and rear crankcase seals to fail.

PRESSURE-TESTING HEADS
When cylinder heads are suspected of leaking coolant, the water jacket is pressure-tested with a pressure gauge that gives readouts in psi or kilopascals (kPa). This testing can be done wet or dry, and there are advantages and disadvantages to each method. It can also be done with the work piece at

ambient temperature or heated to operating temperature.

Before a pressure test can be done, there must be access to the internal area of the piece that is to be tested—i.e., a pressure tap. For example, to do a compression test on a gasoline engine, the spark plug is removed and a test gauge fitting is threaded into the spark plug hole. When the piston comes up, the pressure gauge that is threaded into the spark plug opening registers the pressure in the cylinder.

When a cylinder head is to be pressure-tested, there are often over a dozen openings that must be blocked so that the head will hold pressure, while the pressure source and the pressure test gauge must be plumbed into the water-jacket of the head. You'll have to remove the head from the engine. A plate to block off the water-jacket holes can be fabricated as shown in Figure 16-6. Various sizes

and shapes of plugs are available at plumbing shops, although special plugs or covers must often be fabricated. When test fittings or cover plates are used, they must be suitably sealed with pipe dope, O-ring seals, or gasket material.

Hydrostatic Pressure Testing

A pressure test with the piece to be tested full of water is known as a hydrostatic test (Fig. 16-7). The enhanced safety of this method is due to the fact that liquids are incompressible. What this means is that if the piece under test suddenly ruptures, no one is likely to be harmed, because the pressure drops almost instantly.

Notice that the cylinder head in this drawing is totally filled with water. The pressure source is regulated compressed air, and it enters the head from above. The pressure line between the gauge and the head is filled with air. For the purpose of this discussion, consider that the volume of the air line plus a thin layer of air in the top of the cylinder head is one-half cup, and the volume of the

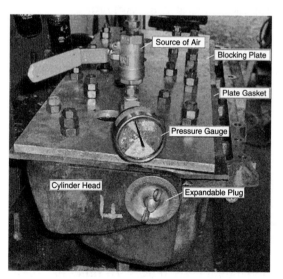

Fig. 16-6. To pressure-test a cylinder head, you'll have to remove it from the engine. All the openings—perhaps over a dozen—must be blocked, as done here with a blocking plate. A pressure gauge is teed into the compressed-air source, which is tapped into the plate.

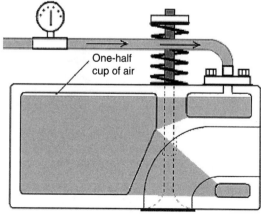

Fig. 16-7. Hydrostatic cylinder-head pressure testing uses water and has several advantages over an air test..

cylinder head being tested is two gallons. Let's say that the pressure on the gauge is 60 psi. If one-half cup of water leaks from the head, this will double the volume of air in the system and will also reduce the pressure reading on the gauge by half, bringing it down to 30 psi.

Therefore, not only is a hydrostatic pressure test much safer than a straight air test, the pressure gauge reading is many times more responsive than a pressure test performed only with air. Another advantage of a hydrostatic test is that the work piece can be located over a dry area, and every drop resulting from leakage will be easy to see.

PRESSURE TESTING DRY, WITH AIR PRESSURE

Pressure testing only with air (Fig. 16-8) and no water at all is far more dangerous than hydrostatic testing, because air is compressible, and if the work piece bursts it will take much longer for the pressure to dissipate. Another disadvantage of straight air testing is that the pressure gauge will be unable to measure very small leaks. This test does have the benefit of very quick results when the work piece is submerged in water with high

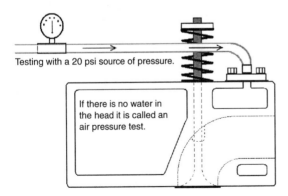

Testing with a 20 psi source of pressure.

If there is no water in the head it is called an air pressure test.

Fig. 16-8. Pressure testing using air can be dangerous but is quicker than hydrostatic testing.

air pressure in it. A small stream of bubbles will quickly show where the leak is.

TESTING HOT

No matter what type of testing is done, it always works better to pressure-test metal pieces as close to their normal operating temperature as possible. It's helpful to test cylinder heads, for example, at 180°F, the normal operating temperature of a cylinder head. Testing hot causes the metal to expand and open even very small cracks, thereby making them more detectable. There are several ways to heat the water in the head, and one of the best is to attach an automotive (electric) tank heater to recirculating tank-style water through the head, while it's under pressure. Another good way is to test a head with air pressure and submerge it into a tank of hot water while it's under pressure to check for leaks.

TESTING LARGE ASSEMBLIES

While the discussion so far has centered on testing parts of engines, it's important to note that the water jackets of complete engines can also be pressure-tested in a fully assembled state.

Sealing materials such as gaskets and O-ring seals are made of materials that are especially good at containing either high pressures or high temperatures. Take care to use the manufacturer's suggested part number, and if the instructions say to put an O-ring of a certain color in a certain position, be sure to do it! Often, gaskets must be made at sea for doing temporary repairs. At times like these, pay close attention to the thickness of the original gasket material, and try to duplicate that thickness.

Where O-rings are concerned, there are kits available to make new ones by cutting the appropriate diameter of round rubber stock to length and then gluing the ends together to form the right seal circumference. When this is done, try to stay as close as possible to the original diameter of the O-ring material, which may be neoprene, Buna-N, or silicone rubber.

The pressure test of a complete engine cooling system is a hydrostatic test because the engine and its cooling system are filled with coolant. Such a test will reveal the integrity (or lack thereof) of the cylinder walls, head gasket, and the cylinder liner seals. Pressure testing such an engine would consist of first connecting a regulated air pressure line, or hand pump, to a point high up on the engine and then supplying between 20 and 30 psi to the system, often through the pressure cap opening.

A pressure test will also indicate the integrity of the cylinder head, the aftercooler core, and the jacketed exhaust system. The jacketed exhaust system, if so equipped, may also have a jacketed turbocharger.

A bore scope (Fig. 16-9) can also be used to watch for a leaking head gasket, head, or cylinder liner while the engine is under pressure.

LIQUID (DYE) PENETRANT AND MAGNETIC PARTICLE TESTING

Fluorescent penetrant testing and magnetic particle testing are nondestructive inspection methods capable of detecting flaws or defects in metal parts with very good accuracy. These methods work for many objects that would be impossible to check with pressure, such as solid shafts.

Liquid penetrant inspection is the first of the modern nondestructive inspection methods. It originated in railroad maintenance

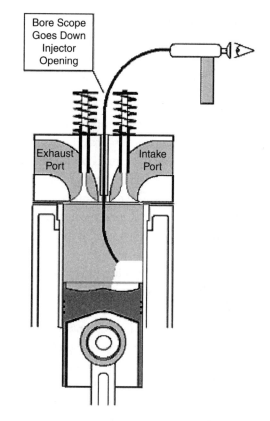

Fig. 16-9. A bore scope in use to provide an internal visual inspection while the cylinder is under pressure (engine not running).

shops in the late 1800s. Parts to be inspected would be immersed in used machine oil. After immersion, the parts were withdrawn from the oil and the excess surface oil was wiped off. The surfaces of the parts would then be coated with powdered chalk or a mixture of chalk suspended in alcohol (whiting). Oil trapped in cracks or flaws in the metal would bleed out, causing a noticeable stain in the white chalk coating.

The oil-and-whiting method was replaced by magnetic particle inspection on steel and ferrous (iron) parts in 1930. However, industries using nonferrous metals, such as bronze, aluminum, magnesium, and titanium, needed a more reliable and sophisticated tool than the oil-and-whiting method. In 1941, fluorescent dye materials were added to a penetrating-type oil to make a penetrant material.

THE BASIC PENETRANT PROCESS

Penetrant inspection is a simple, inexpensive, and reliable way to detect cracks on the surface of metal objects. It can be used on metals and other nonporous materials that are not harmed by the penetrant oils. The technique will detect a wide variety of cracks ranging in size from those readily visible down to the microscopic level, as long as the cracks are open to the surface and are sufficiently free of foreign material.

The steps in the penetrant process have not changed from the oil-and-whiting days. In the first step, a penetrating liquid containing dyes is applied to the surface of a clean part. While cleaning is not part of the penetrant process, it is emphasized because of its effect on the inspection results. Contaminants, such as soils or moisture, either inside the flaw or on the part surface at the flaw opening, can reduce the effectiveness of the inspection. The penetrant is allowed to remain on the part surface for a period of time, which is learned by experience, to permit it to enter and fill any openings.

After the immersion time that is suggested by the instructions, the second step is the removal of the penetrant from the part surface. Care must be taken to prevent over cleaning and removal of penetrant contained in the cracks. The third step is the application of a material called developer. The developer acts to draw any trapped penetrant from cracks and improves the visibility of defects, as shown in Figure 16-10.

Penetrant materials are available in aerosol spray cans and in small containers that can be used on installed parts. A wide variety of materials, including ferrous and nonferrous metals and alloys, fired ceramics and cermets, powdered metal products, glass, and some types of organic materials can be inspected this way.

EFFECTS OF MECHANICAL WORKING

Mechanical working, such as machining, scraping, sanding, sandblasting, shot peening, and even steam cleaning, removes soils and contaminants by physical action. This action also removes or deforms some of the part's surface. Even a small amount of deformation, such as that caused by fine sanding or vapor blasting, will reduce the surface opening of small cracks, resulting in a decrease in the effectiveness of the penetrant inspection process. Severe mechanical working processes, such as metal removal, shot peening,

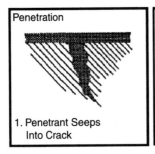
1. Penetrant Seeps Into Crack

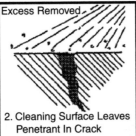
2. Cleaning Surface Leaves Penetrant In Crack

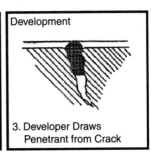
3. Developer Draws Penetrant from Crack

Fig. 16-10. The basic dye penetrant process.

plastic media bead blasting, coarse sanding, or grit blasting, can seal or close the surface openings of large cracks and prevent the formation of penetrant indications. Penetrant inspection must be done prior to mechanical work processes (Fig. 16-11).

LIGHTING FOR FLUORESCENT DYE PENETRANT TESTING

The eye is not too responsive to black light, especially if visible light is present. However, in a darkened testing booth the sensitivity of the eye increases, yielding better results.

Low-pressure fluorescent bulbs are similar to standard fluorescent tubes and are not strong enough for use in detecting fluorescent indications. High-pressure, mercury-vapor bulbs are the most common testing sources for black light. No less than a 100-watt bulb should be used for penetrant inspection, and only after the bulb has warmed up for at least 15 minutes before the inspection is performed.

For safety, black lamp bulbs need filters. Cracked, chipped, or ill-fitting filters must be replaced before using the lamp. High-intensity super black lights that use bulbs with integral filters must have a splash guard, as supplied by the manufacturer, attached to the front of the lamp housing to prevent accidental implosion of the bulb. Prolonged direct exposure of hands to the main beam of the filtered black light may be harmful. White cotton glove liners or other suitable gloves must be worn to protect the skin from burns when exposing hands to the main light beam.

Caution: The temperature of some black lamp bulbs reaches 750°F or more during operation. This is above the ignition or flashpoint of fuel vapors. These vapors will burst into flames if they contact the bulb. Black lights must not be operated in the presence of flammable vapors. Extreme care must be exercised to prevent contacting the housing with any part of the body.

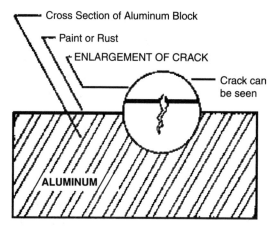

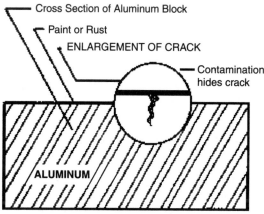

Fig. 16-11. **Effects of mechanical working. In the top drawing, the crack is evident by its raised, sharp edges. In the bottom drawing, after sanding or sandblasting, those edges are gone, and the crack is filled in and may be invisible.**

MAGNAFLUX TESTING (MAGNETIC PARTICLE INSPECTION)

As mentioned above, cracks can exist even in newly smelted metals, can form during fabrication of parts, or can appear as fatigue cracks or cracks due to excessive service stresses. Not all cracks are considered defects. However, if the crack prevents usefulness of the parts, it is a defect. Magnetic particle inspection can often locate cracks in ferromagnetic material. Magnetic particle inspection is another nondestructive method for revealing surface and near subsurface cracks in parts made of magnetic materials. The process consists of three steps:

1. Application of magnetic particles
2. Establishment of a suitable magnetic field
3. Examination and evaluation of particle accumulations

If the part to be inspected is made from an alloy containing a high percentage of iron and can be magnetized, it is in a class of metals called ferromagnetic and can be inspected by this method. If the part is made of nonmagnetic material, it cannot be inspected by this method. The magnetic particle inspection method will detect surface cracks, including those that are too fine to be seen with the naked eye, those that lie slightly below the surface, and, when special equipment is used, more deeply seated cracks.

ELECTRICITY AND MAGNETISM
Electricity is used to cause magnetic fields in parts made of magnetic materials. Magnetic lines of force are always aligned at right angles to the direction of electric current flow. Since it is possible to control the direction of the magnetic field by controlling the direction of the magnetizing current, it is important to know how to use electricity to induce the magnetic lines of force so that they intercept and are as near as possible to right angles to the defect or crack.

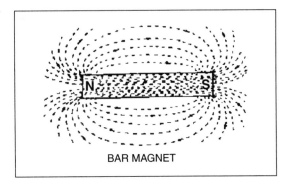

BAR MAGNET

Fig. 16-12. Magnetic flux lines.

MAGNETIC ATTRACTION
The concept of flux lines includes flow, distribution, directional, and attraction-repulsion properties. Each flux line is considered to be a continuous loop, which is never broken but must complete itself through some path. The flux lines always leave a magnet at right angles to the surface. They always seek the path of lowest reluctance (opposition to the establishment of magnetic flux) in completing their loop. When a piece of soft iron is placed in a magnetic field, it will be drawn toward the magnetic source. This is the action that causes magnetic particles to concentrate at leakage fields at cracks. Since the magnetic particles offer a lower reluctance path to the flux lines, they are therefore drawn to the crack and bridge the air gap (Fig. 16-12).

EFFECTS OF FLUX DIRECTION
The magnetic field must be in a favorable direction to produce indications. When the flux lines are oriented parallel to a crack, the indication will be weak or lacking. The best results are obtained when the flux lines cross a crack at right angles. If a crack is to produce a leakage field and a readable magnetic particle indication, it must intercept the flux

lines of force at some angle. When an electrical magnetizing current is used, the best indications are produced when the path of the magnetizing current is flowing parallel to the crack because the magnetic flux lines are always at right angles to the flow of magnetizing current (Fig. 16-13).

While stationary magnetic crack detection equipment is common in large shops, portable equipment is often used on board boats and works well for examining small areas in large components, such as cylinder heads, blocks, and crankshafts. Handheld electromagnetic probe yokes are U-shaped cores of soft iron with a coil wound around the base of the U. When alternating current or rectified alternating current is passing through the coil, the two ends of the core are magnetized with opposite polarity.

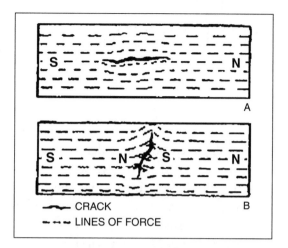

Fig. 16-13. Cracks alter the lines of force. Finely ground iron particles are sprinkled on the steel or iron surface to be tested. When a handheld Magnaflux unit is laid on the surface and activated, the particles align themselves with the magnetic flux lines, and any cracks running across those lines will show as distortions in the particle alignments.

CHAPTER 17

SHAFT AND ENGINE ALIGNMENT

Proper alignment of propeller shafts and engines ensures that the vessel will run smoothly under power, prolongs the life of the equipment, and contributes to the safety of the crew. The shaft and engine need to work together and must be in perfect harmony. Engine power is transferred from the rear of the transmission, through the shaft couplings, intermediate shaft, bearings, stuffing box, rear shaft, the stern bearing, and finally the propeller. *Note: Not all boats have intermediate and rear shafts; these are more typical of large motoryachts and commercial fishing boats.* At times, alignment of the shaft and engine will need adjusting. There is a specific order that must be followed if the job is to be done right, and there are three important factors to consider when the boat is in the water and loaded to normal running weight:

1. The bores of all shaft bearings and the stuffing box must all be aligned within the tolerances specified by the bearing manufacturers.
2. Propeller shafts must be centered within the shaft bearings and the stuffing box.
3. Only after the above two conditions have been met can the engine and transmission assembly be aligned to the shaft.

To summarize, the shaft is first aligned to the boat, and after this work is done, the engine and transmission assembly is aligned to the shaft. *Caution: Be sure to disable the starter motor before doing any of the work described in this chapter!*

Unlike land-based heavy machinery mounted on thick concrete, marine propulsion systems are designed to take considerable twisting and flexing of their platform (the boat) and keep on working. As they are hauled out and blocked for repairs, boats are subject to bending and twisting. In addition, thermal expansion and contraction occur due to temperature changes of the water and air, internal heat sources, and uneven heating when one side of a vessel is in sunlight and the other is in shade. These fluctuations will change the stresses in the hull and the shafting and thereby slightly change shaft alignment.

Weather and sea conditions always require the hull and the shafting to bend and flex as the vessel moves through the water. Marine propulsion systems routinely operate in conditions that land-based machinery, such as stationary diesel generators, would only encounter during a severe earthquake.

Sailboat shafts and engine alignment are fairly stable because of the low power ratings at which they operate. High-performance yachts and workboats are designed with fairly light and flexible hull structures, and often the shafts run at high speeds. Fishing boats or freighters differ from other boats because they are heavy on the ends when empty, but, when loaded, they are heavy in the middle.

When properly designed, built, and maintained, shafts and supporting bearings will last and be relatively free of vibration in any application. As we'll see, there are low levels of normal vibration, and then there are severe vibrations. It's the variation from the norm that tips off the troubleshooter.

FINDING THE SOURCE OF VIBRATION

When vibrations become noticeable due to a change in intensity, alignment checks are in order. Increasing levels of vibration foretell of mechanical damage to the system.

To begin looking for shaft and alignment problems, remove all covers and access hatches so that the shaft can be observed with the transmission engaged. We'll be watching for an obvious wobble of the shaft as it turns and for hot pillow block bearings, which are sometimes found on motoryachts and are often found on commercial vessels. Note: There are many ways a shaft can bend (Fig.17-1). *Caution: Be very careful not to get your clothing or limbs caught in the shaft mechanism while watching the shaft!*

As the shaft turns, a 0.020-inch (20 thousandths of an inch) bend or wobble in the shaft is easy to spot visually. The surface of the shaft can be cleaned with a belt of abrasive emery cloth and a dial indicator set up to verify the visual observations. (A dial indicator has a spring-loaded plunger connected to a dial at one end. The other end has a clamp or a magnetic base for mounting. The device is mounted with the plunger resting on the shaft. See also Fig. 17-8.) After finding a severe bend or wobble, the next thing to do is remove the bent shaft. After the shaft is straightened

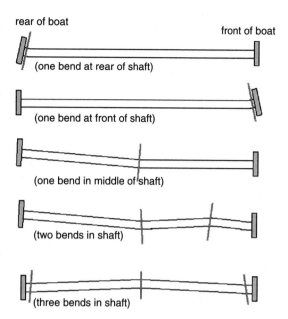

rear of boat
front of boat

(one bend at rear of shaft)

(one bend at front of shaft)

(one bend in middle of shaft)

(two bends in shaft)

(three bends in shaft)

Fig. 17-1. Shafts can have simple or compound bends.

and reinstalled, a complete alignment will be required. If the vibrations are due to misalignment rather than physical damage such as a bent shaft, bent propeller, or failed shaft bearing, see the discussion below.

Every part of a propulsion system has a working tolerance, an allowable degree of imperfection, which permits the new part's specifications to vary a small amount from the specifications of a perfect or ideal part. When checking the alignment of equipment, the working tolerance will keep coming up, and it's important to keep on the low side whenever possible to achieve the best results. The final alignment procedures must be done with the boat in the water.

As we describe the process, it will be easy to see why most boats aren't aligned as well as they could be. The shaft and engine alignment of a boat is often a functional compromise that lets the boat keep operating with a minimum of wear and vibration. However, we'll cover the ideal way to align the equipment.

When vibration is a problem, the propeller must be inspected to spot any damage. A propeller can look great yet have a slightly bent or out-of-pitch blade. This will cause vibration. Furthermore, the stern (Cutless) bearing must be tight enough to control shaft movement according to specifications published by the stern bearing manufacturer.

ALIGNMENT BY THE NUMBERS

Using the reference numbers in Figure 17-3, we will start with eight and count down to the rear of the boat, covering the basic checks that must be made to identify a problem that causes vibration. We will do it this way because the forward end of the shaft is where people normally start looking, mainly because

the front of the shaft is so much easier to check than the rear. Because there are many shafting configurations, this discussion will cover a long shafting system with an intermediate shaft, even though many boats have no intermediate shaft.

8. The transmission output shaft bearings control fore-and-aft, up-and-down, and side-to-side movement of the shaft. The transmission's shaft coupling must be tight on the output shaft. When oil leaks from the rear of the transmission, it comes from the inside through the lip-type output shaft seal, or past the output shaft splines in the output shaft coupling. When there is a vibration in this area, check to ensure that the transmission's rear coupling is tight on its shaft and that the face of the transmission coupling runs true when checked with a dial indicator.

FOR THE WORKBOAT

The Kink at the End of the Shaft

By 2:30 a.m. we had been through the shaft alignment tests several times to verify the results, and it was clear that the boat's intermediate shaft was badly bent at the rear end, only two inches from the coupling. The skipper, Len, had been sitting with me for hours in the engine room bilge, just behind the transmission, helping to turn the shaft and writing down my readings.

We were tired but happy to have found the source of the boat's terrible vibration. All that was left was to take the shaft to the machine shop and have it straightened. Making the opening of the halibut season would be close, with less than twenty-four hours left to go. But it was likely we'd have it ready in time, depending on how fast the machine shop could straighten the shaft.

The next morning, after a short night, I awakened to a call from a very angry boatowner. They had been able to get the machinist to chuck the intermediate shaft in his lathe, and it ran perfectly true (Fig. 17-2). I assured him my findings were right-on and headed for the machine shop. It's important to note that this machinist was very well trained and highly competent; he had been a machinist in the navy.

To my surprise, when the machinist rolled the shaft, the dial indicator needle remained still. There was no sign of the plus thirty-thousandths readings we were getting down on the boat the night before. The skipper was also in hot water with the owner for letting a "little vibration" worry him. Standing in the machine shop, with the crowd who had gathered to watch the fireworks, I was baffled as to why my readings at the boat were so different!

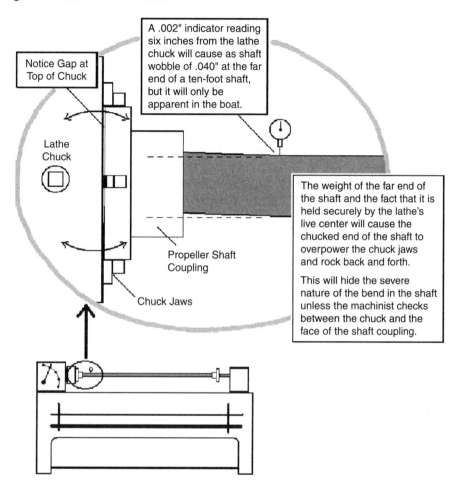

Notice Gap at Top of Chuck

A .002" indicator reading six inches from the lathe chuck will cause as shaft wobble of .040" at the far end of a ten-foot shaft, but it will only be apparent in the boat.

Lathe Chuck

Propeller Shaft Coupling

Chuck Jaws

The weight of the far end of the shaft and the fact that it is held securely by the lathe's live center will cause the chucked end of the shaft to overpower the chuck jaws and rock back and forth.

This will hide the severe nature of the bend in the shaft unless the machinist checks between the chuck and the face of the shaft coupling.

Fig. 17-2. A kink at the end of a shaft.

It wasn't until a few months later that I happened to carry something back to the same machinist. As I looked at his lathe, it dawned on me that I should have had him swap the shaft end for end and recheck it.

Because the bend was so close to the end of the shaft, I saw that he must have installed the bent end of the shaft in the chuck. The straight end of the shaft was held by the point of the live center as shown in the accompanying drawing, which made it seem as though the shaft ran true. The shaft was so heavy that even a new chuck in a new lathe would have allowed the kinked end to slip inside of the jaws as the shaft rotated.

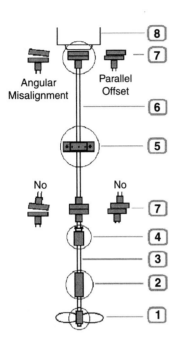

Angular Misalignment

Parallel Offset

No

No

Fig. 17-3. Shafting checks by the numbers. (1) propeller; (2) stern bearing (also called Cutless bearing); (3) tail shaft, if so equipped; (4) stuffing box; (5) intermediate pillow-block bearing, if so equipped; (6) shaft or intermediate shaft; (7) couplings; (8) transmission.

7. The shaft couplings must be tight on the shaft, and the faces of the couplings must be flat and true with the shaft to ensure that the shaft will run true when turning. The ultimate test to determine whether the coupling is running true with the shaft is in a lathe after the shaft has been verified to be straight. However, a skilled marine mechanic can check the trueness of the coupling to the shaft by first turning the shaft with a dial indicator set up on clean places along the length of the shaft. Clean places are made by using belts of abrasive and running it all the way around the shaft to remove rust before setting up the dial indicator.

After the shaft is verified to be within tolerance, the coupling faces can be checked with the dial indicator after separating (splitting) the couplings and using a dial indicator on the face, while turning the shaft. Shaft couplings come in male and female configurations. It is this pilot and pocket system that keeps the couplings concentric with one another. The coupling faces and the pilot and pocket must be free of burrs (Fig. 17-4). There must be a snug hand-tight fit between the pilot and the pocket in the couplings. The final alignment must cause the coupling faces to be parallel and with no offset.

Propulsion coupling bolts are normally Grade 5, as specified by the Society of Automotive Engineers (SAE), and need not be Grade 8 unless these better bolts have been specified by the boatbuilder. Remember, the shanks of these coupling bolts will *never* be in shear unless the nuts are left loose. The only job of the coupling bolts is to create intense friction between the coupling faces. It is friction that transfers the engine's power to the next coupling, and finally to the propeller, and not the shank of the bolt.

Fine-thread bolts with self-locking nuts are often used instead of coarse threads in this location. For ease of removal in the future, point the threaded end of the *front* coupling bolts to the *rear* of the boat. Also, point the bolts in the *rear* coupling of the intermediate shaft with the threaded end pointing *forward.* This makes it easy to put a coat of Anti-Seez compound on the bolt threads before the self-locking nuts are installed. After appying a liberal coat of marine grade anti-seizing compound, the nuts are tightened to specifications.

6. The intermediate shaft has to be straight (Fig. 17-5). Most often this shaft, being somewhat protected from the elements by the shaft alley, is steel rather than stainless steel.

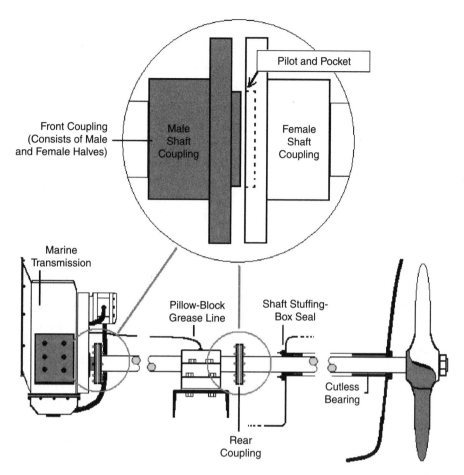

Fig. 17-4. The pilot and pocket arrangement of a shaft coupling.

The reason for this is that a bronze, stainless steel, or monel intermediate shaft represents a needless expense since the intermediate shaft is protected from salt water.

Unfortunately, this shaft can be destroyed in short order by lack of lubrication, such as after the grease line to the pillow block bearing breaks! The intermediate shaft can also degenerate if it is exposed to salt water.

5. When well lubricated, the pillow block bearing is made to carry a heavy, slow-turning shaft for many years. To do so it has to be installed at the right height, not too high and not too low, in relation to the other fixed points of shaft support. The bearing cap must be shimmed to allow clearance for grease on top of the shaft under the cap. Molydisulfide grease is a superior lubricant for such applications and is the lubricant of choice among professional mechanics.

Pillow-block bearings come new with extra paper shims installed between the cap and the bearing's body. This allows for the removal of shims in those instances when there is some wear on the shaft and bearing-to-shaft clearance is too great.

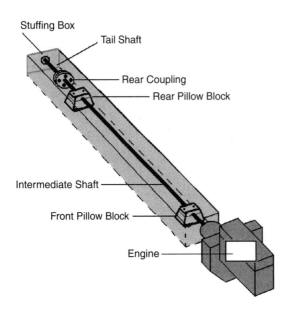

Stuffing Box

Tail Shaft

Rear Coupling

Rear Pillow Block

Intermediate Shaft

Front Pillow Block

Engine

Fig. 17-5. The contents of a shaft alley.

Each bearing manufacturer has its own guidelines for bearing clearance, which is based mainly on shaft diameter. Pillow block bearings have a grease fitting installed to enable greasing with a grease gun. They can also be plumbed to allow remote greasing to take place from the engine room. Remote greasing is more convenient and easier on the crew. The drawback to remote greasing is that you don't know for sure that the grease is getting to the bearing without a visual inspection. Unfortunately, many boats use copper tubing as their grease lines to the pillow block bearings. It is better to use high-pressure hydraulic hoses that are made to length before installation.

While it is normal for pillow blocks to run warm, even as hot as 170°F, cooler is always better. A noncontact infrared thermometer works well for monitoring bearing temperature, especially during the sea trial that must be done after alignment work or any other major repair. It is during the sea trial that the boat is checked for vibrations and heat at the bearings and stuffing box.

4. The stuffing box provides a means of controlling water flow past the same packing that keeps water out of the boat. The water flow through the stuffing box lubricates the packing inside and prevents accelerated wear of the propeller shaft. There is often a grease fitting on the stuffing box.

On workboats, the crew can use this grease fitting to their advantage when they arrive in town and can't wait to get off the boat for a few hours. To stop the stuffing box from leaking for a little while, they may grease the stuffing box fitting, and this stops water from leaking past the packing until the shaft turns again. This keeps the bilge from filling quickly with water.

The only alternative for temporarily stopping stuffing box leakage is to tighten the adjusting bolts (or packing nut) on the stuffing box until the water stops dripping. If this is done, the same adjustment must be loosened before the shaft starts turning again. The rate of water dripping must be several drops a minute, or damage to the shaft and stuffing box will follow. The area where the stuffing box is fastened to the rear of the shaft alley must be well sealed against leaks (Fig. 17-6). There is either a gasket in this area or a durable sealant.

3. The rear shaft is made of either bronze or stainless steel alloy for corrosion resistance. On recreational boats with only one shaft, the same material is used. *Note: Watch for cracking at the end of the shaft keyway during propeller sevice.*

2. The rearmost support for the wet end of the shaft is the stern tube (Cutless) bearing

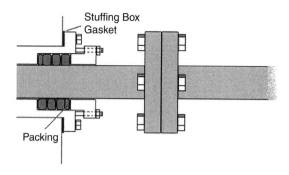

Fig. 17-6. The stuffing box shaft seal.

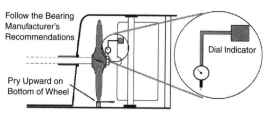

Fig. 17-8. Checking the stern bearing clearance.

(Fig. 17-7). The stern bearing is lubricated by water, and it has an ideal range of clearance that is specified by the manufacturer. The clearance must be small enough to control shaft movement, but great enough to allow water flow through the bearing. It is the stuffing box packing adjustment that controls the flow of lubricating water through the stern bearing. The stern bearing's inner rubber

bearing material must remain attached to the bearing's outer bronze sleeve.

The stern bearing can be checked underwater by an experienced diver. To do so, the diver pries between the rudder shoe and the propeller to lift the shaft while observing shaft movement in the bearing. When the boat is on the hard, the actual bearing clearance can be measured with a dial indicator (Fig. 17-8).

1. Les Christensen of Kodiak Metals, Kodiak, Alaska, told us that propellers must be installed in such a way that the key is not binding between the keyway and the propeller (Fig. 17-9). With the key in a bind, the propeller cannot advance fully onto

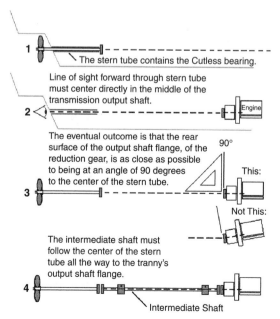

Fig. 17-7. The stern tube points to the engine's best position.

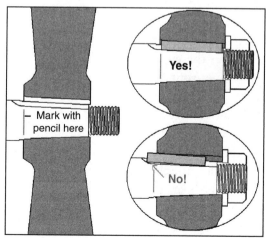

Fig. 17-9. Precautions for propeller installation.

the tapered shaft. This causes two problems: (1) the prop is thrown off-center, and (2) the plane of center of the blades is no longer perpendicular to the shaft. Not only will it vibrate, but it may well come loose as it runs. When this happens, the propeller may fall off.

The best way to install a propeller is to slide it on the shaft without the key in the keyway and put a mark on the shaft at that point, showing that the propeller is all the way on the shaft. When the propeller is installed with the key in place, it's obvious that the key is in a bind if the propeller won't slide all the way up to the mark.

STARTING AT THE REAR

When a vibration seems to be related to the shaft or alignment, the crew will normally unbolt the couplings behind the engine and transmission and check there first for obvious misalignment. Sometimes the crew finds it there. If, when the shaft is pulled back from the coupling pilot, it springs into some other position, you have found a bent shaft or an obvious alignment problem, but you do not yet know where the problem is.

At first it might seem that the answer is to loosen the engine mount bolts and slide the engine around so that it lines up with the shaft. However, this seldom works. When the shaft springs away from the transmission coupling, it indicates there is a problem, but the cause of the problem cannot be tracked down unless the alignment check starts at the back of the boat. The shaft may be straight or it may be bent, but the only way to know for sure is to start at the back of the boat.

When couplings are unbolted and still won't come apart, it helps to use a flange ax

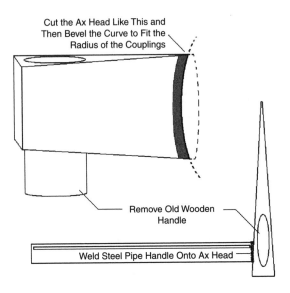

Fig. 17-10. To fashion a flange ax for separating stubborn shaft couplings, remove the wooden handle from a standard ax, cut its blade from a convex to a concave curve as shown, bevel the newly shaped blade, and weld a steel pipe to the flat of the ax head to use as a handle.

(Fig. 17-10) to part them. Not a store-bought item, the flange ax must be fabricated from an ax head.

To repeat: The final outcome of an engine alignment cannot be certain unless the shaft alignment is first verified by starting at the rear of the boat. Notice again that engine alignment and shaft alignment are two completely different things. Now, before starting the alignment check at the rear of the boat, it's important to note that the method varies slightly for boats with steep shaft angles (Fig. 17-11).

When the angle of the shaft is steep and the coupling bolts are removed, the tail shaft tends to slide rearward as it is turned to perform the necessary checks. This makes it very difficult to get consistent readings with a feeler gauge or a dial indicator. For boats with

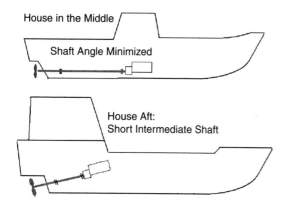

Fig. 17-11. A steeply angled shaft (bottom) requires a somewhat different approach to alignment. See Figure 17-12.

a steep angle, fabricate the fixtures shown in Figure 17-12 to set up the rear couplings.

This tooling system keeps the rear shaft from sliding toward the rear of the boat while alignment checks are being made. Note: This method also depends on the front coupling of the intermediate shaft remaining connected to the transmission output shaft coupling. Mark and number four points on each coupling half, equally spaced around the perimeter. Measure the gap at each point with a dial caliper. (Note: It is normal for the gap to be 0.001 or 0.002 inch larger at the top of the coupling.) Next rotate the shafts, together, one-half turn and measure again. If the gap is consistent at top, bottom, port, and starboard before and after the half rotation, all is well. If not, either the tail shaft or the intermediate shaft needs to be straightened. *Note: If you can't get consistent readings due to rocking and rolling of the boat in the water, chances are the Cutless bearing needs to be replaced before you*

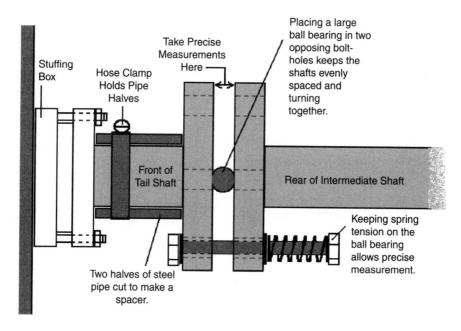

Fig. 17-12. Alignment tooling for use with steep shaft angles. A spacer is cut from two halves of steel pipe, long enough to permit a gap of about ¾ inch between the coupling halves when placed over the tail shaft. Take out the coupling bolts, let the tail shaft slide back far enough to open up the coupling, insert a steel ball bearing as shown, then take up on a spring-loaded bolt as shown to stabilize the coupling with a ¾-inch gap.

can complete the alignment. Finally, note that a wider gap port or starboard is your clue that the engine and transmission will need to be moved port or starboard by adjusting engine mounts.

ORDER OF ALIGNMENT OPERATIONS

To do a thorough check of the alignment of a shaft and engine, follow these steps, starting at the rear of the boat. Verify the following:

1. The propeller retaining nut is tight.
2. The propeller key is properly positioned in its keyway.
3. The propeller is advanced all the way into the tail shaft taper.
4. The propeller blades are undamaged, all blades are pitched the same, and the radial centerline of each is equally spaced with the others around the hub.
5. The rear and front ends of the tail shaft are straight.
6. The stern bearing is tight and secure in its bore (not turning with the shaft), and there is no excess clearance between the shaft and bearing, according to the bearing manufacturer's specifications.
7. The area of the tail shaft upon which the stuffing box packing resides is not excessively worn.
8. The tail shaft coupling is tight on the shaft, and the face is flat. Dress the coupling faces with a file to make them flat if necessary.
9. The rear intermediate shaft coupling is tight on the shaft. Also, file the face of this coupling as needed.
11. The rear of the intermediate shaft is straight.
12. These two couplings are aligned to one another within specifications.

13. The rear pillow-block bearing is in good shape (within specifications), has a way of getting lubrication, and has been getting lubrication.

Continue with the steps below.

14. If the rear of the intermediate shaft needs adjustment up or down or side-to-side, do so now. This is done by loosening the pillow block bolts and sliding the bearing left or right, by shimming the bearing to raise it, or by removing shims to lower the bearing. The forward pillow block bearing may also need to be moved to accomplish this change.
15. Moving forward, check the forward pillow block bearing just like you checked the rear one, and make changes as needed.
16. Continue by removing the droop (see page 288) in the shaft, and then you will know where the engine goes and which way to point it.
17. After verifying that things at the wet end of the shaft (propeller and rear of tail shaft) are all right, the shaft alignment process starts with loosening the rear coupling bolts. Loosen the bolts just enough to see if the coupling flanges spring apart on the top, the bottom, or on either side. If the couplings do spring apart, then this gap must be measured with a feeler gauge (see below).

WATCH THE CLOCK

Upon loosening the bolts, any gap that does open up must be referenced to a clock face (Fig. 17-13). Is the opening at 12 o'clock or is it at 3 o'clock? At the end of the alignment process, when the eventual engine position is right,

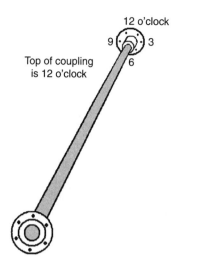

Fig. 17-13. Clock terminology for describing shaft position.

there must be a slight opening at 12 o'clock (on top) on all shaft couplings.

For workboats and fishing boats with slow turning shafts, a maximum opening between couplings of 0.001 inch per inch of coupling face diameter is allowable. For example, the opening between the faces of 8-inch couplings would be a maximum of 0.008 inch. For a high-speed motoryacht, a maximum of half the workboat specifications, or 0.0005 inch per inch of coupling diameter, is required.

Alignment specialists like to see a slight opening straight up at the 12 o'clock position on all couplings. The reasoning is that when the boat is loaded, the shaft coupling alignment would only improve as the boat flexes and the keel drops slightly. If, however, there is an excessive opening at 12 o'clock, or any other position, it is time to check for a bent shaft or an engine that is in the wrong position.

To do so, mark the place where the opening is and rotate the shaft by putting a chain wrench or a pipe wrench on the shaft with a leather welding glove between the turning tool and the shaft. Turn the shaft one-quarter turn in either direction and measure the gap again. If the widest gap moves with the turning, then it is time to suspect that the shaft is bent. When the shaft is straight, the widest opening will stay at the same "clock" position where you first found it.

Note: As the shaft is turned, it may slide apart due to the loose bolts. This may result in a gap opening all the way around the coupling faces. This is not a problem unless the pilot and pocket in the coupling disengage with each other. You can still stack up feeler gauges and calculate the difference between the widest gap and the narrowest gap.

After turning the shaft and finding that the opening moves, it is time to learn which shaft is bent, either the intermediate or rear one. To do this, turn one shaft at a time while keeping the other from turning. For example, if turning the rear shaft causes the opening to move, then the rear shaft is bent. If however, holding the rear shaft still and turning the front shaft causes the opening to move, then the front shaft is bent. Often, however, the opening between couplings will move just slightly, indicating a slight bend. At this point, the mechanic will need to determine how much of a compromise in straightness the equipment can handle and if one or both shafts must be removed from the boat.

THE COUPLING'S PILOT

If you have loosened the coupling bolts and found an excessive opening on the port side of the coupling that does not move or change when the shaft is rotated, then your shafts are straight, but the intermediate shaft is pointing too far to the starboard side. At this point, the rear shaft must be moved back slightly to allow the two couplings to move apart until they are no longer engaged in the pilot or pocket (shown above in Fig. 17-4) of the couplings.

When the couplings slide apart, the intermediate shaft may spring to one side or the other, as well as either up or down. Only one thing decides the position of the intermediate shaft, and that is the direction that the tail shaft points. The boltholes in the base of the pillow block bearing are slotted to allow left- and right-hand movement of the bearing.

REMOVING SHAFT DROOP

Shaft droop is the distance that the unsupported shaft hangs down when it is disconnected from the transmission output shaft coupling. The engine can be aligned only after shaft droop is eliminated by one of two methods.

Note: Droop is normally only a problem at the front of the intermediate shaft because the unsupported span is so great, much greater than the unsupported span between the pillow block bearing and the rear shaft coupling.

Method One: Determine (from tables) the weight (per inch) of the unsupported shaft and also the weight of the coupling. Add these sums together, because this is the weight that is hanging on the pillow bearing. (Example: The shaft weighs 2 pounds per inch and the pillow block is 50 inches aft. Therefore the unsupported shaft weight is 100 pounds. The coupling weighs 10 pounds, so the total unsupported weight is 110 pounds.) Then hang a weight scale on the bottom of a ratchet hoist and zero the scale (Fig. 17-14). Next, take up on the hoist until the

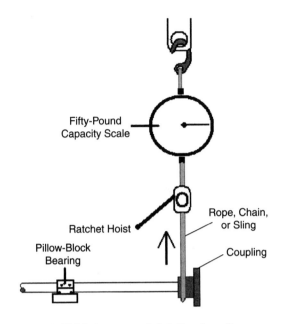

Fig. 17-14. Weigh the unsupported shaft and coupling.

unsupported weight of the shaft and coupling registers on the scale. The droop has now been eliminated by this method.

Method Two: This method is done without a scale and instead uses a dial indicator (Fig. 17-15) mounted on the pillow block bearing. First, zero the dial indicator. Next, attach the hoist to the shaft coupling and take up until the dial indicator reads upward shaft movement of 0.001 inch. This is the shaft height that the engine must be aligned to.

ALIGNING THE ENGINE

After the droop has been eliminated, it is time to align the engine. Aligning the engine really means aligning the *engine and transmission assembly* to the shaft, because the transmission is attached to the engine. Since these two are bolted to each other, they will move as a unit as you take the following steps. The following instructions rely on the couplings

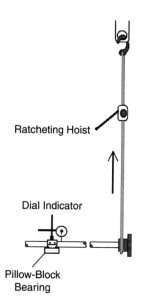

Fig. 17-15. **Removing the shaft droop with a dial indicator.**

being close enough to touch. The two couplings will be aligned to each other.

With the shaft supported in the no-droop position, and the shaft pulled forward and the two couplings touching, check the position of the transmission coupling to the shaft coupling. It is the orientation (Fig. 17-16) of

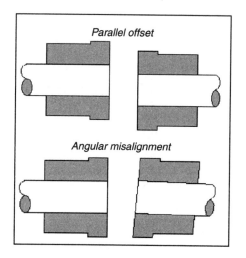

Fig. 17-16. **Coupling misalignment.**

the front coupling to the rear that will tell us which way to move the engine.

If there is a parallel offset in any direction, both ends of the engine must be moved to eliminate it. On the other hand, if there is angular misalignment, then only one end of the engine will be moved to eliminate the problem. Once the engine is moved into position and the couplings are lined up within specifications, the engine can be bolted down. The coupling bolts are installed and tightened only after the alignment is verified with a feeler gauge.

The final alignment of the shaft couplings is done with the boat having been in the water overnight. This time frame is enough to let the keel settle into its normal position. When you check the openings between shaft couplings with a feeler gauge, you should find no gap larger than 0.0005 inch per inch of coupling diameter. For example, a pair of 6-inch couplings (in a high-speed shafting system) should have a clearance between them at 12 o'clock of no more than 0.003 inch.

Lubricate the bearings and confirm visually that grease is coming out from under the bearing cap at the front and rear of the cap. After lubricating the pillow block bearings, it is time to align any power-take-offs (PTO) that are ahead of the engine. Of course, a PTO must be aligned in a way that is consistent with the methods we've covered so far. If all is well, the boat is ready for a sea trial.

THE SEA TRIAL
When running the boat to check it after the alignment, you'll be watching for heat and vibration. An infrared thermometer is great for quickly monitoring the heat of several points as the sea trial commences, and for

checking bearing heat after the repairs and during the sea trial.

Check the tightness of the intermediate bearing by slipping the feeler gauge between the top of the shaft and the bearing cap. The bearing manufacturer publishes specifications for intermediate bearing clearance. If the clearance is too large, the grease will come out at the ends of the bearing cap rather than traveling around with the shaft. To reduce the bearing cap clearance, remove shims from the stack of shims under the cap until the clearance is within specifications.

While the feeler gauge is available, see if it will slide in at the front or back beneath the shaft. If the feeler gauge slips in under the shaft, then the intermediate bearing is tilted. Tilted bearings don't distribute the weight of the shaft evenly on the bottom of the bearing. Uneven weight distribution will cause either the front or rear of a pillow-block bearing to overheat, because one small area of the bearing surface is carrying too much of the load. Shimming (Fig. 17-17) with a wedge as shown will help distribute the load all the way across the lower bearing surface.

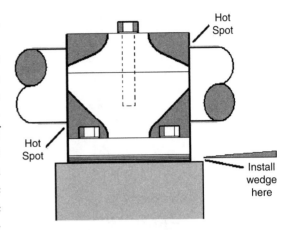

Fig. 17-17. Shimming under a pillow block to eliminate hot spots. In this example the bearing is binding the shaft slightly at the hot spots. Installing a shim as shown will eliminate this binding.

Note: *Shimming under the bearing as shown will lift the whole bearing and the shaft. Therefore, if a wedge shim must be used, then a thin shim may have to be removed from under the whole bearing.*

The last step of the alignment process is to go back over every bolt in the system to verify that all fasteners are tight before replacing all inspection covers.

TABLES AND CONVERSIONS

FRACTION, DECIMAL, AND METRIC EQUIVALENTS

Fractions	Decimal In.	Metric mm.	Fractions	Decimal In.	Metric mm.
1/64	.015625	.397	33/64	.515625	13.097
1/32	.03125	.794	17/32	.53125	13.494
3/64	.046875	1.191	35/64	.546875	13.891
1/16	.0625	1.588	9/16	.5625	14.288
5/64	.078125	1.984	37/64	.578125	14.684
3/32	.09375	2.381	19/32	.59375	15.081
7/64	.109375	2.778	39/64	.609375	15.478
1/8	.125	3.175	5/8	.625	15.875
9/64	.140625	3.572	41/64	.640625	16.272
5/32	.15625	3.969	21/32	.65625	16.669
11/64	.171875	4.366	43/64	.671875	17.066
3/16	.1875	4.763	11/16	.6875	17.463
13/64	.203125	5.159	45/64	.703125	17.859
7/32	.21875	5.556	23/32	.71875	18.256
15/64	.234375	5.953	47/64	.734375	18.653
1/4	.250	6.35	3/4	.750	19.05
17/64	.265625	6.747	49/64	.765625	19.447
9/32	.28125	7.144	25/32	.78125	19.844
19/64	.296875	7.54	51/64	.796875	20.241
5/16	.3125	7.938	13/16	.8125	20.638
21/64	.328125	8.334	53/64	.828125	21.034
11/32	.34375	8.731	27/32	.84375	21.431
23/64	.359375	9.128	55/64	.859375	21.828
3/8	.375	9.525	7/8	.875	22.225
25/64	.390625	9.922	57/64	.890625	22.622
13/32	.40625	10.319	29/32	.90625	23.019
27/64	.421875	10.716	59/64	.921875	23.416
7/16	.4375	11.113	15/16	.9375	23.813
29/64	.453125	11.509	61/64	.953125	24.209
15/32	.46875	11.906	31/32	.96875	24.606
31/64	.484375	12.303	63/64	.984375	25.003
1/2	.500	12.7	1	1.00	25.4

INCHES TO MILLIMETERS CONVERSION TABLE

Inches	Millimeters	Inches	Millimeters	Inches	Millimeters
0.001	0.0254	0.010	0.2540	0.019	0.4826
0.002	0.0508	0.011	0.2794	0.020	0.5080
0.003	0.0762	0.012	0.3048	0.021	0.5334
0.004	0.1016	0.013	0.3302	0.022	0.5588
0.005	0.1270	0.014	0.3556	0.023	0.5842
0.006	0.1524	0.015	0.3810	0.024	0.6096
0.007	0.1778	0.016	0.4064	0.025	0.6350
0.008	0.2032	0.017	0.4318		
0.009	0.2286	0.018	0.4572		

TORQUE CONVERSION TABLE, POUND FEET TO NEWTON METERS

Pound-Feet (lb.-ft.)	Newton Metres (Nm)	Newton Metres (Nm)	Pound-Feet (lb.-ft.)
1	1.356	1	0.7376
2	2.7	2	1.5
3	4.0	3	2.2
4	5.4	4	3.0
5	6.8	5	3.7
6	8.1	6	4.4
7	9.5	7	5.2
8	10.8	8	5.9
9	12.2	9	6.6
10	13.6	10	7.4
15	20.3	15	11.1
20	27.1	20	14.8
25	33.9	25	18.4
30	40.7	30	22.1
35	47.5	35	25.8
40	54.2	40	29.5
45	61.0	50	36.9
50	67.8	60	44.3
55	74.6	70	51.6
60	81.4	80	59.0
65	88.1	90	66.4
70	94.9	100	73.8
75	101.7	110	81.1
80	108.5	120	88.5
90	122.0	130	95.9
100	135.6	140	103.3
110	149.1	150	110.6
120	162.7	160	118.0
130	176.3	170	125.4
140	189.8	180	132.8
150	203.4	190	140.1
160	216.9	200	147.5
170	230.5	225	166.0
180	244.0	250	184.4

FEET TO METERS CONVERSION TABLE

Feet – metres
1 foot = 0.3048 m

ft.	met.	ft.	met.
1	0,305	31	9,449
2	**0,610**	**32**	**9,754**
3	0,914	33	10,058
4	**1,219**	**34**	**10,363**
5	1,524	35	10,668
6	**1,829**	**36**	**10,973**
7	2,134	37	11,278
8	**2,438**	**38**	**11,582**
9	2,743	39	11,887
10	**3,048**	**40**	**12,192**
11	3,353	41	12,497
12	**3,658**	**42**	**12,802**
13	3,962	43	13,106
14	**4,267**	**44**	**13,441**
15	4,572	45	13,716
16	**4,877**	**46**	**14,021**
17	5,182	47	14,326
18	**5,486**	**48**	**14,630**
19	5,791	49	14,935
20	**6,096**	**50**	**15,240**
21	6,401	51	15,545
22	**6,706**	**52**	**15,850**
23	7,010	53	16,154
24	**7,315**	**54**	**16,459**
25	7,620	55	16,764
26	**7,925**	**56**	**17,069**
27	8,230	57	17,374
28	**8,534**	**58**	**17,678**
29	8,839	59	17,983
30	**9,144**	**60**	**18,288**

METERS TO FEET CONVERSION TABLE

Metres – Feet 1 metre = 3.2808 feet	
met.	**feet**
1	3,28
2	**6,56**
3	9,84
4	**13,12**
5	16,40
6	**19,69**
7	22,97
8	**26,25**
9	29,53
10	**32,81**
11	36,09
12	**39,37**
13	42,65
14	**45,93**
15	49,21
16	**52,49**
17	55,77
18	**59,06**
19	62,34
20	**65,62**

INCHES TO CENTIMETERS CONVERSION TABLE

Inches – centimetres 1 inch = 2.54 cm	
inches	**cm**
1	2,54
2	**5,08**
3	7,62
4	**10,16**
5	12,70
6	**15,24**
7	17,78
8	**20,32**
9	22,86
10	**25,40**
11	27,94
12	**30,48**

DEGREES FAHRENHEIT TO DEGREES CELSIUS/CENTIGRADE CONVERSION TABLE

°F	°C	°F	°C	°F	°C	°F	°C	°F	°C	°F	°C	°F	°C	°F	°C
-454	-270	-31	-35	19.4	-7	70	21.1	120.2	49	171	77.2	225	107.2	660	348.9
-450	-268	-30	-34.4	20	-6.7	71	21.7	121	49.4	172	77.8	230	110	662	350
-440	-262	-29.2	-34	21	-6.1	71.6	22	122	50	172.4	78	235	112.8	670	354.4
-436	-260	-29	-33.9	21.2	-6	72	22.2	123	50.6	173	78.3	239	115	680	360
-430	-257	-28	-33.3	22	-5.6	73	22.8	123.8	51	174	78.9	240	115.6	690	365.6
-420	-251	-27.4	-33	23	-5	73.4	23	124	51.1	174.2	79	245	118.3	693	370
-418	-250	-27	-32.8	24	-4.4	74	23.3	125	51.7	175	79.4	248	120	700	371.1
-410	-246	-26	-32.2	24.8	-4	75	23.9	125.6	52	176	80	250	121.1	710	377
-400	-240	-25.6	-32	25	-3.9	75.2	24	126	52.2	177	80.6	255	123.9	716	380
-390	-234	-25	-31.7	26	-3.3	76	24.4	127	52.8	177.8	81	260	125.7	720	382
-382	-230	-24	-31.1	26.6	-3	77	25	127.4	53	178	81.1	265	129.4	730	388
-380	-229	-23.8	-31	27	-2.8	78	25.6	128	53.3	179	81.7	266	130	734	390
-370	-223	-23	-30.6	28	-2.2	78.8	26	129	53.9	179.6	82	270	132.2	740	393
-364	-220	-22	-30	28.4	-2	79	26.1	129.2	54	180	82.2	275	135	750	399
-360	-218	-21	-29.4	29	-1.7	80	26.7	130	54.4	181	82.8	280	137.8	752	400
-350	-212	-20.2	-29	30	-1.1	80.6	27	131	55	181.4	83	284	140	760	404
-346	-210	-20	-28.9	30.2	-1	81	27.2	132	55.6	182	83.3	285	140.6	770	410
-340	-207	-19	-28.3	31	-0.6	82	27.8	132.8	56	183	83.9	290	143.3	780	416
-330	-201	-18.4	-28	32	0	82.4	28	133	56.1	183.2	84	293	145	788	420
-328	-200	-18	-27.8	33	0.6	83	28.3	134	56.7	184	84.4	295	146.1	790	421
-320	-196	-17	-27.2	33.8	1	84	28.9	134.6	57	185	85	300	148.9	800	427
-310	-190	-16.6	-27	34	1.1	84.2	29	135	57.2	186	85.6	302	150	806	430
-300	-184	-16	-26.7	35	1.7	85	29.4	136	57.8	186.8	86	310	154.4	810	432
-292	-180	-15	-26.1	35.6	2	86	30	136.4	58	187	86.1	320	160	820	438
-290	-179	-14.8	-26	36	2.2	87	30.6	137	58.3	188	86.7	330	165.6	824	440
-280	-173	-14	-25.6	37	2.8	87.8	31	138	58.9	188.6	87	338	170	830	443
-274	-170	-13	-25	37.4	3	88	31.1	138.2	59	189	87.2	340	171.1	840	449
-270	-168	-12	-24.4	38	3.3	89	31.7	139	59.4	190	87.8	350	176.7	842	450
-260	-162	-11.2	-24	39	3.9	89.6	32	140	60	190.4	88	356	180	850	454
-256	-160	-11	-23.9	39.2	4	90	32.2	141	60.6	191	88.3	360	182.2	860	460
-250	-157	-10	-23.3	40	4.4	91	32.8	141.8	61	192	88.9	370	187.8	870	465
-240	-151	-9.4	-23	41	5	91.4	33	142	61.1	192.2	89	374	190	878	470
-238	-150	-9	-22.8	42	5.5	92	33.3	143	61.7	193	89.4	380	193.3	880	471
-230	-146	-8	-22.2	42.8	6	93	33.9	143.6	62	194	90	390	198.9	890	477
-220	-140	-7.6	-22	43	6.1	93.2	34	144	62.2	195	90.6	392	200	896	480
-210	-134	-7	-21.7	44	6.7	94	34.4	145	62.8	195.8	91	400	204.4	900	482
-202	-130	-6	-21.1	44.6	7	95	35	145.4	63	196	91.1	410	210	910	488
-200	-129	-5.8	-21	45	7.2	96	35.6	146	63.3	197	91.7	420	215.6	914	490
-190	-123	-5	-20.6	46	7.8	96.8	36	147	63.9	197.6	92	428	220	920	493
-184	-120	-4	-20	46.4	8	97	36.1	147.2	64	198	92.2	430	221.1	930	499
-180	-118	-3	-19.4	47	8.3	98	36.7	148	64.4	199	92.8	440	226.7	932	500
-170	-112	-2.2	-19	48	8.9	98.6	37	149	65	199.4	93	446	230	940	504
-166	-110	-2	-18.9	48.2	9	99	37.2	150	65.6	200	93.3	450	232.2	950	510
-160	-107	-1	-18.3	49	9.4	100	37.8	150.8	66	201	93.9	460	237.8	960	516
-150	-101	-0.4	-18	50	10	101	38.3	151	66.1	201.2	94	464	240	968	520
-148	-100	0	-17.8	51	10.6	102	38.9	152	66.7	202	94.4	470	243.3	970	521
-140	-96	1	-17.2	51.8	11	102.2	39	152.6	67	203	95	480	248.9	980	527
-130	-90	1.4	-17	52	11.1	103	39.4	153	67.2	204	95.6	482	250	986	530
-120	-84	2	-16.7	53	11.7	104	40	154	67.8	204.8	96	490	254.4	990	532
-112	-80	3	-16.1	53.6	12	105	40.6	154.4	68	205	96.1	500	260	1000	538
-110	-79	3.2	-16	54	12.2	105.8	41	155	68.3	206	96.7	510	265.6	1004	540
-100	-73.3	4	-15.6	55	12.8	106	41.1	156	68.9	206.6	97	518	270	1022	550
-94	-70	5	-15	55.4	13	107	41.7	156.2	69	207	97.2	520	271.1	1050	566
-90	-67.8	6	-14.4	56	13.3	107.6	42	157	69.4	208	97.8	530	276.7	1100	593
-80	-62.2	6.8	-14	57	13.9	108	42.2	158	70	208.4	98	536	280	1112	600
-76	-60	7	-13.9	57.2	14	109	42.8	159	70.6	209	98.3	540	282.2	1150	621
-70	-56.7	8	-13.3	58	14.4	109.4	43	159.8	71	210	98.9	550	287.8	1200	649
-60	-51.1	8.6	-13	59	15	110	43.3	160	71.1	210.2	99	554	290	1202	650
-58	-50	9	-12.8	60	15.6	111	43.9	161	71.7	211	99.4	560	293.3	1250	677
-50	-45.6	10	-12.2	60.8	16	111.2	44	161.6	72	212	100	570	298.9	1292	700
-40	-40	10.4	-12	61	16.1	112	44.4	162	72.2	213	100.6	572	300	1300	704
-39	-39.4	11	-11.7	62	16.7	113	45	163	72.8	213.8	101	580	304.4	1350	732
-38.2	-39	12	-11.1	62.6	17	114	45.6	163.4	73	214	101.1	590	310	1382	750
-38	-38.9	12.2	-11	63	17.2	114.8	46	164	73.3	215	101.7	600	315.6	1400	760
-37	-38.3	13	-10.6	64	17.8	115	46.1	165	73.9	215.6	102	608	320	1450	788
-36.4	-38	14	-10	64.4	18	116	46.7	165.2	74	216	102.2	610	321.0	1472	800
-36	-37.8	15	-9.4	65	18.3	116.6	47	166	74.4	217	102.8	620	326.7	1500	816
-35	-37.2	15.8	-9	66	18.9	117	47.2	167	75	217.4	103	626	330		
-34.6	-37	16	-8.9	66.2	19	118	47.8	168	75.6	218	103.3	630	332.2		
-34	-36.7	17	-8.3	67	19.4	118.4	48	168.8	76	219	103.9	640	337.8		
-33	-36.1	17.6	-8	68	20	119	48.3	169	76.1	219.2	104	644	340		
-32.8	-36	18	-7.8	69	20.6	120	48.9	170	76.7	220	104.4	650	343.3		
-32	-35.6	19	-7.2	69.8	21			170.6	77	221	105				

COMPARATIVE SHEET-METAL THICKNESSES

Gauge No.	Uncoated Steel and Stainless Steel*	Aluminum, Brass, and Copper
28	0.015″ (1/64″)	0.012″
26	0.018″	0.016″ (1/64″)
24	0.024″	0.020″
22	0.030″	0.025″
20	0.036″ (1/32″)	0.032″ (1/32″)
18	0.048″ (3/64″)	0.040″
16	0.060″ (1/16″)	0.051″
14	0.075″ (5/64″)	0.064″ (1/16″)
12	0.105″ (7/64″)	0.081″ (5/64″)

*Galvanized steel is slightly thicker than uncoated or stainless steel.

EQUIVALENCIES

Square Measure Equivalents

1 square yard = 0.836 square meter
1 square foot = 0.0929 square meter = 929 square centimeters
1 square inch = 6.452 square centimeters = 645.2 square millimeters

1 square meter = 10.764 square feet = 1.196 square yards
1 square centimeter = 0.155 square inch
1 square millimeter = 0.00155 square inch

Cubic Measure Equivalents

1 cubic inch = 16.38706 cubic centimeters
100 cubic inches = 1.64 liters
1 Imperial gallon = 4.546 liters
1 Imperial quart = 1.136 liters
1 US gallon = 3.785 liters
1 US quart = 0.946 liter

1 cubic centimeter = 0.061 cubic inch
1 liter (cubic decimeter) = 0.0353 cubic foot = 61.023 cubic inches
1 liter = 0.2642 US gallon = 1.0567 US quarts = 0.2200 Imperial gallon

Weight Equivalents

1 Imperial ton (UK) = 2240 pounds (long ton)
1 short ton (USA) = 2000 pounds
1 ton (of 2000 pounds) = 0.9072 metric ton
1 ton (of 2240 pounds) = 1.016 metric tons = 1016 kilograms
1 pound = 0.4536 kilogram = 453.6 grams

1 metric ton = 2204.6 pounds
1 kilogram = 2.2046 pounds

Miscellaneous Equivalents

1 Imperial gallon (UK) = 1.2 gallons (US)
1 h.p. = 2,544 Btus
1 kw = 3,413 Btus

INDEX

Numbers in **bold** indicate pages with illustrations